Challenging the Status Quo

A Political Memoir

Challenging the Status Quo

A Political Memoir

Derek Quigley

TE HERENGA WAKA
UNIVERSITY PRESS

Te Herenga Waka University Press
Victoria University of Wellington
PO Box 600 Wellington
teherengawakapress.co.nz

First published 2024

ISBN 978-1-77692-220-8

A catalogue record is available from
the National Library of New Zealand

Printed in New Zealand by Ligare

Contents

Preface

In the 1950s New Zealand WAS one of the wealthiest countries in the world, with a per capita income of 147 percent of the OECD average and 114 percent of that of Australia.[1] The expectation was that the good times would continue. By then, the country had recovered from the ravages of the Depression and World War II, and in 1949 it had for the first time elected a National Party government, publicly committed to private enterprise and minimal government interference in people's lives.

National proved highly successful at winning elections and was on the Treasury benches for 29 of the next 35 years. But, as this book shows, there is more to good government than winning elections. By the mid-1960s the country was on an accelerating slide down the OECD rankings, although most people didn't realise it until New Zealand was nearly bankrupt in the mid-1980s. Even after dramatic and painful reforms, the per capita income in 2019 was only 94 percent of the OECD average and a mere 77 percent of that of Australia.[2]

In 1949, near the end of my last year at secondary school and in the company of a small group of senior boarders, I had my first introduction to two senior politicians. They were Sidney Holland, or Sid, as he was commonly called, and his fellow Christchurch MP Jack Watts. Holland had become leader of the National Party in November 1940. With a business background, he described himself as 'a Britisher through and through' and was fiercely opposed to the ruling Labour government's socialism. Holland believed in individual freedom, the free market, personal initiative, opportunity, enterprise, responsibility and reward. He wanted less bureaucracy, fewer business restrictions and reduced government intervention, and was highly critical of the Labour government's expanded social security system, which he claimed made people dependent on welfare.

The day we met with them, Holland and Watts were on their way to a formal evening function. Both were dressed for the occasion and oozed confidence in the expectation of what was to become an historic election win for National later that year, when Labour's 14 years on the Treasury benches came to an end.

Although my memory of the occasion is less about what was said than the way Holland and Watts were dressed — with both decked out like talking penguins in black pants, white shirts, bow ties and tails, and obviously on their way to a much more important event than the meeting with non-voters like us — the occasion nevertheless sparked in me a lifelong interest in politics. Little did I know at the time where it would lead: to my eventual election as an MP; 12 years of parliamentary service with two political parties including four years as a Cabinet minister; the end to my Cabinet membership in an acrimonious parting of the ways between me and Prime Minister Rob Muldoon in 1982 over policy, leadership style and ideological differences; the formation of a new political party, ACT New Zealand, with Sir Roger Douglas; and my return to parliament as an ACT MP following the introduction of the Mixed Member Proportional electoral system (MMP) in 1996.

The initial attraction of the National Party for me back in 1949 was its expressed support for individual freedom, personal responsibility and limited government, but over the years in power, pragmatism began to water down these objectives.

By the mid-1980s New Zealand's growth rate had slipped to 30 percent of the OECD average. Ironically, it was Labour, not National, that began long-overdue reform after 1984. Although I was not in Parliament at that time, I was both hands on as a consultant and an eye-witness to those reform as they gathered pace. But soon key Labour ministers began to fight amongst themselves, stumble and fall, and National was re-elected in 1990 with a huge majority. But it too was punished for its broken promises and nearly lost office three years later.

However, before then its leader, Jim Bolger, had promised a referendum on the electoral system which had served his party so well in the past. MMP followed, and now in the new political environment National and Labour are both beholden to the whims of smaller third parties before they can form a coalition government.

This book covers the key events and the roles of various individuals involved over the years 1975–84 when I was a National Party MP, and

1996–99 when I was an ACT MP. It also covers some of my involvement as a government consultant reviewing and recommending changes to entities such as Defence, the Treasury, Justice, the Police Force and the Fire Service. It is written from the perspective of a senior National Party official, an MP in both the first-past-the-post (FPP) and MMP electoral systems, a committed supporter of private enterprise, and a Cabinet minister and consultant who was prepared to stick to his principles and accept the consequences of doing so.

The book also discusses my role as co-founder of the ACT political party and the reasons for that party's failure in its formative years to replace the status-quo-orientated National Party as New Zealand's dominant centre-right force; my role as a select committee chair under MMP; ACT's involvement in ending the first coalition government between the National Party and New Zealand First; and my efforts in attempting to reshape New Zealand's defence capabilities.

It is a history of New Zealand's evolving maturity from the 'golden' years when we were beholden to Britain to its current status as an independent nation in today's uncertain world. It highlights some of New Zealand's successes and failures during that progression, and makes suggestions on what could be done to avoid the mistakes of the past.

Hon Derek Quigley LLB QSO
2024

CHAPTER 1

The National Party

Principles vs Pragmatism

The National Party was formed in May 1936 and came into existence as the result of the earlier merging of the United and Reform parties. Historically, those parties had competed against each other for votes, but from 1931 to 1935 — in the face of increasing electoral support for the Labour Party — they had formed a coalition government that contested the 1935 election as the National Political Federation. This was an attempt to show that the new grouping was intent on representing New Zealanders from all backgrounds rather than sectional groups.

The National Party's founding principles were to

- Promote good citizenship and self reliance;
- Combat communism and socialism;
- Maintain freedom of contract;
- Encourage private enterprise;
- Safeguard individual rights and the privilege of ownership; and
- Oppose interference by the state in business and state control of industry.[1]

Fourteen years in Opposition

But in the aftermath of the Depression and amid a perception that earlier coalitions had handled that situation poorly, the formation of the federation and the National Party did not attract enough support to defeat Labour in 1935 or indeed in 1938, when the National Party contested its first election. On that occasion it made little headway, winning 25 seats to Labour's 53. And although it did better after Sid Holland became leader in 1940, the party faced an uphill battle, along with conservative political parties around the world, for a number of reasons.

One was the impact of the Depression, which had begun in the United States and by 1932 was in full swing. In the US, industrial stocks fell by 80 percent; 40 percent of all banks failed, and unemployment increased to 23.6 percent of the workforce. Conditions were worse in some parts of the United Kingdom, particularly in the northeast which was heavily reliant on shipbuilding. Unemployment there reached 70 percent as ship production fell away almost completely.

Demand for New Zealand's primary products collapsed, with export prices falling by 40 percent between 1929 and 1932 and consumer prices by around 20 per cent. Unemployment rose sharply and a sense of national crisis developed. The decline in commodity prices increased the burden that many faced in servicing and repaying farm mortgages, and as freezing works, woollen mills and dairy factories were caught in the spiral of decline, farmers had less to spend in the towns. With rising unemployment, some of those in the cities drifted back to the family farm or went on the road looking for food and work, where there was little of either available.

A second reason was the need for a different policy response, with the Depression resulting in major policy changes not just in New Zealand but around the world. In the US President Roosevelt abandoned the former hands-off approach to economic management in favour of more interventionist policies, with the focus of his New Deal on 'relief, recovery and reform'. The result was an increased role for the federal government in the national economy.

In all countries in Europe where there were democratic governments, demands for parliamentary change increased. In the UK and France politicians were forced to accept multi-party coalitions and new economic ideas. In Russia, the industrial machine created by the five-year plan — previously admired by many in the West — was lubricated by the blood of millions as Stalin's totalitarian regime instituted vast economic restructuring. In Germany, where the impact of the Depression was particularly severe, Hitler and the National Socialist (Nazi) Party took over.

In New Zealand in 1932 and 1933 the United–Reform coalition government had successfully negotiated continuing access to the British market for New Zealand products, exempting them from tariffs in return for increased preferences for British goods. But also, to the anger of many right-wing elements within the Reform Party, its leader, Gordon Coates, in his role as Minister of Finance, introduced mortgage relief, forced interest rates down and devalued the currency against sterling. The objective was to inflate farmers' incomes and to share the burden of the recession more evenly. As most exports were sold for sterling, which was then converted into New Zealand pounds, farmers' incomes were boosted at the stroke of the pen and imports became more expensive. The devaluation also increased the money supply which in turn boosted confidence and lending. Confidence was further boosted when an independent Reserve Bank was established and began operating to enable better monetary planning and to ensure that decisions about New Zealand's currency were made in New Zealand rather than overseas.

Helped by an increase in the volume and price of exports, the New Zealand economy began to recover by 1933, with unemployment peaking at around 25 percent of the workforce that year, and improving reasonably rapidly over the second half of the thirties. But despite this, the United/Reform government was seen as the hated face of the Depression, and its offspring, National, after it was formed, as its clone.

A third reason, which helped the Labour government, was the decline in support for the teaching of the Scottish philosopher and pioneer of political economics, Adam Smith, whose views had strong support among many New Zealanders, including Sidney Holland.[2] Smith and his followers believed that economic development was best fostered in an environment of free competition that operated in accordance with universal 'natural laws', and that individuals should be allowed to pursue their own private economic interests as much as possible, provided they did not violate basic principles of justice. If individuals had this freedom, Smith argued, they would do much more to further the public good than by governments trying to help the public deliberately and intentionally.

But in the face of persistent unemployment throughout the world, a contrary view was put forward by the British economist John Maynard Keynes. Keynes' thesis was that classical economics rested on a fundamental error. It assumed, mistakenly, he argued, that the balance between supply and demand would ensure full employment. In his view, the overall world economy was chronically unstable and subject to fluctuations, and because of this, during a depression the only remedy was for governments to step in and pump up the economy — if necessary — by financing increased activity through borrowing to replace the missing private-sector investment. If the borrowed money was spent on things like public works, it would boost demand and purchasing power, which in turn would create jobs, he argued.

Keynes' view that governments had a major role to play in economic management, and that socially successful economies required significant contributions from both the government and the private sector, resonated strongly in New Zealand during the Depression. The country's overall mood, conditioned by a high degree of state intervention from New Zealand's early development, was in favour of this type of approach to improve its social and economic affairs.

The long-held view of New Zealanders towards state intervention was that its basis was necessity rather than ideology. This was noted as early as the late 1890s by the French writer Albert Métin, who wrote after visiting New Zealand that the country's radical social legislation had been implemented in a series of pragmatic steps to address specific issues and had little grounding in political theory. Métin coined the phrase for this type of development as 'socialism with no doctrines'.

A fourth reason the National Party did not find sufficient electoral purchase before 1949 was Labour's policies of full employment and expanded social welfare. These were not only widely accepted domestically: the government's social welfare policies became the envy of many countries around the world. As a result the National Party, despite initial opposition, accepted the basic principles of both policies as early as the 1943 election campaign, and reconfirmed that commitment in its 1949 election manifesto.

World War II was a fifth reason. Thousands of young New Zealand men and women enlisted in the armed forces, with numbers under arms peaking in 1942 at over 154,000. 'The war effort' became the predominant national cause. This dampened opposition from the free-trade elements within the community and enabled the government to extend its trade, social and economic experimentation. Prices and wages were controlled; bulk purchase agreements were established with the UK that ensured guaranteed prices for New Zealand farm products; and surplus trading income was deposited in special reserve accounts to smooth payouts and to provide funds the government could borrow against to finance other projects.

Petrol was strictly rationed, with travel mainly restricted to tram, bicycle or shanks' pony. Rationing also regulated the consumption of food, clothing and other consumables, with as much food as possible sent to the UK.

Each person was allowed 26 coupons every six months for clothing. A full-length coat 'cost' 12 coupons, a gym frock and a blouse four. Men's suits lost their trouser cuffs and lapels became narrower, with the single-breasted style developed to save more material. Cigarettes and tobacco were in short supply and people queued for chocolate, sweets and biscuits. Due to the lack of shipping space for mail, letters for overseas had to be written on standard forms which were photographically reduced, transported on film cassettes and enlarged and printed before delivery.

In all towns and villages, in phone booths, on trams and at railway stations, wartime posters reminded people that 'Careless talk costs lives', and that 'Walls have ears'. Posters at railway stations asked 'Is your journey really necessary?' In rural areas in particular the war changed the focus of everyday life to a unified community effort to support the 'boys overseas'.

In order to promote national unity on the political front, in July 1940 the government established a War Cabinet — outside the formal Cabinet — comprising three Labour and two National Party MPs. The National representatives were Gordon Coates and party leader Adam Hamilton. As part of Sid Holland's (successful) campaign against Hamilton for the leadership of the party in November 1940, he claimed that Hamilton could not lead National while he served on a Labour-led body. But despite this, when Holland himself became the party's leader in 1942 he joined the War Cabinet, with ministerial responsibility for war expenditure. In that position he criticised economic waste, bureaucratic regulation and press censorship, all of which he saw as extending and consolidating state control.

Later that year, when Labour intervened in a court case involving coalminers convicted of striking illegally at the Huntly mine, Holland withdrew from the War Cabinet. Coates and Hamilton, critical of Holland's move, then left the National Party caucus and rejoined the War Cabinet as independent MPs. Their defection strengthened Holland's leadership, and from then on he attacked the government without reservation.

Prior to that, National had made little progress in reducing Labour's majority, only increasing its number of MPs in 1938 from 19 to 25 in an 80-seat Parliament. But in the runup to the 1943 election (which was delayed for two years because of the war) a rejuvenated National Opposition party under Holland's leadership aggressively campaigned for free enterprise as opposed to state regulation, and criticised the government for growing shortages, continuing intervention in the economy and what it termed Labour's hypocrisy in introducing wartime conscription after numerous Labour MPs had been jailed for sedition as a result of opposing it during World War I. However, despite National increasing its MPs by nine, largely as a result of the rural vote moving back to the party following improved product prices, Labour was re-elected with a 10-seat majority.

The reality was that the focus on the war effort, Labour's policies of full employment and guaranteed access to the UK market for farm produce were seen by many as an acceptable trade-off for state intervention at that time.

In 1946 Labour again retained power, this time more narrowly, and probably because of the abolition of the 'country quota' which had previously favoured National. But by then Labour was progressively losing support, returning to the government benches with a majority of four seats due to winning all four Māori seats. Voter turnout was 93.5 percent, the highest so far recorded, and the indications were clear: there would be a change of government in 1949.

From 1949: 'No more socialism in New Zealand'

In the lead-up to the 1949 election National campaigned for the private ownership of production, distribution and exchange, and criticised Labour's attitude to the growth of communism in Eastern Europe, with the inference that Labour was sympathetic to that cause. It also strongly castigated the government for weakness against the union movement and in particularly against waterfront militancy, its continuation of war restrictions, top-heavy government, rising inflation, and its poor handling of what had become an acute housing crisis following a virtual halt to house construction during the war.

Two of National's 1949 pamphlets are reproduced below.

On 30 November — with the contest for the four Māori electorates held the day before — National received 51.9 percent of the vote, from an overall turnout of 93.5 percent (the same as in the preceding election), and obtained a 12-seat majority. The big question now was: would the new government stay true to its private-enterprise philosophy, reverse the expanded controls Labour had introduced, revert to a free-market model and make a real difference?

At his press conference in December 1949, immediately after being sworn in as Prime Minister, Sid Holland's comments were encouraging.

NZ National Party: 1949 election pamphlet.

'There is going to be no more socialism in New Zealand. The peg went in this afternoon,' he said.[3] Did this mean National was about to unravel 50 years of interventionism and get rid of import controls, tariffs and wartime price controls, people asked? The eventual answer was a resounding no.

Although food subsidies were initially lifted, they were subsequently reintroduced. Taxes stayed high, and the government backed off abolishing compulsory unionism despite a massive win in the 1951 snap election following a prolonged waterfront dispute. Far from trimming government involvement in industry, successive National governments undertook,

NZ National Party: 1949 election pamphlet.

with taxpayer funding, major industrial projects such as the Tasman Pulp and Paper Mill and New Zealand Steel, and, under Muldoon governments from 1975, a range of 'Think Big' projects.

Rigid social controls — which had led Lord Beveridge to observe in 1948 that New Zealand was a puritan country with two Sundays each week — persisted until the 1980s. Indeed, successive National governments added to them. Pragmatism quickly became National's secret weapon and eventually led to an ideological rift between private-enterprise advocates such as myself and the party's status-quo politicians. The ultimate irony is that it was a Labour rather than a National government that eventually unwound — in the mid-1980s — decades of centralised control of the New Zealand economy.

There were two basic reasons for National's pragmatism. One was the party's prolonged electoral success after 1949. This initially confirmed in the minds of many of its successive MPs that National was the 'natural party of government' and could remain so indefinitely — albeit with the occasional three-year break in favour of Labour — provided it gave its supporters what it thought they wanted.

The second reason was the ongoing time and energy required by day-to-day government. In that sort of environment, the party's founding principles soon took a back seat to immediate problem-solving and issues of national significance.

Several examples illustrate this.

Security was an immediate concern. The Malayan emergency — a guerrilla war between the British and pro-communist independence fighters — had begun in 1948 and in August 1949 the Labour government held a referendum to test whether compulsory military training (CMT) should be introduced. The vote was over 72 percent in favour and resulted in the Military Training Act 1949, with the first call-up in 1950. I was part of the first intake and did 14 weeks of full-time basic training.

My fellow conscripts in the First Canterbury Regiment were my North Canterbury contemporaries but, unlike me, most of them had never been in School Cadets (where I had been an under officer) or experienced the discipline of boarding school. For some, it was their first time away from home, so army life was a traumatic experience as they were forced to adjust to living, training, eating and sleeping in the close company of their peers. Some barely made it, and even today I can still hear the quiet night-time sobs of some of my barrack companions who were having difficulty adjusting to this foreign environment.

While we were in camp the Korean War broke out, and for a short time we thought we might be sent to fight there. It didn't happen, but my parents' concern was heightened when I told them I had been asked to join the regular force and take a commission at the end of my basic training. My father's response, clearly influenced by his own experience in World War I, was an unequivocal no. I accepted this, though I did gain a commission later.

The Cold War was in full swing and with general unrest in the Asian region the government entered into two defence arrangements, SEATO (the Southeast Asia Treaty Organisation) and the ANZUS Alliance. All this took up government time, with George Laking, New Zealand's ambassador in Washington during this period, commenting:

> 1949 to 1956 saw the Embassy devoting most of its resources to defence questions ... [with] Fraser's immediate successor, Holland, slow to recognize or acknowledge that there could be identifiable New Zealand interests different from those of Britain on whose infinite wisdom we had been content to rely for more than a hundred years.[4]

The state of the New Zealand economy was another 'status quo' distraction for Holland governments, as the early to mid-1950s saw New Zealand enter a new economic world. It enjoyed bulk-purchase agreements with the UK, good terms of trade, and a phenomenal wool boom in 1950–51 which saw prices increase by 130 percent when the US military ordered large quantities of wool products during the winter campaign of the Korean War.

New Zealand and its wool producers were suddenly prosperous, but with concerns about inflation, the government froze half of farmers' wool cheques for 12 months. 'Bloody socialists' was my father's response, but despite this, we — along with our farming neighbours — at long last had money to spend. A new TD6 tractor arrived, which I operated for the next decade or so, and a much-needed extension to our farmhouse followed.

Although the spike in wool prices didn't last, New Zealand's per capita GDP in the mid-1950s was the third highest of the OECD countries. The country's economic prosperity then was based on the twin pillars of the security of the British market and the high prices for wool, which accounted for more than a third of the country's total export earnings.

Significant public works followed. Highways were sealed, new bridges built, a major hydroelectric scheme was completed in the South Island and a major housing initiative was maintained into the 1960s. But despite the government's private-enterprise rhetoric, the economy remained highly regulated, limiting innovation and the potential for new internationally competitive industries to develop.

The 1950s were prosperous but the writing was nonetheless on the wall for the next phase of New Zealand's role as Britain's offshore farm. The country was 'effectively a monoculture', with all its exports classified as 'processed grass' and most of them going to a single market.[5] In December

1966 wool prices fell by 30 percent and as a result unemployment and inflation rose steadily. In 1967 the currency was devalued for the first time since 1948. Commodity prices temporarily strengthened until the first oil shock in 1973–74, which confirmed a sharp downturn in New Zealand's fortunes.

Also in 1973 the UK joined the European Economic Community, reducing its dependence on New Zealand's primary products. In 1965 exports to the UK were over 50 percent of total sales; five years later they were 36 percent; and within another decade they were down to 15 percent.

Although the New Zealand–Australian Free Trade Agreement of 1965 helped with access for manufactured goods to the Australian market, by 1966–67 New Zealand was sliding down the OECD rankings and, although most people, including the country's governing political party, did not realise it, the country's period of prosperity was coming to an end.

And it got worse. From 1960 to the mid-1980s New Zealand's income per capita grew by 1.4 percent compared with the OECD average of 2.9 percent.[6]

The abolition of the Legislative Council was another early Holland government initiative which — in my view — has had disastrous (if unintended) long-term consequences.

The council was originally established in 1841 when New Zealand split from New South Wales. The country's governing structure was reconstituted in 1852, with the Legislative Council to operate along the lines of the UK's House of Lords. Its main role was to oversee and review bills that emanated from the Lower House, and it had the power to amend or reject bills other than those involving finance. Members were appointed on renewable seven-year terms from the 1890s, and frequently held views in conflict with those of Lower House MPs. The resultant tension, frequent legislative delays and ballooning membership eventually saw the council become (mainly) a haven where loyal party members and outgoing MPs could be rewarded for long-term service.

Prior to the 1949 election, Holland promised to abolish the Legislative Council and to consider a more appropriate replacement. But following the introduction of legislation on 1 January 1950, and the appointment of additional council members as a 'suicide squad' to guarantee sufficient numbers to ensure its demise, it went out of existence without any replacement body taking its place. As a result, from 1950 until 1996 the prevailing FPP system gave either National and Labour, depending on who won the latest election, almost unfettered power.

From 1954, when candidates representing the newly minted Social Credit Party contested the election in force, agitation for electoral reform built as National and Labour increasingly become closed policy shops. Matters came to a head after the 1981 election, in which Social Credit — the only realistic vehicle for protest votes — secured around 21 percent of total votes cast but finished with only two MPs. The perception was that National's and Labour's dominance under FPP had led to a disregard for alternative points of view. Electors were dissatisfied, several alternatives were exhaustively debated, and the MMP electoral system was eventually introduced.

In retrospect, the Holland government should have given more thought to what the introduction of a unitary parliamentary electoral system would spawn before it abolished the Legislative Council and failed to replace it with a more practical and representative Upper House.

Industrial conflict was another preoccupation of the early Holland government.

Industrial relations were dogged by ongoing government intervention when the Holland government was first elected. The Economic Stabilisation Commission (ESC) had been central to economic management from 1942 and had all-embracing power over the activities of producers and consumers. During the latter part of the war the ESC was effectively under the control of a triumvirate of appointed office-holders: Bernard Ashwin from the Treasury, together with representatives of the labour movement and the farming industries. During 1945 Ashwin and Fintan Patrick Walsh, the president of the Federation of Labour (FOL), worked on a postwar stabilisation regime, which retained most controls. And Walsh — with difficulty — sold the concept to the union movement.

Overall, the workplace environment was heavily regulated and collectively organised. A 40-hour, five-day working week was mandated, and most workers were required by law to belong to the state-registered trade union that covered their particular occupation. Wages were fixed centrally and taxpayer financed conciliation meetings between unions and employer representatives were subject to the quasi-legal rulings of the government-appointed Arbitration Court.

In this system, and because of 'egalitarian creep', award wages tended to move up without much change in wage relativities. Rewards for skills were small, if they existed at all, and only 10 percent of the workforce had formal qualifications. Where occupational shortages arose, government-assisted immigration, mainly from Britain and Ireland, was an easy quick-fix solution. Economic growth was taken for granted. Businesses operated on a cost-plus basis in protected markets, and living standards were regarded as capable of being internationally underwritten by the country's rich endowment of natural resources and its special market access to Britain.[7]

In this environment and in an attempt to reduce the power of the militant hierarchy in some of the key unions, National promised in its 1949 campaign to introduce voluntary unionism and to limit the ability of unions to make political donations — which invariably went to the Labour Party. After the election, the new Minister of Labour, Bill Sullivan, told Parliament during the debate on the Political Disabilities Bill: 'Our aim is to make it clear to all unions that they can make use of their members as a majority of members think fit.' He then went on to say — in an attack on union executive as opposed to union membership decisions — that 'a minority should have no right to commit the remainder in the matter of expenditure of funds', with Jack Watts interjecting 'Where there is compulsory unionism' and Sullivan responding, 'Yes.'[8]

This clear attack on union executive decision-making, coupled with the wage restraint that applied as a result of the stabilisation regime, led to escalating confrontation between the Waterside Workers' Union and the Holland government.[9] In the Cold War climate, allegations flew that the union was controlled by communists, and the eventual upshot was a strike/lockout that lasted 151 days and involved up to 22,000 participants.

Emergency Regulations enabled the navy and army to move goods, and eventually moderate unions affiliated to the FOL called on watersiders to 'abandon their communist-dominated misleaders'. This split the union movement and the industrial action collapsed. With the Labour Opposition adopting a 'neither for nor against' stance, Holland took a chance and called a snap election for 1 September 1951, in which the government's majority increased from 12 to 20 seats.

The two reproductions below, a National Party pamphlet attacking communism within some unions and a 'non-scab' Waterside Workers' Union loyalty card, illustrate the extent of the divide that existed between the government and some unionists.

NZ National Party: 1951 election pamphlet (top);
NZ Watersiders' Union: 1951 Loyalty Card (above).

Housing was another dominant issue. Labour in 1935 had inherited a rental accommodation shortage and blamed it on market failure, arguing that only the state could fix the problem. The government's housing initiatives were part of a wider plan to cut unemployment and stimulate the economy, with the overall objective to:

- give the jobless a trade,
- boost manufacturing industries,
- raise New Zealand housing standards, and
- give tenants security of tenure equal to home ownership.

But despite accelerated state housing construction, a return to direct housing assistance, the establishment of a Department of Housing Construction[10] to oversee state house building, rent controls and rental subsidies for low-income people who were earning too much to qualify for a state house, demand for housing still dramatically exceeded supply by the late 1940s. The situation was exacerbated by a halt to construction during the war and demand for additional accommodation once service personnel came home.

By then there was widespread criticism of the Labour government's handling of the situation, and in particular of the state housing policy. Rents were now covering only half the cost of new state houses, which meant middle-income state housing tenants were receiving hefty subsidies while those who could not get state-housing had to pay market rates for private rental accommodation, often of lower quality.

The government's response was that raising rents would breach its security-of-tenure promise, but many saw the situation as biased and unfair. During the 1949 election campaign the National Party exploited this discontent by promising to reform the system and provide state tenants with the opportunity to buy their state house.

Part of this policy was still in place when I became Minister of Housing in 1978, but by then there were numerous other problems to solve, including competing housing objectives stemming from ongoing adherence to Labour's original policy that house construction and the activities it generated were primarily about employment rather than the interests of renters or low-income first-home buyers. When I became Minister of Housing one of my self-appointed tasks was to try to sort this out.

NZ National Party: 1951 election pamphlet.

In 1956, in the midst of the Suez crisis, Sid Holland suffered a mild heart attack or stroke, and his health failed progressively from then on. I can still vividly remember his 'resignation speech' in August 1957 at the annual party conference. He clearly didn't want to stand down but he knew he had to.[11] As he half-heartedly passed the leadership baton to his deputy, Keith Holyoake, the mood of conference delegates was sombre in the expectation that National would lose the forthcoming election, which was only three months away.

Holland presented Holyoake to delegates and the country as his 'capable, efficient and experienced deputy', and his successor, and Holyoake was sworn in on 20 September 1957. As most people anticipated, Holland had given Holyoake a hospital pass and National lost to Labour in November.

But Holyoake was back as Prime Minister in 1960, after three years in Opposition, following a foreign exchange crisis and the 'Black Budget' that Labour's Finance Minister, Arnold Nordmeyer, introduced to solve it.

Holyoake sought to establish two key touchstones that he thought would characterise his time in office. The first was a focus on civil liberties. The second was a low-key approach to economic management, based on an election slogan of 'steady as it goes'. But in the years 1960 to 1972 the former fell by the wayside as New Zealand became embroiled in the Vietnam War. 'Steady as it goes' went out the window too after Robert David Muldoon became Minister of Finance in 1967.

The rise (and fall) of Robert Muldoon

Muldoon was first elected in 1960, the same year I stood against Mabel Howard in the Labour stronghold of Sydenham. I had met Muldoon briefly at the candidates' conference that year. He became under-secretary to the Minister of Finance, Harry Lake, in 1963, and by 1966 had established a reputation for aggressiveness. He was both admired and disliked, with some of his main detractors within his own party caucus.

As a divisive figure he failed to be appointed to the Cabinet immediately after the 1966 election, with Holyoake later stating that he 'look[ed] for the qualities of a "judge" rather than those of an "advocate" in considering candidates for Cabinet rank'.[12] Clearly Holyoake was intent on teaching Muldoon a lesson, because when he finally did appoint him to the Cabinet in February 1967, the post he gave him was Minister of Tourism.

Muldoon was the most junior minister in Cabinet and clearly regarded the Tourism portfolio as the lowest of the low, as I found out later when I was appointed to that position by Muldoon as — I believe — a slap in the face for my recalcitrance. At the time he joined the Cabinet, Muldoon was also reappointed to the party's Dominion Council. I was also a member of that body and began to get to know him there.

In February 1967 Finance Minister Harry Lake died and Muldoon became Minister of Finance after Deputy Prime Minister Jack Marshall declined the position. Muldoon remained at the bottom of the cabinet ranking but was given seat number eight on the front bench in the debating chamber, from where he began his domination of Parliament. But he had inherited a raft of serious economic problems. Wool prices had collapsed again in 1966, and although commodity prices were temporarily strong again a few years later, New Zealand again began slipping down the OECD rankings.

Warning signs had gone unheeded. For example, a 1962 report of the Monetary and Economic Council — under the chairmanship of Sir Frank Holmes with whom I later worked — pointed out that since 1949 the New Zealand economy had earned the unfortunate distinction of 'having the slowest rate of productivity growth amongst all the advanced countries of the world ... We have persistently sought to increase money incomes and spending in New Zealand more rapidly than our productivity and the real value of our exports have justified.' This was a dramatic reversal from the period after World War II when New Zealand was one of the most prosperous countries in the world, with living standards not far behind those of Switzerland. But New Zealand society was rather self-satisfied and inward-looking, with many regarding theirs as 'God's own country'.

Muldoon's approach as Finance Minister was to introduce a series of short-term measures and 'mini-budgets', based on his view that the New Zealand economy was changing virtually on a weekly basis in response to events overseas. By 1984, with Muldoon now Prime Minister as well as Minister of Finance, New Zealand was nearly bankrupt and resembled a communist society in terms of state control.

CHAPTER 2

Farmer, Student, Lawyer

I was born in 1932 to Frank and Amy Quigley who farmed at Waipara, North Canterbury. My father's family had migrated from Northern Ireland in the early 1880s. My mother's family arrived in New Zealand in November 1908 from the Rossendale Valley near Manchester. My only sibling, my sister Joan, was five years and one day older than me.

I suffered from bouts of rheumatic fever as a child. Those were the days before penicillin was widely available, and because of the possibility of damage to my heart, I was sent off to boarding school at the age of 10 on doctor's orders, so that I had a 'more settled environment'. First it was Medbury School in Christchurch, then Christ's College, at the time New Zealand's most prestigious boys' secondary school. That was where I came to meet Holland and Watts.

Medbury for me, a supposedly sickly and completely spoilt brat with unpolished country manners and very little relevant education, was a traumatic experience. During my initial bout of rheumatic fever I had spent seven months in bed at home and in hospital — in a vain attempt to keep me still — and I had been lavished with attention and handled with kid gloves. Now I was in a regulated environment, just another 'new boy' to be treated as one of the lowest of the low by the senior boarders. Worse still, I was humiliatingly behind in basic subjects like reading, writing and arithmetic, and knew nothing about French or Latin, which were also compulsory subjects.

'Doing the right thing' was drummed into us at Medbury and, despite my initial homesickness, over time I began to enjoy the conformity that the school provided. Also, despite my earlier health problems I soon did well at cricket, boxing and athletics, winning the junior, intermediate and senior athletics championship in my three years there. On the academic

At Medbury school, aged 13.

front, while I initially struggled playing catch-up, by the end of my time at primary school, after a lot of hard work, I was in the middle of the class in most subjects.

Like Medbury, life at Christ's was strictly regimented. By 1949 I was a house prefect, had been accredited University Entrance and had also done well at sport, obtaining my 'blue' in gymnastics and performing well at cricket. I had also won my weight class in boxing.

I was supposed to stay on at Christ's for another year, become head of my boarding house and a school prefect before going on to university. But late in the year I decided — without consulting anyone — to leave at the end of the term and work on the family farm. I still wasn't sure what

I wanted to do long term. In the meantime I focused on farming and the wide range of off-farm activities that were available in the district.

Branch politics

I knew I was interested in politics, and the National Party in particular, so in early 1950, at the age of 18, I became secretary of the party's local branch. As such I was a delegate to Hurunui electorate meetings and one of three electorate representatives to Canterbury/Westland divisional meetings and the party's Dominion Conference. The latter, in 1950, was a celebratory affair, with Prime Minister Holland and senior Cabinet ministers in top form following the party's first-ever election win in 1949.

Later, I became the Hurunui electorate chairman, a division deputy chairman, a member of the party's Dominion Council and Dominion Executive, and a regular attendee at party annual conferences.

The army

The army also started to take up more of my time. After my 14 weeks' basic training in 1950 — following the urging of my company commander, who rated me 'one of his first choices as an officer to take into action'[1] — I attended a weekend officer training course. There, my performance was deemed only 'fair', as a result of my reluctance to take part in what I regarded as some of the silly team games other attendees fell over themselves to play. I was 'deferred' and marked as 'doubtful' officer material.

My company commander was furious and as a result of his vigorous representations I attended another officer training course, this time at the Waiouru Military Camp. I didn't get off to a good start. I arrived a day late, enrolled and proceeded to my allocated bunk-house, where, within minutes, I was placed on report for untidiness (along with a number of fellow trainees). We were ordered to assemble at dawn next morning fully kitted.

Next morning's parade began with an order to raise our rifles at full stretch above our heads and jog around the parade ground. Initially I thought this was pathetically funny, but after some time it certainly wasn't. My rifle become unbearably heavy and I decided I would throw it down — immediately after someone else did so. No one obliged.

Several days later it became clear that my deferral and the representations of my company commander had raised some interest when Major-General Walter McKinnon — Chief of General Staff and father of my future parliamentary colleague Don McKinnon — visited our course. During his inspection General McKinnon asked, 'Which one is Quigley?' 'Me, sir,' I replied, and after a brief look at me he moved on.

All officer trainees were subjected to intense pressure to see who would crack, and several dropped out before it was over. But I managed to hang on and eventually became the first CMT officer commissioned in Canterbury, with 'above average' grades in most subjects. One comment on my report noted that I was 'somewhat unjustifiably self-opinionated' and another that I 'appeared highly strung'.[2]

Shortly after receiving my commission, I attended a two-week annual camp with No. 1 Platoon, A Company under my command. It comprised locals of my own age and many were my mates which meant some challenges to my command responsibilities. One occurred early. On the way to the camp we came across a broken-down convoy vehicle within half a mile of the Belfast Hotel. It was empty and it was obvious where the occupants were.

The bar was lined with very drunk soldiers and I was greeted with a call of 'Have a beer, Quig!' I declined, and after a great deal of difficulty everyone was shepherded outside to the one usable vehicle, where numerous bladders had to be emptied in full view of passing traffic before everyone was on board.

At the camp the truck was unloaded and the occupants were formed up in total disorder by a newly commissioned military police officer who asked, too loudly, 'What have these bastards been up to?' One of the soldiers who had urged me to have a drink with him overheard this and staggered forward. 'What did you say?' he said. 'You can't speak to us like that.' From then on, none of the assembled troops would respond to any instruction from that officer and eventually he had to dismiss them.

My task now was to get my platoon under canvas and settled in. But my two experienced fellow platoon commanders had got there before me and there was no gear left. As I had few options, I instructed my NCOs to quietly pinch back whatever was needed. This worked superbly and we were eventually well equipped.

My commanding officer, Colonel Jim Williams, later gave me some useful advice. 'Don't fraternise with the ranks,' he said, which made sense in command terms but of course was much more difficult in practice. Eventually I settled on a 'semi-cooperative' approach, which must have worked, as we won top place in the regiment's inter-platoon competition.

Young Farmers Club

My involvement with the Young Farmers Club organisation (YFC) also mushroomed at this time. By 1953 I was the North Canterbury district chairman, and thought I was a shoo-in for a Lincoln College scholarship for which there was only one other local applicant.

Unfortunately my over-confidence meant I did not do any research or other preparation for the selection interview, and I failed. But this turned out to be a blessing, as it prompted me to go for a much more prestigious Meat and Wool Boards scholarship to the UK. And this time I prepared properly — over 12 months. I made sure that I achieved as much as I could during that time within my own district, winning the North Canterbury YFC shepherding competitions; leading the winning district debating team where I was judged best speaker; and being a member of the local club team that won the National Miniature Rifle Competition.

My greatest pleasure was winning the district speaking competition. My topic was 'South East Asia', which was very pertinent in the aftermath of the Korean War, with continuing unrest in the area and ongoing concern about the 'domino effect' of communism spreading towards Australia and New Zealand. The topic also had the advantage of being out of the ordinary for a farming contest.

Eventually two of us, both from Canterbury — Derek Fechney and myself — were selected, and sailed for Sydney on Christmas Eve 1954, on the first leg of our voyage to the United Kingdom.

The UK and North America

We arrived in the UK on 4 February, in the depth of winter. My diary notes that London was as I expected: grey and drab.

> The people in the Young Farmers office who are looking after us seem to be financially fairly poor. Taxi drivers have long hair and big noses; and the railway porters are from the moaning lower class. Around the City the homburg, umbrella and trimmings are much in evidence. A Londoner is

expected to rise at exactly the same time every morning, have the same things for breakfast, catch the same train and arrive at and leave work strictly to the clock. Pooh!

Although many of the industrial cities were still showing signs of major war damage, rural areas were prospering. Most of the farms we stayed on were family owned, but, unlike in New Zealand, a farm manager and a number of employees did the actual farm work while the owner supervised the overall 'business'. Consistent with this, I wrote in my diary: 'There is little idea of labour-saving practices, compared with the New Zealand situation.'

My first farm stay was on the west coast of Scotland, where, in addition to what I learnt about local farming, another lesson concerned the Scots' view of the English. The history of conflict between the two 'countries' was very much at the top of people's minds.

It wasn't long since the removal to Scotland of the Stone of Scone (also known as the Stone of Destiny) from under the Coronation Chair in Westminster Abbey in 1950, and it turned out some of the people we met had been involved. The stone had originally been used for the coronation of Scottish monarchs but had been taken from Scotland by Edward I in 1296 to bolster his claims to the throne of Scotland. The actions of those who had removed the stone (albeit temporarily) had reignited Scottish pride and were applauded as a symbolic triumph of Scottish nationalism.[3]

I also learnt a bit about whisky while in Scotland. On a visit to a stud farm where our host intended to buy a bull, we were ushered inside and given a 'wee dram' from a bottle of Johnny Walker Black Label. Soon after, the livestock agent said, 'Let's go and see this bull,' but our host unexpectedly announced that he wanted to go home. In the car the bemused agent asked him what that had been about. The reply was, 'Anyone devious enough to try to pass off ordinary whisky as Black Label can't be trusted as a stud breeder either.'

Probably the most important farming lesson I learnt while I was in the UK — one that is relevant to New Zealand today, given its huge trade reliance on China — is that it's dangerous to have all your eggs in one basket. In other words, diversification of both products and markets is crucially important.

We visited the US before we came home. We had carefully worked out all the places we wanted to visit but hadn't factored in the tremendous size of the continent and the time it took to cross it. A 16-hour bus trip from New York to Indianapolis seemed to make little progress on our map.

It was approaching winter when we visited a Wool Growers Conference in Cheyenne, Wyoming, which looked like a 'wild west' town then and probably still does today. Our host was America's biggest Corriedale owner, with a flock of 4000, but sheep were not high on the agenda among American farmers at that time. However, we were made well aware of their strong opposition to New Zealand meat imports, which were regarded as a threat to local sheep and beef producers.

In California it was extremely hot, with oranges and grapes still to be harvested. This vast country boasted many different climates simultaneously.

Los Angeles and Hollywood were musts to visit for these two Kiwi boys, but it was good to finally travel north to San Francisco and board the ship for the voyage back to Auckland, where we arrived exactly 12 months after leaving New Zealand

National politics

Not long after we were back home, Derek Fechney returned to the UK to do an economics degree and work for the New Zealand Meat Board. Sometime later, when I was married to Judith Dickson, had bought the family farm and was looking for further challenges, Derek's move provided the spur I needed. As I sat on my tractor laboriously cultivating one paddock after another, I used to say to myself, 'If Fechney can get an economics degree, I can too.'

But politics rather than economics was my first choice, and in 1960 I contested the Labour stronghold of Sydenham in Christchurch for the National Party. The seat was held by Mabel Howard, a national icon who had become New Zealand's first woman Cabinet minister in 1947. She had the biggest majority of any electorate in New Zealand and, among other things, was widely remembered for having waved two large pairs of bloomers in Parliament in support of her successful campaign to have clothing sizes standardised.

The Sydenham National Party membership was dedicated, but small and mainly old. A young exception was the electorate secretary, a former Warsaw Resistance fighter named Zbigniew Maciaszek, who had settled

With Mabel Howard, election night 1963 when I stood there again.

in Christchurch in 1950. He was known as Mac by his friends, and Mr McIsaac by those who couldn't handle the Polish pronunciation.

Mac and I decided to run a more aggressive campaign than was traditional in a safe Labour seat. I spoke on street corners, at factory meetings, at the Railway Workshops, and outside pubs when the patrons came out after 6 o'clock closing.

All these venues were hotbeds of Labour supporters who had probably never previously seen, let alone heard from a National Party candidate. Fortunately, the reaction I received was mostly good natured, although I had an anxious moment on one occasion outside the Sandridge Hotel in Colombo Street immediately after closing time. There was a large horse trough in the street by the pub exit, and for a moment I had visions of finishing up in it, given the tone of some of the rather drunk non-National voters who seemed to think I was trespassing on their hallowed ground. Salvation came in the form of a very large police sergeant who must have got wind of my audacity. He initially stood quietly by, but when things heated up he said, 'Are you all right, mate?' This was the cue for us to go home while I was still intact.

To add to the fun, we had people walking the streets with sandwich boards advertising my candidacy, and also made up two big signs that were fitted onto a car trailer in pyramid form. The car and trailer were driven around the electorate continually, and on one occasion, when they were slowly proceeding along Colombo Street during the evening rush hour, the police pulled the driver over. In response to the question 'What do you think you are doing?' he replied, 'We are only trying to make an impression.' The officer's reply was, 'Well, you certainly are, for a mile back. Get moving!'

Our hard work made little difference — Mabel retained her seat, and still had the highest majority of any electorate in New Zealand.

In April 1961 Bill Gillespie, my local Hurunui MP, died. With the electorate regarded as safe for National, nine candidates, including me, sought the nomination. One was Lorrie Pickering, a local farmer aged 42 with a university degree, who was a more acceptable choice in those conservative days than a 29-year-old unqualified youngster like me. He duly won the nomination, but as a consolation prize I was chosen as electorate deputy chairman shortly after.

I was now well and truly infected with the political bug and began looking around for a seat to contest in the 1963 election. The only possibility was the marginal Labour-held electorate of Timaru. But before I could give serious thought to this, Tom Hayman, MP for the Waitaki electorate, died in early January 1962, necessitating another by-election.

During the 1935–38 Parliament my mother's brother, David Barnes, had represented Waitaki for Labour during the influx of workers to build the Waitaki Dam, but in 1962 it was regarded as reasonably safe for National. The electorate was a long way from where I lived so I didn't rate my chances very highly, as I would be seen by some as a 'carpet-bagger'. But I put my name forward on the basis that a good showing there would improve my chances in neighbouring Timaru in 1963.

Allegedly, I came in a close second behind the local farmer candidate, Alan Dick. In retrospect, had I won the nomination, the seat may well have been lost to Labour, as Dick only held it in the by-election by a few hundred votes.

With no further seats in the offing, I enrolled to do Stage 1 economics extramurally at the University of Canterbury, some 70 kilometres away from my farm.

University — and more politics

Maciaszek enrolled to do economics too, attending lectures in person, so we agreed to study together. But I didn't find it that straightforward. I had no university experience, little idea of what was required for Economics I, and, unlike Mac, was not attending lectures. Consequently, after reading my first assignment, the lecturer wrote, 'Although all you have written is true, none of it is relevant to the topic. I suggest you concentrate on the following ...' He listed five specific areas to focus on, all of which subsequently came up in the end-of-year exam.

Armed with this advice, passing the exam in November should have been easy, but on 31 May 1962 the MP for Timaru resigned and a by-election was scheduled for late July. I put my name forward and was selected as the National Party candidate.

Street-corner and factory meetings were organised, and I set out to call on as many local businesses and shops as I could within what was little more than a four-week timeframe. But because by-elections are run by party head office, I didn't have complete control of my campaign. This was confirmed at the end of the last week when I still had a number of businesses to call on and was anxious to complete the task. However, I was told to 'stay close by', and when I objected, I was told that the prime minister — who was coming to Timaru to give the final campaign address — would probably want to see me.

Sure enough, that afternoon I was taken to the Grand Hotel where Prime Minister Keith Holyoake had taken up residence. I was escorted to his room by the party's general secretary, who knocked on the door.

'Who is it?' came the call from inside.

'Mr Quigley is here to see you, sir.'

'Who's Quigley?'

'The candidate, sir.'

It was an inauspicious start but I was ushered into Holyoake's hallowed presence to find him stretched out on his bed resting. After a couple of questions that confirmed my irrelevance, I was dismissed, but at that night's meeting I was presented as one of Holyoake's lifelong friends and a person who, like him, would become an MP after winning a by-election and eventually become prime minister.

I lost by 1307 votes and went back to the farm with my tail between my legs.

Lambing was in full swing when I got there and it was soon time to cut the grass that had been saved for hay, do the baling and cart the hay bales into storage. I was hopelessly behind with my university studies and told Mac I was going to quit. He objected, insisting I could catch up easily.

We agreed to spend the long Labour Day weekend at the farm swotting for the forthcoming exam after we had carted the last hay bales into the shed. They were quite heavy and there was a knack to lifting them without back strain. I wore rubber hand grips with finger holes to stop the baling twine cutting into my fingers, and offered Mac a pair as I showed him how to lift the bales. He would have none of it, claiming he knew what to do.

There were about 400 bales and after an hour or so I could see that Mac was struggling. He still wouldn't listen, but we eventually completed the task and spent the rest of the weekend concentrating on the five topics the lecturer had given me. Later, Mac confessed that the hay carting experience was one of the worst he had ever had.

Changing to law

Somehow, we both passed Economics I, and after the Christmas break I suggested to Mac that we do two more economics units during 1963. 'No,' he replied, 'let's do law.' And that's what we did, enrolling as part-time students to do English, Legal Systems and Criminal Law.

The farm schedule was rearranged to fit in with the university lecture schedule. Ewes were mated early; fat lambs and cull stock were sold when there was high market demand for them; haymaking and harvesting took place after lectures had ended for the year; and all the autumn work was undertaken before university resumed at the end of February. This enabled me to attend two of the three weekly lectures on each subject by staying one night a week in Christchurch, while Mac attended and updated me on the lectures I missed.

Three subjects made for a big workload on top of my full-time farming job. English involved two papers, Legal Systems covered a wide variety of topics, and Criminal Law was a 'failing subject' — designed to weed out those who should be studying something else or shouldn't be at university at all. It was a lot to do.

I found out early on that I was too uptight to get reasonable results if I adopted the traditional student method of sailing along and then cramming for three weeks before exams. So, from the start of July, Mac and I began preparing answers to the questions we thought were likely to come up in the November exams.

The standard law paper at that time required answers to five of 12 or more questions, so we went back and tabulated the topics that had featured in the previous five years of exam papers, and focused on preparing eight answers, sometimes working on subjects before they came up in lectures. On one occasion, because of time constraints and work pressure, we went into an exam room with only seven answers prepared. To my horror there was nothing I could answer on page one, and page two was the same. Beginning to panic, I went to the last question on the back page. When I found I could answer it, I did so without looking at the rest of the paper. Then I moved progressively upwards and found three more I could answer, and a fifth one I knew a little about. Somehow, I got a B pass.

I had appointed a farm manager by this time so that I could sit exams in five subjects, and the following year – in addition to my university studies – I worked four days a week in my uncle's Christchurch law firm. A law student then needed at least three years' office experience before being able to either practise on their own account or join a law partnership. A minimum of a solicitor's qualification was required before this could happen, and I worked out this could be achieved before completing the full degree course. I consequently scheduled my university and office working time to achieve this, despite the fact that I hadn't yet decided whether I wanted to be a farmer with a law degree or a practising lawyer with a farm.

Moving to the city

By now I had passed nine of the 20 subjects needed to complete an LLB but I needed more office experience if I wanted to practise as a solicitor before graduating. It made sense to live in Christchurch, so I leased the farm, took a law clerk's job with Millar & Kerr, and Judith and I and

From left to right, Derek, Mac Maciaszek, Philip Davies and Neil Maclean, Christchurch, 2012.

our four children — Jane, Pamela, Mark and Christopher — moved into town.

I had decided I wanted to do court work after I qualified, but then I was invited to join Helmore, McDonald and Stanley, a firm that specialised in conveyancing. The senior partner was retiring at the end of the year so there was a vacancy to fill. Initially I wasn't interested, but when a starting salary of £1500 was mentioned — almost double what I was earning — I began to have second thoughts. Eventually I concluded that I couldn't afford to turn the offer down and joined the firm after that year's exams.

Exam results were posted on a noticeboard outside the office of the Christchurch *Press*, then located in Cathedral Square, and on the appointed day I went to find out how I had got on. To my horror, my name didn't appear anywhere and I concluded that I had failed all five subjects. This meant I would have to repeat them, delaying my partnership prospects.

In despair I went to the Law Faculty and found that the results for my courses were yet to be posted. In fact I had passed all five. Thus far I had not failed any subjects and was now entitled to be admitted as a solicitor. I still had to pass Conflict of Laws and International Law papers to complete my LLB. This I did the following year.

At that time, most law students studied full time for five years. Mac and I had taken six years to gain our LLBs, counting our first year doing Economics I. Although our grades weren't great, we had made it. We were quite pleased with ourselves.

After graduating, in what now looks like a pretty stupid decision, Mac and I, along with our friends Neil Maclean and Philip Davies, enrolled to do law master's degrees. At that time this degree could be done in two ways: either by passing four papers (covering two subjects) in the first year and then completing a thesis; or by sitting exam papers over two years. All four of us opted for the first route, despite strenuous opposition from our professor.

'Most people don't do the thesis,' he said, but of course we knew better. Although all of us passed our first-year papers, none has yet finished his thesis.

Practising law

Life was good as the 1970s approached. I had a job I enjoyed which, unlike farming, was not dependent on international product prices or the weather; and I was getting on well at work and prospering financially. I was also attracting a number of new clients, particularly from North Canterbury, where I was still well known. My work was more complex and varied, with estates to administer, trust law to master, property transactions to handle, and the occasional court appearance.

On joining the firm I had been shown four extremely old dog-eared files and been told that when someone new joined the practice they had to complete the remaining work on one of these files. I did all four together.

My first Supreme Court appearance was to determine the validity of a last will and testament. The deceased woman in question had executed a number of wills in her final years, their content varying depending on whom she was with when she signed them.

The most recent version had been drawn up by a senior lawyer who was with her when it was signed and witnessed, and he was called to assist the court in deciding whether she had been of sound mind at the time. He told the court that they had had tea together before the will was signed, that she had answered a number of detailed questions, and that she had lucidly recited a poem to him. The court held that the will was valid and that the charities nominated should receive the bulk of the estate, rather than the family members who were named in the earlier documents.

Another case was on behalf of the National Girl Guides Association, which had built a lodge near the bottom of Cashmere Hills as a centre for training, conferences and courses. Part of the building provided accommodation, but it had not been described in the plans as a boarding house. With the building nearly complete the local council ruled that it was a boarding house and had to comply — at considerable extra cost — with new regulations. The association's board demurred and the council issued court proceedings. I was asked to appear on behalf of the Girl Guides. The case was heard by a magistrate who liked his drink, had a large backlog of undecided cases, and gave the impression he was uncomfortable about having to rule on this particular matter. After hearing witnesses and submissions he said he was considering entering a conviction, but would adjourn the case to see if the two sides could reach agreement.

My client board members were akin to an old-time western posse, determined not to dismount until they 'got their man'. Consequently, their message was to tell the magistrate to convict the association if that was what he was determined to do. When I reported back, a very unhappy magistrate entered a conviction and imposed a nominal fine, clearly hoping that no appeal would eventuate. He was out of luck, and in the Supreme Court the Chief Justice found in the association's favour. For several years that ruling was the leading authority on what was and was not a boarding house in terms of the regulations.

Another case I was involved in concerned crayfishing. A Marine Court of Inquiry had been set up following the deaths of seven people in a convoy that had sailed from Lyttelton Harbour to the Chatham Islands to take part in the 'crayfish bonanza' there. Our client was regarded in the industry as a meticulous fisherman who had established a reputation for big crayfish catches. Local Chatham Islands folklore was that you had to 'follow the *Kingfisher*' (his boat) if you wanted to secure good catches too.

A convoy of several registered and approved vessels sailed from Lyttelton, with a second smaller fishing vessel (a dory), also owned by our client, under tow by the *Kingfisher*. A mariner with previous convoy experience was appointed convoy commodore. However, when the convoy passed through the heads into calm open waters an unauthorised yacht, which had been converted to catch crayfish and had five people on board, joined the end of the convoy and continued to sail with it.

Two days later the weather turned and huge seas developed. The tow rope from the *Kingfisher* to the dory broke but was reconnected. Later it broke again and was reconnected a second time. When the tow rope snapped a third time, two of the *Kingfisher* crew boarded the dory, started its motor and proceeded to sail it independently.

The storm worsened, and the dory with its two crew, along with the converted yacht with its five people on board, were never seen again.

The Marine Court of Inquiry was set up to determine what had happened and why, and to apportion blame if that was thought to be appropriate. It was conducted under the provisions of the antiquated Shipping and Seamen's Act 1877, with magistrate Kenneth Headifen presiding. He was known locally as 'Mad Jack' because of his propensity to lose his temper in court, and under the act was the only person allowed to call and question witnesses. So although our client and others had their lawyers present, we could not participate in the proceedings.

Headifen had two people in his sights. One was the commodore, with Headifen claiming he should have taken more notice of the long-term weather forecast and returned the convoy to port when the crew of the unauthorised vessel refused to abandon its attempt to join it. The other person was our client.

The inquiry was held in a large room where those present could see a beautiful, windless, sunny day outside. It was not an ideal atmosphere to get a feel for what it may have been like on the *Kingfisher* being lashed by hurricane-force winds and 10-metre swells.

Headifen repeatedly asked our client if he had 'ordered' the two crew to get aboard the dory and sail it independently. Our client said the two men had decided that getting aboard was the only practical option, and that no 'orders' had been issued.

Headifen refused to accept the evidence of either the commodore or our client. He suspended the commodore's master's licence for three months and fined our client several hundred dollars. I appealed on behalf of both, and although we were unsuccessful, I believe I may be one of only a handful of people in New Zealand to have appeared before this particular type of appeal authority.

A further case illustrates the folly of counting your chickens before they hatch. I was pursuing a debtor who owed my client several hundred dollars. A court judgment had been obtained for the amount owing but we were having difficulty getting repayment. Then a friend phoned to say he had been at a party the previous evening and heard the debtor boasting that he had 'beaten Quigley' and was off to Australia the next day. Armed with this information, I assembled the necessary papers for an urgent court application and duly had the bailiff arrest the 'absconding debtor' on the plane just before it took off. Once in jail, he quickly made arrangements to repay what he owed.

Wills and estate administration were the bread and butter of old, established firms like the one I was in. The preparation or revision of a will often resulted in estate planning transactions to minimise estate duty, which at that time was potentially substantial. Also, the administration of an estate when a client died was a good money earner for the practice, particularly when valuable farm land was involved. But even the simplest will, such as a husband-and-wife disposition, where the first to die leaves everything to the survivor, had to be handled carefully, as I subsequently found out to my potential embarrassment.

On that occasion, mutual wills had been prepared. But when the clients came to my office without an appointment (as often happened with country people) to sign the wills, I was away in court. As a result, office staff handled the signing and witnessing of the documents.

Unexpectedly, the husband died shortly after, and I thought the administration of his estate would be straightforward. But when I looked at his will, I found that he had mistakenly signed his wife's will and she had signed his. He had no earlier will and because he had signed the wrong document, he had effectively died intestate. I decided not to tell his widow immediately — she was already extremely distraught about his death — and set about obtaining full details of the estate's assets.

It soon became clear that even without a will everything could go to the widow. However, the problem was a life insurance policy, which under normal circumstances required a court order before the proceeds could be released. I decided to visit the life company's CEO and explain the situation to him. He understood, and after an offer of appropriate undertakings he agreed to pay out to the widow in full. Shortly after, I made sure that she signed her own valid will!

Joining Bell Taylor

During 1971 I accepted an invitation to join another legal firm, Bell Taylor. The decision was an excellent one, and I stayed on as one of four partners until I became a Cabinet minister after the 1978 election. During my first year there my friend Mac, who still had family living in Warsaw, began to talk about doing his LLM thesis on comparative New Zealand and Polish criminal law. He had done some preliminary research but said he could not complete the writing without a visit to Poland. However, he felt he couldn't absent himself from his current legal practice, which I had helped him buy – so I offered to cover for him for up to three months by going in for an hour or so each morning, while his excellent personal assistant effectively ran the practice.

Mac accepted and I quickly found out that I had taken on more than I had anticipated. Mac had become a 'cause' lawyer, often acting for people he thought were getting a raw deal from 'the system' — be it lending institutions, real estate agents, government bureaucracy, or the occasional magistrate. These cases took up a lot of his time, meaning a large number of 'non-urgent' files sat awaiting completion on his desk. I set myself the task of clearing the pile by the time he returned home, and did so.

My efforts had two unanticipated consequences. One involved the PA. She had the firm's normal business to attend to while Mac was away, and new client work that flowed from people either she or I saw. When I had completed all that needed to be done on a 'desk clearance file', and a fee had been set, I passed the documents to her to action, type up and file away. Later, she said, jokingly, that the increased workload from everything I had passed on to her had nearly killed her.

The second consequence was a very substantial increase in the firm's income for the year, because of all the files that had been billed. The downside was the higher income tax impost that had to be paid, but, as I said to Mac, he had a clear desk when he returned home and good cashflow to pay the Inland Revenue Department.

What Mac hadn't done while he was away was any work on his thesis. Instead, he had got caught up in a concerted attack on the Polish bureaucracy, which brought on a mild heart attack.

CHAPTER 3

Entering Parliament

A Reality Check

Shortly before the 1972 election Lorrie Pickering announced that he was retiring from Parliament because of ill-health. Given that my father had died earlier in the year and my mother still needed a lot of support, plus the fact that I had recently joined Bell Taylor, I decided against seeking the party's nomination for the seat (now renamed Rangiora).

However, a good friend, Adrian Hyatt, got the nod, and as I was approaching the Canterbury/Westland National Party rooms close to election day, I bumped into him. I wished him luck and then added, 'If you don't hold the seat, I'm going to stand next time.' This remark was overheard by another electorate delegate who reminded me of it in 1974, when nominations were again called for the seat after National had lost it and 12 others to Labour in the 1972 election landslide.

In 1972 I was campaign chairman for John Blumsky, National's Lyttelton candidate. John was a senior journalist at Radio New Zealand and was well known and liked locally.[1] Although he worked hard he was never going to win the seat in the face of such a strong swing to Labour. Even so, we ran a vigorous campaign, assisted by a team of helpers from among my legal colleagues and Lyttelton National Party activists. In addition to street-corner, factory and hall meetings, we walked up and down the electorate's steep hills, door-knocking and delivering pamphlets. Interestingly, several of my legal friends who had helped later told me they had voted Labour on the day. Their motivation, they said, was that it was 'time for a change', which proves that you can take a horse to water but you can't make it drink!

On election night we headed off to the party rooms in the centre of the city, where the atmosphere was like a pope's wake. Everyone had long faces, and Murray Hunter, the division chairman, told us — as though this were the final electoral humiliation — that even Hugh Templeton had lost his seat. Hugh was a Rhodes Scholar, a former diplomat, and MP for the supposedly safe Southland electorate of Awarua. He was regarded as one of National's rising stars. I was relieved I had not stood in Rangiora.

To escape all this election night despondency, a group of us headed off for a steak dinner. An hour or so later we returned to the party rooms to find them locked — everyone had gone home in despair. As I wasn't ready to retire yet, a friend and I said good night to our respective wives and set off for National's Lyttelton electorate election night party. This was a rip-roaring affair, with everyone focusing on the future. I was a little drunk when I walked up our drive as the sun was rising, but I remember the birds were singing loudly and the world had not come to an end as a result of National's election defeat.

The 1975 selection process

The National Party significantly reorganised itself ahead of the 1975 election. George Chapman was elected president in 1973, and Barrie Leay appointed director-general soon after. Leay was English and had a good political mind, but processing correspondence was not his forte. In no time at all his Wellington desk was piled high with unattended-to files and unanswered correspondence. Barrie's view was that most problems would eventually solve themselves without his involvement, which thankfully turned out to be correct in most cases.

Part of the reorganisation involved an overhaul of the candidate selection process, with two objectives. The first was to have candidates in winnable marginal seats held by Labour MPs selected before Christmas in 1974. The second was to overcome a situation where a weak candidate in an electorate with large numbers seeking the nomination could come through ahead of much stronger candidates due to the party's preferential voting selection system. The solution was the introduction of a two-tiered selection process that reduced the initial candidate pool to no more than five. As the Rangiora and Waitaki electorates had been lost to Labour in 1972, they — along with Lyttelton — were in the 'early selection' category.

When nominations were called for Rangiora for 1975 I was among the senior ranks of the party organisation and had served my electoral apprenticeship. I had a good university degree and was a respected legal practitioner. With my strong North Canterbury connections to boot,

I was the party's preferred candidate. Despite this, I was reluctant to put my name forward, but in the end did so because of my earlier commitment to Adrian Hyatt. A number of other hopefuls, including Colleen Dewe, a well-known and well-liked Christchurch accountant, were also nominated.

The pre-selection panel was chaired by Jim Gerard, the local electorate chairman, who had political aspirations of his own and later succeeded me as MP for Rangiora. One of the questions he asked was: 'If you win the seat, will you move into the electorate?' I wasn't prepared to give an assurance at that stage, but said I would consider the matter after the election. Gerard's retort was: 'If that's your attitude, I'm not going to vote for you.' I told him he could please himself.

Five candidates (including me but not Colleen Dewe, who was subbed out because the party hierarchy wanted her to stand in Lyttelton), were pre-selected. A series of meet-the-candidates meetings followed, where my ambivalence about standing began to show.

The final pre-selection meeting took place near the Labour stronghold of Kaiapoi, where Norman Kirk had been mayor. The area had been virtually ignored by National as a lost cause but I was convinced the party's vote there could be improved substantially, and had decided to outline how this could be achieved in my speech.

But before my turn came, a political enthusiast and family friend of mine asked Jim Gerard, who was chairing the meeting, if he could tape my speech. The answer was yes, but once I started speaking Jim changed his mind. He walked down into the audience and took my friend's recorder from him. I was furious and vented my anger from the stage with a strong speech. Apparently, my comments about Kaiapoi's importance appealed to the local branch delegates, who decided to vote for me if their own candidate was knocked out of the selection proceedings before me.

On selection night each candidate was to speak for 10 minutes and answer two questions. One was set by dominion headquarters and the other by the local divisional chairman. I expected a question on housing, as house prices had doubled under three years of the Labour government, and the other would be: 'How do you propose campaigning to win the seat back from Labour?' I was right on both counts and gave what I hoped were authoritative answers. The Kaiapoi branch candidate fumbled his questions and was knocked out early in the contest, with his branch delegates switching their support to me. In a marathon elimination process I finally beat Russell Bain, the candidate from the Cust/Oxford area, to win the nomination.

I now had to decide whether or not to move back into the electorate. It seemed clear that from a campaign perspective and in the interests of party morale the answer should be yes, so we rented a house in Rangiora township. As I wasn't prepared to sell our Cashmere house before the election, I began to look for a tenant.

A neighbour showed me an advertisement from someone looking for a house to rent. I rang the number and Susan McAffer answered. She said she had just moved to Christchurch to establish her own advertising agency and had been part of the original Colenso Communications team that was now handling the National Party's election campaign. After some due diligence I agreed she could rent Cloudsly for the princely sum of $40 a week, provided she handled my election communications campaign free of charge. She agreed and joined my campaign committee.

The 1975 campaign

Susan's first decision was to initiate a comprehensive survey to test my electorate name awareness. I was appalled when it came in at only 50 percent, but later learnt that this was actually fairly good. Armed with this information, a campaign strategy was devised to boost recognition of the name Quigley to 100 percent by polling day.

Susan and her team came up with numerous innovative tactics. One involved the use of a London double-decker bus painted prominently with my name in National Party colours. Volunteers were assigned to drive it continually around the electorate to advertise my candidature and create the impression that I was in the area. The bus was also used to ferry teams of volunteers as part of an overall objective to door-knock every residence in the electorate. Specially trained people were tasked with compiling lists of potential and committed party supporters to make sure they voted on polling day. This information is important in New Zealand, as voting here, unlike in Australia, is not compulsory.

I knocked on a lot of doors myself, particularly in the new beachside suburb of Parklands and the Labour stronghold of Kaiapoi. After introducing myself as the National Party candidate, my usual pitch was to give three reasons to vote for National and me. I would then ask, looking the person straight in the eye, 'Can I count on your vote and the votes

1975 election campaign bus.

of the rest of your household on polling day?' In the face of such a direct approach, most people responded immediately with either yes or no, which allowed me to complete fairly accurate voting information sheets.

The important thing, which we warned all our canvassers about, was not to get stuck on a doorstep having long chats, or worse still, successive cups of tea. The electorate was very large, and to cover it our people had to keep moving. Party members were told to show Labour canvassers the utmost hospitality when they called, and to slow them down as much as possible!

My wife and our daughter Jane were active campaigners, with Jane also expressing an interest in the Labour Party. I encouraged her to attend a Labour Party youth conference in Kaiapoi. Kerry Burke, the local MP, initially greeted her warmly, but once he found out who she was he assumed she was a spy and walked off. Despite this, Jane still harboured thoughts of voting Labour and was unwise enough to mention this to her mother, who responded by giving her a resounding slap on the face.

Rodney McMillan, the friend who tried to record my pre-selection speech, door-knocked for me full time for three months during the last part of the campaign. He had a competitive streak and each night he

Another way to campaign.

would ask me, 'How many did you do today?' I usually, rather unkindly, added about 50 percent to my actual number, which spurred him on to even greater efforts.

Kerry Burke had won Rangiora from National in 1972 with a majority of 866 votes. He was an extremely good MP, worked hard for his constituents and was well liked locally. I consequently never criticised him. In fact, on occasions I made it my business to visit the people in Labour's campaign office for a chat. This removed any potential animosity from the campaign, and messages filtered back that they thought I wasn't a bad bloke, despite my politics.

Burke and I had very few joint meetings during the campaign after one well-attended early occasion that focused on superannuation. The venue was my home patch of Waipara, a National stronghold, so Burke was on the back foot. The Labour government had implemented a compulsory superannuation scheme funded by employers and employees (not to be confused with the New Zealand Superannuation Fund, created in 2001). The earlier scheme was the brainchild of Labour Cabinet minister Roger Douglas and promised to provide retirees over time with massive superannuation accounts. An additional objective of the scheme was to create a fund that could be tapped into to finance national infrastructure projects.

Although the scheme was sound in principle, it was easy — in a debating sense — to criticise it by focusing on five points. One was that it had the potential for a government takeover of businesses. This argument was helped dramatically by a highly successful National Party television advertisement created by Hanna-Barbera. It featured dancing Cossacks and depicted Labour's superannuation scheme as a Soviet-style monster that would turn the whole country 'red' in the interests of perpetuating state socialism. A second point was that the scheme was an extra tax on employers and employees, who were already under pressure financially. A third point was that it discriminated against non-employees such as 'non-working' wives and mothers, who weren't covered by the scheme. A fourth point was that the projected massive amounts that Douglas said would build up in individual retirement accounts looked too good to be true and probably were. The final point was that National's counterproposal for a new 'pay-as-you-go' scheme — which promised 80 percent of the average ordinary-time wage to a married couple at age 60 without a means test — was much more understandable and attractive. The Waipara meeting was such a resounding success for me that — as I was told later — Labour cancelled the other planned joint meetings.

Campaign money was limited and there were strict legal limits on how much an individual candidate could spend in the last few weeks before polling day, so we needed to work out how to get the best value for the money available. Susan McAffer had decided early on that it was crucial to overcome the 'faceless candidate syndrome' and that television was the best medium for this. She consequently bought local TV time where for several weeks I appeared just before the 6pm news and simply said: 'Hello, I'm Derek Quigley, the Rangiora National Party candidate.'

It was the first time an individual candidate had used television in this way and, although strict rules limited what could be said, my appearances boosted my candidature significantly. The exercise also used up a large part of my advertising budget, but the impact was pronounced. Towards the end of the campaign another survey showed my name awareness was 99 percent.

Overall, the campaign involved a marathon effort by a large number of local and outside helpers, and by and large it went smoothly. One exception involved my own door-knocking efforts. With election day approaching, I still hadn't visited all the houses in our own street and Judith was adamant I had to do so. Reluctantly — by now I was worn out after almost nine months of near full-time campaigning — I began with the house across the road, which I knew was occupied by active National Party members.

The lady of the house opened the door and almost immediately launched into a diatribe. 'You want to be our member of Parliament and look after the people in this electorate, but you can't even manage your own children properly!' she said. 'Do you know what your son Christopher does?' I was completely taken back and said no. She explained that on numerous occasions she had seen our eight-year-old son and his friend play 'chicken' on the side of the road. When they saw a car coming, they would take turns to ride their bicycles at speed down our driveway, across the footpath, and out onto the road. All the driver of the oncoming car could see was a child on a bike who was going to be run over unless immediate evasive action was taken.

However, as I was to discover, evasive action was part of the 'chicken' game the boys were playing. Just before impact they would brake hard in the shingle strip between the footpath and the sealed road surface, using the loose shingle to skid their bikes parallel with the road. They would then ride off, with no thought for the near heart attack they had caused the car driver. This escapade was one of Christopher's ways of letting off steam after the numerous scraps he got into — again as I found out later — with boys at his local school whose parents were not National Party supporters.

Our campaign efforts were helped immeasurably during 1975 by the failing state of the New Zealand economy and the brilliant nationwide campaign Muldoon and the National Party were conducting. The international downturn had seriously affected New Zealand. Export prices had fallen and the cost of imports had risen due to higher oil prices and increasing international inflation. The public sector was also experiencing substantial cost overruns. To take maximum political advantage of these events, National's election manifesto emphasised that these were symptoms, not the basic cause of New Zealand's economic problems. National claimed that the cause was three years of Labour mismanagement, which had destroyed the country's prosperity, dissipated its reserves, trebled the rate of inflation, and turned New Zealand into an international mendicant with an external deficit per head second only to Iceland. National claimed that Labour's period in government was based on 'borrow and hope' and 'creeping socialism'. To reverse the damage, National's key economic policy objective was 'to restore New Zealand's shattered economy'.

This message became increasingly easy to sell as the campaign progressed because it became clear for most to see that the economy was in bad shape. Between 1972 and 1975 the annual cost of living increase had gone from 5.5 percent to 15 percent, food prices from 2.3 percent to 11.03 percent, and the average house and farm prices from, respectively, $13,697 to $25,205; and $65,464 to $123,889. Ten days before the election — but too late — the government announced some remedial action. It said it would prune immigration; raise charges for rail, electricity and post; and take steps to cool the housing market.

As polling day approached, several factors began to point to a National Party win. These included Labour's visible economic incompetence; Muldoon's barnstorming campaign; his mastery of TV which by then had become a prime campaign medium; and Colenso's skilful input and masterful management of Muldoon. Another key factor was the nationwide effort of National Party candidates and their supporters in key electorates, like Rangiora.

But I was worried that the party might fall just short of winning enough seats to form a government, and that Rangiora would be one where we didn't quite make it. So we stepped up our efforts to frenzied proportions in the last few weeks of the campaign. In the end National won comfortably, with an exact reversal of Labour's 23-seat majority in 1972. My majority in Rangiora was 1386.

I was now the member of Parliament for Rangiora, one of a host of new National MPs. One of our first moves was to sell Cloudsly and buy a house in West Belt, Rangiora.

What have I done?

Bell Taylor had moved to refurbished premises overlooking Cathedral Square just before the 1975 election. My office was spacious, with a magnificent view across to the Cathedral, and my excellent secretary, Susan Simons, was close by. All in all, the location and work environment were superb. In dramatic contrast, my office in Parliament was small and dingy. It had no view and was above the Bellamy's cooking area so that the office reeked of stale food. Secretarial assistance was equally inadequate, with one secretary between two MPs and access to the typing pool if anyone there was free.

My office neighbour was Norman Jones, the newly elected MP for Invercargill. Norman was a real character. He had an artificial leg, a walking stick and a complete disdain for anyone he thought was 'bludging' on the system. His main filing cabinet was the rubbish bin where most of his incoming correspondence ended up. On one occasion early on, when he was contemplating replying to a constituent seeking help in obtaining housing finance, Norman showed me his handwritten draft reply. The intended recipient was accused in the draft of being virtually everything other than a dole bludger (but potentially that too), so I suggested an alternative response:

> The letter is from a constituent who might have actually voted for you. Why don't you write back and say you have referred the correspondence to the Minister of Housing and will get back when you have received his reply? This way, even if the answer is no, the Minister will get the blame not you, and you will be seen to have done your best.

Norman thought this was an excellent idea and followed my advice.

My rotten office accommodation wasn't the worst of it. I entertained serious doubts in my first 12 months about being an MP. I wondered why I and all my supporters had worked so hard to get me here.

As a lawyer in private practice I had complete control over what I did, and was respected for what I achieved. More importantly, I had no one to answer to other than my three compatible partners. But here in Parliament, neither Muldoon nor any other Cabinet ministers took much interest in the views of the new batch of backbenchers. It was made clear to us that we were there to learn, to look after our constituents and — in Holyoake parlance — 'to breathe through our noses' so that we didn't rock the boat. And we were expected to turn up and vote for the government without question when the division bells rang. It was quite a come-down.

To add to my despondency, I was convinced the Rangiora electorate was likely to vanish as a result of impending boundary changes. But this didn't happen. In fact the seat lost some strong Labour-voting areas in Christchurch and moved further north into rural National Party territory. As this meant that I was likely to be re-elected at the next election if I still wanted to be an MP, I decided to become more actively involved in order to find out.

As part of this process I decided to speak my mind in caucus, even if this was contrary to the party line. My first opportunity to do so came early on, and was the result of Muldoon's decision to cancel payments to Labour's superannuation fund without seeking parliamentary approval first. Muldoon was sworn in as Prime Minister on 12 December 1975 and three days later issued a press release stating that the new government would, early in the next parliamentary session, introduce legislation to carry out its superannuation promise, including ensuring that 'the compulsory element in the law requiring employer and employee deductions would be removed retrospectively . . . for pay periods ending after this date'.

However, an Education Department employee claimed that using a press release to announce that the scheme was to be abolished, when Parliament had already passed it into law, was illegal. The Chief Justice agreed, but adjourned the matter for six months — essentially allowing the government time to pass the required amending legislation before then. The court's key finding was significant in constitutional terms: 'The sovereignty of Parliament is such that it has the right to make and unmake laws and no person or body is recognised as having the right to override or set aside the legislation of Parliament.'

My lone-voiced comment in caucus, and my first (but not last) clash with our leader, was to say that he should 'uphold the rule of law'.[2]

Finding accommodation in Wellington was an immediate issue once I was elected. So four other National MPs and I bought a large, old wooden house on the corner of Hobson and Davis streets, within walking distance of Parliament. The other MPs were Colleen Dewe (Lyttelton); easy-going 6-foot-4 Bob Bell, a valuer (Gisborne); Tony Friedlander, another valuer (New Plymouth); and Barry Brill, a Wellington lawyer (Kapiti).

Brill — as well as being intellectually bright — was a little unusual in two respects. One was his claim that he could get by on only four or five hours of sleep each night. As a result, he was always late going to bed. Even so, he invariably compensated by being a late riser too. When he failed to turn up for an early-morning meeting and someone asked, 'Where's Brill?', the usual answer was, 'It's not Brill time yet.' Barry's other trait was that he was a chain smoker. He smoked in bed and often fell asleep doing so, as a result of which, I found out later, his bedspread was covered with burns. Why our old two-storey wooden house didn't burn down in the night is still a mystery to me.

By the end of my first year I was making contributions on economic, housing and legal issues in caucus committees and in caucus itself, and found kindred spirits among a number of my fellow newly elected MPs. Unlike previous National Party caucuses, which were dominated by farmers, a number of the new intake had professional qualifications, university degrees and practical business experience.

One of the new intake was Marilyn Waring, who had won selection against the odds in the safe Waipa seat and had turned 23 just before the election. Waring was the brightest of the new MPs and also a committed feminist. But what I did find slightly bizarre was her assumption that I had one etiquette rule for men and another for women. Quite early on, the two of us were both approaching a closed door. I arrived first, opened it and held it open for her to go through. I would probably have done the same for a male colleague, but Waring's sharp comment was: 'You wouldn't have done that if I was a man, would you!'

There were several other practising lawyers in caucus, including Barry Brill, Dail Jones, Mike Minogue and Jim McLay. Initially we were prepared to 'breathe through our noses' when we found out the economy was in worse shape than we had thought and Muldoon appeared to be taking bold steps to rectify it. In view of this, and more importantly because he was showing strong leadership, I was prepared to walk over broken glass for him in those early days.

Some of Muldoon's closest allies in Cabinet, such as Colin McLachlan and Bert Walker, were much less impressive, with their performance on occasion suspect. But it was Alan McCready who first ran up against the new batch of lawyers in the caucus, in his capacity as Minister of Police. McCready had sought caucus approval to include in the Wanganui Computer (the police's centralised database) the names and charge details of people who had been discharged without conviction in court proceedings. He was knocked back but the following week he tried again. This time he circulated graphic police photographs of mainly women with horrendous facial and other injuries. When asked to explain the relevance of the photos to the issue we were discussing, he replied, 'Where there's smoke there's fire.' He was again turned down.

Bert Walker was harder to pin down — arguing with him was like wrestling with a large balloon. No sooner had you grabbed hold of one policy point than another would pop up that needed amending too. To add to our difficulties, Walker was an unswerving Muldoon loyalist who was regarded by the PM as a constituency MP *par excellence*. Any argument with Walker consequently often became an argument with Muldoon too. Like Walker, Colin McLachlan was one of my fellow Canterbury MPs and was probably Muldoon's closest devotee in Parliament. He has been described by Patrick Millen, Secretary to Cabinet, in two ways. First as '[a]n interesting and likeable man who occasionally had devastating bouts of shrewdness and got the point when everyone else missed it'; and secondly as '[t]he Apostle John in the Muldoon Cabinet' who for 'most of the time didn't know what was going on'.[3]

The 'mixed' performance of some of the members of Muldoon's first Cabinet was thankfully balanced by a number of extremely competent ministers. In this category were Deputy PM Brian Talboys, George Gair and Les Gandar. Another was Hugh Templeton, who had been re-elected as the MP for the Wellington seat of Karori following Jack Marshall's retirement at the 1975 election. All were easy to talk to and work with. Two MPs from the 1972 intake who didn't make Cabinet in 1975 were Jim Bolger and Bill Birch. Bolger became an under-secretary and Bill Birch chief whip — a position he filled brilliantly for the next three years.

Muldoon shows his true colours

One of my worst moments in Parliament was on the evening of 4 November 1976 during what became known as the 'Moyle Affair'. The occasion arose during the debate on the Appropriation Bill (Number 2), which should have been conducted with the House in committee and Muldoon in the chair. However, Labour sought to deal with it as the second-reading debate, for two reasons: to widen the topics that could be discussed, and to attempt to reduce Muldoon's speaking time while Parliament was being broadcast.

Over the next three hours numerous points of order followed, the House Speaker had had to rule on several matters, and Bob Tizard, the first speaker for Labour, claimed that he had only been able to speak for 'nearly five minutes' because of the continual interruptions and points of order.

At 10.30pm Parliament went off the air but the battle in the chamber continued to rage, with tempers on both sides at flash point. I returned there after a visit to the Press Gallery and sensed that no ceasefire was in the offing. Next, Russell Marshall, the Labour MP for Wanganui, referred to the Department of Prime Minister and Cabinet as 'the Goebbels department upstairs', and Muldoon retaliating by calling Marshall 'the Red Reverend'.

Muldoon then added that he assumed the member had a conscience and that he would forgive the effeminate giggles of the member for Mangere (Colin Moyle) 'because I know his background'. Incensed, Moyle retorted by asking if it would be in order to accuse Muldoon of being a member of an accountancy firm that engaged in dishonesty. Not one to be beaten, Muldoon replied, 'It would be in order if it is in order for me to accuse the member for Mangere of being picked up by the police for homosexual activity.'[4]

I was appalled at this turn of events. In my view, Muldoon's attack grossly overstepped the boundaries of propriety and demeaned the office of prime minister, which has a status of its own irrespective of who holds that position. My view was — and still is — that Parliament and the parliamentary process (like the courts) are parts of the fabric of society and that those in positions of authority in those institutions need to act in ways that maintain public support for them.

It was for the same reason that, during my time as a member of Muldoon's governments, I never — even privately — addressed him as anything other than 'Prime Minister'. Another reason I was upset was that Muldoon's comment suggested he had access to confidential information from a police file — or had been fully briefed by the Minister of Police on its contents — and had then wrongly used the information to publicly discredit a political opponent at a time when Moyle was seen as a potential Labour Party leader.

I caught up with Hugh Templeton and made my displeasure known to him. Templeton's take on my reaction is recorded in his book *All Honourable Men*: 'His confidence in a man for whom he said he would once have walked over glass may never have recovered.' Templeton was right, and the next morning I told Bill Birch, in his capacity as senior whip, that if any votes were cast in the House that day he could not count on my support.

Jim McLay later told me that he gave Birch the same message. McLay also asked Muldoon at the next caucus if he intended to discuss what had happened, and was initially knocked back with an agreement to put the matter on the following week's caucus agenda. By then, despite several caucus members promising to support him, McLay told me they all went strangely silent on the day in question. He summed up their attitude this way: 'We are right behind you, Jim, but a long way back.' Many were prepared to roar like lions in private, but became timid little lambs when confronted by Muldoon.

The irony of the Moyle Affair was that the by-election that followed Moyle's eventual resignation from Parliament in 1977 saw David Lange becoming the MP for Mangere and ultimately prime minister in 1984, when the Muldoon government was roundly defeated.

CHAPTER 4

Making Progress as an MP

During part of 1977 I was away from New Zealand as part of a Speaker's parliamentary delegation to China, France and Germany. Sir Roy Jack led the group, consisting of Ben Couch, Merv Wellington and myself as government members, along with Mary Batchelor, Mick Connelly and Mel Courtney from Labour. This was only the second time I had been overseas and it was a brilliant trip.

What we saw in China was particularly fascinating, as the country was just beginning to open up and welcome overseas visitors. From Hong Kong we travelled by private jet for all internal flights and in chauffeured cars through the cities and countryside. Nowhere did we have to stop — even in the biggest cities — for traffic lights, with all of them miraculously turning green as we approached. Everywhere we went we were treated as honoured guests and even had an hour with Communist Party chairman Hua Guofeng. This treatment of foreigners was typical of China at that time, and was part of a propaganda machine to present the host country in the best possible light.

Wherever we went — although we only suspected it at the time — enclaves and even enclaves within enclaves were cordoned off by the authorities so that we only saw what they wanted us to see. This meant we were taken to the best shops, restaurants, guesthouses and scenic spots specifically reserved for visitors like us, with signs in Mandarin reading 'For Foreign Guests Only'.

Ours was one of the first parliamentary delegations to visit the country after the end of the Cultural Revolution[1] and our white Caucasian skins were an oddity. Everywhere we went throngs of locals — hundreds and hundreds of them in the big cities — would stop, stare and point at us in amazement, and then chatter among themselves.

At every meeting the opening formalities were the same. We were given tea, welcomed, and told — in almost exactly the same words on each occasion — that although China still had a lot to do to rebuild its economy and social structures, the time being taken was not the fault of the current regime. It was the fault of 'The Gang of Four' — Mao Zedong's wife Jiang Qing and three men from Shanghai: Zhang Chunqiao, Yao Wenyuan and Wang Hongwen — who had banded together when the ageing Mao was losing his authority and tried to hold the Cultural Revolution together. They had been arrested in late 1976, a month after Mao died, but not before they had wrought political havoc.

However, it was hard to get specific information on what circumstances were like during their reign or earlier, during Great Leap Forward of 1958–62, when an estimated 20–43 million Chinese died from starvation.[2] Either my questions were ignored or I was told to ask someone else. The exception was on one occasion when Ben Couch and I were travelling together and our accompanying official was the former head of the Chinese Christian Church in Britain. He spoke excellent English, and in most cases gave direct answers to questions. He had returned to China during the Cultural Revolution — because he thought it was his duty to do so — and to our surprise was still an openly practising Christian in addition to being a high-ranking Communist Party official.

It was clear the Cultural Revolution had been an horrendous and degrading experience for educated people like him. Yet he was still reluctant, even when pressed, to attribute blame for what had happened, including the huge number of deaths resulting from political purges, poor policies, incompetent administration and the absence of a nationwide food distribution system.

Out hosts' attention to detail was impressive. I dumped a worn-out pair of walking shoes in a rubbish bin when we moved on to another city. The shoes, retrieved and neatly wrapped, followed me and were returned with a smile and a deep bow at our next destination.

In addition to numerous formal functions, we were also able to relax and have some fun. Our host, 'The Professor' as we called him because of his former university position, upright stance, white hair and general bearing, was with us during our whole time in China. He was a charming man and made sure our visit ran as smoothly as possible. A security detachment also accompanied us. Its head was a large jovial man who took it upon himself to educate me into the mysteries of maotai, which he obviously liked and thought I should like too. Maotai is an alcoholic drink — with a foul taste — distilled from fermented sorghum, which has an alcohol content of 53 percent and is usually drunk from shot glasses at formal functions.[3] There was to be no sipping from the glass as far as the head of security was concerned — if I tried to do so I was greeted with *gan bei*, which means 'bottoms up' (literally, 'a dry cup'). He would watch closely until I complied.

By the time we flew out of Beijing (or Peking as it was still mainly called in those days) on an Aeroflot flight for Europe via Moscow, most of us had had enough rich Chinese food and were craving a meal of steak, chips and green salad. Having said that, my visit to China in 1977 was one of the highlights of my first nine years in Parliament, and although I have returned to that country several times since, no trip has matched that initial experience.

As our Aeroflot flight rose into the sky the plane began to rattle violently and most of the baggage lockers flew open. Fortunately, no one was hurt and after an otherwise uneventful flight we arrived in Moscow. There we were immediately given a conducted tour of Red Square, the country's 'House of Soviets' or Parliament, and had a fleeting visit to see the city's impressive underground metro.

From there we were driven to what appeared to be a private hotel with a large meeting room and bathroom facilities. A meal was served and — as we eventually found out — we were expected to stay there until we were driven to the airport for our flight to Paris. Two Russian soldiers stood inside our room on either side of the exit door. Merv Wellington decided to go outside but as he got to the door the soldiers — without comment or fuss, and in a way they had obviously practised to perfection — turned him around so that he was facing back into the room. Only Wellington and I saw what had happened, but he got the message loud and clear, and didn't try to leave again!

Most of our time in France was spent in the Normandy area where heavy fighting had taken place during World War II. We travelled by bus with relaxed but heavily armed guards and, as was the case in China and later in Germany, we received excellent briefings. This part of our trip provided numerous highlights. We visited Mont Saint-Michel, famous for its salty lamb dishes, a tide that comes in faster than a galloping horse, steep streets and an amazing abbey perched on top of what appears to be a very large solid rock. We also spent time in Bayeux (with its grand

Cathédrale Notre-Dame de Bayeux and famous tapestry), the beautiful beach town of Deauville, the port of Le Havre, Rouen and finally, Paris.

I had been in Paris in 1955, but had never previously visited the lower house of Parliament, the Assemblée Nationale. A visit and a meeting with local MPs had been organised for us. The Assemblée was in session and was a colourful spectacle, with the performance of its deputies akin to a cock fight between groups of bantam roosters. This impression was confirmed later when we met with some of the deputies and senators. One of our party naïvely asked about the impact within the European Economic Community of imported farm produce from countries like New Zealand. For the next half an hour the members of various French political parties in the room engaged in vigorous debate. It was as though we weren't there as charge and counter-charge flew and tempers flared, with much of the bile directed at the Communist Party members present. Unfortunately my schoolboy French wasn't up to the occasion and I missed much of what was said!

Germany was the last country we visited, with security much tighter than in France because of the recent activity of the Baader-Meinhof Gang or Red Army Faction, a far-left group engaged in armed resistance against what they regarded as the fascist German state. As they had assassinated the federal prosecutor-general — along with his driver and another passenger in the car — not long before we arrived, our guards had side-arms and automatic weapons, and were on alert at all times.

In the cities we travelled in Mercedes-Benz cars with a contingent of motorcycle guards — wearing white gear and nicknamed 'the white mice' — ahead and behind our vehicles. As we approached an intersection one of the white mice would ride ahead and stop the traffic while a fellow motorcyclist leapfrogged our convoy and did the same at the next intersection.

All the drivers were in their early twenties and were trained to take evasive action if necessary. I still vividly remember how they operated as they drove us from Stuttgart to the airport at Frankfurt before we left to fly home. In light drizzling rain, our team rode in five cars under full escort from the city to the outer suburbs, where the white mice then peeled off. We then continued at more than 160 kilometres an hour, with about half a car length between each vehicle. The speed and following distance were designed to make it difficult for another vehicle to break into the convoy. The trip took us through numerous villages, where, in the interests of safety, the convoy slowed to around 100 kilometres an hour. I was with Sir Roy in the lead car, so our journey was relatively stress free, but the same was not true for the rest of our contingent. Those in car number five arrived at the airport in a state of complete nervous shock.

The Berlin Wall was still firmly in place when we visited that city and — at the urging of the Labour members of our party but against the advice of the New Zealand Embassy staff member who was with us — we took a train trip into East Berlin.[4] At the railway station the East German authorities took our passports, and only handed them back on our return. Boarding calls were only given in German, so we had to rely on the embassy official who reluctantly came with us to tell us where to go and what to do.

My other memories are of the high wire fences and 'no man's land', where escapers were regularly shot. East Berlin was drab and grey, with nothing on display in the shops, in sharp contrast to West Berlin. I was glad to get back to the western side of the wall.

I got on well with most of my travelling companions. Sir Roy was a brilliant tour leader, with a genuine interest in architecture and the arts. He always displayed unbounded courtesy towards our hosts in whatever country we visited. In China in particular he was an instant hit with his attempts to master a little of the local language and his ability on the violin, which he played on several occasions. Earlier I had had some social contact with him in Parliament, and on one occasion we had lunch together in his Speaker's suite when he wanted to pick my brains on some economic issue I had been researching. I can remember sitting at one end of a huge dining table while he sat at the other end. It crossed my mind to say, 'Roy, why don't I come up and sit next to you?' but he was far too 'proper' for that so I stayed where I was.

Roy unfortunately started to have health problems while we were away, which culminated in his death from cancer later in 1977. Merv Wellington and I took it upon ourselves to make sure he took his pills and to check his room to collect the things he habitually left behind.

The one run-in I did have while we were away was with Mick Connelly, who had been in the Cabinets of Norman Kirk and Bill Rowling during the 1972–75 Parliament. Mick was a likeable character but he had an inordinate appetite for beer. In Stuttgart — at a luncheon hosted by Manfred Rommel, mayor and son of Field Marshall Erwin Rommel of World War II fame — he fell asleep with his head on the table. I was furious.

I told him he was a disgrace and that he had let us and New Zealand down. My recollection is that my comments were like water off a duck's back.

Abortion triggers major divisions

Abortion became a major issue in Parliament in 1977 and led to long-term divisions and enmity within caucus. The initial trigger was the introduction of the Contraception, Sterilisation and Abortion Bill put forward by Frank Gill, Health Minister and a staunch Roman Catholic. The Bill foreshadowed a substantial tightening of the law against abortions and was introduced despite the fact that a royal commission on the subject was still sitting.

Pro-choice supporters like me believed that Muldoon, himself a strong supporter of the Bill, was not even-handed in the way he handled debates on the matter as caucus chair. We resolved to fight every clause in the Bill when it was finally introduced.

It was a prolonged and bitter struggle and at one stage, after a particularly lengthy debate in the House led by Gair, Waring, McLay and me, I decided I had done all I could to fight the Bill and was ready to give up. It was late in the night and I went off with McLay to Bellamy's for a hot chocolate and something to eat. When I got back to the debating chamber Marilyn Waring was still there fighting every clause. I decided that if she was going to stick it out, I would too. We fought the Bill all through the night and it was not until well into the next morning, when Muldoon returned to Wellington after some out-of-town function, that David Thomson called an adjournment and closed Parliament down. Later, Muldoon was to claim publicly that if I were elected deputy prime minister, National would lose the Roman Catholic vote because of my views on abortion.

An interesting aside to the debate is that I was much more comfortable, from a personality perspective, with the pro-choice group in Parliament (which crossed party lines) than I was with the so-called pro-lifers. There were obvious exceptions. For example I had, and still have, a lot of time for Birch and Brill. But in general I was more comfortable with the likes of Talboys, Gandar, MacIntyre, Gair, Templeton, McLay and Waring — and all the other women MPs, who were always on the pro-choice side while I was there — than I was with (for example) Muldoon, Gill, Walker, Bolger, Wellington and Warren Cooper.

Despite the differences on abortion, during the rest of 1977 and 1978 I consolidated my position in caucus and began to be listened to on a variety of subjects. For example, when Muldoon and his officials were preparing for the 1978 budget I suggested reducing the existing 19 income tax steps, and as a result they came down from 19 to five. The key steps were a rate of 14.5 cents on income from zero dollars to $4500, and a long flat one at 38c for those earning between $4500 and $10,000 a year. This was at a time when the average annual income was $7500. Beyond $10,000, marginal rates rose progressively to a top of 60c in the dollar from $22,000. The upside was a much simpler tax structure. The downside — particularly for some low-income earners — was that income tax became payable on the first dollar earned. I had asked officials to look at exempting (say) the first $3000 of income, but the cost in lost revenue would have been too high.

I was also able to introduce a member's bill on community service. I wanted 'service' to be compulsory for everyone at age 18. I proposed a total of 12 weeks' service, based first on in-service training and then on community-based programmes. But Muldoon talked caucus out of this, in favour of a shorter voluntary proposal. In retrospect, I should never have agreed to this change as it watered down the whole basis of what I was advocating: the notion of giving back to society; providing opportunities for unskilled young people to obtain skills; producing a national register of fit and unfit young people; and providing an alternative to CMT.

My Bill had been drawn up after extensive consultation in New Zealand and overseas, with consideration given to a scheme in Denmark that formed an alternative to CMT, and the Sunderland scheme in England, based on trade training. My proposal was not designed to overcome youth unemployment. Had it been, the Bill would have been a much more comprehensive measure, providing for specific skills training, relocation assistance and so on. The Bill contemplated a period of service for both genders of 100–200 hours, with an expressed preference for those who enrolled while still at school or shortly after leaving. The director-general of Community Services would control the overall scheme, with local authorities managing the day-to-day administration. There was also a provision for supervision by local service clubs. Trainees would receive no payment, but would receive an allowance for travel.

One of the many responses I received on my Bill was from senior pupils of the Hawarden Area School within my electorate, who wrote:

'The community seems very apathetic, so something like this would encourage a better community spirit.'

Although my Bill was not passed into law, the debate in the House and the consultation I undertook both increased my national profile.

Along with McLay and Brill, I was a frequent speaker in Parliament on a range of topics. On one occasion I was a little late getting to the debating chamber after the dinner recess and was told by the whip immediately after I had sat down in my seat that I was the next — and first — government speaker. It was an important Imprest Supply debate and Bob Tizard was leading the debate for Labour. He was already in full flight and I initially had no idea what to say in reply. Muldoon then sauntered over and handed me an envelope with a few headings scrawled on the back. 'Here's something you can use,' he said, and I did. After I had spoken and was sitting down at my desk, still in a state of nervous shock, he came over again and said 'Well done', which made me feel pretty good.

I was sitting quietly in the House one evening when I was told — again presumably on Muldoon's instructions — that I was to take over the role of Speaker for a period. No sooner was I in the chair than a point of order was raised. Without really listening to what had been said, I responded: 'Overruled. Get on with the debate.' Fortunately, they did, and as soon as I was able to, I handed the job of Speaker to someone else. In contrast, when Brill was told to 'take the chair' on a subsequent occasion, he had to cope with numerous points of order and a running battle with Opposition speakers that eventually led to him having to recall the House Speaker. Brill handled the situation much better than I probably would have done.

Muldoon backs off National's reform agenda

The government had taken some immediate steps within 10 days of taking office in late 1975 to confirm Labour's pre-election cuts to immigration and housing subsidies. It had also announced a cap on the number of employees in the public service, which had risen substantially under Labour.

In March 1976 Interest on Deposit regulations were revised to allow interest rates to rise with the aim of enabling smaller trading banks to compete with the 'big four' banks for funds and to enter the housing mortgage market. Officials thought this was a step in the right direction but that more freeing up was needed. However, Muldoon became uneasy as interest rates rose, inflation continued to climb and the amount of money in circulation dramatically increased. Instead of contemplating reducing tariffs and import controls to free up the economy, or relax price controls, Muldoon thought that intensifying their application would bring inflation under control. It didn't, and by the end of 1976 'the early optimism ... about a new dawn under National was waning'.[5]

In the view of people such as Roderick Deane, who later became deputy governor of the Reserve Bank and a major player in the Lange government's reforms in the 1980s, politicians needed to accept that reducing inflation and the overseas deficit would cause some discomfort, and that for the reform process to succeed, some people were likely to get hurt in the early stages. A degree of political will was consequently required.

However, Muldoon had strong views on what was ideologically and politically right and wrong. Although he was prepared to entertain a degree of deregulation, he did not want New Zealanders divided too starkly into winners and losers.[6] He was also acutely aware — as he continually told caucus — that you cannot achieve anything in Opposition, which meant that staying in office was his key objective. As a result, by the time of the 1978 election the government had started to pursue a more regulated and interventionist approach in the hope that this would ensure its re-election.

CHAPTER 5

1978

A Seat in Cabinet

Although National's share of the vote fell in the 1978 election from 48 to 40 percent we retained power — albeit with 51 seats and a majority of 10 in a 92-seat Parliament. The party's organisation in key marginal seats was what got us over the line. I was re-elected in Rangiora with a slightly reduced majority of 1145. This was consistent with the overall swing against the party but I had some anxious moments during the campaign. Initially I had been sent for a week to hold the hand of another National MP who had separated from his wife, was drinking too much and later figured in a potentially embarrassing situation for me as Minister of Housing and for the government. Muldoon apparently thought that Rangiora was either safe for National or I was dispensable, but either way I was nervous at being away from my own electorate when I knew the tide was running out for the government.

Although we ran a vigorous local campaign in the last few weeks in particular, and our efforts since 1975 to build my reputation as a good local MP looked to have paid off, I thought my nightmare of being a one-term member had come true when we were listening to the preliminary election results as we drove to the Rangiora courthouse on election night. A commentator said, 'It looks as though Derek Quigley has lost Rangiora' and I sat dejectedly in the car outside the courthouse for some time after we had arrived. Eventually I said, 'All right, let's get it over and done with' and entered the building. No sooner were we through the door than the Labour candidate met me and said, 'Congratulations, Derek, you've had a good win.' So much for the accuracy of radio reports!

Shortly before election day all the local National MPs and candidates had met in Christchurch with local business people. After the meeting I stayed on chatting to Eric Holland, MP for Fendalton and Minister of Housing, about housing policy. Eric and I had been officers in the Territorial Army together and got on well, and I had also been an active member of his caucus housing committee in Wellington.

I didn't know at the time that Eric was considered likely to be dropped from the Cabinet if National were re-elected and therefore was surprised when he said, 'You might be Minister of Housing yourself after the election.' Holland was in fact dropped, with Muldoon apparently dissatisfied with his performance. At a brief meeting after the election Muldoon told him of his decision, adding, 'I'm sorry, Eric,' to which Holland replied, 'No you're not, Rob.'

Eventually I did become Minister of Housing, although it was not straightforward. Muldoon phoned me early in the week after the election, telling me to come to Wellington but gave no indication why. When he finally saw me he said I was in Cabinet but he didn't know at that stage which portfolio I would get.

The problem was the Kapiti electorate, where Barry Brill, who was slated for Justice, was marginally behind on election night. Although he finally won the seat and held it until 1984, the 1978 result was for a time on a knife edge. The progressive count and recount seesawed so much that on one occasion one of his constituents called out to him in the street, 'Hello, Mr Brill, I see it's your turn this week.'

In the end Muldoon couldn't wait any longer to appoint his Cabinet. Jim McLay became Minister of Justice and Attorney-General, and I got Housing, Associate Finance, State Insurance, Government Life, the Public Trust Office and the Earthquake and War Damage Commission. I also became a member of the Cabinet Economic Committee and one of the three ministers on the Cabinet Expenditure Committee. Unfortunately, in my view, Barry Brill never made it into Cabinet.

Before being sworn in, I returned to my electorate for the prizegiving at Swannanoa School. This area is staunch National and the atmosphere was like a carnival. I was extremely tired and on edge after weeks of campaigning and the hype of the past two days. As I was giving a short speech I felt dizzy and thought, 'I can't do this.' But I quickly recovered and carried on, eventually settling into my new role as a minister.

One matter I hadn't counted on as a newly appointed minister was indirectly assisting with door-knocking in a Labour-held electorate. At a dinner dance at Government House shortly after the election I was showing little enthusiasm to dance, but when I was approached

New Cabinet Ministers, after 1978 election. Left to right: Wellington, Birch, Quigley, Muldoon, Cooper, Couch and McLay.

successively by Fran Wilde and Ann Hercus, both Labour supporters, I stepped up. Fran became MP for Wellington Central three years later, and Ann had defeated Colleen Dewe in Lyttelton in 1978. By way of introduction, Fran told me that one of her team had dared her to ask me to dance with her, and that if I agreed, she would get a week's door-knocking in return from her supporter. Ann's reason was less prosaic. She said she wanted me to go into 'partnership' with her ... I presumed she meant in a legal practice but I may have been mistaken. The upshot was that over the next three years she had the ability to make me blush at the drop of a hat whenever I caught her eye while I was speaking in the House.

Immediately after the Cabinet swearing-in ceremony there was much administration to be done regarding housing, office accommodation and transport, and it all took time. I still had my room in our Hobson Street house, and late at night, as Jim McLay had nothing arranged, I suggested he use one of the vacant bedrooms there for the night. He accepted and we set off on foot from Parliament.

A nearby clock struck midnight as we approached the Molesworth Street entrance to Parliament. We began to cross the road and a distraught and dishevelled young woman came running towards us from the direction of the nearby National Library building site. She said she had been attacked as she walked along the footpath and dragged into the construction site, and had fought off her assailant as he tried to rape her.

McLay's first question to her was, 'Has anything been stolen?', which was a sensible thing to ask, given that the assailant might subsequently be caught with something of hers in his possession. I can't remember the answer but I do recall that Jim ran back to Parliament to phone the police while I accompanied the woman slowly back there. Several police officers soon arrived with a tracker dog. We explained what had happened and then set off again for Hobson Street.

To our surprise none of the Press Gallery journalists picked up on what had happened, but two days later I was in my office in Old Parliament Buildings when my private secretary, Malcolm Fearn,[1] knocked on the door and said that the police had rung to say two detectives were on their way to see me. I was quizzed about the incident, fielding questions such as 'Was she wearing a bra?' 'Was she cut or bruised?' 'Did she have shoes on?' I answered yes to the shoe question but I didn't have a clue about the other things. I did emphasise that she had been extremely upset.

Conscious of the 'Moyle Affair' and the possibility that homosexual activity may have been involved on that occasion, I then proceeded to explain to the police why McLay and I had been out on the street together at midnight. The detectives replied that what we were doing was entirely our business. Later I learnt that Jim — for exactly the same reason — had also told the police why we were out together that night. Both of us reported the incident to the Minister of Police and to Brian Talboys, Acting Prime Minister at the time. Brian's joking response was, 'Which one of you did it?' We heard nothing more from the police, so presumably the would-be rapist was never caught.

Problem solving

Constituency work was much easier to handle after the 1978 election, although my new responsibilities meant I spent less time in the electorate. I had brilliant office staff in Wellington to handle incoming mail and phone calls, and I developed a system that worked well in dealing with anyone who wanted to see me when I returned to the electorate during weekends. MPs then had no taxpayer-funded electorate staff, so Judith was the message-taker there and did a brilliant job. Her task was to note down the names and telephone numbers of those who called, but not to get involved in the detail of their issue.

Before I left Wellington to return home I would personally phone anyone I was due to see to find out what the meeting was about so that I could be properly prepared. Mostly constituents wanted to see me about either a State Advances mortgage application or a rural telephone connection. In many cases my call established that correspondence was already under way, or more information was needed. As a result, a meeting with me was often not required because the matter could be resolved quite quickly, or referred to another minister.

I soon found out that being a minister provided immediate access to fellow ministers, and through them to their senior department officials. It was consequently much easier to progress a particular issue than it had been as a backbench MP where 'cooperation' at a higher level depended on the minister involved and the willingness of his office and/or departmental staff to help.

I clearly remember three occasions where issues evoked different responses from ministers.

The first was with Les Gandar in his capacity as Minister of Education, while I was a first-term MP. Gandar told me that pupil numbers at the Oxford Area School, in my electorate, had been declining to the point where the school was now uneconomic and would have to close. Les was a practical politician and was aware of the implications of closure. He was also prepared to listen to reason, so when I asked for a few days to think the matter through, he readily agreed. A week later I went back to him with a counter-proposal, which he accepted. He also agreed to let me announce the plan to the Oxford community.

I arranged a public meeting at the school to discuss its 'possible closure' and, as I anticipated, a big crowd attended. Locals assumed a closure decision had already been made and I was coming to announce it. I stood and outlined the decline in attendance numbers, what it was costing to keep the school open, and the minister's initial plan. I then told them about my counter-proposal, which effectively meant that the decision on the school's future was in their hands. This was greeted with warm applause from a crowd that had been expecting the worst, and now realised that they were going to have a say.

For the school to stay open, I said, a demonstration of practical support for it was needed. Pupil numbers would have to increase substantially over the next 12 months to make the school financially viable. This effectively meant the local community rather than the government was responsible for what happened. The message got through, enrolment numbers increased substantially, and the school is still open today.

On another occasion I was approached when I was in Cabinet by a constituent who had a property for sale up a quiet road on the outskirts of a rural township. I made a site visit and saw a near-new dwelling on a section on one side of a small stream, with the local public domain on the other side. The constituent had concluded a sale agreement, but the buyer's solicitor had found out from the Department of Lands and Survey that the Queen's Chain ran through a corner of the garage attached to the house. The department and the buyer were insisting that the offending part of the garage be demolished before the sale could proceed.

Venn Young was the minister involved and, like Les Gandar, was very approachable. I suggested to him that the Queen's Chain be moved across the stream onto the domain, and he agreed that this was a sensible solution. However, two weeks later I received a letter signed by him stating that the offending part of the garage had to be demolished. I went back to him and said that was not what we had agreed. More time elapsed and in due course an identical letter arrived. This time when I went to Venn's office I was not my usual quiet and measured self. The matter was finally fixed with the sale proceeding and the garage unchanged.

A third example involved my Cashmere neighbour and close friend Graeme Walker, who was a brilliant designer and an expert on high-performance motor vehicles. Graeme had no university qualifications but was extremely skilled and knew in intimate detail how engines work. At the time New Zealand was in the grip of the second oil shock and was beginning to look at a range of fuels as alternatives to petrol, and in particular at methanol.

Graeme told me he had been working on a dual fuel carburettor (or throttle body injection system) that could handle a variety of fuels, including 100 percent methanol. I told him to come back to me when his system was working.

Six weeks later it was, and I organised a demonstration through the Minister of Energy, Bill Birch, with the government's chief scientist in attendance. The system worked brilliantly, with methanol and a wide range of alternative fuels. When its basics were explained to the chief scientist, his arrogant response was that anyone without at least four university degrees couldn't have come up with a concept like that without 'fluking it'.

Detailed fleet trials followed, including one involving six new Mazda 626 vehicles, two of which had been built by Mazda to run on methanol. The trial established that the performance of the Walker system was equal to and in some cases superior to that of the Mazda factory-built methanol engines.

Three subsequent international symposiums confirmed the superior performance of the Walker system over most alternatives, but in 1990 the Liquid Fuels Trust Board was disbanded by the new National government and all contracts and research and development involving alternative fuel programmes, including Walker's, were cancelled. Walker's most recent invention is a simplified variable-compression-ratio multi-fuel engine that has overcome the problems major vehicle manufacturers had been struggling with for years. Unfortunately, Graeme has now died, so his inventions have died with him.

One matter that impacted directly on my own ministerial responsibility — and could have been extremely embarrassing — concerned a fellow National MP. I was sitting in the debating chamber one evening when my private secretary signalled that he needed to speak to me urgently. He had the head of the Housing Corporation (HC) with him.

Once we were inside a meeting room with the door firmly closed, I was told that the MP in question had subdivided and sold off some of the land around his house, with part of the proceeds of sale earmarked to pay off his HC mortgage. When it came to settlement, the MP attended to this personally, handing over the settlement documents including the discharged mortgage; receiving the cheque for the purchase of the section; and in due course receiving his house title back from the Land Transfer Office, mortgage free. What he had not done was pay off the mortgage as promised.

I was annoyed and asked the HC head why the documents had been given to the MP rather than to his solicitor. Shamefacedly, he said, 'Because he's an MP.' My response was: 'Get the money back and sue him if you need to. I don't want to hear any more about it.' I didn't, except to be told the mortgage had been paid.

A massive cut to Vote: Housing

Another drama had arisen much earlier, indeed within days of my swearing in as Minister of Housing. During his whole time as Prime Minister, Muldoon was also Minister of Finance, caucus and Cabinet chair, and the person who decided who was and who was not in Cabinet. He was consequently able to exercise inordinate power.

The problem I faced just before Christmas 1978 originated from a Treasury report approved by Muldoon in his capacity as Minister of Finance. It stated that Vote: Housing was to be cut dramatically. Muldoon had told me that housing was a very sensitive political area and that he considered National's loss in 1972 to have been in large part due to the government's inadequate housing policy. I didn't agree with him — and still don't — but said nothing at the time.

Shortly after, I faced a roomful of officials, including my own office staff, senior HC people, the Treasury housing desk officer, the head of the Prime Minister's Department, and the prime minister's housing adviser. Senior HC officials outlined the implications of the required cuts, which were potentially horrific, and after a brief discussion the head of the Prime Minister's Department asked, 'What are you going to do, Minister?' The reply on the tip of my tongue was 'How the hell would I know — I've only been in the job five minutes,' but fortunately I didn't utter those words. Instead, I said I would think about it and we would meet again later. Over the next few days I had intense question and answer sessions with HC officials, with the focus on reining in expenditure in 'easy' areas.

Successive New Zealand governments had, since Dick Seddon's Workers Dwelling Act 1905, been actively involved with providing large-scale 'affordable' housing, with an initial emphasis on rental accommodation. By 1978 the Crown — through the HC — owned thousands of rental properties and was funding the construction of many more each year. It also provided concessional mortgage finance to low-income first-home buyers if they bought a new-built house.

HC spending could consequently be turned on and off on an annual basis by increasing or decreasing the number of houses to be built, or by varying the size and number of mortgage approvals. This was the usual way to regulate the HC budget and was the process I initially instructed officials to follow. However, as I wasn't satisfied that this was a sensible medium-term solution, I took a large pile of housing policy files home to study over the Christmas holidays.

The beneficiaries of existing housing policy

As I worked through these files it became clear that a limited number of major home building companies had captured the market. They had large land holdings and were handling most of the state land subdivisions and building activities that produced new state houses and homes for low-income first-home buyers. The social, economic and employment impact of their activities was huge. It stemmed from Labour's post-Depression full-employment policy and ranged from urban planning and acquiring and subdividing land, to completing state houses and new privately owned homes that people eventually moved into. Numerous supply and service industries were also involved, including the full range of building trades, whitegoods and carpet manufacturers, retailers, landscapers, plant nurseries and so on. Thousands of skilled and unskilled people were involved.

Invariably these houses were built in areas with limited public transport and few shopping facilities, commonly called 'nappy valley' suburbs. I had been critical of the lack of basic facilities in these types of subdivision in my maiden speech to Parliament in 1976.

All the major home builders, starting with Fletchers back in the days of the Depression, had established close relationships with successive prime ministers, and Muldoon was no exception. Knowing this, I was aware that they would quickly lobby him if their economic livelihoods were threatened. I also knew that any fundamental changes I might come up with would have to be not only economically and politically sound, but also visibly consistent with National Party philosophy. I then focused on the two main areas of HC spending: state housing and new home loans.

Of the two, state housing was easier to deal with initially, as the caucus housing committee had done a lot of work on this area when I was a backbench MP. A key National Party policy was to foster home ownership, and moves were already in place to encourage existing state tenants to either progressively move to market rents or to buy the house they were renting. Tenants were, on average, paying well below market rents and tenancies were costing the HC significant money for repairs and maintenance. Detailed calculations had shown that sales of rental properties, even with minimal deposits and a mortgage back for the balance of the purchase price, would save the HC millions of dollars each year.

I was conscious of the social imperative of assisting people into affordable housing, but believed that any financial concessions needed to achieve this aim should be a social welfare responsibility rather than one foisted onto the Housing Corporation.

Back in Wellington after the Christmas break I instructed HC officials to accelerate the state house sales process and the move to market-based rents. I gave three arguments for the latter. The first was equity. Many low-income families were not able to get state houses and were consequently paying more rent than their peers. Second, over time these moves would establish a more even playing field in the rental market, encouraging additional private-sector investment in the sector. Third, it would encourage workforce mobility. This was because there was a policy stopping existing tenants from getting a second state rental property if they vacated the one they were living in. Monetary incentives thus strongly encouraged people to stay where they were, even if employment opportunities arose elsewhere.

I also told HC officials to ensure that as many new state houses as possible were built in established housing suburbs, to alleviate 'nappy valley' syndrome and to provide a better community age mix. A further motivation was that Cabinet approval was not needed for any of these changes as relevant broad-based policies were already in place. I consequently proceeded without it.

The low-income first-home-buyer mortgage policy was much more difficult to change. But what was clear from the start was that despite the policy supposedly being for the benefit of this group, the real beneficiaries were the major home builders, the people they employed, and the business their activities supported. What made matters worse for first-home buyers was that concessional HC finance — as opposed to high interest-rate mortgages from banks or solicitors' clients — was not available for what were then much cheaper privately owned houses in established suburbs. Applicants were consequently not only denied choice — which was at least theoretically National Party policy; they were also pushed into buying more expensive properties in new housing subdivisions with few basic facilities and little employment close by.

A logical solution seemed to be to offer applicants who satisfied the policy criteria the opportunity to decide where they wanted to live and what sort of house — new or existing — they preferred to buy. In other words, to provide them with choice. However, this would involve a major policy change and, because I wasn't initially sure about the best way to proceed, I discussed the options with Hugh Templeton. Hugh and I had worked well together during my first three years in Parliament, and now with him as deputy minister of finance and me as associate finance minister and minister of housing we had continuing overlapping responsibilities, and a good personal working relationship.

Templeton suggested I should discuss the matter with Muldoon, so I made an appointment to do so without telling him in advance what the topic was. It was well into the evening when he saw me, and he was obviously busy and tired. Immediately after I sat down I was asked abruptly what I wanted. I replied that I would like to talk through some possible changes to housing policy. His next question was 'Do you know what you want to do?' and when I replied, 'No, not yet,' his response was: 'Don't waste my time until you do and then come back and see me.'

I left his office more than a little peeved and vowed never to discuss any of my portfolio policy matters with him again. And I never did, apart from a brief discussion much later on about a paper Bob Jones had prepared for me on the 'Beautiful New Zealand' scheme.

Other housing policy changes

Given Muldoon's ongoing interest in the politics of housing, I knew I would have to take control of the total portfolio to avoid his continual interference. Early help came in two areas. The first was in the form of a new community and housing improvement scheme I inherited from Eric Holland that had been held over until after the election.

In early 1979 I released the policy package, which was designed to upgrade inner-city accommodation by providing concessional loans to individuals who wished to improve existing houses. The scheme was such a success that HC officials soon began to worry about a budget blowout. At Wellington Airport, just as I was about to board a plane to return to my electorate, they presented me with a paper and media release announcing a dramatic curtailing of spending on the scheme. In the rush to catch my flight, I signed the paper and authorised the release of the press statement when I should have deferred consideration of the matter until at least the following week.

An avalanche of media criticism followed the announcement, with the result that over the next few days HC and Treasury officials, my office staff and I reconsidered the scheme's funding projections and the potential to augment them, if that became necessary, from other analogous areas within Vote: Housing. We concluded that the scheme could continue in a slightly amended form, and a press release in my name followed. In it I said I had made a mistake in initially curtailing the scheme and that it would continue subject to minor changes. The media welcomed my acknowledgement that I had made a mistake, commenting that such an admission from a politician was unusual.

My second housing initiative, which was important in terms of the party's oft-stated support for private enterprise, was to prepare a paper seeking Cabinet approval to disband the Housing Corporation's Construction Division and allow private-sector architects to handle state house design work. The division drew up plans for new state houses but, despite its name, didn't actually construct anything. I quietly lobbied my colleagues before Cabinet consideration of the matter, and my paper was approved despite reservations by Muldoon, who consistently asked thereafter, 'How are you going to build state houses when you have got rid of the Construction Division?'

Caucus support for the policy was enthusiastic, particularly among the new group of private-sector and reform-orientated MPs elected in 1978. I was seen as a minister who was actually doing something consistent with party philosophy. As a result, Muldoon introduced me to delegates at the party's 1979 conference — to much applause — as 'the minister for private enterprise'.

The third housing initiative concerned the low-income first-home buyers policy. This involved a much bigger change that took longer to prepare, gain approval and implement. As what I was contemplating was likely to have an initial adverse impact on the new home construction sector, and would consequently result in intense lobbying in opposition to it, I knew that detailed homework would be required to convince Cabinet.

In my approach to selling the new policy I emphasised the word 'choice', which was a fundamental part of National Party philosophy. Also the fact that, as existing homes were on average cheaper than new homes, the new policy would allow more HC applicants to be assisted, which in itself was good politics. I further emphasised that buying in an existing suburb would provide a better mix of age groups there. And finally, the change I was advocating was likely to put less pressure on the need for costly infrastructure services.

By the end of 1979 the new policy initiative had been fine-tuned within my caucus housing committee, with input from senior HC officials, John

Buddle (the strongly supportive Treasury housing officer), David Lloyd (the government's research director), and Len Bayliss, a member of the prime minister's think tank and someone I worked with later when I ran the Hugo Consulting Group.

A paper titled *1980/81 Housing Policy* was considered by the Cabinet Economic Committee on 25 February 1980. It contained two simple recommendations:

- that Cabinet confirm that the government's housing lending programmes should be designed to achieve what is in the best interests of prospective home buyers;
- that Cabinet indicate what support (if any) should be made available to the building industry.

The committee referred the paper to officials for comment, but because of my earlier consultation with them, they quickly wrote a report for the Cabinet Economic Committee dated 11 March 1980. In it they commented:

> The house building industry is affected by a number of economic/demographic variables: population, migration, the rate of household formation, the relative price of new and existing houses, real disposable incomes, interest rates and the money supply.
>
> As a result of economic conditions and the high net migration outflow over the last few years, dwellings completions have declined from a peak of 34,300 in 1974/75. This process of adjustment is continuing with 1979/80 completions expected to be 15–16,000. While it is possible that there will be increased demands on the industry in the medium term, the evidence is not such as to suggest that special steps should be taken to maintain the present level of demand into 1980-81. (Appendices I and II set out more detailed information and were intended as a background to the officials' paper.)
>
> Indeed, artificial stimulation of the new house market could hinder the desirable restructuring taking place in the industry. The major dampening influence on demand for new houses is the disparity between new and second-hand prices. To the extent that demand for new houses is artificially stimulated by preferential financing terms offered by the Government, the problem will remain. In addition the needs of prospective home purchasers are not being met.

> Social policy, not outweighed by considerations of support for the building industry, suggests therefore that the present measures of support (notably the suspensory loan but also easier eligibility for new house purchases) be discontinued and prospective home owners allowed a free choice between new and existing houses. The implications of such a policy change for house completions in 1980–81 would be a reduction from the current annual rate of 14,000/15,000 to around 9,800/11,000.
>
> Officials, for the reasons set out above, favour a return to free choice. The alternative would be to develop a package based on existing policies — involving some preference for new home purchasers but with no continuation of the suspensory loan — aimed at financing through Housing Corporation and Maori Affairs some 12,000–13,500 house completions within the COPE [Committee on Public Expenditure] provision of $283.4 million in 1980–81.

Officials accordingly recommended that the Cabinet Economic Committee:

- Confirm that the Government's house lending programmes should be designed to achieve what is in the best interests of prospective home purchasers. This would involve free choice between new and existing houses for Housing Corporation/Maori Affairs clients;
- Agree that the existing building industry support through the Housing Corporation/Maori Affairs should be discontinued and the situation watched closely; but_if the committee continues building industry support, that this should not exceed what is given at present;
- Authorise the Minister of Housing and the Minister of Finance to finalise the details of the 1980/81 Housing Policy.

Cabinet approved the new policy, but to lessen any potential fall-off in demand for new housing as a result of the changes, eligible borrowers who opted to buy a new house rather than an existing property were offered a $4000 suspensory loan in addition to the normal HC first mortgage.

Housing Corporation borrowers reacted positively to choice, with 70 percent opting to borrow to buy an existing house. A second effect was that new house builds suffered an initial dramatic drop-off, which led to major home builders agitating for the policy to be reversed. Over time, some builders switched more of their new house construction activities to cater for a different type of clientele, such as middle-income people and retirees. Some, particularly Dick White, head of Neal Housing, had the good grace — when new starts began to pick up again with a different type of construction mix — to tell me that the policy changes were right and were long overdue. (However, my latest advice from Michael Bassett, a former parliamentary colleague, friend and former Labour Cabinet minister who was still in touch with White, was that he (White) may now have resiled from that view.)

As a further housing initiative, consistent with my view that concessional funding was a social welfare matter and not be an HC responsibility, I submitted a paper dated 27 March 1980 stating:

> I am convinced that our social objectives can be better achieved by massive restructuring. The basic outline of what is proposed is as follows:
>
> - Disestablish the construction and land development section of the Housing Corporation.
> - Discontinue the bulk of new lending.
> - Transfer existing loan administration to non-Public Service agencies (BNZ or Trustee Savings Banks).
> - Transfer the responsibility for public housing to local authorities.
> - The foregoing could lead to a total staff reduction of approximately 850 which is about 40% of the total number employed by both the Housing Corporation and the Rural Bank.

However, these proposals were far too radical for my Cabinet colleagues and were consequently not progressed at that time.

CHAPTER 6

Attempts to Control Government Spending

Early on I had asked Muldoon what my specific tasks were as associate minister of finance. He had said they were expenditure control — particularly as a member of the three-man Cabinet Expenditure Committee — and to give speeches around the country on what the government was doing to balance the books after three years of Labour mismanagement.

Hugh Templeton and I had begun by having a selection of papers prepared by officials, which described a gloomy picture of the overall state of the economy. As work on the 1979 budget accelerated, Hugh and I invited ourselves to the meetings Muldoon was having, where it was clear that the country was facing sustained pressure on overseas funds, high domestic inflation and unemployment, and the potential for a huge internal deficit. All this pointed to the need for major corrective action, which is what Treasury and Reserve Bank officials were recommending. But Muldoon didn't like this advice, and told us in Cabinet that despite his desire to restructure the economy, he feared the government would inherit all the pain and little of the benefit by the next election.

Muldoon at heart was a status quo politician who never seemed capable of balancing all the relevant factors at the same time when doing so mattered. And it did matter, because on 16 January 1979 the Shah of Iran fled his country, and by the start of April New Zealand and many Western economies faced a second oil shock. This caused Muldoon to retreat even further from his earlier commitment to caucus on opening up the economy. This didn't go down well with the reformist members of the Cabinet like Templeton, McLay and me, or others in the government caucus who were now more market orientated in their thinking.

The work I was involved in as a member of the Cabinet Expenditure Committee was fascinating, and I was rigorous in my responsibility for expenditure control, given the need to reduce government spending. I was also determined to practise what I preached within my own areas of ministerial responsibility to retain credibility with my colleagues in the face of the constraints we were imposing on their portfolio spending. Our committee was served by an excellent Treasury officer, Brian Tyler, and he and I in particular 'hunted as a team' looking for departmental 'fat' that we could cut away.

The responses from individual ministers to the overall spending cuts that Cabinet as a whole had agreed to were interesting. They ranged from the cooperative approach of George Gair in both Social Welfare and Health, to outright obstruction from Merv Wellington in Education. All three portfolios faced big spending budgets, and in Gair's case all we had to do was tell him what the target reductions were and then let him come back and advise us how they would be achieved.

The approach of Wellington and his officials was radically different. Their opening stance was that education needed more money, not less. When that failed, they would mount a series of 'do or die' battles over politically sensitive areas of the department's budget in order to distract us.

Wellington and his officials out-foxed us the first time around, but were indiscreet enough to be overheard later boasting about the fact. We consequently won the succeeding battles.

Quite early on in 1979 Muldoon had sat in on the committee's examination of Railways estimates. Unlike court work, where you are not supposed to question a witness unless you already know the answer, I was still learning about the financial intricacies of many areas of government spending. I consequently often asked questions because I simply didn't know the answers. In the case of Railways, my first question, prefaced on that occasion by 'This may be a silly question but . . .', was 'Why do we have guards' vans and guards on trains?' To my surprise, and I suspect to the surprise of all the other MPs present including Muldoon, the answer was: 'They don't serve any necessary purpose. They are only there because of the unions.' A decision followed to get rid of them.

Another experience I remember from around that time, which later caused me to have a good look at the role of the military in peacetime, involved a dinner at Vogel House. Muldoon used this venue as his Wellington residence, and occasionally overseas delegations were invited

No, you can't have more money.

there for talks during a formal evening meal. On one occasion — I think the only one I was invited to attend — the visitors came from China and the mess chefs from the Royal New Zealand Air Force base at Shelly Bay did the catering.

Immediately after the main course and just as Pears Belle Hélène were placed in front of everyone, the speeches started. It was a long-drawn-out affair as everything was translated from English to Mandarin and from Mandarin to English. Gifts were also exchanged, which dragged out the process further. By the time it was all over, our desserts had been sitting in front of us for at least half an hour and the chocolate on the outside of the pears was like concrete. Those few who did manage to crack through it found raw pear inside. Not a good advertisement for military planning — or food preparation!

My work on the Cabinet Expenditure Committee, my private-sector bias, the way I was handling my housing responsibilities and my hard-line response to pleas from most of my colleagues for more money began to attract attention. I became known among officials, and particularly among senior Treasury personnel, as Cabinet's public voice for fundamental economic reform. The draft speech notes officials prepared for me for my public addresses progressively built on this theme and Muldoon — at least initially — seemed to have no problem with it.

However, the committee was still having difficulties with some ministers. Faced with little progress in implementing the October 1979 decision that ministers were to review all functions within their portfolios, I worked with Treasury officials to develop some ideas to better control government spending.

These culminated in my detailed memorandum to the prime minister dated 20 November 1979 which began by showing that between 1974 and 1980 government spending had increased in real terms by about 30 percent, rising from 29.2 percent of Gross Domestic Expenditure to 37 percent. The memo also noted that major variations, for example in energy development, farm support programmes, health initiatives and general 'across the board' constraints, had disguised the incremental 'creep' year on year.

The paper went on to outline the four existing processes designed to control expenditure. The first was the 'base load' exercise conducted by the Committee on Public Expenditure (COPE), in which policies were considered in terms of across-the-board increases or reductions depending on macro-economic or financing considerations. The second process was an attempt to coordinate the consideration of all new policy proposals. The third was the yearly review, in which ministers and departments were asked to review all policies and functions with the objective of identifying savings. The fourth process was the 'sinking lid' policy on staff numbers, to enable departments to shed 'fat' less painfully.

However, the expenditure percentages quoted above clearly showed that these measures were not working. The double-digit inflation New Zealand was experiencing had overtaken these processes with a twofold result. COPE had become a bureaucratic device for preserving existing policies and was also essentially a cost-plus exercise that inevitably resulted in a degree of yearly expenditure increase. This occurred because departments were constantly encouraged to adopt an expansive view of their overall requirements. Once that claim was accepted, it was added to the base figure from one year to the next. An additional factor was that most policies were open-ended. Expenditure on some was dependent on how vigorously policies were pursued, while economic circumstances dictated the cost of other policies, such as unemployment benefits.

There were also problems with the new policy review process because not all policies were brought within the review, and no acceptable system had emerged, even within the Cabinet room, for establishing absolute priorities between competing sectors. This problem was not peculiar to New Zealand — it was a weakness of the Westminster system.

The system actually operated as an invitation for ministers, departments and special interest groups to propose new or expanded areas of expenditure, with little or no incentive for existing policies or functions to be reviewed at the same time.

My view was that the policy review processes offered little hope of achieving the required savings unless ministers were willing to adopt a rigorous approach, and my experience on the Cabinet Expenditure Committee showed that this was not happening. The 'sinking lid' policy had no doubt reduced staff numbers and resulted in departments tightening their operations, but it had also led to unintended consequences. One was that there was now an incentive to replace labour with capital, such as electronic data-processing applications. Another was for more work to be contracted out to the private sector, irrespective of whether this was a cost-effective option.

The mechanisms I proposed in my paper, which would have led to better control of spending both in the aggregate and by sector, included:

- the specific identification of all increases in expenditure over the previous year, by bringing all allocative decisions together and allowing the relative merits of 'unavoidable' extensions of existing policies to be weighed against those of new policies that could otherwise be introduced;
- the placing of specific financial ceilings on all new policies, so avoiding the expenditure creep that arose from the introduction of open-ended basically uncontrolled policies, in the sense that once the 'rules' are set, the Government has relatively little control over the consequential level of expenditure;
- a continuation of the 'tit for tat' policy whereby departments are expected to make room for new policies by specifying how compensatory savings could be achieved in respect of current expenditures;
- the identification, on a selective basis, of major policy spending areas for evaluation, and the responsibility for evaluation being vested in a

Cabinet Committee supported by a small team, probably based in the Treasury; and

- the grouping of a number of votes, making them subject to an overall expenditure limit, and allocating to a Cabinet Committee (comprising the ministers concerned, plus the minister of finance) the primary responsibility for determining expenditure priorities within the sector (i.e. the so called 'envelope' approach used by the Canadians).

My paper concluded that while no magic wand existed that would provide the government with the expenditure control sought, I believed, as did COPE, that the mechanisms discussed in the paper would represent a coordinated and mutually reinforcing approach.

The key concept was more explicit fixing of the limits within which expenditure decisions were to be made, and shifting more of the responsibility for expenditure control and policy review to where it most effectively belonged — with individual ministers and the departments for which they were responsible.

By mid-June COPE officials were considering the proposed new approach and had gone back to first principles in asking the question: 'What is the basic philosophy underlying the "Quigley concept"?' Their answer was that:

- aggregate expenditure should be determined on the basis of availability rather than needs;
- given the flat economy the public sector was already large enough;
- if departments were to do anything new and at the same time do more of the same, by necessity they would need to come under closer scrutiny; and, finally,
- if one department's vote got more, another would get less.

The officials went on to identify what they saw as the two principal mechanisms that needed to be introduced, namely the fixing of expenditure ceilings and a 'tit for tat' requirement for all new expenditures.

Much of what I was advocating is *passé* today, but in the 1970s and 1980s the view that the public sector was somehow different from the rest of the economy and so should not have to follow the same management rules had wide support. The argument was that my recommended approach would weaken the democratic process and/or lead to a savage fall-off in the standard of social services.

My response was that without some measure of performance or price mechanism it was virtually impossible to assess the value taxpayers were getting for the substantial sums they were paying for a whole host of government activities. I also made the point that, unlike in the private sector where inefficiencies could result in losses and the risk of takeover or insolvency, government departments were not subject to these constraints. The government and its ministers therefore had an especially onerous responsibility for supervising public-sector performance, including ensuring the appointment of competent managers.

I was particularly critical of the prevailing system for appointing senior and middle managers in the public sector. I likened it to a situation where the senior employees of New Zealand's leading companies shared collective responsibility for selecting staff, regardless of the wishes of that company's board of directors.

Ludicrous as this may sound, New Zealand's top public-sector CEOs at that time were appointed by a 'committee of cardinals' — a panel of 12 senior public servants. I suggested disbanding this panel and replacing it with a ministerial appointment process, involving appropriate minister–CEO accountability relationships. I also advocated the need for standards of disclosure and reporting to be at least as high as, and preferably higher than, those in the private sector.[1]

However, as time went on, various factors made it difficult to progress my objectives. To name a few: the second oil shock, which increasingly came to dominate the political environment; hyperinflation; rising unemployment; balance of payments problems; increasing handouts to the farming sector. A further problem was Muldoon's innate conservatism. This meant some really big expenditure decisions were not going to be subject to the constraints my proposals suggested, despite the problems I had identified and my suggested solutions. Another problem was that as Muldoon began to realise how isolated he had become in caucus and Cabinet, he was not going to support anything I suggested that might have enhanced my personal standing among my colleagues. This was graphically illustrated in the months to come.

Accident compensation

While I was still in Muldoon's good books he began to give me extra tasks. One was to chair a Cabinet/caucus committee to review the accident compensation scheme. Michael Cox, an accountant, was the main backbench caucus member on the committee, which was once again serviced by David Lloyd.

Back in 1900, New Zealand had followed the example set by Otto von Bismarck in Prussia 16 years earlier and introduced a 'no fault' workers' accident compensation system. The Workers' Compensation for Accident Act lasted, with some changes, until 1974. It provided injured workers with weekly benefits, and in case of death, compensation for dependants. Employers were required to take out insurance cover for potential injuries to employees. Benefits were small and could be paid for a maximum of six years from the date of injury. Injured workers also had the right to sue an employer for negligence. Non-work and motor vehicle injuries were not covered by the act.

Following dissatisfaction with the scheme's coverage and the difficulties of having to establish negligence to recover damages in court proceedings, a royal commission in 1967 recommended a new 'no-fault' approach to compensation for personal injury, which came into force on 1 April 1974. However, by 1979 there were growing concerns about the cost of the scheme, with employers increasingly vocal about paying for non-work-related injuries.

The review under my chairmanship was designed to reduce the cost of the scheme and improve its administration. Although some of the committee's more contentious recommendations were watered down during the select committee's consideration of submissions on the Bill, substantial legislative changes resulted, involving the deletion of more than 60 sections of the 1972 Act, with several new provisions:

- moving the funding structure from 'fully funded' to 'pay-as-you-go';
- reducing employers' payment obligations from 100 percent to 80 percent for the first week following a work accident;
- moving work-related motor vehicle accidents from the earner's account to the motor vehicle accident account
- increasing the maximum amount payable for permanent loss or impairment from $7000 to $17,000, with the maximum amount for pain and suffering remaining at $10,000.

Muldoon was publicly enthusiastic about the committee's report, its recommendations and the legislative changes that followed.

Alternative economic objectives

As time went on, in the face of growing frustration with the direction of the government's economic policy, I began work on a set of alternative economic objectives for the period 1978–81. This culminated in a document that had input from David Lloyd, selected members of the caucus economic committee and (unofficially) from some of the more market-orientated officials in the Treasury.

To my horror, this private draft document was subsequently reproduced in full by Press Gallery journalist Tony Garnier in his 1981 book *Election '81: An End to Muldoonism?* Contrary to Garnier's claim in his introduction, the document was not 'noted' by the government caucus, was not intended for publication, and had been given to Garnier in absolute confidence. Garnier drew a direct line between my preparation of this document and my subsequent sacking by Muldoon:

> Shortly after the 1978 General Election, the new Associate Minister of Finance, Derek Quigley, put pen to paper on what he believed, strongly as it soon turned out, should be the objectives of the National Government's economic policy for the next three years until the 1981 election. The document, compiled with help from Treasury officials, was 'noted' by the government caucus, but never made public. Confirming he had compiled the document, Quigley said much later he did so because he believed it was a responsibility of a government to set out in clear terms what it was trying to achieve. In the absence of suitable economic sign-posting of the future by the Minister of Finance, Mr Muldoon, he had decided to take an initiative of his own. The document is published here in full for the first time, exactly as circulated within caucus. Readers can draw their own conclusions on what has and has not been adopted by the government. Quigley, of course, has since lost his job as Associate Finance Minister, partly because, it is said, Muldoon disagreed that economic objectives should be highlighted.[2]

My alternative economic plan was aimed at improving the productivity and the international competitiveness of the New Zealand economy by removing restrictions on the private sector and reducing government spending. The full document is reproduced as an appendix (see page 335).

CHAPTER 7

Other Ministerial Responsibilities

The Abbotsford slip

In addition to my housing and finance responsibilities, I was also Minister in Charge of the Government Life, State Insurance and Public Trust Offices, along with what was then called the Earthquake and War Damage Commission (now the Earthquake Commission or EQC). These entities were expected to tick along nicely without much ministerial involvement, but this was not always the case.

The first to require my attention was the Earthquake Commission, following a landslip in the Dunedin suburb of Abbotsford. The concept that led to the creation of the commission had evolved over time from 1906, when general insurance companies were required to pay levies to maintain fire brigades. Further impetus followed events such as the Napier earthquake in 1931 and the Japanese attack on Pearl Harbor in 1941, with Parliament passing the War Damage Act that year and foreshadowing the possibility of covering other disasters such as earthquakes.[1] However, it was not until 1944 that New Zealand became the first country in the world to extend coverage to disaster restoration with the establishment of the Earthquake and War Damage Commission.

Premiums were collected through individual fire insurance policies, and in due course a special disaster fund was established to provide a degree of protection against losses from storms, floods and volcanic eruptions. From 1954 the commission was authorised to accept voluntary — but not compulsory — insurance premiums against landslips.

There had been numerous smaller landslips at Abbotsford, notably during the building of the Dunedin–Mosgiel railway line in 1914. Despite this, and a 1951 University of Otago report stating that the land was unsuitable for building, housing construction began in earnest from 1953. Slips resulting from motorway construction in 1966 and 1968 required several houses to be demolished. From 1968 cracks started appearing in houses, with evidence of subsidence and earth movement becoming more common in the following years. Between late 1978 and mid-1979 water mains and sewerage pipes frequently ruptured and four houses had to be evacuated. Another six houses were evacuated before the end of June 1979.

Up until this point the commission had not alerted me about this issue. When it did, and I visited the area in July 1979 with Venn Young in his capacity as Minister of Lands, it was a scary experience as we stood on land that was continually groaning.

Initially, the government refused to declare a state of emergency, but on 6 August, with 13 houses by then evacuated, Civil Defence declared an official emergency and began drawing up plans for the complete evacuation of the area. Although the situation didn't seem immediately urgent, two days later a major slide saw 17 people stranded on a strip of land in the middle of a landslip and having to be rescued by a rope line.

Overall, the slide involved 5 million cubic metres of earth, mud and rock, and eventually led to the loss or relocation of 69 houses. Miraculously, no lives were lost. The Earthquake Commission paid compensation of $10–14 million to those affected.

A commission of inquiry found that the area had a geological predisposition to slippage, with potentially unstable weak clay layers. The commission also considered the issue of landslip cover on a New Zealand wide basis, which led to changes in building and subdivision practices. Also, because neither the Earthquake Commission nor normal insurance policies automatically covered landslips at the time of the Abbotsford 1979 disaster, insurance regulations were substantially rewritten in 1984. Individual claims are now possible for people who have chosen appropriate insurance coverage.

State Insurance and Government Life

Early in 1979 I set up a review of the activities of the Government Life and State Insurance offices to see if they should be amalgamated in the interests of efficiency, effectiveness and potential financial benefits. I was not aware that the State Services Commissioner, Mervyn Probine, had approached Muldoon in his capacity as Minister of Finance in September

1978 on this matter, but that consideration had been deferred until after the election. When I raised the matter with Muldoon he was supportive, and I received Cabinet approval on 19 February 1979 for the Treasury and the State Services Commission (SSC) to prepare a paper on the pros and cons of a potential amalgamation.

By early September the review team unexpectedly concluded that amalgamation provided no clear advantages. Although it was accepted that amalgamation would provide wider career prospects for a limited number of staff working in areas such as investment, accounts, personnel and general administration, the investigation showed that private companies had tended, at that time, to diversify rather than merge their activities.

The officials' report made two key points. First, in the private sector the two types of business (life and general insurance) were carried out within entirely separate subsidiaries or divisions for funds management, with only the ownership and certain management services in common. Private insurers had typically moved to the position the government-owned insurance offices were in. Second, Government Life and State Insurance still retained their historical roles as industry insurance 'quasi' regulators.

But the review did uncover some financial viability problems within Government Life. Initially these were thought to be minor, but when further research and advice from my backbench colleague Ian McLean showed that the office was in serious trouble, I immediately consulted Mervyn Probine. Flowing on from this, an advisory board — chaired by Frank Dickson, head of the Canterbury Trustee Savings Bank — was set up to work with the Government Life CEO, Hutton Peacock, to nurse the business back to full health. Although the board had no statutory authority, Peacock and his staff treated it as though it had, and the whole exercise achieved the required outcome on a completely cooperative basis.

In setting up this advisory board I was determined to appoint people because of their ability to do the job, not because of their political affiliations. Dickson's appointment was a case in point. When I sought caucus approval for him to chair the board (which was then accepted practice), Muldoon asked me about Dickson's politics. I replied, 'I haven't the slightest idea, Prime Minister. I selected him because of his ability to do the job.' His appointment was approved without further comment.

Interestingly, the subsequent practice in the mid- to late 1980s of appointing statutorily constituted boards of directors to oversee the activities of state-owned enterprises drew on the advisory board concept that Probine and I had worked out for Government Life.

Review of cooperatives

As a backbencher I had been a member of a five-person caucus committee under the chairmanship of under-secretary Keith Allen to consider the taxing of cooperatives. However, as there were no substantive decisions on the committee's recommendations before the 1978 election, I progressed the matter in 1980 in my capacity as associate minister of finance.

The issues involved were politically sensitive, as a range of entities could conceivably lose their concessional and in some cases tax-exempt status if the law were changed. Those potentially affected included various producer cooperatives, the Public Service Investment Society, veterinary clubs and similar bodies, building societies, workingmen's clubs, and assorted charitable and educational institutions. Also potentially within the net were retail companies that operated on the basis of distributing surpluses as discounts to shareholders and/or their members.

The usual stated objective of a cooperative is to provide credit and services to members at or near cost. As a result — based on the common law mutuality principle that 'a man cannot make a profit by trading with himself' — the cooperative organisation (in its capacity as agent for its members) could retain any resultant surplus not otherwise rebated to members as tax-free working capital. In contrast, ordinary trading entities, often in direct competition with cooperatives, were required to pay tax on their profits at specified rates. I decided to look at whether inequities were involved and, if so, to recommend changes.

Adam Smith, as far back as 1776 in his book *The Wealth of Nations*, had developed the canons of taxation as equality, certainty, convenience and efficiency. Any taxation system, in Smith's view, should treat all people of a particular country equally, clearly define the tax a person or entity should pay, be convenient for taxpayers and tax collectors, and make it cheap to pay and collect tax.

My starting point was the report of the Ross Committee in 1967 on the New Zealand taxation system.[2] It had suggesting reducing corporate and personal tax rates and abolishing land tax, with increased revenue derived from a new comprehensive sales tax, introducing a wider tax base through taxation of the business activities of charities and educational institutions, taxing fringe benefits and increasing excise taxes.

One complication I faced was that Muldoon — in his capacity as minister of finance in 1967 — had opposed the Ross Committee recommendations on the grounds of the cost of their implementation, and the fact that the tax burden would fall more heavily on low-income earners.

As it was clear that the economic position of members of a cooperative was improved as a result of the activities of the organisation, it seemed valid to ask: 'Is that economic gain a proper subject for taxation and, if so, is the gain a gain derived by the organisation or the member or both?' The answers were important for a number of reasons.

In Canada the Carter Commission's report of 1966 disregarded the common-law mutuality principle of no profit if trading with oneself, and held that 'in our view the important point is that if the economic position of the [cooperative] member is improved as a result of the activity, the economic gain is a proper subject for taxation.'

I agreed. My view was that the tax system should be neutral, neither favouring nor discriminating against any form of legal endeavour. I maintained that neutrality or impartiality required similar treatment for all businesses competing for the same sales and profits and that the mutuality principle should be judged on the basis of the transaction, not the association. Following on from this, if income were derived from a commercial transaction, it should be taxed in the normal way no matter how the entity was structured.

My recommendations were to restrict the tax advantage of 'mutuality' strictly to situation where trading was with the entity's own members; to tax any entity's surplus at prevailing company rates after deducting rebates; to tighten the tax-exempt status of building societies, charities, educational entities etc (some had been set up only to benefit from their tax-free status); and to tax the rebates of individual owners.

Muldoon found all this too hard, but eventually not so the reforming Labour government after the 1984 election.

Practising what I preached

Particularly in my capacity as associate minister of finance, I built up a reputation as a hard-nosed operator determined, where possible, to restrain government spending and reinforce the National Party's policy of support for private enterprise. To maintain my credibility, I was also determined to practise what I preached within my own portfolio responsibilities. As a result, Vote: Housing in the 1980 budget was substantially less than it had been in 1979. This, plus the reviews I had initiated and the speeches I had been giving about the need to restructure the economy, meant I was starting to attract attention, culminating in Geoffrey Palmer, the Labour MP for Christchurch Central, 'criticising' me in his budget speech on 15 July 1980.[3]

Palmer began by castigating the government's budget overall, claiming that it was devoid of positive steps to overcome critical social problems such as unemployment. He went on to claim that the government was suffering from a crisis of confidence resulting from an ideological split between ministers (like the prime minister) who were intent on political survival, and 'the Minister of Housing who believes that it is necessary to implement rigorous economic policies rapidly'.

He quoted from a speech I had given in October 1979 where I said: 'As a private-sector advocate, I want to see the state eventually withdraw from its predominantly financing role, and provide more opportunity to the private sector to encourage it to cater more adequately for the demands of prospective home buyers.'

Palmer contrasted the budget estimates for 45 separate votes, noting that only three had been reduced, while all the others had either increased or remained about the same. Vote: Housing, with inflation taken into account, he claimed, had been cut in real terms 'by [much] more than one fifth and perhaps by as much as one quarter'.

He then outlined elements of the new economic philosophy I was advocating: tighter control over government spending to avoid budget deficits, a sustained shift from public-sector to private-sector activity, an acceleration of industry restructuring with a reduction in protection, and the encouragement of foreign investment.

These proposals were so radical — said Palmer — that they were doomed because they 'fail[ed] to take into account the complexity of the New Zealand economy' and would reverse more than 140 years of government involvement in it. Worse still, I was accused of doing in my Housing portfolio what I had been advocating in my public utterances.

Although most National Party members enjoyed this speech, some of my Cabinet colleagues, such as Bolger and Wellington, were far less enthusiastic. And although Muldoon never chided me at this stage about the things I was advocating, I was sent off shortly after as head of a New Zealand delegation to a meeting in Papua New Guinea on the Pacific Forum (Shipping) Line. The trip coincided with the National Party's 1980 annual conference. I was consequently out of sight and out of mind.

Battling Australia in the PNG highlands

I had previously been to a housing ministers' conference in Australia that was characterised by bickering between state and the federal governments (with Jeff Kennett, Housing Minister in Victoria, in particular at his arrogant and obnoxious worst). I had also chaired a comparable constructive meeting in New Zealand. But the Pacific Forum Line (PFL) meeting was the first time I had led a New Zealand delegation overseas.

The PFL had been set up following a Pacific Forum agreement in 1977, to establish a regional shipping company to enhance trade between the Pacific Islands, New Zealand and Australia. At the time of my involvement, it was owned jointly by the governments of 12 countries in the Pacific, but today the parent company is a joint venture between the Government of Samoa and Neptune Pacific Line.

In 1980 the PFL was losing money, as it did for many years to come. This may have contributed to an associate finance minister being sent to PNG rather than the minister of transport and/or minister responsible for the PFL.

The New Zealand delegation was quite large. Besides me, it consisted of my senior private secretary, transport secretary Jack Healy, officials from Foreign Affairs and the Treasury, and a representative of the PFL. I can still visualise the expression on Healy's face at the first briefing meeting in my office before we left Wellington. It read: How did we finish up with a greenhorn like you heading our team?

The meeting was originally scheduled to be held in Port Moresby, but riots and killings in the capital saw it shifted to the village of Mount Hagen in the Western Highland Province. This happened to be in the electorate of Paias Wingti, PNG's minister of transport and later prime minister (1985–88 and 1992–94). Transport Minister Peter Nixon led the Australian delegation.

Our arrival at Mount Hagen coincided with a visit by the PNG Deputy Governor-General and a school half-holiday to celebrate the occasion. As we drove from the airport to the village conference venue, children threw flowers and fronds over our cars. This was fine for me, in the front car, but the same was not true for those in the following vehicles. When the flowers and fronds ran out, the children improvised with shingle and stones, and in one case, a large piece of wood that cracked a car windshield!

We were all relieved to arrive at the hotel unhurt and to be let through two high security gates. On closer inspection of the hotel grounds, a glaring incongruity became evident. Despite the impressive security gates at the front of the hotel, only a low, rusty barbed-wire fence ran between the back of the grounds and the nearby village, with numerous well-used walking tracks visible between the two.

The two days of meetings were difficult and confrontational. My objective was to try to extract more money from Australia, which, in our view, was not contributing its fair share to keeping the PFL financially afloat and operational. Although I had an excellent team of experienced officials with me, to my initial dismay I found that proceedings were to be conducted like those at the Pacific Forum, where only the head of each delegation is permitted to be present. This meant that my officials were excluded.

Unsurprisingly, Peter Nixon took strong exception to my suggestion that Australia wasn't pulling its weight, and our head-on had a substantial degree of invective. To counter this, I insisted on two adjournments to consult with my officials, and in the end we achieved a satisfactory outcome.

After the conference we played nine holes of golf, which taught me how different it is to play at 5500 feet above sea level. I had hit a good drive down the first fairway and selected what I thought was the correct club for a shot to the green. The ball was struck beautifully and was heading for the pin — or so I thought. Instead, it sailed over the green, the course boundary and the adjoining road, finishing up in a small factory compound.

Back in Wellington I reported to Muldoon that the PFL was in a hopeless financial state, was never likely to be viable, and should be closed down. But as the PFL was one of his pet projects, my advice was ignored.

About two weeks later I hosted a dinner in the Cabinet dining room for all the members of our delegation and their partners. I was about to make a short speech towards the end of the dinner when I was pre-empted by Jack Healy. He congratulated me on the outcome of the PNG meeting and then — to my surprise — said that, despite having been a senior public servant for many, many years, he had never before been invited to dinner by a Cabinet minister. I was extremely annoyed — not with Healy, but with the succession of ministers he had served who had not thought to repay his loyal service.

Locked in late at night

Despite the hard but enjoyable grind of ministerial responsibility, there were lighter moments. One took place shortly after the Cabinet had moved in 1979 from the Old Parliament Building into the Beehive. Hugh Templeton, as minister of broadcasting, had the only TV set in the building (apart from one in Muldoon's office). As Hugh's office was next to mine, I would go there most nights to watch the 6pm news.

On the evening in question Templeton was absent, so after the news had finished I made sure his main office door was locked and left through the back door, which led through his and my separate bathroom suites to the central Beehive lift area. I had snibbed the lock on this second door as I went through, and as I heard it close behind me I realised that the armoured glass doors in front of me were also locked. I was stuck in the common back-door space between Hugh's and my office and I knew I would remain there until I could attract the attention of someone in the lift lobby area!

About an hour later a security guard appeared there and I signalled to him to get a key so that I could get out. He disappeared, and that was the last I saw of him. Hours went by and still no one came. It was about 2.30am when the cleaners arrived and let me out. I found out later that day from two very embarrassed security guards that the first one I had alerted was just about to finish his shift and had told his replacement to let me out. The replacement had gone to my office, let himself in with a master key, seen my suit coat on my chair and assumed — wrongly — that I had somehow already got out.

No one got bawled out, as the original mistake was mine and mine alone, but the incident had a sequel. A Cabinet Expenditure Committee paper had somehow found its way into the public domain a day or so earlier, and when its contents appeared on TV the police were called in to investigate the leak. Their enquiries were still under way at the time I was locked in.

Unsurprisingly, some of my former backbench colleagues who heard about my experience of being locked in thought it was hilarious and asked why I hadn't forced open the door that led back into Hugh's office. I said I had tried but hadn't been able to budge it. Bob Bell responded that all I needed to have done was kick the door hard near the handle and the wooden surround would have split. 'Nonsense,' I said. Bob asked if I wanted him to show me how to do it and unwisely I said yes. Fortunately, my locked office door was used for the demonstration, not Hugh's. Bob was extremely tall and had bigger feet than anyone else in Parliament, and when he kicked the door the wooden surround immediately split and the door flew open.

Next day the police sergeant heading the investigation into the leaked Cabinet committee paper visited me. Eyeing my broken door jamb, he said, 'Minister, I think we have found out how the person who stole the Cabinet paper got access to it.'

I replied, for once without even blushing, 'Sorry, Sergeant, that's not how it happened.'

CHAPTER 8

The Law and the Arthur Allan Thomas Case

Public perception is that decisions of the full Cabinet are based on thoughtful discussion and that 'big ticket' items, in particular, are approved only after rigorous scrutiny during which all members who want to contribute have their say. While this was sometimes true during my time as a member of Muldoon's Cabinets, it was the exception rather than the rule.

Muldoon's style as Cabinet chair was much more dictatorial than when he ran caucus meetings. In addition, most items had already been through Cabinet committees and as such were seen as coming back to be rubber stamped, with limited opportunity for non-members of those committees to have much input.

But there seemed to be plenty of time for discussion of trivial practical matters. When we moved from the Old Parliament Building to the Beehive there were numerous teething problems because of the building's newness and its novel circular shape. A lot of Cabinet's time during those early days was spent discussing the inadequacy of lifts and the non-functioning of toilets. On one occasion, when a discussion of this type seemed to be going on for ever, I handed Jim McLay, who sat next to me for most of my time in Cabinet, a note that read: 'What agenda item do you think will go through next for $160 million without any discussion?'

Later, when major decisions were being made about the impact of the 'Think Big' projects, members of the Cabinet Economic Committee and a small group of ministers who thought officials were too slow in concluding negotiations with potential project contracting partners became impatient. They were more interested in the politics of being seen to make decisions than in the impact of a particular project on the overall economy. This was at a time when thoughtful consideration and maximum input from officials should have been the priority, with the country increasingly facing financial problems from the impact of the second oil shock.[1]

The Arthur Allan Thomas saga

The eventual pardoning of convicted murderer Arthur Allan Thomas was a complex and polarising business in which politics and the rule of law warranted careful consideration. In the end it was meticulously handled by Jim McLay in his capacity as minister of justice and the only person who had the authority to recommend a pardon to the governor-general.

An Arthur Allan Thomas Cabinet Subcommittee was set up to support McLay in whatever decision he finally made. It was to consist of Muldoon, MacIntyre and McLay, but at the suggestion of the latter, my name was added to 'provide balance'.

Background to the case

Right from the time the local Tuakau police received a telephone call on the afternoon of 22 June 1970 about an abandoned and bloodstained farmhouse belonging to Jeanette and Harvey Crewe, the case attracted widespread media and public attention and scrutiny.

The scene was particularly grisly.

The adult occupants were nowhere to be found, although bloodstains and drag marks suggested their dead or injured bodies had been removed from the scene. Their 18-month-old baby, Rochelle, was found alive but in a distressed state in her cot several days after her parents had disappeared.

There were suggestions that Rochelle had been fed in the intervening days. Evidence was also given of a 'mystery woman' seen outside the Crewe house a few days before the crime scene was discovered.

A police investigation eventually resulted in Jeanette and Harvey's bodies being found, in August and September 1970 respectively, in the Waikato River. Both had died of gunshot wounds.

Their neighbour, Arthur Allan Thomas, was arrested and charged with their murders on 11 November 1970.

A jury trial began in the Supreme Court on 15 February 1971, in which Thomas was eventually found guilty on two counts of murder.

An appeal against conviction was dismissed four months later. In late 1971 the governor-general was petitioned to grant a new trial. Sir George McGregor, a retired judge of the Supreme Court, reviewed the material that had been submitted and reported on 2 February 1972 that in his view no further reference to the court should be granted. In his opinion there had been no miscarriage of justice.

However, a further petition was put before the Court of Appeal which, after hearing evidence and submissions over four days between 5 February and 16 February 1973, ordered a second trial.

The second trial — again before a jury — began on 26 March 1973, and once again Thomas was convicted on both counts. On 11 July the Court of Appeal dismissed an appeal against this second conviction.

During the second trial the defence questioned some of the police evidence, focusing in particular on the cartridge case found in the Crewe garden that had been a crucial part of Thomas's original conviction. Forensic scientist Dr Jim Sprott — whom I later got to know quite well — testified that the cartridge case did not in fact match the bullets that killed Harvey and Jeanette Crewe.

A campaign of support for Thomas, led by journalist Pat Booth of the *Auckland Star* and aided by Jim Sprott, attracted a high degree of public interest. They pushed for the conviction to be overturned and their campaign eventually attracted the attention of Attorney-General Martyn Finlay, who wrote a memorandum dated 1 November to Prime Minister Norman Kirk.

Although Finlay dismissed much of what Booth had written in his *Auckland Star* articles, claiming that his analysis was not objective, he did accept that one point warranted further inquiry. It involved the two cartridge cases produced by the Crown in the second trial. One was the case that had been found in the garden, while the other came from a box of bullets belonging to Thomas that the police had test-fired from his .22 rifle. While Crown witnesses had stated in court that the two cases were either 'identical' or 'indistinguishable', Booth claimed, citing Sprott's evidence, that their difference was not only significant but demonstrably so.

Finlay's comment in his report to Kirk on Booth's claim was: 'If this could be established, the whole foundation upon which the Crown's case had been built would be called into question if not demolished.'[2] He went on to note that although he had hoped for a 'yes/no' answer following further research in New Zealand and Australia about the cartridge cases and the bullet fragments, this had not eventuated. This meant he was left with drawing out facts from a clash of opinions and inferences.

Finlay added that Detective Inspector Hutton (the police officer in charge of the homicide inquiry) had noted in his report on the murders: '[I]f the Sprott/Booth submission were accepted it would mean that the "Charles" cartridge case [exhibit 350, found in the garden] was "planted" [by police].' Finlay wrote to Kirk: 'I do not accept this.'

Finlay concluded that as a *prima facie* case had been put forward, a (further) judicial review by the Court of Appeal — following an application to the governor-general for the exercise of the prerogative of mercy — was justified. However, in 1975 the five Court of Appeal judges unanimously held that the Thomas defence team had not excluded a reasonable possibility that exhibit 350 could have contained 'pattern 8 bullet fragments', which were found in both Crewe bodies. The court consequently turned down the application.

But Thomas's supporters would not be silenced. Pat Booth's book, *The Fate of Arthur Thomas: Trial by Ambush*, came out in 1975, claiming that the convictions were against the weight of evidence. Thomas appealed to the Privy Council, which advised on 4 July 1978 that it had no jurisdiction to entertain such an appeal. In 1976 the Arthur Thomas Retrial Committee, based in Auckland, published *ABC of Injustice: The Thomas Case*, authored by Booth and Sprott.

The next major development was in 1978 and followed the publication of British investigative author David Yallop's book *Beyond Reasonable Doubt?* Yallop was scathing of the way the police and the courts had handled the case and he included an open letter to Muldoon asking for Thomas to be pardoned. Yallop claimed that Thomas was innocent and that the conviction amounted to a serious miscarriage of justice. The nature and seriousness of his allegations, and in particular his claim that he knew the identities of the 'mystery woman' and the person who fed the Crewe baby reignited public interest.

Muldoon had taken an interest in the case as early as May 1972, and had expressed unease about the guilty verdict at the first trial. On becoming prime minister he had substantial correspondence with both Booth and Sprott, and on 26 November 1976 met with them to discuss 'what could be done'.[3]

Muldoon met Yallop on 24 October 1978 and the following day issued a press release. In it he stated that Yallop had handed him certain documents and that '[t]hese included a letter which purports to identify the woman who is alleged to have fed Rochelle Crewe after the murders'. The PM said he had decided to ask a prominent Auckland lawyer to investigate Yallop's allegations. The lawyer would be given freedom to act as he saw fit, and would report directly to Muldoon. The lawyer, whose name was not initially disclosed, was Robert Adams-Smith QC. He subsequently produced two reports: the first in January 1979, the second in December 1979.

In his first report Adams-Smith stated that Yallop had no proper basis to state that he knew who fed the Crewe child or that he knew the identity of the woman who had been seen on or near the property on 19 June 1970. However, he went on to question the Crown's evidence of the timing of the murders on the evening of 17 June, stating: 'The suggestion that the deaths occurred during the evening [of the 17th] does not accord with the quantity of milk apparently in the house at the time of the deaths.'[4] And later: 'Because the question of the time of the murders is vitally connected with the evidence [of two witnesses] … that there were sightings of a woman on Friday the 19th June and a child on Saturday 20th June … It would appear that further enquiries are necessary in respect of this aspect of the case.'[5]

Muldoon told the media on 25 January 1979 that he had asked Adams-Smith to make further enquiries. In his second report Adams-Smith stated: 'I have real doubt whether the case against Thomas was proved beyond all reasonable doubt … [I]t seems that an injustice may have been done.'[6]

'Personal and Secret'

On Wednesday 12 December 1979, MacIntyre, McLay and I each received an envelope from the Prime Minister's Department marked 'Personal and Secret'. The envelopes contained copies of Muldoon's two press releases on the case, some police documents, the first Adams-Smith report, part of his second report, and a comprehensive comment by the solicitor-general on Adams-Smith's two reports.

After McLay and I had each independently gone through the papers, we met on Friday 14 December to discuss our initial thoughts. At that stage we were both of the view that the papers revealed no reason to pardon Thomas.[7] I therefore thought it likely the Cabinet Subcommittee would be split 2/2. MacIntyre was known to favour a pardon and had already written a lengthy letter to Muldoon in 1977 raising doubts about Thomas's conviction,[8] and Muldoon appeared to be of the same view.

In my view Adams-Smith had raised no new evidence, and his reports were confusing and wrong in law in at least two respects. For example, he stated that he had approached his task as if considering the situation of 'a man accused of a crime as opposed to a man convicted of it'.[9] Had he proceeded on the basis that Thomas had already been convicted by two juries, the key issue for him would have been whether there was any new evidence that raised real doubts. He was also critical that the Crown's case was 'based mainly on circumstantial evidence', which seemed to imply that this type of evidence — which many, many court trials and decisions are based on — is somehow inferior to other evidence. He also appeared to overlook the fact that in the Court of Appeal judgment after the first Thomas trial, Thomas's counsel had unsuccessfully raised several arguments similar to those Adams-Smith himself now raised.

The Solicitor-General had summed up, in my view, the doubtful probative value of the Adams-Smith reports:

> It appears that Mr Adams-Smith has dealt with the matter on which you [Muldoon] first asked him to report. He then raised the question of the timing of the killings arising out of doubts in his mind in relation to the milk, etc. and the two sightings [by the two witnesses]. He satisfied himself about them then went on to explore a new avenue altogether. He explored some possible new evidence and rejected it. He then considered the new avenue on the same material that was before the two juries. In effect he suggests a possible course that neither of the defence counsel in the two previous trials and appeals nor Thomas in the numerous subsequent proceedings has suggested.[10]

In essence there appeared to be three options now to consider: pardoning and releasing Thomas on the basis of the content of the Adams-Smith reports, declining to take any action, or referring the points raised by Adams-Smith to the Court of Appeal. On the first option, as the Solicitor-General wrote:

> [T]o pardon or release Thomas on the basis of this report would be to make a mockery of our justice system . . . To substitute Adams-Smith's opinion

> which has been formed as he says without investigating all aspects of the case for that of the juries and the Courts would in my opinion be quite wrong.[11]

I agreed with this and therefore believed a pardon was inappropriate. This led to consideration of a 'do nothing' decision, which I regarded as untenable. I was therefore left — on the basis of the limited information I had at my disposal — with the third option, a further referral to the Court of Appeal. I thought this was the best course of action as the government would be seen to be deferring to the opinion of the court, rather than to the views of a QC who had heard no opposing points of view.

When I arrived in Parliament on 17 December after a weekend in my electorate, the other three members of the subcommittee were already in discussion. I found that McLay had changed his view over the weekend and was now in favour of a pardon. I said I didn't agree, but that as a minority position would be impractical and unhelpful, I would support McLay's recommendation. I added that the focus should now be on what a pardon was likely to cost the Crown. To the horror of the others, I said I thought $500,000 would be the starting amount for compensation to Thomas. (The amount eventually paid was almost double that, after Thomas had spent nine years in prison for a crime it had eventually been decided he had not committed.)

Why had McLay changed his mind? The answer is contained in a detailed email to me in March 2017, which illustrated why he was so successful in his roles as Minister of Justice and Attorney-General. Some extracts follow:

> I came to the Thomas matter with a fairly open mind — but, I must admit, with some inclination in favour of the convictions (and therefore against Thomas). I took the rather narrow, lawyer's view that Thomas had been twice convicted by two different juries, and those convictions had survived a number of judicial and other reviews. I hadn't heard all the evidence on which those verdicts and decisions were based, so it would take some persuading to get me to a contrary view.
>
> Over the weekend, I started to hand-draft a memorandum to justify a further referral to the Court of Appeal. As I wrote, I came to realise that what I was drafting in fact led, inevitably, to an almost opposite conclusion — namely, that Thomas would have to be pardoned.

My analysis revealed a number of problems. Most significantly, however, in dealing with the matter, the Court would really have only two options — to reject Thomas' claims (thereby, effectively, also rejecting Adams-Smith's views), or to recommend a retrial (it couldn't acquit or otherwise absolve him). *But the Crown could not mount a retrial.* Material (and hotly disputed) items of evidence were no longer available, in some cases had been destroyed (you will recall how the .22 cartridge case finished up in the Whitford tip!).

Furthermore, the Court would have *known* that a retrial could not be mounted ... (Derek, with respect, I think you might have overlooked this point about the practical inability to mount a new trial, which would, effectively, have made any referral to the Court of Appeal quite meaningless.)

In short, we had a report whose 'findings' we had to publish and couldn't ignore (as you rightly observe, 'a "do nothing" decision was politically unacceptable') ... [A]nd yet publication of the report might result in irresistible public presume to release Thomas — and that would do much more damage to the judicial system than any pardon.

Derek, I walked a very careful legal and constitutional path through this difficult issue. It was inevitable that, as Prime Minister, Muldoon would play some role in the matter (he and his Government would have to support me and deal with any consequences). He appointed Adams-Smith, and he established the *ad hoc* Cabinet committee. If he hadn't done those things, I would have had to inform him, in some way, of my proposed action; but he didn't interfere, and he left me to make the decision — and that's what I did.[12]

Thomas was awarded $950,000 in compensation, and in 1980 a royal commission was set up to investigate and report on three key matters:

1. Whether there was any impropriety on any person's part in the course of the investigation or subsequently, either in respect of the cartridge case (exhibit 350) or in respect of any other matter?
2. Whether any matters that should have been investigated were not investigated?
3. Whether proper steps were taken, after the arrest of Arthur Allan Thomas, to investigate any matter or information, if any, which suggested that he was not responsible for those deaths?[13]

The commission's answer to (1) was that '[police officers] Mr [Bruce] Hutton and Mr [Len] Johnston planted the shell case . . . and that they did so to manufacture evidence that Mr Thomas's rifle had been used for the killings.'[14] The Solicitor-General in due course recommended against prosecuting the two officers due to insufficient evidence.

Politics and the rule of law

McLay's well-reasoned and completely justifiable decision to pardon Thomas aside, this case raises some wider issues. Although the pardon illustrates the right of the Crown to exercise the prerogative of mercy where criminal trials and appeal systems produce a result that the public interest cannot sustain, this safety valve needs to be used exceedingly sparingly.

At the risk of repeating what I said on the Moyle Affair, no open democratic society like New Zealand's can function properly unless there is confidence in and support for the integrity of the parliamentary process, the judicial system, the rule of law and the people who represent them. This is why, in the context of Muldoon's roll-back of Labour's superannuation scheme — in the face of an opposing Court decision — I criticised him for his failure to uphold the rule of law.

Initially I saw the Thomas case in similar light. There had been a host of court hearings, appeals and petitions, and to override them was, I thought, tantamount to bringing the judicial process and the integrity of the New Zealand police into disrepute.

As I had told my caucus colleagues in another context, one of the fundamentals of our legal system is the maxim 'better the law be certain than fair', because this way people at least know what the law is. However, the judicial process needs to have appropriate checks and balances built into it. The Thomas case initially had these in abundance, but it turned out this was still not enough.

The decision of the 1980 royal commission clearly further damaged the credibility of the judicial process and the integrity of the New Zealand police in the eyes of the public. There were also questions about why the inquiry was held and whether it followed the principles of natural justice during the course of its hearing.

The reality is that the police were in an impossible position before the royal commission. Thomas was judged to have been innocent, convicted only because the cartridge case had been planted, which was the same question Attorney-General Finlay had decided the other way around in 1973.

The police were of the view that the commission, led by allegedly outspoken Australian judge Justice Robert Taylor, was 'out to get them'. Some regarded the hearings as a trap set by Muldoon, who had taken a strong personal interest in the case and become convinced that Thomas was innocent. The commission's report confirmed the police's worst fears, describing Thomas's imprisonment on false evidence as 'an unspeakable outrage'.[15]

Although Peter Williams QC, who represented Thomas at the commission, had little sympathy for the police complaint that Muldoon overrode the whole legal system, he commented that 'the judicial process hadn't really helped Thomas very much'.[16] Further, he agreed that Muldoon's personal intervention was crucial:

> Muldoon read the file, which was quite extraordinary for a politician. He sat down with us at the Intercontinental Hotel and he discussed it with us at length. I'm talking about hours of discussion and he had an amazing knowledge of detail.[17]

Williams remembers DCI Bruce Hutton giving evidence to Justice Taylor at the commission. Williams noted: 'They had the court packed with police and they booed Taylor because he was so direct in his questions. I've never seen anything like it in my life.'[18] In his memoir, *A Passion for Justice*, in 1997, Williams recalls that 'some politicians and certain judges regarded Thomas's crusade as an attack upon the whole New Zealand judicial system … the vast majority of police saw the Thomas saga as an all-out attack on them.'[19]

I agree.

CHAPTER 9

The Colonels' Coup

During late 1979 and 1980 there was increasing unhappiness throughout the country and also in caucus about Muldoon's style and leadership. The media speculated that he was becoming isolated within the National Party, and that younger and more right-wing MPs and party officials no longer respected him personally or approved of his tactics or policy decisions.[1]

Caucus disaffection came to a head in 1980 in the form of the so-called Colonels' Coup, but had started building up well before then in two main areas. The first was Muldoon's failure to recognise that the world economy had changed and that New Zealand had to adapt too. Instead, he kept adopting a series of short-term measures based on his view that the New Zealand economy was simply reacting (almost on a weekly basis) to overseas events.[2] As a result, he had no coherent long-term strategy. In the words of Professor Gary Hawke, he

> was an inveterate meddler, an overconfident, self-proclaimed economic manager ... [who] thought of the balance of payments today, the fiscal deficit tomorrow, but never seemed capable of balancing all the relevant factors at the same time. He had the misfortune to be in office when this mattered.[3]

My own response was to produce the paper referred to earlier.

The second area of concern was over Muldoon's style. Although he was unusually intelligent, a strong leader and a brilliant communicator, his aggressive style often descended into the unseemly. His conduct during the 1975 Moyle Affair was only the beginning. Some of his behaviour, in my view, demeaned the office of prime minister, and all raised questions about his judgement. These instances included:

- a series of public spats with former Prime Minister Sir John Marshall;
- his attacks on Justice Mahon's findings as sole royal commissioner in the Mt Erebus Inquiry;
- his comments that President Jimmy Carter was a dangerously naïve politician ('a peanut farmer from Georgia'), concerned with morality rather than realism in foreign policy;[4]
- his conduct towards party president George Chapman, who was frequently refused permission to convey the view of the party organisation to caucus;
- his reluctance in caucus to consider tax reform and the removal of import licensing, despite public undertakings to do so;
- his continuing support of non-performing ministers such as Colin McLachlan, who was appointed (ahead of Bolger, to the latter's anger) to the front bench when another minister retired;
- his recourse to bullying when he couldn't win an argument on logic;
- his refusal to promote individuals with different economic views — for example his 1982 bypassing of Roderick Deane for Reserve Bank Governor in favour of Spencer Russell;
- his description of Robert Mugabe, Prime Minister of Zimbabwe as 'just out of the bush';
- his approval of Frank Gill's retirement from Parliament and appointment as ambassador to the United States, precipitating the disastrous East Coast Bays by-election loss to Social Credit on 6 September 1980;
- his confrontational and unhelpful contribution at the opening meeting of Don Brash's East Coast Bays by-election campaign.

The final straw for his detractors was Muldoon's public comments that poor National Party organisation had been responsible for the by-election defeat in East Coast Bays. Large sections in the party openly criticised him for trying to shift the blame when it was clear that the initial trigger was his agreeing to Gill's mid-term retirement.[5]

The Colonels' Coup

The two main Cabinet conspirators in the attempted 'coup' were McLay and me. We had limited support from George Gair, and initially from Bolger before he turned tail. It was Paul East, known for his impish humour, who coined the title 'the Colonels', a reference to the Greek military junta of the 1970s, and the nickname clearly appealed to the press. The key 'non-commissioned officers' were Michael Cox, junior whip Tony Friedlander, Doug Kidd, Ian McLean and Bruce Townshend. Cox was the most active NCO, and at his and McLay's suggestion, 28 caucus members signed letters calling for Muldoon to be replaced by Deputy Prime Minister Brian Talboys. This number, with a few others reluctant to put their names to paper but nevertheless committed to change, represented a caucus majority. The signed letters were deposited with Eric Holland for safe keeping and were eventually returned to the signatories.

The initial intention of the conspirators was to 'teach Muldoon a lesson', but this evolved early on into a move to replace him with Brian Talboys. Despite Barry Gustafson's claim in Muldoon's biography that the dissenters may have contemplated a candidate other than Talboys to replace Muldoon — such as Gair, McLay, Bolger or me — this was not the case. Talboys was always the only candidate.

Muldoon had left for a long overseas trip before the by-election, visiting India, China, Bermuda, Washington, New York and Mexico. In his absence, Talboys had performed well in the House. At 59 he was still relatively young, physically impressive, had held a wide range of ministerial posts and, most importantly, never descended into personality politics. Like Muldoon, he was himself overseas (in Bonn) when the coup was coming to a head, and was showing increasing reluctance to have his name put forward. Initially he had said he would not challenge Muldoon directly but would accept a draft. But as time progressed, he wavered even on that.

Towards the end of his trip Muldoon got wind of the revolt, and on a stopover in Hawaii on Sunday 12 October he spent the best part of a day on the phone rallying support. Back home his key caucus supporters were Acting Prime Minister Duncan MacIntyre, David Thomson, Bill Birch, Barry Brill and Aussie Malcolm, along with outsiders such as Des Dalgety, his lawyer. However, senior National Party officials and party members showed little support for Muldoon. Even George Chapman, at a meeting with McLay and me, expressed the view that we 'had to leg-rope him'. We took this as tacit approval from the senior levels of the party.

On 12 October McLay, Kidd, Cox and I met with Bolger in his ministerial house in Bowen Street to discuss the situation. While we were there Bolger took three long phone calls. One was from Bill Birch. Another was from the man I described as 'the chief lobbyist for the Catholic Church',

Des Dalgety. From then on, Bolger, a staunch Catholic who had clearly had his ear seriously bent by Dalgety (and possibly also by his own wife, Joan), started to have second thoughts about his involvement. One of Bolger's strong points is his ability to advance his own interests. Consistent with this, when Muldoon arrived back in Wellington three days later, Bolger was the first to jump ship and pledge his continuing loyalty and support.

Muldoon was met at Auckland Airport on 15 October by MacIntyre and the Auckland party divisional director. They told him that caucus was split 28 to 19 in favour of Talboys, with three members not identified. Muldoon then flew to Wellington, arriving at Parliament late that evening. Friedlander and I were leaving the building for the day when Muldoon came through the door. He stopped, looked at us and said, 'What have you two been doing, plotting against me?' I replied, 'Yes, Prime Minister.' Muldoon turned to Friedlander and said, 'See me in my office at 9 o'clock tomorrow morning.' He went on his way.

Before caucus next morning I had a long phone conversation with Talboys — who was still in Bonn — to try to get a firm commitment from him. Despite my telling him that a large number of us had 'put it on the line' for him, he eventually said that even if caucus voted for him later that day he wouldn't accept a draft until he was back in New Zealand.

In light of this prevarication and Bolger's defection, along with the eye-balling I knew several of the 28 signatories had been subjected to (including Friedlander), it was clear to me that the coup was dead in the water.

Gustafson's account that the potential coup spluttered on over the next few days until Talboys told caucus on 23 October he would not contest the leadership is wrong, and was an attempt by Muldoon to rewrite history. The only thing that spluttered on were the recriminations, with some coming to a head almost immediately (in Talboys' case), and for others (McLay and myself) continuing for years.

Because of my lengthy phone call with Talboys, McLay and I had not been able to meet before caucus to discuss tactics. However, McLay had talked to Bolger and had been brought up to date on Talboys' position. He was also aware of a comment by Talboys around the same time that if Muldoon were ousted 'Rob would grab the pillars of the temple and pull the whole place down'. This proved very prescient.

The atmosphere when I walked into the caucus meeting was electric. A group of Muldoon supporters were angry that he had been publicly humiliated. Their views were countered by those of us who had had enough of Muldoon's confrontational style, his support for sycophants in the Cabinet and his poor judgement. Now there was a third group: people who had signed up for Talboys but were petrified that they would be found out.

I had two options. To either call for a leadership vote that I knew we were likely to lose and could not guarantee would be conducted by secret ballot, or have my say. I chose the latter option, as did several other caucus members, outlining the extent of our dissatisfaction — and that of numerous party members — with Muldoon's leadership style.

Muldoon and his team had won a pyrrhic victory, but their champion was substantially wounded.

Apologise and grovel or else!

The Colonels' Coup taught me a lot about human nature. The first lesson is that some people cannot be trusted. I also learnt about the different ways people respond to pressure. Bruce Townshend had to be assisted from the House shortly after the failed coup when he collapsed from a mild heart attack while speaking in the debating chamber. Tony Friedlander, who maintains he never apologised to Muldoon despite being told that he wouldn't make Cabinet unless he did, eventually became minister of housing and a Muldoon supporter.

Cox, McLean, Kidd and Townshend were told they 'were wet behind the ears' when they tried to reason with Muldoon, but along with Robin Gray maintained their integrity. None of them made it into Cabinet under Muldoon's leadership, despite being miles more able than some who did.

McLay, along with Marilyn Waring and a handful of others, never apologised to Muldoon. McLay had been called to his office, but before doing so he came to ask me if I had received a similar 'invitation' and, if so, what I was going to say. I hadn't — nor did I subsequently, presumably because I was thought beyond redemption. This meant that I didn't have the early opportunity that McLay had to express my views on a one-to-one basis, and wasn't able to until later in the year. McLay later reported to me: 'The meeting didn't last long and I didn't resile, nor interestingly, did he ask me to.'

Rob Talbot's post-coup reaction was the most pathetic. The letter he signed in McLay's and my presence in favour of Talboys was the one that put us over the top in terms of numbers. But his subsequent actions suggest that he had assessed how the trend was running and just wanted to be on the winning side. Within hours of the coup's collapse he came to me asking for his letter back. Shortly after, he became one of Muldoon's staunchest cheerleaders and eventually made it into Cabinet. I reminded him in 2008 of his original letter. He replied, 'I cannot recall the precise details or what I signed up to, which are now irrelevant when my loyalty to Muldoon continued till the end of his career.'[6]

The three people who attracted Muldoon's ongoing, deep-seated dislike and occasional expressions of public vitriol were George Gair, Brian Talboys and me. Gair was a brilliant portfolio minister who by and large kept his head down and had not been particularly active as a coup participant. But he undoubtedly had leadership ambitions, was liberal on abortion and worse still — as far as Muldoon was concerned — had the tendency, because of his personality and public relations background, to want to debate all the options in considering a particular matter, and then opt for the middle ground. Muldoon characterised this as indecisiveness, and in my view this, along with Gair's refusal to apologise or concede anything after the coup, led Muldoon to despise him.

No doubt angered by my refusal to 'make up', Muldoon continued to bait me over the years. My stock reply, that I wasn't going to get involved in personality politics, clearly infuriated him but I believe heightened my public support and standing within the party.

The deputy leadership contest 1980

Back in control, but sensing that Talboys could come again, Muldoon decided to get rid of him. Unfortunately, Talboys went quietly, though he still had years of good politics before him and enjoyed strong caucus support. As Hugh Templeton later wrote:

> Personal antagonisms, long held in check, were unleashed. Muldoon would take no account of his own shortcomings. All he wanted was Talboys' head on a charger. Brutally he blamed his deputy for encouraging the coup. Talboys' loathing of Muldoon made it impossible for him to stay any longer in the same room … With contempt, he flung his resignation at Muldoon … [and] the National party lost the able, fair and imaginative leader that Muldoon could never be.[7]

I've asked them to remove the cap.

Talboys' public announcement that he wouldn't be standing again in 1981 was preceded at the caucus meeting in early December 1980 by Muldoon announcing: 'As Mr Talboys is not standing at the next election, caucus needs to elect a new deputy leader. We will do that next Tuesday and it will be Duncan MacIntyre.'

MacIntyre had had a distinguished career during World War II, serving in Australia, the Middle East, Italy and Japan, and had attained the rank of brigadier. At one time he commanded 28 (Māori) Battalion in Jayforce. First elected as the MP for Hastings in 1960 he was, along with Muldoon and Peter Gordon, one of the 'Young Turks' in his early caucus days. He was respected and liked by all his caucus colleagues during my time as an MP but he faced two problems in the contest for the deputy leadership position. The first was the way Muldoon 'anointed' him for the position before any vote was held. The second problem was the finding of a Commission of Inquiry set up to consider the part he (and the Minister of Lands, Venn Young) had played in an application for a loan by MacIntyre's daughter and son-in-law to the Marginal Lands Board, while he (MacIntyre) was acting as the board's chair.

The commission cleared MacIntyre of having acted improperly but described his conduct as 'extremely unwise'. But before the inquiry was set up, the matter was referred to Parliament's Privileges Committee, which McLay chaired and I was a member of for this particular hearing. My membership worried Duncan because (he told me) he thought I was 'too tough' and might push for a finding against him. He needn't have worried, as he was cleared by the committee. Later, I learnt from Jim McLay that MacIntyre was also worried that I might use my membership of the Privileges Committee to discredit him and advance my own prospects as a rival deputy leader. Such Machiavellian thoughts never entered my thinking. I never sought promotion while I was in Parliament, and even when I did ultimately put my name forward for the deputy's position it was for one reason and one reason only — my determination that caucus, not Muldoon, should decide who the new deputy prime minister would be.

Muldoon's dictatorial approach in promoting Duncan for the deputy position infuriated me and a number of other caucus members. And because Muldoon's public comments in support of MacIntyre were fast leading towards a win for him by default, I told Duncan that at least one other hat would be in the ring. He responded, 'I thought there would be', and he wished me all the best. We shook hands and both of us knew there would be no animosity between us whatever caucus decided. At that stage, I had no idea that I might have a chance of winning.[8]

I invited Duncan up to my office for a drink and he accepted. 'Do you want to bring your mate with you?' I asked, thinking that Muldoon and I might be able to resolve our differences in a more relaxed environment. He went over to Muldoon and put the invitation to him. 'That's a good idea,' said Muldoon, and in due course the three of us walked out of the chamber together, which in itself was a pretty rare sight. Before this I had asked Bolger if he wanted to join us as McLay — my first preference — was away from Parliament that evening.

Muldoon, MacIntyre, Bolger and I arrived in my office and were joined by David Thomson, who turned up uninvited. I turned to Muldoon and said, 'This is the first time you have been in my office, Prime Minister.' He replied, 'Yes, it's small, isn't it?' which was the first rebuff of my contemplated reconciliation and a precursor of what was to follow.

We then moved to the meeting room off my main office where the drinks cabinet was located. After I had given everyone a drink, Muldoon told us, laughing, that as Talboys was down south at a meeting with his electorate people, he (Muldoon) had issued a press release, embargoed until 8.30am, announcing that Talboys would not be standing for re-election in 1981. He went on to say that normal electorate business had been taken before Brian had been scheduled to speak to the meeting, so he hadn't yet been able to tell them or speak to the media about his decision to retire.

Muldoon then turned to me and said loudly, 'So I've announced his retirement for him, and next Tuesday we're going to elect a new deputy leader and it's *not* going to be you.' I said, 'You don't need to shout. I'm not deaf.' Muldoon then moved right up to me and repeated exactly the same words in a whisper. I took no notice and over the next several hours continued refilling everyone else's glasses. As the night progressed, the invectives directed at me came thick and fast, becoming so vicious that at one stage Bolger's face became as white as a sheet and he left.

I was told in no uncertain terms not to stand as deputy leader, and I responded with my reasons. I was then accused by Thomson of being disloyal to Muldoon, with a demand that I kiss his shoes, to which I responded by laughing. Muldoon then asked me why I had led the coup, and when I told him it was because of the way he handled himself and that we had initially only set out to teach him a lesson, he suddenly seemed very hurt. 'Why didn't you tell me?' he asked. I said we had decided that when you have a mad bull in a china shop, the best solution is to put it down.

Muldoon responded by inviting me to resign from Cabinet. He said my alternative economic strategy paper — which according to him I planned to release before the next election — meant I could not stay. I denied intending to release the document and was accused of lying. My retort was: 'Say that again and I'll thump you.' Muldoon did repeat it, and I thought, what do I do now?! I had visions of myself lying on the floor being kicked and thumped in turn by Muldoon, Thomson and MacIntyre.

Thankfully, discretion won the day. I stood up quickly and offered everyone another drink.

It was extremely late by now. The House was still sitting, and Muldoon was fairly drunk. MacIntyre and Thomson left to close the House down for the night — fittingly the subject of debate had been sale of liquor legislation — and Muldoon and I were the only two left in my office. But before I could say anything he got up and headed unsteadily for the door leading to my bathroom, nearly falling over the seat by the door. I sat waiting for him to return, but after five minutes or so when he didn't, I said to myself, assuming he had gone, 'You rotten little bastard.' I began to tidy up the room when the door burst open and MacIntyre and Thomson came back in. 'Guess who we found asleep in your toilet?' Muldoon had flaked out in there, but shortly after he rejoined us and continued over the next hour or so to abuse me further.

It was fully daylight when they left my office and I went back to my apartment for a few hours' sleep. For his part, Muldoon never made it home that night and was late arriving in his office the next morning, according to his office staff. That same day I had a visit in my office from David Thomson, who said, 'You did well last night.'

The blatant attempts to frighten me out of standing for the deputy's position only strengthened my resolve to contest the role, which illustrates how little Muldoon knew me. I have always been amenable to a low-key, well-reasoned approach, but invariably dig my toes in if I'm faced with threats or bullying.

The meeting in my office had a sequel. Over the next day or so four different Press Gallery journalists approached me, having been told — almost certainly by someone in Bolger's office — about my confrontation with Muldoon. The first three didn't know how to handle the story and were looking to me for confirmation. I responded with comments like 'That's interesting' and 'Where did you get that story from?' and they eventually went away.

The fourth approach was from Richard Long, the *Dominion*'s political reporter and a very experienced operator. Richard tried the same tack as the previous three, without getting anything from me, and finally said, 'Well, Quig, it's such a great story, I'm going to run it anyway.' And he did — on the front page. The headline read 'Muldoon advises Quigley he should quit Cabinet' and the accompanying editorial commented that the unseemly haste of the move to install a new deputy reflected badly on the prime minister:[9]

> As we suggested yesterday there is no need to replace Mr Talboys so soon after the announcement of his intention to retire late next year . . . When a new deputy is selected he needs to be a younger, more creative man, not a politician even older than a parliamentary veteran who feels he is ready for retirement.[10]

As 'next week's caucus' approached, Muldoon lobbied intensely for MacIntyre, and summoned a number of caucus members to his office. Doug Kidd, Tony Friedlander and Rob Talbot, in one group, were subjected to a bitter tirade against me that lasted for nearly two and a half hours. MacIntyre and David Thomson were also present.

Other National MPs — such as Pat Hunt, the member for Pakuranga, who was one of my supporters — were openly harangued in the debating chamber. Muldoon was fairly drunk when he approached Pat, and I and a number of MPs overheard his pitch. When Pat said he would be voting for me, Muldoon asked him if he had thought about what would happen if he (Muldoon) opposed Hunt's renomination for the Pakuranga seat. The reply was a classic: 'Actually, Prime Minister, I think it would help.'

At the caucus meeting I had the numbers, and when the Muldoon/MacIntyre camp realised this they ducked for cover and argued in favour of leaving the vote over until after the Christmas break 'so that party members can be consulted'. And that's what was finally agreed to after Eric Holland in particular — a supporter of mine — spoke in favour of a delay, not realising I was ahead.

Intense lobbying continued over the holidays, with Muldoon publicly accusing me of being a right-wing extremist and someone he couldn't work with. Gustafson claims that what apparently really stuck in his craw was the possibility of seeing 'one of the most unrepentant leaders of the rebellion against him rewarded by being made his deputy and heir apparent'.[11]

The evening before the first caucus meeting for the year on 4 February 1981 — with final lobbying still taking place — I had finished up in Bolger's office before retiring for the night. As I was about to leave, and the two of us were there alone, I said to him, 'If I'm out first tomorrow, I'll be voting for you in the second ballot, and I expect you to reciprocate.' He agreed, and we shook hands on it. He didn't keep his word, which was par for the course, as later events confirm.

Earlier, when I was still unsure of my numbers given Muldoon's campaign against me, McLay and I discussed the possibility of him also standing, despite his public support for me. The basis for this suggestion was that his candidature might split the MacIntyre/Bolger vote in my favour. We decided against it, but there was an attempt to get McLay to keep his head down. The messenger on the morning of the caucus meeting was Lance Adams-Schneider, who said to McLay, possibly tongue in cheek, 'Rob really admires you and will probably be moving you to

Delayed deputy PM vote to avoid wrong result.

the front bench.' McLay listened but didn't respond, and an hour or so later nominated me for the deputy's position, with McIntyre and Bolger also standing. McLay had a follow-up visit after the vote from Adams-Schneider, who commented that he hadn't realised how committed McLay was in his support for me and he was 'disappointed'.

Bolger was knocked out in the first ballot and a second vote followed. Muldoon declared MacIntyre elected and told caucus there was no need to disclose the numbers. Subsequently, he is reported as saying that on the first ballot I had 23 votes, MacIntyre 20 and Bolger 7, and that the final vote was MacIntyre 26 and me 24. I doubt this for a number of reasons. The two scrutineers, McKinnon and Friedlander, have consistently refused to disclose the count.

I believe the vote was tied and that MacIntyre was elected on Muldoon's casting vote. Hugh Templeton, who was caucus secretary, has publicly suggested this possibility. The other reason I believe this was Muldoon's

Duncan finally makes it.

comment to me across the table in the Cabinet dining room in early February 1982, after Michael Cox narrowly won the position of junior whip from Robin Gray. The Cox/Gray vote had been tied and they agreed to resolve the matter by tossing a coin. During the dining-room incident Muldoon leaned across to me and said — without anyone else hearing — 'I thought I was going to have to have another casting vote.' As Muldoon never said anything without a reason, his message was clear: 'I got you on the deputy leadership vote!'

Rewards and demotions

A Cabinet reshuffle was announced shortly after the deputy decision, with its size increased from 18 to 20. McLay was demoted to number 17 for his role in the coup and his support for me for the deputy's position. Birch was rewarded — for his ability and his support for Muldoon — with a move up to the front bench from number 13 to number 4. Bolger was also rewarded, going from number 9 to number 5. Both leapfrogged George

Cabinet reshuffle to bolster support for PM.

Gair, who had experience and ability but had continued to transgress by openly supporting me for Deputy PM.

Other beneficiaries in the reshuffle were two of the under-secretaries, Aussie Malcolm and Ian Shearer, and Warren Cooper. Muldoon presumably didn't know that Shearer had voted for me. Brill, another under-secretary and a Muldoon supporter, was again passed over, presumably because of his heavy involvement with Birch in the 'Think Big' projects.

I moved up from 16 to number 9 but was kept off the front bench. I stayed on as a member of the Cabinet Expenditure Committee and gained Tourism, but lost Associate Finance and my position on the powerful Cabinet Economic Committee to Warren Cooper, who also joined the front bench.

My loss of Associate Finance denied me access to Treasury officials and reports, with officials specifically instructed — despite Muldoon's public denials to the contrary — to keep me out of that loop. Tourism was regarded by Muldoon as inconsequential, and in commenting publicly he stretched credibility when he said that the transfer was to enable me to get wider portfolio experience and not a rejection of my stance on financial matters.[12]

Around the same time I was approached by the US ambassador to New Zealand, Anne Martindell, and asked if I wanted to go to the US on a leader's fellowship. As the timing would have enabled me to be there for Present Reagan's Inauguration early in 1981, I was very interested and told Muldoon of the invitation. His response was emphatic. 'No, you can't go. I decide who does.' In due course Don McKinnon made the visit. Later he told me he was there when Reagan was shot. He had not been aware that anyone else had been considered for the trip, saying, 'Knowing the LPSM [little pear-shaped man, our nickname for Muldoon], he would most definitely have stopped you going to R's inauguration — that would have given you far too much importance.'[13]

CHAPTER 10

Tourism, 'Think Big' and the Springbok Tour

Hanmer Springs

One location I took a particular interest in after the 1978 election, when my electorate dropped the Christchurch suburb of Parklands and moved further north, was Hanmer Springs — the township, the area surrounding it, and in particular the hot springs and adjoining accommodation lodge. I already knew that part of my electorate well and was impressed by its existing and potential tourist attractions, which — in addition to the lodge and hot pools — included a magnificent golf course, walking tracks, a quality ski-field, horse-riding facilities, jet-boating and a good fishing river.

Hanmer is one of a limited number of South Island resort areas with a range of year-round attractions that young and old could enjoy. It is also within easy driving distance of Christchurch and I believed the area was capable — without losing its special and unique characteristics — of absorbing many more visitors as New Zealand's tourism industry expanded. To that end I was keen to see the lodge and hot pools upgraded.

The pools were renovated first, with three hexagonal pools and a fresh-water pool installed in 1978. The lodge sorely needed major improvement so I approached the Tourist Hotel Corporation (THC), while I was still a backbench MP, to consider acquiring and upgrading it. I was convinced the lodge was an essential part of the area's tourism potential. Some preliminary investigations followed, but little progress was made until I became minister of tourism.

As minister, I had to be careful not to be seen to be promoting a matter that might benefit my own electorate. With this is mind, I brought together in Hanmer the THC's general manager, the Government Life Insurance Commissioner, and an independent property investment specialist.

I then stepped back and left it to the other three to progress matters as they thought fit. By 3 November 1981 I was able to write to the chairman of the Amuri County Council and advise him that 'negotiations are now proceeding to purchase the Lodge but there is no guarantee that these will be successfully concluded'. I went on to say that if a sale were finalised, the prospective buyer had assured me that all lodge employees would continue to be employed, adding that the prospective buyer was not the THC, which had only been involved in the initial visit I had organised as minister.

The prospective buyer was a company called Financial Services Limited and on 27 October 1981 it issued a letter of intent to proceed, subject to certain conditions being satisfied. The vendors and the potential buyer met twice more, but unfortunately concluded no binding sale and purchase agreement. As a result, the lodge upgrade languished until Houghton Investments bought the property in the late 1990s.

Other tourism initiatives

Tourism was a fascinating portfolio, with the Tourist Department never before having had a senior minister. As a result, top-level staff responded enthusiastically to the challenges I gave them. One of my first requests was to see an up-to-date list of the department's tourism planning and development projects so that they could be prioritised within budget for maximum impact. A three-page document followed, listing items such as negotiation with the Treasury and the Development Finance Corporation on budgetary assistance for tourist accommodation and facilities through tax deprecation and grants in lieu; the 'liquor link' levy on tavern sales to fund the Hotel Investment Account; and negotiations with the Treasury and the Housing Corporation, to extend the Tourism Facility Development Scheme.

I wasn't very interested in such matters, preferring to leave them to officials. I wanted to concentrate on areas where tourism potential could be improved in the national interest. First I needed to know the economic value of the industry to New Zealand, and where the major earning areas were, so that they could, if necessary, be improved. This resulted in facilities such as those at Ruapehu, the Wairakei Thermal Valley and Tourist Park, Waitangi, Milford Sound and Mount Cook (plus the airport there) being placed high on the list for upgrades. Special attention was also paid to attracting more visitors from Australia and developing more high-quality ski resorts, given that New Zealand was a close winter destination for our trans-Tasman cousins.

Australia was New Zealand's largest and most important market in 1981, supplying nearly half of our visitors that year. Despite this, Australian visitor numbers had declined significantly, especially in the holiday segment of the market, falling 26.6 percent between 1976 and 1981.

After in-depth analysis I announced a joint-venture advertising campaign, which I launched in Brisbane. Funded by the government and the private sector, it focused on people, and stressed the diverse activities and scenery that New Zealand had to offer. In a press release I noted the economic benefits that would flow from a successful campaign, and emphasised that Australian tourists travelled throughout New Zealand and were especially important for the smaller operators in the South Island.

One of my overseas trips as minister was to Mexico, where my hostess was that country's minister of tourism and its first-ever female Cabinet minister.

It was extremely hot when we arrived in Mexico City, and when we got to our hotel I was desperate for a beer. My driver, personal bodyguard (the son of the Commissioner of Police) and the rest of the Mexican team were sitting on the other side of the bar room and I signalled to them to come over and have a drink with me. Initially they didn't understand what I meant — Cabinet ministers apparently didn't do that sort of thing in Mexico — but they soon caught on. From then on, our team was lavished with extra attention, including visits to offbeat places (necessitating an extra security contingent), singing at restaurants, and requests to be photographed with them. The only downside of the visit was a case of Montezuma's Revenge, which hit me when we got back to Los Angeles.

Before the trip to Mexico I had met up with an American, Peter Dailey. He and his wife Jackie (a member of the Disney family) had attended a tourism conference I was opening in Christchurch. After my time there, my team was scheduled to fly to Queenstown in one of the air force's VIP planes to inspect the THC hotels in the area and see the site of the proposed Remarkables ski-field. As we had spare seats in our plane, I asked the Daileys if they would like to come with us, and they did. More on Peter Dailey later.

The trip to see the Remarkables site was both exhilarating and terrifying. We travelled in two helicopters, with the mountain shrouded in mist and — in my view — the distinct prospect of a mid-air collision. I wasn't used to helicopter flights and had near heart failure when the chopper I was in — with me sitting next to the pilot in the front glass-bubble area — suddenly flew off the highest peak to disclose a drop of thousands of metres immediately below us as we started our flight back to the airport. In contrast, the flight into Milford Sound in a small plane on a beautiful still day showed that part of New Zealand at its best, with the location one of the most picturesque in the world.

Tourism and the environment

What these visits and others like them brought home to me during my time as minister of tourism was the potential for tourism to become a major earner of foreign exchange for New Zealand. However, a lot of money needed to be spent on upgrading current facilities; private-sector capital was clearly needed; and an assessment was needed to establish the likely impact of increasing visitor numbers on the environment.

I instructed officials to initiate detailed research on these issues so that an overall strategy could be developed. The impact on environmentally sensitive areas had not been investigated at government level before, and it was not a straightforward exercise. This was because many of the prime locations — other than the THC-owned hotels — were outside the direct control of my portfolio, with the departments and agencies concerned often having other agendas and spending priorities.

Milford Sound was chosen first and subsequently became the blueprint for cooperative developments at other locations. On 2 April 1981 a new policy proposal for Milford was ready to go before the Cabinet Expenditure Committee. The paper sought approval for the modest sum of $54,000 to be paid to the Department of Lands and Survey for the design and preliminary investigation work required for what became known as the Milford Sound Development Plan.

The study had already progressed through the senior-level Milford Sound Consultative Committee, involving the Department of Lands and Survey, the Fiordland National Park Board, Lake County Council, the

Tourist and Publicity Department, the THC, the Ministries of Transport and Works and Development, and fishing interests. The committee had defined the objectives for the study, which were: to develop clear and positive guidelines for all future development at Milford Sound; to recognise the planning principles and levels of agreement already established; to provide adequate opportunities for effective public and organisational input; and to provide a firm basis for the commitment of special funds for the Milford development. The overall objective was to provide for greatly improved facilities for visitors and at the same time to minimise the impact that increasing visitor numbers would have on the outstanding environmental qualities of the area. Before Covid-19, Milford Sound attracted between 500,000 and a million visitors each year.

The Beautiful New Zealand scheme

Another proposal for which I gained Cabinet approval and launched just before the 1981 election was the Beautiful New Zealand scheme: a concept businessman Bob Jones had originally raised with me. Jones was to go on to establish the New Zealand Party in 1984 and to ask me to lead it.

In its simplest form, the scheme was aimed to brighten the roadside verges of main routes and other areas with trees, shrubs and flowers to enhance the appearance and view. The scheme built on the beauty of the tree-lined streets in the Waikato town of Cambridge, the colour and attraction of the Garden City of Christchurch, and the varied autumn landscapes of parts of Otago and Canterbury. Although it was designed primarily to boost tourism, its main objective — which sold it to my Cabinet colleagues on the eve of the election — was to improve the lives of New Zealanders as they travelled to and from work, visited other parts of the country on holiday or just enjoyed a heightened awareness of the beauty of their own country. The scheme had the added potential benefit of softening the government's hard-edged image.

As I told the media:

> The concept of New Zealand as a 'garden country' is a natural extension of our growing reputation as a horticultural country. Fruit growing areas such as New Zealand's 'fruitbowls' in Hawke's Bay, Central Otago and Nelson have already recognised the visitor potential during the blossom season. Orchid farming near Napier has recently been put on the list of

> local attractions in that area. Parts of Otago and Canterbury have drawn visitors for decades when the deciduous trees turn the countryside golden in autumn. Alexandra's Blossom Festival last month is an example of the drawcard [that] flowers can be to an area.

Initially, I was unsure how to present the concept to Cabinet because of Muldoon's antagonism towards me, but in the end I went directly to him. Bob Jones' paper was quite long and when I gave it to Muldoon in his office, I suggested leaving it with him to read later. He said, 'No, sit down,' and proceeded to go through it page by page without comment. I later learnt that he met with Jones over a private dinner and the scheme was approved by Cabinet.

The logical person to chair the committee set up to implement the scheme was Bob Jones, who would apply his trademark drive and energy and political skills to make it a success. However, he told me he was not available and Sir Miles Warren, an eminent Christchurch architect, was appointed. Much, much later — in 2011 — Jones told me he had not taken on the chairman's job because Muldoon had specifically told him he didn't want him involved. Presumably Muldoon wanted to ensure neither of us got too much positive public exposure.

After I left Parliament the scheme was canned, allegedly because of financial constraints but more likely because my detractors didn't want any lasting public reminders of me and my achievements.

That aside, from small beginnings in 1980, the tourism industry in New Zealand, before the shock of Covid-19, grew to become one of the country's highest earners of foreign exchange, generating a direct annual contribution to GDP of $16.2 billion, and a further indirect contribution of $11.2 billion in the year ending March 2019.[1]

PR personified: Nixon, Reagan et al.

The Daileys reciprocated my hospitality in flying them to Queenstown with an invitation to spend time with them in the US after my Mexican trip, and again on a second occasion shortly afterwards when I visited the US west coast on tourism business. On that second trip we enjoyed a specially conducted tour of Hollywood courtesy of Jackie's Disney family connection, and then were flown in the Dailey/Disney private jet — which was much more modern than the VIP plane the Daileys had flown in with us in New Zealand — to their ranch in Washington State near the Canadian border.

I was invited to come back two or three months later for the yearly turkey shoot but declined. I had already been away from New Zealand several times that year, and if I wanted to shoot turkeys, my preference would have been to have several of my caucus colleagues in my sights.

Peter Dailey was an interesting person to talk to and to learn from. He ran a successful advertising agency and had been involved in several US presidential campaigns. One was for Richard Nixon whom he knew well and regarded, Watergate aside, as one of America's most intelligent and able presidents. He contrasted the security presence when he had visited President Nixon at his beachside home with a later visit after Nixon had resigned as president. On the latter occasion virtually no security was on view — an illustration of how the mighty had fallen.

Dailey was briefly involved in President Gerald Ford's re-election campaign in 1976 until he and the Ford team had a mutually agreed parting of the ways over how the campaign should be run. Peter said that Betty Ford was determined in the wake of the Watergate scandal that her husband should be projected as the complete opposite of Nixon, whom he had replaced. As a result, Peter said, Ford finished up looking like 'just another candidate', rather than the president seeking re-election, and lost to Jimmy Carter.

Dailey was also involved in Ronald Reagan's campaign against Carter in 1980. A third candidate vying for the presidency at that time was John Anderson, an independent from Illinois. Reagan and Anderson had agreed to a TV debate, and in preparing for it, the Reagan team organised a practice run in a garage mocked up to look exactly like the TV studio set where the actual debate was going to take place.

Before the practice run, Reagan and someone standing in for Anderson were given a detailed background folder to swot up from. 'Anderson' appeared in a neat suit and tie and demolished Reagan, who had turned up in his Saturday morning casual clothes, completely unprepared. But Dailey said Reagan was a quick learner and never made the same mistake again. Reagan was also so impressed by the performance of Anderson's stand-in, David Stockman, that he appointed him his budget director on becoming president.

I found the detail of the Reagan media campaign fascinating. Reagan had been an extremely successful governor of California and had turned that state's finances around. He had also been a film star and was best known outside California in that capacity. Dailey told me that the campaign team deliberately tried to play down the film-star aspect and highlight the candidate's financial management skills. They used less glamorous photos in their advertising material so that people were not continually reminded of Reagan's Hollywood appearances.

Towards the end of the campaign the Reagan media strategy was pitched at 'middle America' rather than the staunch Republican vote. As election day approached, this strategy began to attract such violent criticism from within the Republican Party hierarchy that the people running it had to be physically locked away from their detractors while the campaign continued.

It wasn't until just before the end of the campaign — after polling showed that support from middle America had been locked in — that the focus switched back to courting the party faithful. The result was a 50.7 percent vote for Reagan, 41 percent for Carter and 6.7 percent for Anderson. And for the first time since 1952 the Republicans controlled the Senate.

'Think Big'

Muldoon claimed through 1979–80 that New Zealand was facing the worst economic crisis since the Depression of the 1930s and sought to remedy the situation with incentives and subsidies rather than freeing up controls and protection. As a result, as the 1981 election approached, the economy, held back by years of in-built rigidities, was also being buffeted by rising oil prices. The state of the economy looked likely to be the issue that would bring the government down.

However, two things could still be used in National's favour. The first was to somehow turn the oil crisis into a political success story. The second was to take advantage of the Springboks' planned rugby tour of New Zealand, scheduled for just before the election.

The 1972–75 Labour government had already committed to utilising the giant Maui gas field off the Taranaki coast, with a 30-year 'take or pay' clause inserted in the contract with the oil companies. When the price of oil began to rise dramatically — it was NZ$12.88 a barrel in March 1979 and some commentators were suggesting it could go as high as NZ$100 — the government saw this as a twofold opportunity. It could make

New Zealand less dependent on limited supplies of increasingly expensive overseas liquid fuels, and at the same time diversify the New Zealand economy away from its dependence on a narrow range of agricultural commodities.

By now Bill Birch was minister of energy, with Barry Brill as his under-secretary. Time was of the essence, according to Muldoon, who believed that 'New Zealand was in a survival situation'.[2] Given this, in Hugh Templeton's words:

> [a]s a crisis manager [Muldoon] felt justified in pressing ahead. The public face of the crisis was the second oil shock in early 1979 following the Iranian Revolution which spawned the 'Think Big' programme in New Zealand. By then he could see 'Think Big' as his wizard's wand for the 1981 election. The oil shock, despite its disastrous effects on New Zealand, need not, after all, destroy his intensely held three-term ambitions.[3]

'Think Big' had started out as a series of unrelated policies and projects, but by the time of the 1981 election the concept had become a key element in an overall growth strategy that also included initiatives to increase traditional farm exports and to rapidly develop fishing and forestry. The energy-related components of 'Think Big' — some of which were not related to the Maui field — included a methanol plant at Waitara, an ammonia/urea plant at Kapuni, a synthetic petrol plant at Motunui, the expansion of the Marsden Point Oil Refinery, the expansion of the New Zealand Steel plant at Glenbrook, the electrification of the North Island main-trunk railway between Te Rapa and Palmerston North, a third reduction power line at the Tiwai Point aluminium smelter near Bluff, and the construction of the Clyde Hydroelectric Dam on the Clutha River.

Not everyone favoured either the frenetic way the 'Think Big' projects were progressed or their philosophical basis. Skilled workers were already in short supply, and as their pay increased, wages rates ratcheted up nationwide through the wage-bargaining system. The Treasury, the Reserve Bank and officials from the Prime Minister's Department were divided about the merits of several of the projects, and questioned the economic assumptions underpinning them. However, to quote Gerald Hensley, when a 'department's view differed from his, as it did on some aspects of the projects, [Muldoon] simply ignored it'.[4]

Cabinet was also divided over the extent that New Zealand taxpayers should be involved in the projects, and this came to a head over the methanol plant. Muldoon and his supporters favoured the New Zealand government-owned and -financed entity Petrocorp — which was to hold a 51 percent interest — teaming up with Alberta Gas. The other side — which included Birch, Talboys, Bolger, McLay and me — wanted the contract to be given to a 90 percent privately owned consortium comprising British Petroleum, Fletcher Challenge, Shell, ICI Petroleum, Japanese interests, the government and public shareholders.

Before the decision went to Cabinet our side was certain it had the numbers, but we hadn't thought to lobby Warren Cooper, given his previous outspoken public support for private enterprise. To our surprise he voted with Muldoon and we lost by one vote, largely due to Muldoon's masterly handling of the debate. He had received a detailed briefing from Birch the day before and in Cabinet claimed that because he had a sore throat, he had prepared a short paper which he circulated and spoke to briefly, to limit debate. What I regretted later, when Cabinet reconvened after the methanol plant decision and the lunch break, was mentioning how pleased my colleagues and I were that his sore throat had miraculously recovered …

Over time, 'Think Big' became synonymous with increasing inflation, industrial strife and project cost overruns. Again, in Hugh Templeton's words:

> Where the private sector would not gamble, Muldoon and the sovereign state bet on high oil prices. It was an unusual risk to accept. When supplies increased and prices fell, that burden was Muldoon's legacy to his successors. It was no longer his problem.[5]

The 1981 Springbok rugby tour

The Springbok tour, like the Vietnam War and the anti-nuclear issue, turned into a source of major social division in New Zealand. In 1973 Prime Minister Norman Kirk had gone back on an earlier undertaking and had banned a proposed tour by the South African Springbok rugby team. In contrast, National's 1975 election policy was that 'there will be no interference in sport, in any form', and Muldoon took this further when he indicated just before the election that the Springboks would be welcome to visit New Zealand.

The first test of this policy had been in 1976, when the All Blacks toured South Africa following the death of hundreds in the Soweto riots there. The tour under those conditions attracted widespread condemnation in New Zealand and internationally, with black African nations boycotting the 1976 Montreal Olympics in protest. Yet Muldoon maintained that a free and democratic country could not restrict the rights of its citizens to travel overseas, and reiterated his belief that sports and politics should be kept separate.

The Gleneagles Agreement followed in 1977, whereby the Commonwealth Heads of Government unanimously agreed to 'discourage' contact and competition with sportspeople and sporting organisations, teams or individuals from South Africa. The word 'discourage' had replaced 'ban' in the draft at Muldoon's insistence. The Gleneagles Agreement saved the 1978 Edmonton Commonwealth Games, but Muldoon doubled down and restated that his government would not allow political interference in sport in any form. The New Zealand Rugby Union took this as a green light and in September 1980 invited the Springboks to tour the following year.

When the Rugby Union's invitation was discussed in caucus, I expressed the view that we had made a firm commitment in our 1975 policy and should stick to it. Naïvely I thought that although protests would take place, once the team arrived the scheduled games would proceed without disruption. I was wrong.

I was overseas in Mexico, the US and Australia in my capacity as minister of tourism during most of the tour but watched the violence it engendered on TV. It was not going to be helpful in promoting New Zealand as a brilliant destination for tourists.

I had intended to watch the final Auckland test back in Wellington, and had been picked up by an air force plane near Cheviot after seeing constituents there. The take-off was smooth and uneventful, but over Cook Strait the plane hit an air pocket and dropped dramatically. My wife, who was wearing a lap belt, hit her head on the ceiling, where a loose screw was protruding from one of the light covers. Blood spilled everywhere and an ambulance was waiting for us at Wellington Airport. As I watched the game on TV from the hospital emergency department, while Judith received medical attention, my memory is of a light plane circling the rugby pitch during the match and dropping flour bombs on the players.

With the benefit of hindsight our 1975 policy was wrong, and we compounded that mistake by not cancelling the tour when we were in office. However, the upside of the tour, in purely party-political terms, was the impact it had on votes in provincial cities. Muldoon stood up at the party's pre-election annual conference as a resolute leader, a champion of law and order, and (unlike Kirk before him) a prime minister who had given a clear policy commitment and stuck to it. But the cost was in the form of deep domestic divisions, and substantial damage to New Zealand's international reputation as a tolerant multicultural nation.

On the economic front Muldoon was still unwilling to face up to reality. By May 1981 private-sector credit was expanding again and had recorded an annual increase of 33.8 percent, despite the statement in the budget of 9 July 1981[6] that the government was 'determined to maintain a firm grip on the growth rates of the money supply and credit aggregates', actions belied these words. At one stage Muldoon even suggested to officials that he was considering reducing interest rates.

As the election approached, inflation was at a crippling 16 percent. The country's growth rate had declined to about 30 percent of the OECD average, and export growth was the slowest in the OECD. Government-imposed regulations and controls, which were supposed to overcome New Zealand's problems, were destroying the country's capacity to adapt to the rapid changes taking place in other parts of the world.

The solution that Treasury officials put forward was to rely more on market prices so that resources were allocated to their best use. The analysis in the Treasury's *Economic Strategy Overview* sent to Muldoon in late 1981 — but withheld from junior finance ministers on his written instructions — was blunt: 'There are in fact no soft options on the restructuring/protection front, or rather the soft options are likely to result in a continuation of the slow growth of the past twenty or so years.'[7]

CHAPTER 11

Resignation from Cabinet

As an extremely busy Cabinet minister I had found it difficult to do much campaigning in my electorate before the 1981 election. However, I had gained considerable local and national publicity during the preceding three years, and closer to home when I hosted Prince Charles at that year's Oxford A&P Show. It was wet on the day of the show, which kept the numbers attending to about double the normal turnout rather than attracting an unmanageable crowd.

The Prince was relaxed and easy to talk to. Local A&P committee members, however, seemed overwhelmed by the occasion and huddled together in the far corner of the president's tent. So I went over to them and said, 'For Christ's sake, come over and talk to him,' which they then did.

National's 1981 election campaign officially kicked off in Christchurch, with me introducing Muldoon to the town hall audience of mainly party faithful. Muldoon had expressed reservations about my performing this task but needn't have worried — I was just as committed as he was to ensuring the government's re-election.

A major upside for me in the Rangiora electorate was that the party was well led, had uniformly strong branches and was also well off financially. I had also been able to enhance my personal support base over the years in some of the parts of the electorate that did not traditionally vote National, with the result that Labour seemed to have given up on any thought of winning the seat.

Given all this, I was incredulous, hurt and furious in equal measure — and showed it — when Jim Gerard told me I was completely out of touch with what was going on locally. And yet within days I realised he was right. I redoubled my efforts, running a strong campaign that saw National hold the seat with a majority of 923.

What saved me and many other sitting National MPs on polling day was Labour's failure (still in an FPP voting system) to pick up the support of former National Party voters who had progressively begun to desert the party after 1975. An article in the *New Zealand Listener* following post-election Heylen analysis of voting figures from the 1981 election illustrated this.[1] In 1975 National had secured 47.58 percent of total votes cast. In 1978 that percentage had dropped to 39.82 percent. By 1981 it was 38.78 percent.

In contrast, Labour's vote over those three elections stayed virtually static at 39.56 percent, 40.41 percent and 39 percent respectively. What National lost appeared to have gone to Social Credit, which increased its vote from just below 7.5 percent in 1975 to more than 20.5 percent in 1981. The two ironies of the final 1981 result — which saw National returned with a working majority of one seat after reappointing Dick Harrison as Speaker — were Labour's failure to unseat National despite securing more votes, and Social Credit only winning two seats despite its high percentage of the overall vote. In his typical style, Muldoon blamed the media for National's poor result and suggested that by 1984 'the growth strategy would be more visible'.[2]

The post-election Cabinet

When Muldoon announced the post-election Cabinet in December 1981, the pro-market intake of 1978 was again completely ignored, while Jonathan Elworthy, John Falloon and Rob Talbot were brought in. McLay had been partially forgiven for his earlier 'indiscretions' and moved up from 17 to 9. I was demoted one place to 10. Muldoon held on to the key position of minister of finance, despite strong pressure from within the party to appoint someone else.

Possible contenders for the position included Gair, Templeton, McLay, Birch and Bolger. Muldoon disliked Gair intensely, despite his demonstrated competence. Templeton desperately wanted Foreign Affairs, but had Finance experience and would have handled it competently. McLay was too valuable in Justice to be moved from there. Birch was already frantically busy with the Energy portfolio and had just lost his offsider, Barry Brill, at the election. Bolger had the Labour portfolio and no finance experience. And although I had strong party support for the position, there was no chance Muldoon would give me the job. Instead, I was given the Works portfolio, in addition to continuing with Housing and my other four minor responsibilities.

When Muldoon rang me to tell me about Works I asked — because I liked the portfolio and had made some good progress with it — 'What about Tourism?' He said he had given it to someone else. The surprise appointments were Cooper gaining Foreign Affairs and Falloon gaining Deputy Finance. Warren Cooper had no Foreign Affairs experience, which meant that Muldoon was frequently involved with this portfolio. Falloon was the most junior minister in Cabinet and had no previous finance role, which also increased Muldoon's workload substantially. The work previously handled by two senior finance associates was now being given to one newly appointed minister. Muldoon also maintained his continued involvement (and interference) in Bolger's Labour portfolio.

The first meeting of the new Cabinet in mid-December considered a brief Treasury paper stating that export prospects had deteriorated, import volumes were rising, and the balance of payments situation was worsening. In the face of a projected increase in the budget deficit and rapidly rising inflation, the paper went on, 'the country's economic outlook [is] worrying'.[3] At the same meeting the interim report of the Task Force on Tax Reform was tabled, suggesting that personal tax rates for middle-income earners be significantly restructured, and that any resulting shortfall be recouped from increasing the role of indirect taxation. Muldoon thought the report unhelpful, but I disagreed strongly and continued to express my views over successive months.

In February Muldoon told caucus he would address tax reform in the 1982 budget, but was clearly beginning to resile by April, when he told caucus that 'tax reform was an insoluble problem' and that the forthcoming budget was his most difficult ever. My response in caucus — in my normal diplomatic way — was to say that a pile of disparate taxes on everything from clothing and footwear, to trees and flowers, books and periodicals (which was contemplated) was stupid and no answer to his budgetary problems.[4]

CER and liberalisation

One ongoing issue during 1982 was the potential for a closer economic relationship (CER) with Australia, Hugh Templeton was given responsibility for New Zealand's side of CER in the post-election Cabinet. I had earlier been on a flight with Hugh and Doug Anthony, the Australian Deputy PM, back to Wellington from a Waitangi Day celebration and had taken particular notice of Anthony's comments. He said the existing New Zealand–Australia Free Trade Agreement was effectively dead and that Australia was now prepared to offer New Zealand a new deal (CER) that would result in a progressive liberalisation of trade between the two countries and, more importantly, would provide an opportunity for New Zealand to modernise its economy.

Anthony was extremely pro-New Zealand, but said that what was on offer was a one-off opportunity. If New Zealand didn't take up the deal, Australia would move on and deal with other countries. Templeton was enthusiastic and, to his lasting credit, was finally able to bring CER to fruition, despite Muldoon's concerns in the face of claims by the New Zealand Manufacturers Federation that New Zealand could lose up to 400,000 manufacturing jobs.

My own view was that we should go ahead with the proposal based on the belief — supported by most senior officials — that the New Zealand economy needed to be opened up. I was also of the view that because most industries in Australia at the time were inefficient, we would not be throwing ours into the deep end of international competition if they only had to compete with Australia. A further potential benefit I saw was that better access to Australia would provide much-needed market diversification for our primary products. All of this was consistent with the speeches urging reform that I had been making throughout my time in Cabinet. I saw CER as an attractive practical step in the right direction.

However, my public utterances had started to unsettle some within the 'status quo' sectors of the economy, and particularly manufacturers who were doing nicely financially under the protection of import licensing. The chairman of the Manufacturers Federation approached Muldoon to get me to tone down my public comments. Muldoon was in a cleft stick. On one hand he was being pressured for reform — by elements within the caucus, the party, the Treasury and the Reserve Bank. On the other hand was the anxious local manufacturing sector. His solution was to tell me not to make any 'right-wing' speeches in the lead-up to the party's annual conference.

A new approach to the Works portfolio

The Public Works Department (PWD) was established in 1876 in response to the rapid growth and development of New Zealand at the time. Its functions then covered areas such as immigration, railway construction, roads, electric power supply, housing, building controls and unemployment relief. And as with Tourism, I was determined to make a success of this new ministerial position.

The Public Works Act 1928 brought the PWD and the Ministry of Works into a single unit under the minister of works. The departmental head was given the title Commissioner of Works. In 1973 the department was renamed the Ministry of Works and Development and when I became minister its various divisions were Architectural, Civil Engineering, Mechanical and Electrical Engineering, Power, Roading, Town and Country Planning, and Water and Soil.

Works' prime role was as an agency carrying out a wide range of design, construction and maintenance activities, including associated supervisory services, on behalf of clients. Total expenditure in 1980/1981 was $705.6 million, of which $538.8 million was in respect of work commissioned and funded by other departments or agencies. Expenditure instigated and funded by Works totalled $166.7 million. These were large amounts of yearly expenditure.

Bill Young, the minister I succeeded — and indeed successive ministers before him — had spent considerable time travelling around New Zealand by bus in the company of Works roading staff, meeting with local government officials and elected representatives who wanted to push for central government funding for their pet road and bridge projects. I believed the department had competent officials who were more than capable of recommending how best to allocate scarce resources. I also believed that no important roading decisions should be made (and indeed should not be seen to be made) in response to local on-the-ground lobbying.

After participating in one brief tour — so that I could show that my decision was based on practical experience — I suspended my participation in these events. They were a waste of my valuable time. I was also determined to show that things would be run differently with me as minister.

In the past, rank and file Works head office personnel had rarely had a chance to meet their minister. In contrast, I wanted to give them an opportunity to question me on my background and beliefs and what I wanted to achieve, so I set up a schedule of meetings with each division in turn, starting with Architecture. The Commissioner was opposed to the idea and said so, but when he realised I was determined to go ahead, he asked if I wanted him to come with me. I said no, and his rather supercilious response was that he would go around after me and 'tidy up'.

At the first meeting I gave a thumbnail sketch of my background and what I sought to achieve as an MP and Cabinet minister. Then I asked those present to tell me how they thought the general public viewed the department and what they thought were its strengths and weakness. After a slow start, we had a full-on discussion over the next two hours and I left with the feeling that I had made considerable progress in getting them on side.

Meetings with the other divisions followed, and the Commissioner did not have to go around afterwards tidying up! Indeed, on a later occasion when I was having drinks with senior personnel from around the country who had come up to Wellington for one of their six-monthly roundtables, the Commissioner commented: 'One of our problems as senior officials has been spending too much time telling ministers what we think they want to hear instead of telling them the truth.' I took this as a major change in attitude, but was disappointed that I appeared to be the only one present who noticed.

Although the prime minister had sidelined me from the Cabinet Economic Committee, I was now, as minister of works, chair of the Cabinet Works Committee, which was important as it was the gateway through which most major departmental building projects had to pass before they could receive Cabinet approval.

As final approvals depended on the state of the government budget, the overall programme the committee considered — as with Housing — was subject to frequent stops and starts. Many projects took a decade or more from concept stage until they sat before the Works Committee, with this long gestation period having some unfortunate consequences. One was that a culture of 'it's our turn' had developed among sponsoring departments. Another was that any major plan modification was a no-no because it invariably resulted in a project losing its place in the queue. This meant no one would acknowledge that a particular design was out of date or could benefit from modification.

The worst feature of the process was that the Works Architectural Division people who serviced the committee, and should have been offering independent advice on the merits or otherwise of a particular project, were loath to tell the committee what they actually thought, for fear of dropping the sponsoring department in it.

Following on from my meetings with head office divisions, an opportunity arose to change the culture within the ministry. In early February 1982 a proposal sponsored by the Department of Scientific and Industrial Research (DSIR) came before the committee. It involved plans to build a three-storey building on Lincoln College land next to a proposed Ministry of Agriculture and Fisheries (MAF) research facility that was to be run in conjunction with the college. Initially, the committee didn't know about the MAF proposal, but when we found out I decided that DSIR Minister Ian Shearer and I should visit the site, with a view to considering more effective use of the staff, buildings and equipment of the two departments. I was sure some cost savings could result.

However, bad weather delayed Shearer and the two backbench MPs who were to join me, and they never left Wellington. In Christchurch I met up with DSIR senior scientist Harvey Smith, and as were driving to Lincoln College together I asked him if his department's building had any design problems. He said, 'Yes, but no one you meet today will acknowledge that.' He added that they thought I was there to say no to the proposal. I assured him I wasn't.

At Lincoln I met up with James Stewart, head of the college, and local departmental officials, and asked how long the buildings had been on the drawing board. The answer was 10 years. Next, I asked them the same question I had asked Smith about the appropriateness of the current plans, given the passage of time. Sure enough, I was assured they were completely fine.

At the Works Committee meeting the following week I asked Works officials the same questions. The reply was: 'Can we come back to the committee next week with an answer?' At the following week's meeting the committee was told it might be possible to build one building to house both departments. I then asked: 'If there is no delay in the approval process before the committee, how long do you need to reconsider the matter?' The answer was six weeks and the date was set.

When the committee duly met to consider the matter, we were presented with a set of revised drawings that had been agreed to by Works and the two sponsoring departments. Instead of two separate buildings, each with a lift, the revised plans showed one two-storey building with no lift. The ground floor was to be concrete blocks and the second floor was to be clad with wood. The overall cost saving was in the millions. The committee approved the new proposal and reiterated that the building schedule was not to suffer any delay.

Architectural Division personnel were now like cats with two tails. At long last they were being treated as professionals and being required to provide the government with independent advice on projects. This was a major departure from past practice where the expectation was that plans drawn up and promulgated — in the case of big departments such as Education by that department's own in-house architects — would be approved without question.

However, the way ahead was not without problems. These came to a head when the Department of Education presented plans to rebuild parts of Wellington East Girls' College near the Basin Reserve. The Works chief architect came to see me before the meeting to say his division had looked closely at what Education was proposing, and thought there was a better and more cost-effective way to achieve the desired outcome.

When the Works officials expressed their view at the committee meeting, Merv Wellington and his officials were furious. The matter was adjourned and I arranged to visit the school and meet members of the school's board. Before the visit I received a detailed briefing from the chief architect on what Education wanted to do on site and why Works architects opposed it.

The central issue was the assembly hall area, which was full of history and a focal point for the school's achievements. The Department of Education wanted to demolish this building, as a senior departmental official explained while we walked around the school grounds before meeting board members. He pointed to the mix of children we saw, and told me that their backgrounds were now so diverse that the history portrayed in the assembly hall area meant nothing to them. He was adamant that the pupils and the school would be much better off with a new building, without being continually reminded of an irrelevant past. I remained non-committal and we went off to meet the board.

The board members were all women, and after tea and scones we sat in a semi-circle and discussed the redevelopment. I said I had been impressed by what I had seen of the school so far, and that they could be justifiably proud. We then moved on to the contrasting redevelopment proposals from Education and Works. I asked what significance they attached to retaining the character and historical content of the assembly hall area, emphasising that the revised plans Works had put forward could proceed without any additional delay.

Initially no one responded, but then one of the members said that, subject to no loss of project timing, she supported the Works proposal. I then asked each member individually for their view and all eventually said they preferred what Works was advocating ahead of the Department of Education's proposal. As a result, the Works Committee approved the Works plan.

However, that was not the end of the matter. Within days — after I had resigned from Cabinet — Merv Wellington reversed the Cabinet Works Committee decision in favour of his department's plan. However, his victory was pyrrhic. No redevelopment had started before the 1984 election, which National lost. When the new Labour government's minister of works was briefed on the two plans, the Works proposal was reinstated and eventually implemented.

The Clyde Dam

Before I became minister of works and development after the 1981 election, Cabinet had approved, in July 1981, the construction of a high dam on the Clutha River at an estimated cost of $580 million. The Kirk Labour government had planned a lower dam, but the Muldoon government overturned this in favour of a higher-capacity dam on the basis that additional electricity was needed, in part, to power the new aluminium smelter about to be built at Aramoana.

Earlier, the Contractors' Federation had been lobbying the government for more private-sector involvement in infrastructure projects in general, and the Clyde Dam project in particular. Their efforts were successful when Bill Young, the then minister of works, announced in December 1980 that Cabinet had decided that private contractors would build the dam and the Ministry of Works and Ministry of Energy staff would build the powerhouse. Later, Young promised more private-sector involvement in Taranaki projects, in the Aramoana smelter and in the Otaki geothermal power plant.

In December 1981 — immediately after the election and my appointment as minister of works — the first part of the Clyde dam project was put out for tender. The work involved building the greater part of the concrete gravity dam, treating the foundation, making and erecting the 7.8-metre-diameter steel penstocks, and installing the gates to control the flow of water. At this stage, several contractors were already busy on site doing preparatory work. For example, J.W. Connolly of Cromwell was building a 20-metre tunnel near the dam's eventual crest, while Downer was erecting the main concrete batching plant. Wilkins & Davies was close to completing its second excavation contract, having formed a number of platforms and access roads, and Baker Construction and Cooper were operating their heavy earthmoving plant.

Before this, an application for a water right for the high dam had been lodged with the National Water and Soil Conservation Authority, with approval eventually issued in January 1982 after various reviews and Planning Tribunal decisions on appeal.

On 29 March 1982, on my recommendation, Cabinet approved a tender from an Ed Zublin–Williamson joint venture to build the dam, and on 21 April 1982 I announced that 'subject to satisfactory resolution of legal issues concerning water rights',[5] my intention was to award the contract to this consortium at a tender price of $102.6 million. Bidding had been keen, with six of the seven tenders within $10 million of each other. All were from joint ventures between New Zealand and overseas firms — from Australia, Britain, South Korea, Japan, West Germany, Switzerland and the US. The bid from the Ministry of Works, which was also allowed to tender, was initially for $156.4 million but was revised down to $117.3 million.

Ed Zublin was a major civil engineering contractor in West Germany. It had a turnover in the hundreds of millions of dollars, 30 percent of which was involved in overseas civil engineering contracts. In Austria it had recently built a large concrete arch dam that was more than twice the size of the Clyde Dam. The company was also currently working on dams in Iraq and Honduras, and part of its arrangement with Williamson was to provide nine key project managers to initiate the work at Clyde, and for them to be matched by Williamson employees who could be trained to take over as soon as possible. Williamson had been involved in previous international joint ventures, including building the Manapouri tailrace tunnel and the first Wairakei geothermal power station.

The contract decision was a major change for this type of work, described in *Contractor* magazine as marking 'the dawn of a new era that would eventually see private companies replacing the Ministry of

Works and Development and local authorities as the builders of public infrastructure'.[6]

However, as I had stated in the press release announcing the successful tenderer, the water right decision was still the subject of an appeal to the High Court on points of law. The central issue advanced by disaffected landowners[7] before the court was Bill Young's chairmanship of the Water and Soil Conservation Authority — which was required by statute — and whether this, associated with his active promotion of the Clyde Dam project as minister of works, represented a conflict of interest.

The landowners' application was successful and the water right was held to be illegal. However, the Crown had lodged an appeal before I announced the successful tenderer, and I had made it clear the water right issue had to be resolved first. In practical terms, the government faced a choice of either mothballing the construction site, which was already employing a substantial workforce, while it applied for a fresh legally challengeable water right, or putting special empowering legislation through Parliament. It chose the legislative course and my responsibility as minister was to get it through.

In drafting terms the matter was relatively straightforward, as the National Development Act 1979 had been enacted for the express purpose of streamlining the planning process for 'works of national importance'. That act gave the government the power to designate such works and to refer them directly to the Planning Tribunal for review and recommendations. The final decision on whether such works would proceed was retained by the government, and significant constraints were placed on the ability of affected persons to challenge or review those decisions.

The legislation developed for the Clyde Dam, titled the Clutha Development (Clyde Dam) Empowering Act 1982, went one step further than the National Development Act by containing provisions to grant water rights to the Crown in respect of the operation of the Clyde Dam on the Clutha River. This provision superseded any power in the Water and Soil Conservation Act 1967 or any other enactment, and overrode decisions already made by the High Court and the Planning Tribunal to decline the Crown's application for such consent.

The drafting of the legislation might have been relatively straightforward but it was much harder to persuade a majority of MPs to support it. The government had a slim majority and at least two National Party caucus members — Ruth Richardson and Simon Upton — were signalling their potential opposition. Fortunately, I had people in my office with public relations expertise and this was crucial in getting support for the legislation from all the members of the government caucus, and ultimately also from the two Social Credit MPs.

In the lead-up, I briefed the Labour Party caucus and arranged for interested MPs and key journalists to visit Cromwell. The unpublicised objectives were for them to see how much had already been built on site (with the dam walls already stretching well up into the sky). It must have been clear to them that the project would be difficult to unwind. Also, we arranged for them to talk to management and workers and hear about their work prospects in the area if the project was mothballed for an indefinite period.

A special team was set up in Wellington to provide MPs and the media with detailed briefings. These officials were instructed to answer all and any questions put to them, including providing information on the likely economic impact on any private-sector contractors and subcontractors likely to be affected by any delay.

My staff and I made a special effort to ensure that Richardson and Upton received all the material they wanted, and additional meetings were arranged with officials to discuss their questions and concerns. The approach ultimately paid off, but years later Ruth Richardson claimed that her back was covered with my sprig marks.

I was no longer in Cabinet when Parliament passed the special empowering legislation.

A speech to Young Nationals

In late May 1982 and before my resignation from Cabinet I gave a speech in Wellington to a group of financial service sector people, with my speech notes largely based on material supplied by the Treasury. I discussed the role of government in the economy and the conclusions of the taskforce of the New Zealand Planning Council in its July 1980 publication. The taskforce had recorded that the government should not attempt to lay down a detailed blueprint for the level and pattern of investment over the next decade. Rather, its role should be to provide the right climate for private and public investment decisions, give better signals, and reduce the negative influence of regulations, licensing and controls.

I went on to discuss the major government decisions over the past four or five years, making the point that they would influence New Zealand's development for many years to come. I added that there were 'substantial risks associated with the energy projects if not carefully handled', and cited the potential for problems similar to those that Britain had faced with its North Sea oil fields if New Zealand did not pursue appropriate macro-economic policies.

Next, I said that I saw risks for New Zealand in two main areas. First, the large amounts of money being spent on the 'Think Big' projects could result in a shortage of funds for other businesses such as farms and factories. Second, New Zealanders might reject the structural change taking place unless the justification for it was 'sold' to them appropriately. I added that in the past New Zealand had focused too narrowly on earning overseas funds, and on the quantity rather than quality of development. I concluded by saying that today's dirty word was not 'profit' but 'inefficiency', and that we needed to use the total resources available to the country to best advantage. Unfortunately, I said, 'the theory and the practice are still poles apart and will remain so until governments accept that their role is not to dictate but to listen, explain and guide.'

Copies of my speech were distributed widely, yet attracted no media attention or comments from my Cabinet or backbench colleagues.

New Zealand celebrates the sovereign's birthday on the first Monday of June, and on 7 June 1982 I was scheduled to speak to a meeting of Young Nationals at their conference at the Chateau Tongariro in the centre of the North Island. The weekend before was spent with friends whom I had first met in the early 1950s when I led a group of North Canterbury Young Farmers Club members on a tour of the Hauraki Plains.

I hadn't asked for speech notes to be prepared in my office as the presentation was to be at a party function, but I had taken several documents with me as background material so that I could prepare my own notes to speak from. They included some polling material, a copy of my earlier speech to the Wellington financial service group, a selection of newspaper cuttings and articles, and some papers on the 'Think Big' projects.

One newspaper cutting was a full-page reproduction, dated 4 June, of a speech by one of my constituents, farmer-economist John Bayley, who had worked in the head office of the Bank of New Zealand. In a speech that week to North Canterbury Federated Farmers, Bayley noted: 'In the aftermath of the election I am very fearful that inflation has faded from the official priorities and ... that the government regards its election win (by default) as a mandate to continue the same policies as they had through 1980 and beyond.' He went on to say he would be looking at Table 2 in the forthcoming budget for the level of projected expenditure, 'not the platitudes in the front which have long since lost their credence, to see if the government was intent on doing something about inflation'.[8]

I had brought two other press cuttings with me. The first related to a speech by Bill Christie, president of the Manufacturers Federation, in which he criticised the government's record in integrated medium-term economic planning 'because real commitment at the top has not been forthcoming'.

The second cutting contained criticism by the minister of energy, Bill Birch, of a statement in a speech by John Hunn, chairman of the Development Finance Corporation, that the 'Government has not provided sufficient information for an informed debate on the viability of each [energy] project'.

The speech I finally prepared for delivery at the Chateau conference was typed up over the weekend by my hostess, and, contrary to later public comments by some of my parliamentary colleagues, was not discussed with the media or distributed in any way before I delivered it. It contained major extracts from the Wellington financial service group speech and referred to the Bayley, Christie and Hunn comments.

It started — as was fitting for a group of Young Nationals — with a question: 'What has happened to the National Party since it was swept back into office in 1975 with an overwhelming majority?' I went on to discuss some of the decisions the government had taken since that time, but added that we were now attracting less and less popular support at the polls — 47.58 per cent in 1975, but only 38.78 per cent in 1981.

Later I asked a further question: 'Has the individual New Zealander been involved enough in the decision-making process so that he not only understands it, but also supports it?' As a part answer I referred to an article in the *Listener* earlier in the year noting that only 7 percent of those who voted National in 1981 did so because of the growth strategy. My conclusion was: 'Clearly "Think Big" is neither understood nor supported at this stage by the majority of New Zealanders.'

This was the headline that TV picked up and widely reported on that evening. The comment was taken out of context, disregarding the overall content of my speech and the nature of the audience it had been prepared for.

In full flight.

A media frenzy erupted. To put the TV headline in its proper context, I had copies of the speech distributed to the Press Gallery and to my fellow MPs. I declined to comment to any media.

Initially Muldoon didn't raise the matter with me; nor was the matter discussed in that week's caucus while I was there. However, he did say, in response to media questions, that he disagreed with my comments. Bill Birch for his part was furious because I had referred to him by name in the speech. He claimed I had intruded into his area of ministerial responsibility and asked me to issue a public apology. I declined, and Birch sought Muldoon's intervention.

Nothing further eventuated until the *Dominion* announced it was going to publish the full text of my speech later in the week. Muldoon immediately phoned me to tell me to stop the impending publication. When I replied that it might be difficult to do so, he said that was my problem. He then left Wellington on a brief visit to Australia.

Thinking that any direct approach to the *Dominion* would only heighten publicity and the speech would still be published anyway, I sought advice from Brian Lockstone, the prime minister's press secretary, whom I knew well and respected. Brian agreed that any attempt to gag the paper would backfire and suggested I write to the editor, 'putting the speech in proper context'. I followed his advice, and also wrote to the prime minister telling him I had discussed the matter with Lockstone, and was following his advice.

The *Dominion* published the speech, together with my letter, and made its own comments on the matter:

> **Quigley writes to The Dominion**
>
> THE EDITOR of The Dominion yesterday received the following letter from the office of The Minister of Works and Development:
>
> > *I note that you are proposing to publish the full text of the speech I gave last Monday 7 June and felt that it would be helpful if I provided some additional comments to put the speech it its proper perspective.*
> >
> > *As you will be aware it was prepared for and delivered to a group of young people with a common interest in National Party matters. They were holding a conference to discuss a wide number of topical subjects including the Clyde Dam issue and the Government's growth strategy. I was also aware that a remit was to be moved on the subject of special legislation for the Clyde Dam.*
> >
> > *The speech was deliberately designed to stimulate discussion, because, in my view, it is most important that a group such as this has the opportunity to debate the issue of the day in an informed manner and appreciate the role the Government plays in the decision-making process. The debate on think big has to date concentrated on a limited number of large scale projects rather than the part each of these plays in an overall development strategy.*
> >
> > *Yours faithfully*
> > *D F Quigley*
>
> The Dominion responded:
>
> > The Prime Minister, Mr Muldoon, and other ministers involved yesterday maintained their silence on Mr Quigley's controversial weekend speech. Mr Quigley arrived very late at the National Party caucus

> meeting — just a short time before it rose for lunch. Mr Muldoon, speaking at a lunch-time press conference, said he did not know the reason for Mr Quigley's late arrival. Mr Muldoon said Mr Quigley's speech, which raised fundamental questions of party philosophy, was not mentioned by the minister.
>
> The Leader of the Opposition, Mr Rowling, said Mr Quigley had deserted the Government's sinking ship when he questioned its growth strategy this week. 'What's really happened is that Quigley's the first guy — not to think about it, I'm sure, in the National caucus — that's decided he's really going to say something about it.'[9]

Towards the end of the week I was approached by journalist Ian Fraser, who fronted the hour-long primetime Sunday evening TV programme *Newsmakers*, to appear on that weekend's show. I had still made no public comments on my speech and was also in the thick of the Clyde Dam special legislation controversy as the responsible minister. Thinking that the TV programme would provide an opportunity to explain the government's position to a nationwide audience, I agreed to participate, subject to strict criteria.

The agreement that Fraser and I came to was that the first part of the live interview would focus exclusively on the Clyde Dam issue, and after that we would move to the Young Nationals speech, putting it clearly in context. All Fraser's questions were discussed and agreed to in advance to avoid the potential for any ambush. The TV station widely pre-advertised the forthcoming interview.

On Saturday morning when I was back in my electorate I received a phone call from Muldoon. In typical direct fashion he said that he had seen that I was scheduled to appear on *Newsmakers* on Sunday and asked, 'Is the programme pre-recorded or live?' When I said it was live he responded: 'If you go on that programme I want your resignation from Cabinet on my desk on Monday morning.'

'Wouldn't it be sensible to discuss what I intend to cover?' I said.

'I told you to stop the publication of your speech in the *Dominion* but you didn't do that, and now you are going on television.'

'But I wrote to you about the *Dominion* matter,' I quickly said.

He was taken aback at that, said he hadn't seen any letter and would phone me back. He did so shortly after and said the letter didn't make any difference. He repeated his ultimatum.

On page 146 of his fourth autobiography, *Number 38*, Muldoon records that the first thing he told me was that he required an apology 'to be made to those Ministers who were offended by [my] statements, and second, that [I] should not go on television to repeat [my] criticism'. These comments are completely untrue. The ultimatum I was given at that time related only to my appearing on the TV programme.

I flew up to Wellington on Saturday afternoon. In anticipation of my possible resignation from Cabinet on Monday, and not wanting to be accused of lagging behind with innovative housing policy, I arranged to meet with senior Housing Corporation staff and John Buddle, the Treasury housing official, on Sunday morning. I asked them to prepare a Cabinet paper on state house rental policy that would pave the way for the Crown to exit from that activity and for local authorities and the private sector to pick up this responsibility, with, if necessary, financial support from central government. The Cabinet paper was completed the next day and arrangements made for it to be referred to the Treasury for comment. None of the officials at the meeting were told of Muldoon's ultimatum to me.

On Sunday evening I went on the *Newsmakers* programme without mentioning Muldoon's resignation threat before, during or after the interview. After an initial slightly nervous start I warmed to the task, and the feedback I got was that it was an excellent interview. I was told I had explained the need for special legislation for the Clyde Dam well; and that the overall thrust of my Young Nationals speech had now been fully explained. Later in the evening when I saw Jim McLay at his Oriental Bay apartment he praised the interview and expressed the view that whatever sins Muldoon might have laid at my door had been fully remedied. 'You certainly didn't criticise your colleagues,' he told me later.[10]

The programme attracted a huge nationwide audience and on Monday morning, 14 June, I deliberately made myself unavailable, and so I hadn't yet seen Muldoon when I walked into the Cabinet room before the start of the meeting. Duncan MacIntyre was the first person I saw. He shook my hand and warmly congratulated me on what he said was a 'brilliant' *Newsmakers* performance.

Muldoon arrived shortly after and immediately told me to come with him to his office, before the Cabinet meeting started. There he made no comment on my *Newsmakers* interview, but said my Young Nationals speech had offended, embarrassed and angered some of my Cabinet colleagues and I had the option of either publicly apologising or resigning from Cabinet.

'You must know what I will do in those circumstances, Prime Minister,' I said.

He responded by offering me the wording of a short apology. I thanked him, shook his hand, wished him all the best, and said I would think about it. I then went down to my office and started to draft my resignation from Cabinet and the Executive Council. I was joined there shortly after by Jim McLay, who — when he saw that I was determined to resign — suggested some minor changes to my resignation letter.

By now it was nearly lunchtime so I returned to the Cabinet meeting. Just before Cabinet adjourned, Muldoon — as usual — went around the table asking if ministers had any additional matters they wished to raise. When it was Bill Birch's turn he started to raise his dispute with me but was immediately stopped by Muldoon, who said it was a matter between himself and me.

When it was my turn, I told Cabinet members I had been given the option of apologising or resigning from Cabinet, and I was resigning. Hugh Templeton tried to open up discussion but Muldoon shut him down. The meeting broke up, and as I went down in the lift Ben Couch was in tears, saying, 'I thought we were all meant to be mates.' A few days later he penned me the note shown below. In contrast, Warren Cooper's comments in the lift were: 'You're a bloody idiot.'

At a press conference later that afternoon I mentioned Muldoon's attempt to get me to resign from Cabinet when I opposed Duncan MacIntyre for the deputy prime minister position, and detailed the events of the past week. I concluded by saying that I would be considering my position as an MP over the next few days. This raised the possibility of a by-election in Rangiora and — because of the government's slim majority — a general election. I remember David Thomson visiting me to urge me to stay on.

Response to my resignation

I received thousands of letters of support following my resignation, as well as a few that were critical. There was also a flood of media comment. Some was to the effect that I got what I deserved, but most people

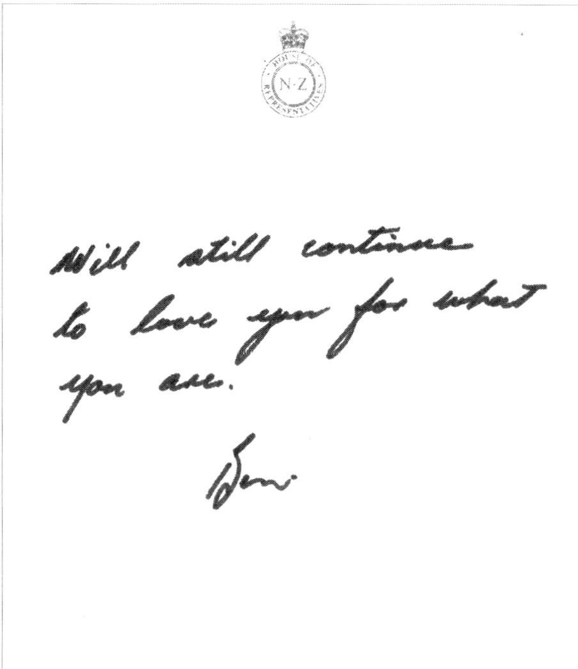

HOUSE OF REPRESENTATIVES N·Z

Will still continue
to love you for what
you are.

Ben

Note from Ben Couch following my resignation, 24 June 1982

were supportive of the need to publicly discuss the issues I had raised. A *Dominion* editorial summed up the issue:

> Mr Quigley draws attention to the need to take stock of the quality of administration while the party is in office. He challenges party youngsters to consider the matter, possibly because it isn't as easy to get the whole Cabinet examining its priorities, from the point of view of political philosophy rather than the scraping back into power again. Maybe a clash of personalities is inevitable . . . But the matters raised matter most.[11]

A summary of events appeared much later in an article by Philip Worthington in the Christchurch *Press*:

> To many people, the most significant political event in New Zealand during 1982 will be what has become known as the Quigley affair. The forced resignation of a Cabinet Minister who publicly questions the directions and effectiveness of the Government to which he belongs is rare enough on the New Zealand political scene to warrant this importance . . .

> In essence, the facts are simple enough. Mr Quigley, as Minister of Works and Development, addressed a conference of Young Nationals on June 7. He cast doubts about the wisdom of concentrating energies on the big development projects that form the cornerstone of the Government's growth strategy. He said the strategy was neither understood nor supported by most New Zealanders …
>
> These comments upset the Prime Minister, Mr Muldoon, who said that Mr Quigley had breached the principle of collective Cabinet responsibility and offended Cabinet colleagues. Mr Muldoon asked Mr Quigley to apologise or resign. Mr Quigley re-affirmed his comments and resigned …[12]

Despite Muldoon's assertion that my resignation was a matter of a breach of 'collective Cabinet responsibility', this was not the case.

CHAPTER 12

A Backbencher Again

Some in caucus, particularly Ruth Richardson and Marilyn Waring, criticised Muldoon for his high-handedness in sacking me. Others remained silent. While most quietly conceded that dramatic changes in the direction of economic policy and leadership style were needed, they were more concerned about the government's narrow parliamentary majority and the destabilising effect that another confrontation with Muldoon would have on the party's and their own electoral prospects than they were in siding with me. The Bob Brockie cartoon below with the little figure of George Gair saying 'Hang on in there Derek' sums up the situation nicely. It was one of many that appeared over the next few weeks.

Muldoon appointed two new ministers to take over my former responsibilities, with Friedlander getting Housing and Works, and Keith Allen taking over Government Life, State Insurance, Public Trust and the EQC. In addition, he became minister of customs. To publicly emphasise the two-for-one changeover, I attended the new ministers' formal swearing-in ceremony at Government House.

Bolger was the big winner from my resignation, as it enhanced his leadership prospects. His crowing to the effect that 'we have got rid of Quigley' reverberated throughout Parliament for days. In contrast, the wider National Party was overwhelmingly supportive, with a large contingent greeting me — much to my embarrassment — at Christchurch Airport on my arrival back home after my resignation. Business and party activists had seen me as virtually the lone voice in Cabinet for reformist economic policies. Now, with my departure, they viewed Cabinet as unbalanced at a time when a change in policy direction was clearly needed.

Hang on in there Derek.

I need consistency.

Damn the National Party.

That's got Quigley safely tucked away.

Private-sector credit had increased by 28 percentage points since the easing of credit restrictions early in 1981, there was growing pressure on interest rates, and the Federation of Labour was signalling it was not prepared to forgo wage increases in return for tax cuts. To add to this, officials were warning that the inflation rate for the second quarter of 1982 was running at 5 percent and was likely to reach 20 percent for the year. Meanwhile, inflation internationally was falling. Tax reform had been in the party's 1981 election manifesto and for some time had been pushed aggressively in caucus by, in particular, Michael Cox, Ian McLean and newly elected MP Ruth Richardson. All three advocated a broad-based GST consumption tax to replace a raft of existing indirect taxes, and favoured cuts in personal and company tax.

But Muldoon saw things differently. His answer was to impose a wage/price freeze, which was initially supposed to last for 12 months from June 1982 but was still in place by the time of the snap election in mid-July 1984. This was seen as public confirmation of his opposition to freeing up the economy, and further enraged those who disliked him and his economic policies. Some saw the timing of the freeze as an attempt to divert public criticism away from his sacking of me. An Eric Heath cartoon featuring Muldoon, Birch and me captures this nicely.

Where Muldoon got the idea for a freeze is not clear. I myself had advocated a temporary ban on general wage orders in my alternative economic policy document, but this was part of a total package to restructure the economy and nothing like Muldoon's initiative.

Inflation had been a major agenda item at the OECD meeting Muldoon attended in Paris the month before. It has been suggested that 'an unidentified American economist with whom Muldoon had discussions there seems to have suggested a freeze'.[1] The idea was run past Hugh Templeton, who was also in Paris at the time, and the matter was raised with officials once they were back home. The officials were so strongly opposed that they produced a joint memo for Muldoon listing their concerns.

Despite this, the idea was put to the Cabinet Economic Committee during the week of 14 June, without advice or briefing papers from officials, and was approved by the full Cabinet as an oral item on 21 June. Only Jim McLay spoke strongly against it. The freeze was imposed by regulation the following day, without the need for reference to Parliament, and applied to wages, salaries, prices, rents and subsidies. It covered all forms of remuneration, including dividends, directors' fees and professional charges.

The wage/price freeze was supposed to shut them up.

Interest rate controls gazetted the previous November were extended to cover all forms of deposits and commercial bills. A fixed exchange rate replaced the 'crawling peg' system, with some scope remaining for adjustments to the dollar's value.[2]

Against the backdrop of my sacking and the introduction of the freeze, another government measure added to the anger of many traditional National Party supporters. It was contained in the No. 2 Income Tax Amendment Bill, which sought to outlaw retrospectively previously legal investment contracts to stop the loss of tax revenue through an array of tax shelters — special partnerships; horticultural, livestock and film schemes — that enabled individuals (in the prevailing inflationary environment) to offset their other income against their investments in these schemes.

Initially, the measure was only intended to stop syndicate members from writing off their personal income tax. However, to also catch so-called high-income individual taxpayers, the final legislation provided for a maximum of $10,000 to be written off in any one year, and for property sold within 10 years of purchase to be effectively subject to a capital gains tax.

It all became too much for some party loyalists and, in Hugh Templeton's words, irretrievably damaged the image of the third Muldoon administration:

> The business community shuddered collectively at the loss of the most outspoken ministerial proponent of the market. Muldoon's tax-avoidance proposals undermined that foundation support. Key party members in electorate after electorate simply folded their tents. Muldoon's dictatorial power raised too many hackles. Players who believed in a fairer, more civilised game rallied in Quigley's support, forgiving his betrayal of Cabinet unanimity.[3]

The issue of Cabinet unanimity — or Cabinet collective responsibility — that Templeton refers to raises the question of whether my 'sacking' was because of a breach of that doctrine — which is a constitutional matter — or an act of political expediency. The evidence suggests the latter for three reasons. First, Muldoon was able to get rid of a recalcitrant minister who had challenged him and his policies. Second, despite his later rewriting of his ultimatum to me, he initially did not criticise me for the content of my Young Nationals speech, only demanding my resignation from Cabinet later if I went on *Newsmakers*. Third, my resignation was a rare instance of others making the bullets that Muldoon was eventually pressured into firing. The two bullet-makers were Birch and Bolger. Birch had been genuinely upset at some aspects of my speech and wanted an apology. In contrast, Bolger seized on the opportunity to get rid of a potential opponent and egged Birch on.

For my part, given that what I said in my speech was factually correct, was designed to stimulate discussion among a group of Young Nationals, and needed to be said, I felt I had nothing to apologise for. Resignation was therefore the only option I was prepared to entertain.

Resignations from Cabinet were extremely rare at that time, with only three or four before me and Sir Apirana Ngata's in 1934 (following a commission of inquiry into the administration of the Native Department) the most recent. Because of this, and the background to my departure, my poll rating among National MPs as preferred prime minister rose from just under 5 percent to about 12 percent, second only to Muldoon at the time I resigned.

Some of this support was clearly an expression of anti-Muldoonism rather than personal support for me. But what I did demonstrate was that I was not only prepared to stick to my principles, no matter the personal cost,[4] but was also prepared to stand up to Muldoon publicly when few others were. Given this, one of my prized possessions is a copy of Michael Bassett's book *Three Party Politics in New Zealand 1911–1931*, which the author inscribed: 'To one of the few politicians with real guts.' Later, Richard Prebble constantly referred to me — when he and I were back in Parliament in the 1990s as members of the ACT New Zealand Party — as 'the only National Party Cabinet minister who was prepared to stand up to Muldoon while Muldoon was still alive'.

Further mini-dramas followed my resignation, one of them at the party's annual conference. I arrived at the venue late, with the meeting already in session. To the dismay of my many supporters — who without telling me had decided to stand up, cheer and clap when I entered the hall — I came in by a side door and quietly joined my Rangiora delegates without too much disruption. The result was that when I spoke on a remit on redundancy, commenting that the topic was one I knew a lot about from personal experience, I received widespread applause. At the same conference there was friction over my replacing Warren Cooper, at the request of the Dominion Council, to give the keynote speech to female delegates. The Muldoon camp were not keen, so as a compromise I agreed to have no media present when I spoke, and not to circulate copies of my speech notes. In retrospect this was a mistake. The speech was one of my better ones, and went to the heart of what I had been advocating.

I began by saying I was happy to debate with anyone — either at the meeting or elsewhere — issues like service to the National Party, loyalty, concerns about the nature of New Zealand society and the direction it was heading.

I referred to the changes in voter support between the 1975 and 1981 elections — National falling 47.58 to 39.82 percent; Labour virtually static at 39.56 percent and 39 percent; Social Credit going from just below 7.5 percent to more than 20.5 percent — and said these figures illustrated two things. One was National's fragile hold on the Treasury benches. The other was the emerging presence of a substantial block of 'footloose voters' who could be captured by National or Labour if 'either of those two parties could break with their present orthodox approach and present themselves in a more attractive way'.

In a recent Heylen poll, only 7.6 percent of National voters had cited an economic reason for supporting the party. Crucially, this percentage figure was half of that recorded among voters at large. In marked contrast, 28.4 percent of Labour voters had supported their party in 1981 on the strength of its economic policies. Clearly, National's economic policies were less effective in persuading voters. Also notable was that the 'growth strategy' did not feature strongly as a positive or negative influence on voters.[5]

The same poll showed that despite 29.4 percent of those who voted National citing support for Muldoon as their principal reason for supporting the party, 'the anti-Muldoon vote was higher than any other principal reason provided by switchers (people whose 1981 vote was different from 1978) going to Labour, and apart from third-party factors, was the main cause of voters voting for Social Credit'.

My conclusion was that had any adverse 'personality' row involving Muldoon occurred during the campaign, National could have lost the election. To emphasise the significance of this, I highlighted the poll's conclusion that of those who switched to National in 1981 after having voted for another party in 1978, 15.2 percent decided as late as election day to cross over.

National was a party at risk, I said. There was a danger of further erosion to Social Credit in crucial National seats, and on the other hand a distinct possibility that Labour — which was already starting to attract support in some policy areas — might be able to gather up a sufficient number of protest voters who were temporarily lodged with Social Credit, to win the next election. I emphasised that time was of the essence:

> It is necessary for the party and its politicians to be much more constructive than we have been in the past. We need to get out in the electorates and work for the things we believe in; to canvass for subs; and to leave aside personality politics.

I went on to discuss my concerns about New Zealand's future, and began with an extract from a recent article in the *Australian*: 'New Zealanders live in a social climate tinged by an uncertain economy and dominated by a political arena which is more unstable and turbulent than at any time since the 1930s.' The same article concluded: 'The result is a social system under stress.'[6] I said that for many New Zealanders the Springbok tour epitomised the anguish of an angry and uncertain people. Tens of thousands had seen the issue in one-dimensional, uncompromising terms. There were widespread breaches of the law, with civil and social disobedience. Hundreds of decent New Zealanders had finished up in New Zealand courts:

> It was then, as it is now, as though we are suffering from a crisis of identity . . . The world has changed, New Zealand has changed, and many of us are having difficulty adjusting to those different circumstances. We have got confrontation in all aspects of our society — in politics, in industrial relations, in social protest and in economic planning. The list is endless. We have legitimised personal attack; our procedures and institutions are increasingly being viewed as irrelevant.

As examples I cited the Erebus Inquiry, the Clyde Dam saga, and Parliament's preoccupation with trivia and party-political expediency.

> And if you think that perception is only limited to a small number of people, you are wrong because public opinion polls tell us that more than half the community believes that the present political system is in need of reform.

I pointed to the extent of change already under way, saying that by the 1984 election 70 percent of New Zealanders would be aged under 42, and yet the current Cabinet was all male, with only two of its 20 members aged under 40. 'No wonder it has difficulty at times relating to the average Kiwi.' I continued:

> There are now vast differences in attitude between town and country as the Springbok tour and the 1981 results in individual electorates showed; and even cities vary dramatically one from the other. Auckland has its race relations problems (Bastion Point); Wellington is dominated by the political scene; and Christchurch is still more conservative than many parts of England. It is little wonder that the government's offer of tax cuts (or was it tax reform?) and the growth strategy have been seen by many as an inadequate response to the ferment and the mood for change that is evident out there in the community.
>
> . . . We need growth and a growth strategy, plus a lot of other things too. But more than anything else as a political party we need to communicate better. That's why I said in my speech to the Young Nationals that 'Think Big' was neither understood nor supported at this stage by the majority of

New Zealanders. The polls prove that I am right; my correspondence proves that I am right; and so too does Report No. 5 by the Economic Monitoring Group of the New Zealand Planning Council, which was released on Monday 14 June 1982, the same day I resigned from Cabinet.

I then quoted from page 36 of that report:

> The energy programme is generally seen solely as a response to the oil crisis, and export incentives and supplementary minimum prices as exclusively related to the stimulation of exports, and not as part of a comprehensive plan to cure balance of payment problems. This is understandable as there is no broad programme of government measures designed to actively encourage replacement of imported goods and services or economy in their use. Furthermore, these policies have been part of the government operations which have resulted in an internal deficit accommodating a high level of inflation … And inflation has encouraged a general feeling that increased import prices can readily be passed on, so that there is no need to search for alternatives to increasingly costly purchases from overseas.

I said a package of measures was needed, where all parts worked together, adding that this was crucial because no government could control all aspects of an economy, and the way people responded to policy measures was more important than the intentions of their designers. 'It is important to get the market signals right. People are more likely to respond to them than to mere rhetoric.'

I then quoted from a National Party election pamphlet titled *It's People that Really Matter*:

> Our democratic system is founded on the principle that individuals have the right to voice their opinions on issues that concern them. These voices must be heard. Equally, individuals have a responsibility to become more involved in the decisions that affect them. Each one of us must be prepared to be accountable for the effects of our actions on our neighbours. The key to further involvement of the individual is knowledge and, the National Party, is committed to keeping New Zealanders both informed and involved.

New Zealanders had a desire to participate: 'to be 'listened to' rather than 'talked at', I concluded.

A chance to debate the freeze

Despite the freeze, by the time of the 1982 budget in early August the deficit was approaching $2 billion, partly due to increased assistance to farmers, family assistance rebates and tax reductions. In theory, these measures had been introduced to honour an election undertaking but in fact they were an attempt to reduce the pressure from the FOL for wage increases. The view of most officials by this stage was that the freeze would increase the deficit and worsen the distortions already adversely affecting the economy.

I believed a long-term freeze could not possibly work in an economy like New Zealand's, which was subject to the vagaries of international trade. Further, I believed that the longer the day of reckoning was postponed, the more difficult and painful the solution would become. One frustrating aspect was that the freeze had been brought into effect by regulation. This meant there had been no way to test its basis or merits other than in caucus where any dissent was slapped down with the retort 'Don't you want to reduce inflation?'

However, in late 1983 the government found it could not regulate skyrocketing mortgage interest rates without the approval of Parliament, because of restrictions imposed by the Economic Stabilisation Act 1948. The purported solution was introduced in Parliament on 17 November 1983 in the form of a Finance Bill, which would enable mortgage rates to be regulated. The Bill was referred to the Public Expenditure Committee for submissions and I was nominated as a member of that committee.

When the Finance Bill was reported back, Dail Jones and I made it clear in caucus that we would vote against the Bill's second reading on the basis that it would interfere with existing contracts. In response to Muldoon's claim that the majority of the public favoured interest rates being forced down, Ruth Richardson argued that the market should decide. Muldoon's response was: 'We can't go through the session next year like this. If this continues on smaller issues, we will have an election before the session next year.'[7]

Hugh Templeton's verbatim caucus record differs from Gustafson's account in *His Way*, which states 'that if defeated on the Bill he [Muldoon] would call an early election'.[8] In caucus Muldoon had not specifically connected an early election to the defeat of this Bill. Again, this is an example of his frequent attempts to rewrite history in his favour.

Before Christmas, in a follow-up to Muldoon's caucus comments and his concerns about caucus disunity, Sue Wood, the new party president, and Barrie Leay, the party's director-general, approached Waring, Minogue, Jones, Richardson and me. We were asked to give an assurance that we would support the government on confidence and supply through to the next election. I was annoyed that my loyalty was questioned in this way, but even so gave the requested undertaking.

However, that was after the Finance Bill. Before the second reading debate, Richardson and I decided to put amendments before Parliament, and obtained private-sector legal advice on their drafting.

During the debate Muldoon criticised his dissenting backbenchers for supporting 'usurious interest rates' and being so ideologically driven by their free-market beliefs that they thought that 'if everything was let go things would be all right. They are wrong,' he said. 'Everything will not be all right. Everything will be all wrong.'[9]

In my response, I began by expressing concern for all those home owners and young farmers who were struggling to pay very high interest rates, and said that in that context I would be dealing with three basic questions about the Bill and the government's draft regulations attached to it. The first was: Will the proposed controls work in a sensible and practical way or is the government's sympathy for the home owner or the young farmer merely words without practical effect? My second question was: Is the proposed remedy consistent with the rights of the individual by preserving the bargain that the borrower and the lender agreed to, or is the state rewriting the contract those two parties entered into? My third question was: Is the proposal consistent with what we in the National Party say we support? I then said that the answer to all three questions would be no.[10]

I gave practical examples showing that some rates would be held up and some would be increased as money flowed from the controlled to the uncontrolled lending sector, reflecting what the Reserve Bank had noted in its paper on the Bill to the Public Expenditure Committee: 'The problems highlighted in the submissions illustrates the extreme difficulty in applying rigid controls over such a vast, fluid structure as the financial system.'

I also quoted the submission from the Law Society: 'The Bill would permit grave interference by regulation with contracts of loan already made and being implemented in good faith.'

On the question 'Is the proposal consistent with what National stands for?' I answered unequivocally 'No', adding:

> Most Government members have a fear of regulation, based not just on a philosophical approach but also on a practical concern that controls beget controls. If one proceeds down that particular path it eventually becomes socialism under another name — and there are already enough socialists in the House. Again, the principle is inconsistent with the freedom of the individual.

I concluded by saying:

> I want to put the record straight, because what is being advocated, as far as the free marketers are concerned . . . it is not an absolute free economy or the law of the jungle, and anyone who says that is the case is little more than a fool. With controls and regulations we need disciplines, standards, and limits on what should be applied in all regulation-making powers. For the reasons I have outlined I do not support the Bill and will be moving a series of comprehensive amendments . . . which provide . . . that the regulations — will not apply to existing mortgages . . . In other words [they] will relate only to new contracts . . . The Bill before the House will not achieve the results that people hope of it, and that is why I oppose it.

Dail Jones, to the surprise of Richardson and me (as we had not discussed our amendments with him), then also spoke against the Finance Bill.

When it came to a vote, the government, with support from Social Credit and two dissident Labour MPs who had failed to get re-endorsement for the next election from their party, won with 43 votes to 40. It was another illustration of the divide between Muldoon and me; and when we both spoke later during the committee stages, the bitterness engendered was clearly evident.

But I was not alone. One of Muldoon's traits was that once he had identified someone as not being on his side — either as a result of perceived disloyalty or because they had advocated views that conflicted with his own — he would invariably seek an opportunity to get his own back. Two examples illustrate this.

The first concerns Brian Talboys, whose acrimonious relationship with Muldoon, particularly in the aftermath of the Colonels' Coup, has been discussed earlier. In 1981 Brian had been awarded the Order of the Companions of Honour by Her Majesty the Queen. The order was instituted by King George V in 1917, and persons eligible as members are those who have 'rendered conspicuous service of national importance', which Talboys clearly had. Membership of the order is limited to 65 although in certain circumstances the statutory quota can be exceeded. In New Zealand, the order is traditionally reserved for prime ministers and long-serving ministers of the Crown. The honour does not confer any title, but ranks immediately after Knights and Dames Grand Cross of the Order of the British Empire. Members may use the letters 'C.H.' after their name.

On numerous occasions after Talboys had left Parliament, caucus members raised the possibility of putting him forward for a knighthood. Muldoon continually rebuffed such suggestions with the retort 'That's not appropriate, he already has a higher award.' Annoyed, and suspecting this was untrue, I approached Philip O'Shea, New Zealand Herald of Arms Extraordinary to Her Majesty and the representative in Wellington of Her Majesty's College of Arms, London, England. O'Shea's written response to me dated 27 October 1983 states, among other things: 'Appointment to the Order does not preclude the conferring of another honour, including a Knighthood.' O'Shea went on to give several examples — Holland, Nash, Holyoake and Marshall — who were all made 'C.H.' before being given a knighthood. Talboys finally received a knighthood in June 1991, long after Muldoon had lost office.

Roderick Deane was chief economist (and later deputy governor) of the Reserve Bank during Muldoon's last few years as prime minister and minister of finance. In the early 1980s Deane had referred a broad range of reforms to Muldoon but had 'made little progress' on them.[11] Muldoon taught Deane a lesson in 1982 when both the bank's governor and deputy governor signalled their intentions to retire from the bank's board. The directors' unanimous decision was to promote 40-year-old Deane as governor. Muldoon would have none of it, and approached deputy governor Dick Wilks to take the top job, telling Deane that he didn't get it because of policy incompatibility.[12]

Deane was offered and accepted the position of deputy governor. The new governor didn't last long — in October 1983 Muldoon told the Secretary of the Treasury he wanted Wilks to retire, so he did. Muldoon again put the knife into Deane by selecting Spencer Russell, an outsider, to be governor. In caucus, when I and others questioned the failure to promote Deane, we were told that had been passed over because he was too young, and an appointment of someone his age would mean he would likely be there too long. No one believed this.

But Muldoon disliked me more than anyone else in caucus. I was accused of staying on in Parliament until '[I] fortuitously qualified for [my] parliamentary pension', and my judgement was publicly questioned for planting grapevines on my North Canterbury farm at a time — so Muldoon said — 'when New Zealand was clearly heading for an oversupply of grapes'.[13]

However, I had the last laugh. When I found out he had had his aortic heart valve replaced in 1989 after a foot injury and subsequent blood poisoning I had considerable sympathy. I had previously had the same operation — but without his complications and near death. My sentiments in a letter to him in the early 1990s wishing him a speedy recovery and ongoing good health were genuine and were occasioned by a photograph on the front page of the *Dominion* of a still clearly unwell Sir Robert — whose knighthood had been conferred in the 1984 New Year's Honours — and Dame Thea outside Parliament before its formal opening after the 1990 election. With my letter I enclosed a bottle of gold-medal chardonnay from my property. His reply is reproduced below.

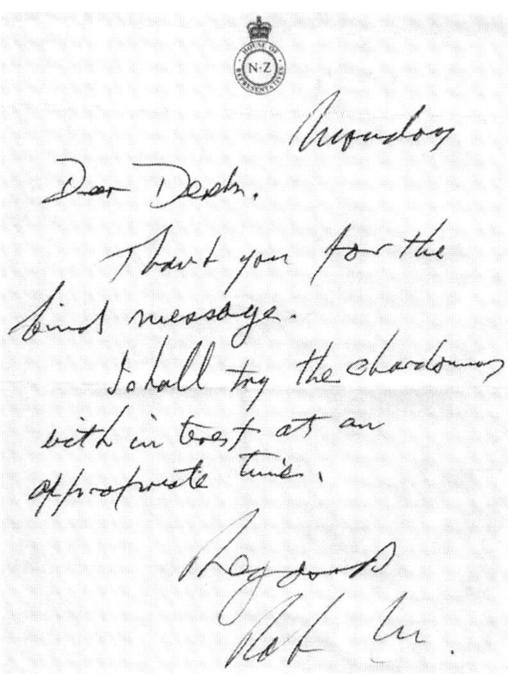
House of Representatives N·Z

Wednesday

Dear Derek,

Thank you for the kind message.

I shall try the chardonnay with interest at an appropriate time.

Regards

Rob M.

Muldoon's reply to mine wishing him good health.

CHAPTER 13

Research and the Bob Jones Party

In an environment of Muldoon's continuing antagonism towards me, my colleagues keeping their heads down and with the media continually hanging on my public utterances looking for evidence of division, it became difficult for me to get my policy messages out there.

Caucus was no longer an appropriate forum, and the debating chamber also created challenges. An effective presentation in the House needs to be free flowing, not a wooden and colourless delivery from speech notes. But there is always a risk with a free-flowing speech — often interrupted by interjections and responses to them — that it provides the opportunity for a word or phrase to be taken out of context and put into a headline by a commentator intent on finding ongoing differences within the government. So I said little in caucus and spoke infrequently in the House. Instead, I progressed my reform agenda either through a former Cabinet colleague — with him presenting the idea as his own — or in the form of well-researched articles, often circulated among all MPs, and offered for publication through key media outlets.

My work on the Cabinet Expenditure Committee on New Zealand's compulsory vehicle Warrant of Fitness (WOF) regime is an example of the first method I employed, with Hugh Templeton in this case picking up and running with what I had initiated and continued to research. My in-depth work on the meat industry illustrates the alternative approach at work.

The meat industry

I had been interested in the meat industry since my time on a Meat and Wool Boards scholarship. I had also been a meat producer, and then a barrister and solicitor advising farming clients. As an MP I was acutely aware of the industry's importance to the New Zealand economy, and also its appalling performance; lack of coordination; and complete absence of short-, medium- and long-term policy. To make matters worse, some senior government ministers seemed intent on legislative changes that would result in even more problems.

The industry was an important foreign exchange earner with, at the time, almost 94 percent of its slaughtered product exported. Processors had been required to spend substantial sums of money in the 1970s to improve their hygiene and inspection regimes as a result of pressure from the US and the European Union. When the government de-licensed the industry in 1981 an influx of new entrants led to an excess in killing capacity, fierce competition for supply at certain times of the year, and financial problems for some operators.

Some officials and politicians believed the solution lay in using the existing provisions of the Meat Export Control Act — which allowed the Meat Producers' Board[1] to control the marketing of all export meat — to establish a single-desk, export-selling regime similar to that run by the supposedly historically successful New Zealand Dairy Board. As a follow-up in 1982, the Meat Producers' Board — on a temporary basis — took over the marketing of all export sheep meat.

Along with a minority of caucus members I was opposed to centralised control *per se*, and so were many farmers, despite the fact that they were receiving substantial taxpayer assistance. This largesse was the result of the introduction in 1978 of a supplementary minimum price (SMP) scheme designed to stabilise farm incomes and provide a buffer against rising inflation. Later, more taxpayer money came from a livestock incentive scheme introduced to encourage increased production.

Two major problems within the meat industry were a lack of cooperation between its various players — producers, processors, exporters, marketers, unions, scientists and industry body representatives — and political interference. At that time the industry was highly seasonal, and producers were and still are fiercely individualistic. This meant they were understandably more interested in the price they received for their product than the wellbeing of the processing sector, which, in any event, they believed was operated at the behest and in the interests of the militant Freezing Workers' Union.

The Meat Producers Board's constituency — as its name suggests — was producers, not other industry players. My view was that this resulted in a threefold problem. First, as constituted, the board functioned on behalf of a narrow range of players in the overall industry, whereas under its statutory mandate and because of the country's reliance on the industry's export earning capacity, its real responsibility and accountability should have been the wider community.

Second, the board tended to think of producers in isolation, instead of recognising them as part of the total food market. And finally, the board's organisational structure was unsuited to modern-day requirements, with its members elected not for the contribution they could make to the efficient operation of the industry as a whole but because they could attract enough votes from an electoral college that itself owed no allegiance to anyone.

So the task I set myself was to devise an industry structure that took account of the roles, responsibilities and accountabilities of each of the players within it.

A key feature of my approach — outlined later in more detail — was to confirm the status of the Meat Producers' Board as a producer body rather than a marketing organisation. I recommended that it should focus on:

- the benefit of the industry to the overall economy,
- the management of export quotas, and
- the allocation of research funding.

Guest of the UK government

Early in 1983 I took up an invitation to spend time in the United Kingdom as a guest of the government, and met there with key politicians and think-tank leaders interested in economic reform and social policy.

Margaret Thatcher, whom I had met in Christchurch and dined with in the company of Barrie Leay in September 1972 before she became the Conservative Party leader in 1975, was prime minister at the time of my visit.[2] The Falklands War was still a recent memory, with New Zealand highly regarded for its contribution to the war effort by making available one of the RNZN's frigates for non-combatant patrol duties. I was still in Cabinet when the frigate decision was made, and was a firm advocate of assisting Britain, saying that our involvement was 'the right thing to do' and, in any event, 'would not harm our trade prospects'.

By 1983, although the Falklands War was over, another conflict — this time a domestic one — was building up in the UK, with the Thatcher government on one side and the militant National Union of Mineworkers, (mis)led by Arthur Scargill, on the other. This 'war' became a symbolic struggle over the issues of parliamentary democracy and the rule of law.

Ian MacGregor, who had previously headed British Steel and had dramatically restructured that industry, had been appointed to head the National Coal Board with a brief to turn the industry from making a loss into making a profit. It was obvious that widespread industrial unrest would follow. The background to what was taking place, and the consequences, formed the basis of several reform-based articles I wrote for publication back in New Zealand.

On the terrace of House of Commons. Left to right: Michael Ryle, Clerk of the Overseas Office, Rt Hon Bryant Godman Irvine MP, Quigley, and James Lamond MP.

At the time of my UK visit, Peter Dailey was the US ambassador to Ireland and he invited us to stay with him and Jackie in the magnificent official residence in Dublin's Phoenix Park. During our time there the Daileys hosted a dinner for me which was attended, among others, by Tony McMullen (president of the Irish Rugby Union), Alan Dukes (the serving Minister of Finance), and Ray MacSharry (a former Fianna Fáil minister of agriculture and finance).

At the time New Zealand's access for lamb into the EEC was a hot political topic. MacSharry told me it was an issue he and I should be able to resolve on a one-to-one basis, but that we couldn't talk about it because of its political sensitivity among his constituents. Unfortunately, MacSharry lost his opposition front bench position shortly after, over a phone-tapping scandal, so the two of us were unable to progress the matter.

While I was London I visited what was left of the Smithfield market, and took various opportunities to carry out research on the New Zealand meat industry from a UK perspective. I had lunch with the Borthwicks board, and talked to various local meat wholesalers and retailers. I was particularly interested in the increasing impact that the UK's EEC membership was having on its own production and on New Zealand's export opportunities.

On the way to the Borthwicks board luncheon in the company's Rolls Royce, I gained an interesting insight into British politics from my chauffeur, once he discovered I was an MP. He said he had been a Labour voter all his life until Labour leader Michael Foot opposed Britain's involvement in the Falklands War 'when our boys were on our ships on the way there', and would be voting Conservative in 1983. I was interested in this because Foot had actually *supported* deploying British forces. But my chauffeur and clearly others like him were sceptical of that support, as Thatcher was re-elected with an extra 58 seats, her party collecting 43.5 percent of the vote in contrast to Labour's 28.3 percent.

At lunch the Borthwicks board chair asked me a question out of left field: 'What should we do about our current investments in New Zealand?' My answer was unequivocal: 'You should sell,' and they did — initially to the Waitaki Meat Company in 1986.

One article I wrote while I was overseas was published in *Straight Furrow*. It began: 'New Zealand is kidding itself if it thinks that it can dictate the price it gets for its lamb on the British market. It has tried that before and failed and the mess that we are in now is largely the result of not learning from past mistakes.'[3]

I went on to discuss what I believed needed to be done to put the meat industry on a sounder footing because of its importance to the overall New Zealand economy. I pointed to the precedents in the UK in restructuring the textile and steel industries, and recommended that a working party be formed to report, as a matter of urgency, on all aspects of the industry. I emphasised that the working party should comprise people who understood and were representative of production, plant operation and ownership, employment, finance, transport, marketing, and taxpayer interests.

When I returned to New Zealand I did more research and circulated a detailed paper in March 1983 discussing what I saw as the two main barriers to better meat industry performance. The first was domination of a fragmented industry by producer representatives. The second barrier was the emphasis on volume production and throughput rather than consumer preference.

The paper concluded that a comprehensive industry review was required, and I suggested that the following terms of reference be considered:

- The nature of the product
- Livestock production trends
- Marketing
- Government/producer board/quasi government involvement
- Fragmentation of ownership
- Human resources
- Capital expenditure
- Financial strength of the industry
- Domestic market

I also included a suggested new industry structure.

On 26 May 1983 the government announced a meat industry taskforce made up of two Meat Producers' Board representatives, two industry representatives and the director-general of the Ministry of Agriculture and Fisheries (MAF) as chair. The brief was:

> to identify any weaknesses in New Zealand's approach to meat marketing and in the light of changing market conditions define the requirements for the industry to develop and operate a global meat marketing strategy

to maximise returns to the nation; and having done this to recommend an appropriate industry structure to achieve these requirements.

The taskforce's key recommendation when it reported was 'that the Meat Board take control of all export lamb and mutton and handle them as a national pool'. This effectively put meat exports on a similar basis to dairy exports, namely monopoly export control in the hands of the Meat Board.

This was approved by the government in late 1983, despite submissions in opposition from groups such as MAF (with input from the agricultural universities, Lincoln and Massey), the Department of Trade and Industry, Wattie Industries Ltd and the Treasury. The Treasury submission of 14 October was particularly scathing:

> Incentives to efficiency are absent from the Task Force's proposals and no case is made — or even argued — that centrally-administrated discipline can effectively substitute. Features such as monopoly control, cost pooling and compulsory schedules of producer prices are not compatible with the objectives of the efficiency throughout the industry and responsiveness to consumer requirements. Of special concern is the proposal for compulsory acquisition [of lamb and mutton exports] as this would permanently sever the link between the producer and the market. Finally, incompleteness of the Task Force's proposals presages both continuing and costly uncertainty in the meat industry and pressures for the government to arbitrate between conflicting interests.

In the face of this widespread opposition, I and like-minded caucus members were keen to know why the government had decided to give the Meat Producers' Board this degree of control. Barry Brook from the Prime Minister's Department provided the answer in a briefing session on 31 October 1983. He confirmed 'that the PM was quite sympathetic to a centralised marketing "solution" and was attracted to pool selling'. Brook further commented 'that the lack of acceptable public alternatives (including [Quigley's] and the Lincoln College suggestions) and the influence of [Fred] Dobbs (a board member and close friend of Muldoon) were the prime factors influencing the PM'.

Although the campaign by those of us opposed to long-term exclusive board control of export marketing eventually prevailed, it was not until after the election of a Labour government in 1984 that marketing responsibility progressively moved from the board to private exporters.

Further policy suggestions

At the National Party annual conference in Dunedin in 1983 I was again given a key speaking role at one of the side meetings. This time I spoke on 'Learning to like new technology'.[4] The thrust of the presentation was that innovation was an area where New Zealand could do much better than it had done during the past 25 years, and that one solution was to give priority to developing human rather than material resources:

> If we place material resources first then the major issues are producing more of them or further processing them . . . However, if we defined resources in human terms, our highest national goals would be the raising of educational standards, improving people's participation in meaningful employment, increasing our emphasis on research and development in traditional and innovative areas, developing our high-technology industries and improving our intellectual capacity.

Straight Furrow reported that my speech 'gave one of the clearest and most comprehensive analyses of the topic yet provided'.

As a backbencher again, I had no access to the departmental and in-house speech writers some ministers relied on, but I still had some good sources elsewhere. For example, for the technology speech, Tony Hall, one of my Rangiora team supporters, had been able to access excellent basic research material from the Auckland head office of whiteware manufacturer Fisher & Paykel, an innovator in its field.

However, I missed the detailed input from officials when I began to prepare a speech for the Dan Watkins Memorial Lecture, to be delivered at AGPOL '83 in Wellington in August.[5] I was to be the keynote speaker (the request was received when I was still a Cabinet minister), and also one of 21 speakers on the general topic of 'The formulation, implementation of and response to agricultural policy'. My contribution was likely to attract a lot of attention so I wanted it to be good.

The topic I chose was 'Objectives of New Zealand agricultural policy'. Had I still been a Cabinet minister, the Treasury would have provided detailed speech notes for final polishing in my office. As it was, I was on my own — or so I thought. I still have a clear recollection of what took place in my cramped 'Siberian' office when I received a visit from three very bright senior Treasury officers: Roger Kerr, Bryce Wilkinson and Paul Bevan. All three would later play a key role in reforming the New Zealand economy.) They handed me a number of books and articles, with Roger Kerr, who acted as their spokesman, telling me that because they were not able to produce speech notes for me, they had highlighted various pieces of research they thought might be helpful. And of course they were.

I began my speech by saying that I had been unable to discover a clearly defined strategy for New Zealand agricultural policy, but instead had unearthed a string of uncoordinated decisions that often appeared to be working one against the other. I had consequently decided to focus on priorities rather than objectives. The main priority, I said, should be to define the respective roles of those associated with the agricultural industry and to remove the constraints that limit their ability to perform to optimum capacity.

I concluded that New Zealand agriculture had an exciting future, but that its full potential would not be realised unless rational priorities were established and implemented. To this end, it was essential that those who made and implemented policy did so in a way that avoided ad hoc and unpredictable decisions.

My full speech, and those of other participants, was published in a post-conference booklet with mine becoming for several years one of the core texts for Massey University students on relevant courses.

The New Zealand Party

From late 1982 National had begun to face a further decline in electoral support following a falling-out between Muldoon and his longstanding friend and supporter Bob Jones — property developer, self-made millionaire and author. Jones strongly opposed the government's interventionist policies, comparing them to what he had recently observed in the Soviet bloc.

He spoke out against the government in a series of newspaper articles, claiming that it had betrayed its principles of individual liberty and free enterprise. Then, on 20 January 1983, he announced that in protest he would stand as an independent at the next general election — against Hugh Templeton in the Ohariu electorate. His campaign would, he said, be 'to counter National's shift to socialism, attempt to turn Muldoon around and ... wake him up'.[6]

Jones' announcement of his candidacy led to a groundswell of support among disaffected National voters fed up with the government's interventionism. A number of people encouraged Jones to go further and start a new political party to split National's vote and bring the government down. The idea took hold and Jones, along with some of his supporters, began to lay the foundations for a new party.

I had got to know Bob Jones quite well during my time in Parliament and had been to his Wellington home on several occasions. His views and mine on economic matters and the role of government were similar, although at that stage we were poles apart on defence policy.

Before the launch of what became the New Zealand Party, Jones rang me and asked if we could meet. He said his wife Jane could pick me up 'travelling incognito', so no one would know we were meeting. I agreed to the meeting, but said not to worry about Jane being disguised. So she picked me up by the main Parliament steps in broad daylight.

Back at the Jones residence, Jane was dismissed after preparing afternoon tea, and Bob and I went through to a room that had sea views and two sets of seats facing each other in front of a fireplace. Bob sat down on a couch and said 'Sit down,' indicating the other couch. I preferred to keep standing by the fireplace. We began to talk and after a few moments he again asked me to sit down. I said thanks, but I was happy standing. By now I could see he was getting twitchy, and he confirmed this when he suddenly burst out: 'For Christ's sake, sit down, you're making me nervous!' This time I obliged.

Bob doesn't like to be reminded of events like this and prefers to relate what happened at a second meeting later in Christchurch. We were sitting across the table from each other and he suddenly said, 'Pass me your glasses.' When I obliged, he retorted, 'Muldoon would never have done that.' Supposedly — in Bob's view — I should have responded with 'Why?' or 'No', or 'Get stuffed.' However, I never wanted to act like Muldoon.

The purpose of the meetings was that Jones wanted me to lead the new party. At the Wellington meeting — after we had been joined by local businessman Trevor Beyer — I was pushed hard to say yes. On that occasion I remained non-committal. At one point Jones accused me of being a mouse and I responded that he should watch out, as I too had boxing experience. However, in Christchurch I delivered a definite no.

I had several reasons. The main one was my early commitment to support National to the next election, which I had previously conveyed to Sue Wood and Barrie Leay. The second reason was that my defection would undoubtedly have precipitated an early election, given the government's slim parliamentary majority. I had no intention of wearing the responsibility for that. Third, I was pretty certain (we were still in an FPP electoral environment) that even a good showing by the New Zealand Party in the election might not result in winning any seats. Rather, it might make it easier for Labour to become the government.

Added to this, I could see that Jones was keen to be the leader himself, and that if he wasn't, he would be extremely difficult to work with. Finally, I wasn't sure at the time that I wanted to continue as an MP, despite having already been confirmed as the National Party's Rangiora candidate.

The New Zealand Party was officially launched on 22 August 1983 with the slogan 'Freedom and Prosperity' and the promise to get rid of the Muldoon government because Jones and other former National Party supporters 'could not stand what was happening any more — retrospective legislation, the abandonment of philosophy, a totally controlled economy, bullying tactics'.[7]

The party's policies differed substantially from those of most of the country's other political parties, with an emphasis on liberalising the economy, ushering in a flat tax regime and adopting open-market principles — most of which I supported. The manifesto contained a number of other significant proposals. One was a large reduction in military expenditure and the abandoning of defence links with Australia and the US (and, in particular, the ANZUS Treaty).

The National Party caucus responded predictably to the new threat. Some claimed that Jones was just rattled by the personal attacks on him by Muldoon and a few others, but in fact it was National that was rattled. The free-market backbenchers in caucus toned down their criticism of Muldoon and his policies, and the government proceeded in bunker mode at a time when its only hope of re-election was decisive action to restructure the economy.

My view has always been that good policies properly sold will always win ahead of political expediency, and that when the electorate is eager for change and knows that it is needed — as was the case in 1984 after years of fortress-type government — it will reward politicians who have the guts to take the hard decisions. This is exactly what happened to the

Lange Labour government three years after winning in 1984, when it was re-elected for a second term in 1987 with an increased majority.

However, with a quiescent caucus as National approached the 1984 election, Muldoon, in Templeton's words, 'was able to delay or abandon the removal of subsidies, the lowering of protection and the introduction of a broad-based and efficient tax system. Our best-laid policies were caught in a web of missed opportunities.'[8]

In March 1984 Duncan MacIntyre stepped down as deputy prime minister for health reasons and announced he wasn't standing for re-election in 1984. Jim McLay was an obvious choice to replace him as deputy. In his roles of attorney-general and minister of justice he had helped Muldoon and his government out of numerous tight political/legal spots. But Muldoon didn't trust him because of his role in the Colonels' Coup, his economic views, and his friendship with me and other reform-minded MPs such as Cox, McLean and Richardson. So Muldoon put up Birch for the position. Bolger was also nominated, but McLay won by four votes on the first ballot, with Birch and Bolger splitting the remaining votes between them.

As an indication of how successfully Muldoon had been in isolating me and my views from the majority of my caucus colleagues, no one suggested nominating me for the position, even though I would not have been interested. This was despite my continuing to poll ahead of all other National MPs (other than Muldoon) as preferred prime minister.

By now the New Zealand Party was making big inroads into National's support base, and also appeared to be pulling people away from Social Credit. Jones' engaging style, his ability to attract media coverage and the party's policies attracted a considerable following, with some polls showing that his party could possibly receive 20 percent of the vote.

However, the party also had its opponents. Muldoon labelling New Zealand Party supporters 'the greedies', pointing to Jones' personal wealth and the fact that much of the party's support came from the wealthier sectors of society. Left-wing groups also attacked it, objecting to its support of free-market economics. Both they and Muldoon claimed that the party was out of touch with ordinary New Zealanders, and that it was merely 'the Bob Jones Party' and not a fully fledged political movement. Jones was frequently criticised for his blunt and 'politically incorrect' style, although clearly some found this refreshing.

CHAPTER 14

The 1984 Election and Labour in Office

I had been exploring job options outside Parliament since late 1983, with one possibility being the Australian pastoral company Elders IXL, headed at that time by the Australian Liberal Party acolyte John Elliott. Elders had a strong Australian rural servicing base, plus interests in breweries and food processing, so I got in touch with the company.

As a result, I was contacted by Peter Shirtcliffe, CEO/managing director of the New Zealand Goodman Fielder group of companies, an extensive supplier of consumer foods in Australia and New Zealand and a group that had business connections with Elders. At our meeting I made it clear that I still hadn't decided to quit politics, but if I did, I was interested in joining an 'Elders-type company'. Peter then asked me to prepare a paper setting out what I would like to do if I were to join Elders or the Goodman Group, and how I thought my presence could add value to either of them. I did so, and at our next meeting we agreed to await my political decision, with both of us assuming we had plenty of time before November — when the election was scheduled.

At that stage only one MP — my caucus colleague Ian McLean — knew that I was contemplating not standing in 1984, and no one in Parliament was aware that I had been approached to lead the New Zealand Party.

In early 1984 some polls were suggesting National might win again, but late in the evening of 14 June 1984 a very drunk Muldoon went on national TV to announce a snap election. By then Labour was at 46 percent in the polls and National was down to 39 percent. Muldoon was somehow still preferred prime minister at 33 percent to David Lange's 18 percent.

The announcement had been preceded by a caucus meeting during the day where Muldoon first announced his plan to call a snap election. Everyone either supported his recommendation or didn't oppose it. However, the decision created a dilemma for me, as I hadn't finally decided whether to stand again or not. Ian McLean was beside me when the meeting concluded and said, 'You'll have to stand now, Quig.' I said I would have to think about it, but probably wouldn't stand.

Ian, whom I respect highly as an individual, an MP and as an economist, shortly afterwards followed up with a four-page handwritten note that began:

> I am taking the unusual step of putting my thoughts on paper in view of the major significance to the Party of your intentions. In my view, your resignation as a candidate could cost us 1 to 2% of the vote at the next election.

He wrote that his conclusion was based not only on my standing in the polls, but more importantly on the reaction he was getting door-knocking throughout his electorate. He thought a substantial number of traditional National Party people were staying with the party because I symbolised their hopes that the Muldoon style would not ultimately prevail. He concluded:

> I have and will respect your confidence without any exceptions. We each have only one life to lead and people of our age with other challenges and opportunities must take them. Whatever you decide, I respect your reasons.

The decision was not an easy one — the election was only a month away. Fortunately, the Rangiora electorate organisation was in excellent shape, under the able leadership of Isla McFadden, my electorate chair, and my personal support was such that I would have won comfortably had I stood again. However, the same could not be guaranteed for any replacement if I stood down. Labour had held the seat for three years from 1972 when Lorrie Pickering pulled out late, and I didn't want to be the cause of that happening again in 1984.

And yet I decided to leave. Two things finally confirmed my course of action. One was that my childhood bouts of rheumatic fever were starting to catch up with me. Increasingly I was having problems breathing if I exercised vigorously, and I knew I was heading for major heart surgery. The other reason was the thought of spending three years (at least) in Opposition. In my view the National caucus was dominated — with several exceptions — by a group of gutless 'born-to-rule politicians' who had lost track of the party's ideals. The party had too often said one thing in Opposition and done the opposite in government. The bottom line was that I was tired of banging my head against a brick wall, so I decided it was time to do something else.

What I hadn't appreciated — and didn't realise until quite some time later — was how much support I did have in caucus from people like McLay, Cox, McLean, Richardson and a few others, 'as a symbol of the sort of policies they would have liked to have pursued', as Jim McLay later put it.[1] There was also wider community support than I appreciated for what I had been advocating.

My first job was to break the news in person to Isla McFadden. She is a brilliant woman and was personally supportive of me, but was also aware of the burden I had just placed on her and her electorate committee. She and I agreed to keep my decision confidential until I had spoken to the party hierarchy and announced it publicly.

I then rang McLay from my electorate and asked him to pass my decision on to Muldoon, along with my unequivocal commitment to support the re-election of the party. Next, I flew up to Wellington where all the party's candidates were attending a candidates' conference. On arrival, I arranged a press conference, announced my decision not to stand and flew back home that evening. Muldoon told the assembled candidates about my decision, but later commented that he thought my not standing would not have much effect on the outcome of the election. Post-election, he told a different story.

The Rangiora selection for 1984

Time was short, and there was a distinct possibility that, unless the right person were chosen, the party would lose Rangiora. My view was that Jim Gerard was the only person who had any chance of holding it. He had earlier been my electorate chairman; had extensive party experience at a local, divisional and national level; and as the son of a former National Party Cabinet minister he had politics in his blood.

I actively supported Gerard as soon as he nominated. This caused some disquiet, particularly in the Oxford area where the branch chairman was an active anti-Quigley Muldoon supporter and Gerard had ruffled some feathers following a marriage break-up. As a result, the local Oxford party branch was supporting Robert Johnson, a well-known and respected local farmer and Wool Board member. Johnson may well have made an excellent MP in other circumstances, but if he had been the candidate this time around, I was certain Labour would win the seat.

In the event, four or five people were cleared by the division for the selection meeting at the local hall just down the road from where I lived. One candidate devoted much of his speech to a bitter criticism of me for my late withdrawal. I would have none of that. Far from apologising, as some thought I might do, I gave a spirited speech while the votes were being counted, emphasising the good shape the electorate organisation was in, and reconfirming my commitment to see that the successful candidate was elected.

Finally, I reminded delegates that if the seat did change hands — as had happened in 1972 and again in 1975 when Labour's well-liked and respected MP lost the seat to me, it would probably be due to a nationwide swing against the party. Fortunately for electorate unity, and for me and my reputation, Gerard was selected on the first ballot. My number one priority from then on until election day was to make sure he was elected.

During my time as an MP we had built up extensive 'street lists', which not only recorded committed National Party supporters, but also those identified as likely to vote for us. Swing voters were also noted. It was the latter two groups I concentrated on during the campaign. Many of them leaned more towards National than Labour but were strongly anti-Muldoon. Most said they supported me and what I stood for, but because I wasn't standing, they would probably vote for the New Zealand Party candidate. To counter this, my pitch — which was sometimes delivered face to face but more often over the phone because of time constraints — was simple, although not always quite this 'bald':

> The National Party and its policies are more important than personalities and that's why I'm campaigning for it. In Rangiora, because of New Zealand's first past the post voting system, the contest is between National and Labour. A vote for the New Zealand Party will only help Labour to win the seat. If you really want Labour to win, don't hide behind a protest vote, have the guts to vote for it directly.

Gerard held the seat for National, with a narrow lead on election night and a final majority of 346. The New Zealand Party candidate got 2631 votes. Gerard stayed in Parliament until 1997 when he became New Zealand's high commissioner in Canada. He was an excellent local MP.

On top of my efforts in Rangiora during the campaign, I visited a number of other electorates at the request of local candidates (Rangitikei, Rotorua, Tauranga, Fendalton and Whangarei). My success rate was six out of six, although National's MP numbers dropped from 47 seats in 1981 to 37.

Muldoon's post-election take on the party's loss — set out in a long critique to the party's dominion councillors — was that it was due to poor advertising and inadequate organisation — from party headquarters through to divisions. He also claimed that his TV addresses had been too informal, that he had failed to convince the public he had 'a real problem with two recalcitrant members' (Waring and Minogue)[2] and that the media were uniformly hostile. In a complete about-face he also wrote: 'The resignation of Mr Quigley, who was also well aware [like Minogue] that he had qualified for parliamentary superannuation, was another major blow which set us back substantially right from the beginning of the campaign.'[3]

Voter reaction to my resignation would have been much worse for the party had I not vigorously supported both it and the leader during the campaign. I received numerous letters commending my efforts. A typical one was from Muldoon's close friend Harry Julian, who wrote: 'I am particularly pleased at the public support you are giving the Prime Minister and the Party at a time when I know you must have many mixed feelings.'

The reality was that I suppressed my personal feelings during the campaign, working as hard as I could to see that National held Rangiora, and supporting other party candidates where I could, despite personal reservations about some of them. In Gerard's case my 100 percent commitment to his election was in repayment of the support he had given me through some difficult times, and because he was, in my view, the only person who could hold the seat.

Philip Burdon — who had become the MP for Fendalton in 1981 following Eric Holland's retirement — was another local candidate I supported during the campaign. This was despite his lack of support for me after my resignation from the Cabinet. Philip was an enigma as a parliamentarian. Despite being successful in business, he was a reluctant supporter of much-needed reform in the sector. Instead, he became a self-styled 'enlightened pragmatist' who was continually testing the political wind. He later claimed that one of his major successes was to defeat the so-called 'scorched earth' policies advocated by Ruth Richardson during her time as minister of finance.[4] Philip also clearly harboured leadership ambitions, and once famously asked Lesley Miller (one of Muldoon's press secretaries who had earlier stood for the party in Taupo) 'Do you think I have charisma, Lesley?' Her reply was: 'Philip, if you had charisma you wouldn't need to ask.'

As I predicted, the New Zealand Party won no seats (under the FPP voting system), despite capturing 12.2 percent of the overall vote. It came second in several electorates, and Bob Jones himself came third in Ohariu with a credible 29 percent of the vote, allowing Labour to win the seat. NZP's votes came from both National and Social Credit, with the result that the Lange Labour government was comfortably elected. National won 37 seats to Labour's 56.

Having achieved his objective of getting rid of Muldoon, Jones unilaterally announced that the New Zealand Party was going into recess. In 1986, with its policy platform largely implemented by the Labour government, the party opted to 'merge' into the National Party in an attempt to keep its free-enterprise and libertarian philosophy alive.

National outlives its welcome

By the time of the 1984 election the National Party had been on the Treasury benches almost continuously since 1949, apart from 1957–60 and 1972–75. Muldoon's influence on the New Zealand political and economic scene had been felt for 24 years, from soon after his election as an MP in 1960. It had accelerated in 1967 when he became minister of finance, and had continued unabated thereafter.

Although New Zealand had suffered a number of external shocks during that time, including Britain joining the EEC in 1973,[5] two massive oil price hikes, a 30 percent decline in the country's terms of trade and the dumping of subsidised primary products on its export markets, most of the country's economic problems were self-inflicted.

Inflation through most of the 1970s and 1980s was rampant, at a rate 50 percent higher than the OECD average. The 1970s also saw further welfarism and state intervention with the introduction of the world's first no-fault, universal accident compensation scheme; new legislation designed to settle Māori land claims; an overly generous universal taxpayer-funded superannuation scheme; and 'social welfare' for sheep farmers in the form of SMPs to compensate them for falling meat and wool returns. The SMP scheme resulted in many recipients getting more money from the government than they earned from their farms. Also, before the 1981 general election a massive energy self-sufficiency programme, 'Think Big', had been initiated, largely funded by the taxpayer.

Not surprisingly, these actions led to increasing government deficits, a sharp acceleration in public-sector borrowing, tax increases, rising unemployment and successive credit rating downgrades.

The extent of New Zealand's economic decline from the heady heights of the 1950s was dramatic. From the 1960s to the early 1980s per capita income growth averaged a mere 1.4 percent a year compared with the OECD average of 2.9 percent, with middle income earners bearing the brunt of this deterioration. In the 30 years to the early 1990s the government's tax take increased by 190 percent in real terms, or by 106 percent per capita if population growth is taken into account.[6] By comparison, the gross wage of the average one-income family went up by only 20 percent, with take-home pay declining because of tax increases.

Productivity also declined dramatically, with probably the biggest fall in the public sector, which by the mid-1980s accounted for 24 percent of all activity and consumed 29 percent of all investments, excluding income transfers from one part of the community to another. Government trading entities alone were responsible for 12 percent of GDP, but cumulatively produced a nil profit. Some, such as the New Zealand Forest Service, never got into the black in 70 years of existence.

But New Zealand's decline in performance was not just the result of excessive government involvement in the economy. Two other factors played a role. First, the *quality* of its involvement was suspect. Second, particularly from 1977 onwards, Muldoon's stop/go style of economic management — coupled with a refusal to embrace change at a time when change was essential — led to years of poor relative economic performance.[7]

Even so, Muldoon was not wholly to blame. Although a substantial number of National MPs were well aware of the need for reform, others saw National's continuation in office as their prime objective. This idea was continually reinforced by Muldoon's comments about the hopelessness of previous Labour governments as economic managers, and reminders that you can't do anything in Opposition. As a result, some MPs were convinced that they had to stay in office for the good of the country, come what may. But in reality, by 1984 National had been in government too long. It was arrogant, tired, out of touch, riven by internal conflict and reluctant to move against the myriad special-interest groups it had created.

Yet, even when it became clear on election night that Labour had won a resounding victory, Muldoon didn't go easily. When he rang Lange at the Auckland Metro Theatre to congratulate him, he added, 'I've got some bad news for you tomorrow.' Before Lange could reply, Muldoon hung up.[8] What followed was a temporary constitutional crisis of Muldoon's making, which his deputy McLay and a handful of senior ministers were forced to resolve.

The crisis was ostensibly over whether or not the defeated caretaker government was required, in the 12-day interregnum, to follow the established convention of acting on the advice of the incoming government. Muldoon didn't care about convention; he was more interested in having the final say.

The background to the crisis, its extent and how it was resolved are discussed in detail in the Bassett book on Roderick Deane's *Life & Times*.[9] Essentially, Labour was widely expected to devalue the currency on becoming government, but Muldoon in his caretaker role refused to do so, despite being advised to devalue by the Treasury. Immediately Labour won, there was a run on the dollar, causing the Reserve Bank to briefly close the foreign exchange markets, but not before millions of foreign exchange dollars had left the country through the actions of currency speculators.

His actions — as far as I and many others were concerned — were the last straw, and ended any vestige of respect I had for him, leaving aside his considerable personal attributes. To paraphrase Hugh Templeton, in defeat Muldoon tried to drag down the temple. He had told Cabinet there was no need to devalue and that was what he would advise David Lange. But he did not explain that he would *refuse* to devalue, even if that was the will of the incoming government.[10]

When Lange and his finance team — led by Roger Douglas — were fully briefed by officials they accepted that a 20 percent devaluation was needed.[11] Muldoon was instructed to implement this, but that evening he stated on television that he wouldn't be obeying Lange's instructions. However, following pressure from his Cabinet colleagues, Muldoon eventually regained his 'constitutional poise' and in typical style at an emergency Cabinet meeting on 17 July implied that he had made the decision himself, telling ministers he was ready to devalue.[12]

Overseas borrowing to finance the dollar outflow amounted to $1.7 billion and forward exchange contracts totalling $1.2 billion were signed by the Reserve Bank. The taxpayer ultimately footed most of the bill for the benefits obtained by those purchasing the forward exchange.[13]

Muldoon's economic policies, and years of refusing to heed advice, had finally caught up with him.

Reforming the economy

With this rocky start, an immediate concern for the Lange government after being sworn in was dealing with an economic crisis that was so serious that the country was on the verge of defaulting on its international obligations.

Given the extent of the problem, Labour's Cabinet opted for radical action, introducing a series of sweeping reforms that affected most sectors of the economy. The New Zealand dollar was floated, interest rate controls were removed, producer subsidies were cancelled, taxpayer support was withdrawn from a host of special-interest groups such as the farming sector. Eventually many government enterprises were sold, and major changes were introduced to public-sector management and accountability.

I was highly supportive of what the government was doing, because, in the words of historian Michael King, '[the] economic controls were also shed in an enactment of the kinds of policies that Quigley had been trying to sell to his National colleagues'.[14]

The New Zealand electorate had endured nine years of authoritarian government and was ready for change. This view was reinforced by a well-run and well-publicised post-election economic summit on the state of the nation that brought together representatives from all sectors of the economy. Then, in a first for New Zealand, all the departmental briefing papers for the incoming government, including a full range of Treasury reports showing the country's parlous financial state, were released to the public.

Labour had been in Opposition for a long time and was hungry not only for office but also to improve the nature of New Zealand society. Its senior ministers, particularly those in sympathy with the views of Finance Minister Roger Douglas were imbued with a reforming zeal based on years of thinking about the issues but with little previous opportunity to implement their ideas.

Unsurprisingly, not everyone within the government caucus and the party's senior echelons favoured the 'right-wing' economic line the government was adopting. Yet many who would otherwise have been vehement critics of the speed and direction of change, as well as its impact on New Zealand society, were diverted by a war of words that developed between the Labour government and the US administration over proposed visits by American nuclear ships.

Often overlooked is the part that senior officials in the Treasury and the Reserve Bank played in the reform process. Both entities had been in the wilderness for at least the last two years of the National government's term when Muldoon refused to heed their advice on how to reverse the country's declining economic circumstances. But reform-minded individuals such as Roger Kerr, Graham Scott, Bryce Wilkinson and Rob Cameron with crucial input from Roderick Deane in the Reserve Bank — had been using this time well. They had gone back to a theoretical framework for reform and had identified six major elements of economic and management theory that they believed would help New Zealand's recovery.

The six elements were agency, public choice, contracting, finance, accounting and management. As a result of this work, officials were able to articulate the policy implications of the various theories at appropriate times during the course of the government's reform programme. This was particularly noticeable in the public sector, which by this time was too big and therefore too important to be allowed to continue to hold back the rest of the reforming programme.

One aspect of the reform process was of particular interest to me and accorded with my own approach to problem solving. Although economic theory was important, the underlying basis for reform was not driven by ideology or by some simple process or model to resolve management functions or to separate out different roles. Rather, it was based on in-depth thought about institutional settings and how these shape and motivate decisions. The fundamental objective of the reforms was to raise the quality of decision-making at all levels of the economy by subjecting decision-makers to competition without undue government interference. And, by and large, it worked.[15]

The reform process was helped by the fact that Labour's key Cabinet ministers represented the generation born after World War II, who viewed New Zealand in less insular terms than their predecessors. They took the view that the ideas, productive energies and confidence needed for New Zealand to make its way in the world and to overcome its problems would only emerge by exposing all sectors of the economy to the forces of competition. The focus was therefore on creating appropriate incentives and conditions to encourage these ideas to flourish throughout the whole community.

The state sector, with its traditional focus on resource distribution, regulation and control, was still seen to be lacking transparency in its processes and activities. This was despite the positive impact of the 1982 Official Information Act, which 'had completely changed — for the better — the manner in which [senior officials] advised Ministers'.[16]

The public service was New Zealand's largest employer, with more than 20 percent of the total labour force either directly or indirectly on the state's payroll.[17] The government's view was that rather than being a tool for reform, the sector was a major part of the problem. Ministers consequently decided that it too should be exposed to the same market rigours that had been applied to farming, manufacturing and other businesses. Virtually all the state's activities were to become open and competitive, 'in the belief that this transparency would eliminate unnecessary functions and inefficient processes and clarify accountability'.[18]

This led to the adoption of a set of organising principles that underpinned the reform process within the state sector, namely:

- That the state should not be involved in activities which could be performed more efficiently and effectively by the wider community or by private businesses.
- That state trading enterprises were likely to function most efficiently and effectively if they were structured along private-sector business lines.
- That departments would operate most efficiently and effectively if their functions were non-conflicting and clearly specified. This led to the functional separation of policy from operations, and commercial activities from non-commercial activities.
- That the managers of departments would perform most effectively if fully accountable for the efficient running of their organisations, with the minimum practicable degree of central control of inputs.

- That, as far as practical, the cost of state activities should be based on market factors so that the quality, quantity and cost of products should be determined by the requirements of purchasers rather than the preferences of producers.

Three crucial pieces of legislation reflected these principles. The first was the State Owned Enterprises Act 1986, which came into force on 1 April 1987. Its basis was the conversion of former state trading departments and corporations into businesses along private-sector lines. Many SOEs were later sold off, with the state withdrawing almost entirely from direct involvement in trading enterprises.

The second piece of legislation was the State Sector Act 1988, which created a department known as the State Services Commission, with a State Services Commissioner and deputy commissioner. Where the role of the earlier much smaller Public Service Commission had been employer and manager of the public service, it was changed to employer of chief executives, and adviser to the government on the management of the state sector.

The State Sector Act 1988 also made chief executives in the core state sector fully accountable to their responsible ministers for managing their organisations efficiently and effectively. This resulted in CEOs being placed on formal performance-related, limited-term contracts. The act ended 75 years of centralised control of the public service in New Zealand.

The third piece of legislation was the Public Finance Act 1989, which changed the basis of state-sector financial management from a focus on the cost of production (inputs) to a focus on the relevance and effectiveness of outputs, and the overall results of these outputs from the government's perspective.

A series of financial management and accounting reforms followed, designed to introduce within the state sector as many of the disciplines of the commercial operating environment as practical. In particular, ministers were required to formally purchase the outputs of departments at specified standards of quality, quantity, timelessness and cost, through accrual accounting and capital charging. The apex of these financial and accounting reforms was the production of a rational set of national accounts that, at the time of introduction, was thought to be unique internationally.[19]

CHAPTER 15

Life after Parliament

When I left Parliament I was 52 and we were living on a farm I had bought two or three years earlier. My original Glenmark Drive farm — which I had sold when I bought the new one — was excellent sheep country but, like many others in the area, lacked sufficient rainfall, creek flows and water storage potential to offer many diversification opportunities. A group of locals — led by innovator Ted Whyte, who had already started growing roses and other flowers on his farm on a commercial basis — put together a proposal that received a government subsidy for the Glenmark Irrigation Scheme. Its basis was the construction of large 'turkey nest dams' on individual properties to be filled with surplus winter water drawn (where available) from a nearby stream or from paddock run-off.

My original farm and the new one were both within the scheme's boundary and had been approved for inclusion by the government without my input or involvement. When I was in Cabinet and it became clear that the project was hopelessly uneconomic, I was careful to disclose my interest and took no part in any discussions or the eventual decision to stop any further taxpayer input.

The new farm I bought was bigger, had good creek water access, and consequently irrigation potential. It therefore provided more diversification opportunities. I approached three neighbouring owners about the possibility of planting grapevines on a commercial basis on our individual properties. The area we were all in had a northerly-orientated microclimate that I thought might be ideal for grapes.

The others were interested, and to make sure we were properly informed I sought advice from the vineyard manager at Penfold's in Auckland and Allan Scott, who had successfully planted vines in the Blenheim area. Their initial responses were that our general location would be suitable for grapes, but they would need to look at specific farm sites and soil profiles before expressing a final opinion. The two visited independently, and in preparation for their arrival, a series of 2-metre-deep holes were dug on each farm.

In my case, the profile of the flat land near the Main North Road frontage showed thick, black marbled topsoil over reasonably porous clay and limestone. The paddocks away from the road had a thicker clay subsoil, but one area — which sloped gently towards the northwest — attracted particular comment. Both visitors said the site could produce the best cabinet sauvignon in New Zealand. In the end, for convenience and ease of access, we planted the first vines in the flat paddocks near the highway.

The varieties to be planted, and their locations on each of the four farms, were based on the advice we received. Each property initially had about 4 hectares of vines. We had contemplated that one property would have an 'entity' winery and that the overall concept would be managed communally, but the winery proposal was dropped because of financial constraints. Planting got under way, with gewürztraminer the main variety planted on my place.

The vines established quickly and a first light harvest was handpicked. The following year, when the overall crop looked likely to be sufficiently heavy, the entity paid a deposit on a second-hand automatic harvester, with the balance to be paid nearer harvest time.

However, a late frost caught most of the flowering vines, which meant we could not afford the harvester. The solution unexpectedly came from the Lange government, which, while cutting spending in most other sectors of the economy, announced a vine 'grubbing grant' aimed at encouraging vineyards to pull out less popular grape varieties and think about replacing them with more popular strains.

As gewürztraminer was one of the less popular varieties, I offered to pull mine out, hand over the grant to the entity and have it replant my area with better varieties. The harvester was delivered, but very little entity replanting took place initially as farming in general came under financial pressure due to the Lange government's overall spending cuts. The result was that the entity concept lapsed, as each individual participant dealt with its own business concerns.

Over time, grape growing has been an outstanding success in and around Waipara. The location has long, dry summers, ample sunshine and benefits from the shelter of a range of coastal hills. The diversity of soil types and resulting wines are a feature of the area, including pinot noir, riesling, chardonnay, sauvignon blanc, pinot gris and merlot. Pinot noir in particular is showing huge potential and expanded production is planned, with less reliance on grapes shipped down from Marlborough to be processed in local wineries.

Becoming a consultant

I needed to augment my annual parliamentary pension of $6895.16 — the question was how? Before I got very far I had to deal with my developing heart problem, and arranged an in-house procedure at Christchurch's Princess Margaret Hospital. After it was over the senior theatre nurse asked for my thoughts. I said, 'It looks as though I will have to have a heart operation,' to which she retorted, 'I could have told you that before we started!' But as the advice from the specialist was that surgery was not particularly urgent, I went back to focusing on my employment options.

I couldn't imagine becoming a full-time farmer again, and although law was a possibility, I had sold my share in Bell Taylor when I became a Cabinet minister. Another option was to accept an offer to become a District Court judge, but neither that nor practising law again appealed to me. I talked to Susan Lojkine, my hard-headed accountant, who had earlier advised me to resign from Bell Taylor because, even although I wasn't drawing any profits from the firm, I was still potentially jointly and severally liable for any claims against it, no matter how unlikely.

Her suggestion was that I should consider consultancy, and she strongly advised me to locate my business in either Wellington or Auckland, where there were likely to be more opportunities than in Christchurch. This advice made sense so I returned to Wellington to look for office accommodation to establish my consulting company Quigley & Associates Ltd, and to sift through several approaches I had already received. Around the same time, I sadly separated from my wife Judith.

One of the people I made contact with was Ralph Pyatt, a Deloitte partner and younger brother of Christchurch's Anglican bishop Allan Pyatt, whom I had met and whose judgement I respected. He knew the Wellington scene well. He responded with a generous offer. Deloitte, he said, had a spare office and I could locate there, rent free initially, if that suited me. I accepted and went back to Peter Shirtcliffe to talk further about Elders and the Goodman Group.

Immediately after deciding not to stand for re-election I had also met with one of the other Goodman directors, resulting in the offer of a full-time job with Elders, based in Wellington. I declined because I had decided I wanted a 'bread and butter' job that would pay basic living expenses but still allow time for me to get involved in other interesting areas. I received a good number of offers, including board positions and other part-time roles, one of which arose from my contact with Elders and Shirtcliffe, which I accepted. It was a position on the Goodman Fielder Cereal Foods Board; and later, when the Lange government opened up banking licences in New Zealand, I became a director on the Elders Bank Board.

Cereal Foods was a particularly interesting company, with its main products involving flour mills, pasta products and related consumer goods. Its CEO at the time was Peter Allport, who eventually became an extremely successful and sought-after professional company director.

Elders' banking foray into New Zealand was a disaster and only lasted a few months. Its strategic decisions were driven from Melbourne, and instead of concentrating in the first instance on the New Zealand rural sector, it tried to compete head on with the established large banks. This was a mistake, particularly as it would have had an opportunity, later, to buy the Rural Bank when the government sold it off. The New Zealand board members were paid our director's fee for a full year, yet attended only about three meetings.

Another approach I received was to join the board of a small, new, publicly listed Auckland-based merchant banking company named Qtron. It was the brainchild of two local stockbrokers and the owner of Walker & Hall. The company was an innovator in its field and if I joined its board, its meeting would provide regular trips to Auckland and contacts in that city.

Around the same time financier Frank Renouf approached me to join the board of Renouf Corporation, New Zealand's first established merchant bank. Renouf was a flamboyant and controversial Wellington businessman. I had first met him in my capacity as minister of tourism at a function he hosted at his Wellington residence for two unrelated Singaporean gentlemen named Ho.

The Hos were interested in buying hotels in New Zealand, but 'only if New Zealand was willing to have them'. I thought this a strange basis for an investment decision but could see the tourism potential and urged them to proceed. Their application (in which I played no part) was successful, but their investment in what started off as the Kingsgate Chain made — I suspect — little money either for them or for their business interests.

Renouf had apparently followed my progress as an MP, and when he approached me to join the corporation's board he asked, 'Who did you study to develop your monetarist theories?' I didn't like to say no one, although I had followed the writings of Ayn Rand and Milton Friedman. I said my views were not based on any particular theory but had been built up over time from watching what worked and what didn't.

Faced with competing offers now from Auckland and Wellington, I again talked to Susan Lojkine. Her oral advice was to take the Renouf offer on the basis that 'although you might finish up in prison, it will be a lot of fun'. But I joined the Auckland board instead, and avoided any chance of a jail term when many in the New Zealand business community lost a lot of money during the 1987 sharemarket crash.

One position I sought but didn't get was membership of the Meat Producers' Board. Aubrey Begg, elected the Labour MP for Awarua in the Kirk landslide win of 1972 and in the mid-1980s a member of the electoral committee that selected Meat and Wool Board members, had followed my views on the restructuring of the industry and approached me to stand for election. There were three nominations for two board positions, with one person a shoe-in for one slot, and a contest between me and John Acland for the other.

Acland was a respected South Canterbury farmer and son of the late Sir Jack Acland, a former Meat Producers' Board chairman and one of the numerous people I had sought advice from when I was preparing for selection for my scholarship to the UK in the early 1950s. John was well known by the 25 farmer members of the electoral committee, and had personally visited them all to press his credentials. In contrast, I was too busy with my other work to travel the length and breadth of New Zealand, but did phone some members. I was consequently regarded by most of the selection panel as 'a non-contender'.

In my speech on selection day I outlined my views on the industry and said I thought the board was too heavily orientated towards the interests of producers, and that the board and the industry as a whole would benefit from a wider membership. These comments were well received by some but were too radical for others. As a result, although I tied with Acland on the first ballot, I lost on the second. John Acland later became a very successful board chair.

Hugo Consulting Ltd

The 'bread and butter' opportunity came out of the blue when I was invited to lunch with the managing director of a company I had never heard of, Hugo Consulting. Hugo had four directors: Sir Frank Holmes and Len Bayliss (both of whom I knew well), Geoffrey Datson (a former Trade & Industry deputy secretary) and Geoffrey Goodwin (an Englishman who ran the company but wanted to spend more time in the UK). I was asked if I would take over Goodwin's job of running Hugo.

All four Hugo directors worked on the company's business part time, providing strategic advice and insight to a number of New Zealand's leading businesses. The emphasis was on the international and domestic economies, industrial relations, political trends and government policy, particularly as it affected business. Advice was conveyed via seminars in Auckland and Wellington, and to individual businesses by arrangement. Several senior politicians were regular seminar contributors, as were experts in specialist fields such as industrial relations. One contributor in the latter field was Alf Kirk, an economist and accountant/auditor with a trade union background, who at the time was working part time in the Beehive as a member of Prime Minister Lange's advisory group.

Kirk was a brilliant operator and was full of fun. As a committed socialist, he had some reservations about the ethics of being involved in the corporate world, but had agreed to become a Hugo director at the same time I said I would join. When Alf's appointment was announced publicly, Leader of the Opposition Jim Bolger denounced it, claiming that Kirk was selling information he had picked up as a member of the Prime Minister's Department to the business community and should resign from Hugo.

Alf was incredulous, as he had previously worked closely with Bolger when the latter was minister of labour and was distraught that his personal integrity had been questioned so publicly. He told me he was resigning as a Hugo director and would be taking no further part in its activities. Rather forcefully, I told him that Bolger was only point-scoring and that if he resigned it would give credence to Bolger's claim. He needed to stop being a wimp, I said, and to turn up at the next morning's meeting as usual at 8am. He did. Alf stayed on as a Hugo director, and eventually joined the Quigley & Associates team.

Open heart surgery

The fact that my breathing problems had got worse was brought home to me after a dinner at the Pyatt residence. Next morning, Ralph came to my office and said that his wife — who was a senior cardiology theatre nurse — had been extremely concerned about my state of health and wanted me to see a specialist urgently, which I did. A series of tests confirmed that my aortic heart valve needed replacing urgently.

Before the operation was performed — in Wellington's Calvary Hospital by Australian-born cardiothoracic surgeon Allan Hilless — we discussed in detail the procedure, the associated risks, and the different types of valve replacement I could have. My own research had established that the surgery mortality rate for a person of my age was about 2 percent, with the additional possibility of a stroke during the procedure.

The valve options were either a mechanical one or a bio-prosthetic one from a pig, with advantages and disadvantages for both. The mechanical valve was said to be more durable, with some still functioning nearly 40 years after being implanted. In contrast, a pig valve had an estimated life of 10–15 years, and would therefore probably need to be replaced, with a potential reoperation mortality rate of up to 14 percent, depending on the recipient's age and overall health. But the pig valve — unlike the mechanical valve — would require no ongoing medication, so I chose it, in the hope that surgical procedures might improve and mortality rates decline over time.

Within days of my scheduled operation I had some unexpected luck. Staff at the local blood plasma supply facility gave notice that they intended to strike at the time of my operation. As a result it was decided to draw off a quantity of my own blood ahead of time for use during my procedure. In retrospect this turned out to be a good decision, as normal blood donors were not screened at that time for the hepatitis C virus which can result in cirrhosis, liver failure and a form of carcinoma.[1]

In hospital the afternoon before my operation, numerous further tests and X-rays showed substantial potential damage to the heart wall.

Tree trimming in 1986 shortly after first heart operation.

In the early evening there was a knock on the door and the hospital accountant appeared. 'We forgot to get some money from you when you booked in. Could we have $5000 please?' I handed over my credit card. Like me, he was obviously aware of the mortality statistics associated with my surgery!

When I came to after the operation, the first thing that went through my mind was: I'm still alive! The second was that I needed more air, and I asked for a window to be opened. At that stage I couldn't see all the tubes attached to me. One of my early visitors said, 'Together with all the blood it was a pretty scary sight.'

The nurses were brilliant. One in particular was a mind-reader — I only had to think about wanting something and she would be there attending to it. I wasn't quite so happy with the physiotherapist whose job it was to check that no fluid built up in my lungs. Standing behind me with her arms tight around my chest, she instructed me to cough deeply.

This wasn't great fun given that my sternum was now held together by pieces of wire and was doing its best to heal.

Within days of the operation an X-ray showed that my heart was now back to normal size. Amazingly, that initial 1986 valve only began to deteriorate in late 2015 after 29 years, and was replaced in January 2016 by a trans-aortic valve implant. The surgery was at 10am, I was up and walking about that afternoon, and was discharged home the following day. To celebrate, my partner and I walked to our local pub the next evening for a stiff scotch in my case and a gin in hers. This time around, my recovery time was also dramatically less, even though I was 84.

More job offers

Among the other job offers I received after the 1984 election was one from Government Life to front a TV promotional campaign. I thought about it, and a week or so later phoned the person who had approached me and said, 'Thank you, but no, I'm not interested.' He told me that in any event Mike Moore, the minister in charge of Government Life, had put my proposed involvement to Cabinet, which had declined it. I then asked, as an aside, how much they had been prepared to pay for my involvement. The answer was $150,000 — a very large sum in those days. The Labour Cabinet obviously thought I might be looking to make a political comeback and were not prepared to give me free TV time.

I did accept an offer to join the New Zealand board of Colonial Mutual Life, which was chaired by Noel Lough, former head of the Treasury, whose economic views were similar to mine. The CML advertising team also approached me to front an advertising campaign for their entity. Again I turned it down, despite staff claims — much to my amusement — that at that time I had 'film star status' because of my continuing public profile and support in the preferred prime minister polls.

The CML board position was interesting, and added to the knowledge I had picked up as minister in charge of State Insurance and Government Life. It also provided contact with top-rate directors and, through them, access to consulting opportunities. One of my fellow directors was Roy Mason, who had been appointed chair of Telecom when it was split off from the Post Office conglomerate. For months, Mason and his board had been in protracted negotiations with the government over the transfer value of Telecom's assets, and had belatedly begun to worry about the possibility of the industry being deregulated and how this might affect their status as an SOE. Mason's question to me was, 'Is that something your consultancy company can advise us on?' I replied, 'Yes, of course.'

By 1987 I had formed another consulting company, Strategos Consulting Ltd, in which Quigley & Associates held a 50 percent shareholding. The other two shareholders, Alf Kirk and Rob Campbell, each received a 25 percent holding at no cost. Campbell — like Kirk — was an economist who was publicly regarded as a leftie and Labour supporter. The Telecom contract became Strategos' first assignment, with most work on it done by Campbell, with some input from me.

Following a trip to Australia to examine industry deregulation there, we reported to Mason that deregulation was inevitable, and that it was likely to be progressed very quickly. His board had three options, we said. They were to oppose deregulation, to support it and engage with the government on how to implement it, or to sit back and do nothing. Our recommendation was for the board to proceed with the second option, which it did when the decision to deregulate was announced shortly after.

In late 1987, when Strategos was starting to pick up a number of additional consulting jobs, out of the blue I received a call from Bob Tizard, the minister of defence, asking if I would chair a defence review. I said yes. When we met he told me Defence had initially been exempt from the government's early reforms for three reasons. First, because the initial focus of state-sector reform had been on trading entities rather than the core public-service departments. Second, because of the anti-nuclear stand-off with the US and its flow-on effects. And finally, because Defence's legislative basis meant that the strict application of the government's standard state-sector reform model was deemed inappropriate. But the government now had Defence in its sights, Tizard said.

CHAPTER 16

The Background to Labour's Anti-nuclear Policy

Prior to the start of Strategos' defence review,[1] the Lange government had passed the New Zealand Nuclear Free Zone, Disarmament and Arms Control Act 1987. This followed the government's refusal in February 1985 to accept a port visit by the USS *Buchanan*. But that had not been the first time there was international controversy over US ship visits.

After World War II the US, France and the UK frequently tested nuclear weapons in the Pacific region, but France in particular attracted huge criticism when, after beginning tests in French Polynesia, it — along with some other countries — refused in 1963 to join Britain, the US and the Soviet Union in banning atmospheric testing. New Zealand had consistently protested against testing in the Pacific, and when Moruroa Atoll became the focus of French tests, the government and Greenpeace stepped up their opposition, with a Greenpeace vessel sailing into the test zone in 1972.

The 1972 Labour government of Norman Kirk adopted a more vigorous foreign policy than earlier National governments. Kirk's attitude was that foreign policy should express New Zealand's national ideals as well as its national interests, and the government applied increased pressure on France to stop tests in the Pacific.

In 1973 New Zealand and Australia took France to the International Court of Justice. When this failed, New Zealand sent a frigate to the test area, with the Opposition National Party declining the invitation to send a representative on the protest voyage. National's leader, Jack Marshall, claimed that the dispatch of the frigate was irresponsible, and that this 'futile and empty gesture' would only inflame the situation.[2] He would rather take France back to the International Court, he said.

However, public criticism and New Zealand and Australian protest actions must have had some effect because Valéry Giscard d'Estaing, who was elected French president in 1974, ordered testing to be moved underground.

But with tests still continuing, Moruroa remained a focus for protesters. At the UN New Zealand proposed a nuclear-weapons-free zone in the Pacific, condemned all French tests there and demanded their cessation. The UN General Assembly duly passed Resolution 3477 in December 1975, seeking to make the Pacific nuclear free.

Foreign policy under the Kirk government was also more activist than it had been for many years, signalling an increasing divide between National and Labour on a number of foreign policy issues. Things came to a head in 1985 when the Lange government's anti-nuclearism clashed head on with New Zealand's membership of ANZUS, which involved implicit acceptance of the protection of the US nuclear umbrella. Nuclear weapons were increasingly deployed by the US on its growing fleet of nuclear-powered vessels, and the US military wanted these vessels to visit treaty partners' ports from time to time.

Earlier safety concerns

The first New Zealand ban on nuclear-powered ship visits was in fact imposed by the Holyoake National government in 1971, and was followed by the Australian government in 1972. The reason was concern about liability in the event of a nuclear reactor accident on board.

This had been a growing concern, with a number of overseas ports refusing entry to US nuclear-powered warships. Since 1957 there had been a strict liability provision within the US for civil (on-shore) reactors but this did not apply to reactors on board ships. In 1962 the US and UK governments reached agreement on the liability issue, which allowed the nuclear-powered merchant vessel *Savannah* to birth at Southampton on her maiden voyage.

By then, several European countries had drawn up international agreements for civil nuclear reactors, and the 1962 Brussels Convention sought to establish that, in the case of nuclear-powered ships, including warships, absolute liability lay with operators.

But the US Joint Atomic Energy Committee and the US Department of Defense were adamant that warships should not be bound by international treaties. According to the director of the US navy's nuclear propulsion programme, Rear Admiral Hyman Rickover:

> [W]e simply cannot afford to subject what is now a third of our major naval combatants to the dictates of international regulation under this convention ... surely maintaining the sovereign status of these ships is more important to our national interests than solving the liability question for nuclear merchant ships.[3]

Nevertheless, faced with governments around the world restricting access to its ships, the US needed to adopt a practical approach. Public Law 93-514 was signed by President Gerald Ford on 6 December 1974, specifying that 'the United States ... will pay claims or judgments for bodily injury, death, or damage or loss of real or personal property proven to have resulted from a nuclear incident involving the nuclear reactor of a United States warship'.[4] This provision was designed to provide access to foreign ports by the US navy for 'efficient ship utilization and to provide a place for members of the crew to rest from their demanding duty'.[5]

The US needed to secure port access because its withdrawal from Vietnam meant potential base closures in a region that was showing increasing support for a nuclear-free zone in the South Pacific. Both Australia and New Zealand were active advocates of such a zone, which had implications not just for French nuclear tests in the region but also for transit and port visits by nuclear-powered and nuclear-armed ships. American representatives at the 1974 ANZUS council meeting consequently took the opportunity to point out the problems a nuclear-free zone in the South Pacific would create for them.

In mid-1975 the US sent an *aide-memoire* to Canberra ahead of the forthcoming South Pacific Forum meeting, reiterating its 'objections to the nuclear-free zone proposal and its dissatisfaction that an ANZUS ally should persist in a course which the US had declared harmful to its interests'.[6] Participating states were given an ultimatum: nuclear visits or no security.

This had the desired effect on Australian Prime Minister Gough Whitlam. He wrote to Bill Rowling — who had become New Zealand prime minister following Kirk's sudden death on 31 August 1974 — arguing that a nuclear-free zone could 'stir up controversy with the United States and raise questions about the ANZUS relationship'.[7] Australia duly declined to support a UN resolution in late 1975 sponsored by New Zealand, Fiji and Papua New Guinea.[8]

Since 1947 the US had relied on a document issued by the US Chief of Naval Operations that stated it only required 'service' (i.e. military) clearance — as opposed to 'service, diplomatic and ministerial' clearance — for the entry of its ships to the ports of Australia, New Zealand, and Canada. However, unlike Australia, New Zealand had failed to abide by the spirit of this 'agreement', requiring each visit to receive diplomatic and ministerial clearance in addition to service clearance. With ship visits to New Zealand increasing in the 1950s, the US sought confirmation of the 1947 understanding. This request was rebuffed, with the Prime Minister's Office complaining that 'the Americans were riding roughshod through the proper procedures' and that on several occasions they had 'failed to ask the New Zealand naval staff for operational clearance while claiming to have already received it when applying for diplomatic approval'.[9]

The reality was that successive US administrations had paid little heed to the southwest Pacific since the Korean War, leaving Australia and New Zealand responsible for the stability of the region. Indeed, in 1963 ANZUS was conspicuously absent from the *New York Times*' list of America's top 10 commitments.[10] It was not until the mid-1970s, following the earlier ban by Australia and New Zealand on visits by nuclear-powered warships, that the US began to show a renewed interest in ANZUS and ship visits. The administration therefore applied pressure on New Zealand to end liability suspension. The US argument was that the law it had passed had resolved the issue and a continuing ban was inconsistent with ANZUS.

Australia also weighed in against New Zealand, with its defence minister visiting to press the point. This resulted in Rowling announcing on 10 July 1975 that the Cabinet was re-examining its prohibition but that there were no plans for change at the moment. Activists within the Labour Party, in anticipation of a possible government backtrack, had voted overwhelmingly at the party conference in May for a prohibition on the entry of both nuclear-armed and nuclear-powered vessels. Despite this, the party's 1975 election manifesto made no reference to port visits. Instead, it stated that the American alliance would be maintained.[11]

Following the election in 1975 of the Fraser government in Australia and the Muldoon government in New Zealand, both countries reverted to enthusiastic US cooperation. In New Zealand's case, Muldoon met with members of a subcommittee of the US House Armed Services Committee on 14 January 1976, and announced to waiting journalists immediately afterwards that New Zealand would be lifting the ban on nuclear-powered vessels because the prohibition was inconsistent with the country's obligations as an ANZUS signatory.

A few hours later the incoming Australian government followed suit. In 'a flush of euphoria' the Australian deputy secretary for Foreign Affairs advised members of Congress that a Fraser government would not merely support ANZUS, but would develop the alliance further as a vehicle for solving more 'global' problems, starting with the extension of ANZUS to the Indian Ocean.[12] Given the warm support they had received in New Zealand and Australia, the US delegation went home under the impression that they had experienced a 'unique opportunity to literally be present at the rebirth of ANZUS'.[13]

As a further sign of its earnest support, in 1977 New Zealand joined the maritime and reconnaissance agreement — designed to ensure more widespread maritime coverage of the Pacific and parts of the Indian Ocean — which had been in force between Australia and the US since the early days of the Cold War.

It had long been US policy to 'neither confirm nor deny' (NCND) whether a visiting ship was nuclear armed. This remained a politically sensitive issue in both countries, with the suspension regimes having at least six lasting repercussions into the 1980s.[14] One was that liability for nuclear reactors became inextricably linked to the carriage of nuclear weapons, and led to disquiet about the NCND policy. Concerns were compounded in 1974 when US Admiral La Rocque told a congressional committee that he had never known a US conventionally powered nuclear-capable vessel *not* to carry nuclear weapons:

> They do not off-load them when they go into foreign ports such as Japan or other countries. If they are capable of carrying them, they normally keep them aboard at all times except when the ship is in overhaul or in for a major repair.[15]

Another repercussion was that the Australian and New Zealand governments had given the trend towards nuclear propulsion as one of the reasons for reinstating ship visits. Attention now shifted to the possibility of nuclear escalation at sea involving nuclear-powered submarines which, because of their ability to spend longer periods away from home base, were more likely to seek foreign port visits.

A third repercussion was that reinstatement — unlike suspension which was imposed by Order in Council and did not attract much public attention — attracted greater public attention in Australia and New Zealand in the post-Vietnam War environment.

Although there were protests in Australia when the first nuclear-powered submarine, the USS *Snook*, berthed in 1976, Australian anti-nuclear opinion initially tended to focus on the uranium issue rather than port visits. In contrast, the target for the New Zealand anti-nuclear movement was the deployment of nuclear weapons. Protest groups proliferated, including the New Zealand Campaign for Nuclear Disarmament (CND), the Women's International League for Peace & Freedom, the UN Association, and the small boat squadron that formed to undertake symbolic harbour blockades. The squadron's activities peaked during the Muldoon governments.

There were 160 US naval visits in total to New Zealand ports between 1958 and 1984. Over the 1967–72 period, coinciding with the Vietnam War, there was an average of 16 visits a year by conventionally powered US warships. Numbers dropped off significantly during 1973–75, and there was an average of seven warship visits annually from 1976 to 1984, with the difference being that most of these vessels were nuclear powered and at least half were nuclear weapons capable.[16]

A further repercussion was that liability suspension emphasised the difference, from a political perspective, between the Australian and the New Zealand approach to a range of the anti-nuclear issues. The Whitlam government had heeded US pressure on the Pacific nuclear-free zone and placed more importance on ANZUS than on public opposition to visits by nuclear-powered or nuclear-armed ships. In contrast, in New Zealand, suspension had sown the seeds within the Labour Party for a legislative prohibition against port visits rather than leaving NCND decisions and policy generally in the hands of the executive.

Another repercussion was that suspension revocation widened the anti-nuclear debate. Initially, suspension of ship visits had been about insurance liability, but revocation of that policy was presented by Muldoon as a question of obligation and alliance. He consequently called on the Labour Opposition to state whether or not it wished New Zealand to remain in the ANZUS alliance.[17] This gave support to those within the Labour

Party, such as Helen Clark, Jim Anderton, Russell Marshall and Margaret Wilson, who were pushing for the renegotiation of ANZUS or withdrawal from the alliance. It also shifted CND from a policy of non-alignment to one in favour of New Zealand exiting from ANZUS and SEATO and becoming truly non-aligned. 'We cannot do this if we allow ourselves to be used for the US's naval nuclear weapons systems,' they said.[18]

And finally, revocation heightened environmental concerns.

In New Zealand these various elements began to coalesce — stoked by Muldoon's confrontational style — when the cruisers USS *Truxtun* and *Long Beach* made port visits in August and October 1976. It had been 12 years since the last visit by a nuclear-powered ship and these visits attracted widespread public opposition. As the 1978 election approached, former prime minister and now Opposition Leader Rowling stated in a speech on United Nations Day that a Labour government would again close New Zealand ports to nuclear military vessels. Although National was returned to office on 25 November 1978, Labour's opposition to visits by both nuclear-armed and nuclear-powered ships now seemed set in concrete.

The next visit was in January 1979 by the USS *Haddo*, a nuclear-powered submarine, followed by a second visit by the *Truxtun* to Wellington in September 1980. Around 5500 people visited the vessel during its week-long stay, with some polls showing that 48.6 percent favoured continuing visits by nuclear-powered ships, compared to 33.7 percent against.[19] 'But by the end of 1982,' wrote Michael Pugh in his book *The ANZUS Crisis, Nuclear Visiting and Deterrence*, 'the hitherto fragmented peace movement began to develop greater co-ordination, and with a neighborhood nuclear-free zone movement also gathering momentum, anti-nuclearism was poised to influence the [New Zealand] middle ground.'[20]

The buildup to the 1984 election

The anger within the Labour Party and the broad-based anti-nuclear movement increased when a third visit by the *Truxtun* was arranged to coincide with the Labour Party conference in May 1982. There, Rowling declared that ANZUS was 'no longer acceptable in its present form'. Delegates cheered and stamped their feet as he added, 'Nuclear weapons will not be allowed into New Zealand ports under a Labour government and that's the message!'[21]

At Labour's 1983 conference, Rowling told delegates:

> Our task is therefore to produce foreign policy … which tells the world that our decisions will be made in Wellington — not Washington, nor London, nor Canberra. The kind of independence which we will maintain under a Labour Government will not be negotiable. Neither will our anti-nuclear stance, which will be an important element of that policy.

Rowling went on to say that many other policy elements would be capable of negotiation and refinement, but added:

> If, of course, our allies are not prepared to accept our anti-nuclear position as the bottom line, it will be they who have to do the withdrawing from existing arrangements. We should give them a chance. Under no circumstances should we walk away from any agreement. Such an action would considerably weaken our own bargaining position for the future.[22]

This approach was strongly endorsed by the conference and subsequently became official party policy. Thus it was no surprise when the incoming Lange government sought to enact its nuclear-free policy.

The reality was that from the early 1970s through to the election of the Lange government in 1984, an alternative defence perspective had been gaining currency in New Zealand, in opposition to the more traditional National Party approach. The main theme of this alternative perspective was the need to establish an independent national identity separate from American militarism. A range of considerations supported this approach:

- the risk of superpower confrontations escalating into a nuclear war;
- membership of a defence alliance with a superpower could act more as an incentive rather than a deterrent to attack;
- in the event of conflict, self-defence or non-violent resistance was less risky than being defended by a superpower;
- New Zealand should concentrate on developing its own resources and potential rather than assisting others to achieve their defence objectives;
- an independent New Zealand could make a more effective contribution to the promotion of goals such as global disarmament; and
- the benefits of an increased trade base with a wide range of partners were likely to exceed any loss of trade with traditional alliance partners.[23]

It was not only Labour Party supporters who held these views — they had much wider currency. A feature of the runup to the 1984 election was the extent to which most of the parties — other than National, with its support for ongoing membership of ANZUS and continuing ship visits, but nevertheless with a long and active history on disarmament and non-proliferation issues — campaigned on what could be termed anti-nuclear but pro-ANZUS policies.

The exception was the newly formed New Zealand Party. Its manifesto deplored the amount New Zealand spent on defence, denied that the Soviet Union was an enemy, and advocated armed neutrality. Because it was generally seen to be advocating right-wing policies, its views on defence and security made Labour's stance look mainstream and moderate.

In this environment, and given increasing public disillusionment with the government, it was difficult for National to be heard. Despite this, early in 1984 Deputy Prime Minister McLay, shortly after he was elected to that position, gave a speech stripped of hubris on the government's policy towards the ANZUS alliance and what was realistic in a nuclear-armed world.[24]

He began by referring to comments by Pope John Paul II in Japan in 1981 where the Pope had defined two steps towards the survival of humanity: a 'conscious choice' and a 'deliberate policy', with the inference that the resolution of the nuclear predicament had to pass through both these stages.

In terms of conscious choice, McLay made the point that successive New Zealand governments had consistently opposed nuclear testing, had been among the earliest signatories to the limited test ban and non-proliferation treaties, and had in November 1983 with Australia jointly sponsored a UN resolution calling for a comprehensive nuclear test ban treaty, as well as supporting another resolution seeking a prohibition on the production of fissionable material for weapons purposes.

He went on to say that conscious choice on its own was not enough and that 'deliberate policy' in a real-world context — where at that time the nuclear arms race rested with five acknowledged nuclear weapons states — also had to be considered. In terms of New Zealand's foreign policy interests in the Pacific and the wider Pacific/Asian region at a time when the Soviet Union was extending its military presence in the region, he pointed to the importance of the balance of power that the United States provided, describing New Zealand's membership of ANZUS alongside Australia as the cornerstone of the country's regional foreign policy.

McLay then discussed a number of counter-arguments that were being advanced: that as there was no immediate threat to New Zealand's security the country could safely withdraw from ANZUS; that armed neutrality was an option; and that there was a halfway house where New Zealand could maintain membership of the alliance but retain the right to considerable dissent and independent action. In other words remain in ANZUS but say no to nuclear-powered ships (which by then accounted for almost 42 percent of all US combat vessels).

Although McLay acknowledged it was a matter of opinion how far one member could depart from the spirit of a treaty without jeopardising the whole alliance, the key question he asked was: 'Could our commitment to the treaty be taken seriously if we denied port access to nearly half the naval ships of the largest treaty partner?' His answer was effectively no. 'A halfway house is at best a half-hearted commitment.'[25]

McLay's attempts at rationality aside, it is clear that Muldoon had been working on the issues he wanted to fight in the 1984 election well before he announced the early election. Michael Bassett put it this way: '[Muldoon] had a fine eye for those sorts of dividing issues where he knew he could win [and] he would strike at the right moment to make sure the cards fell his way.'[26] Muldoon hoped that ANZUS — where there were real points of policy difference between National and Labour — might provide salvation for the government in 1984, and had begun to set the scene much earlier.

His practice, Bassett noted, 'appeared to be to request a visit whenever he was floundering in the polls, because he calculated that he could win from the protests'. In fact Bassett's research shows that Muldoon sought more ship visits than the Americans felt comfortable making, and had even planned one for September 1984, anticipating a tight general election.[27]

Marilyn Waring also recorded that Muldoon was counting on ANZUS:

> Muldoon had also received support for the type of campaign he wanted the focus of the election to be on from the July 1983 ANZUS Council meeting. The Communiqué of 21 July following that meeting stressed the importance of upholding the principles of freedom of navigation and over-flight as provided in international law. It also noted the importance to the alliance and the region of security considerations, including access by allied aircraft and ships to airfields and ports in accordance with the sovereign right of States to receive such visits.[28]

The next ANZUS council meeting was scheduled in Wellington in July 1984. As it happened, this took place immediately after the early election but before the reins of power had officially passed to the Lange government. Had the election been held at the normal time of October or November 1984, the meeting and the presence of senior American officials in New Zealand in July would almost certainly have attracted a substantial degree of protest from anti-nuclear, anti-America groups. This would have provided Muldoon with an ideal launchpad for the planned US ship visit in September and another abrasive election campaign.

Muldoon's main aim in government was to stay there, and he had no compunctions about using any tactic available to him to achieve this end. Ship visits were part of this, as evidenced by the response to questioning during the Disarmament and Arms Control select committee hearings and Richard Prebble's comments on his briefing in Washington by State Department officials:

> When I said that the Labour Party's policy was to have a nuclear free Pacific, and asked if that would mean the end of ANZUS, they replied, just as former Vice-President Rockefeller said publicly, 'Of course it would not.' I should be less than frank if I were to say that a nuclear free Pacific is the Americans' No. 1 option. It is not, but they believe that they can live with such a concept. Indeed, I went further and asked, 'Why do you send nuclear powered warships to New Zealand?' The House ought to know that their reply was: 'We have never, never requested that a nuclear-powered ship visit New Zealand. Every single visit has been in response to a particular request from the National Government.'[29]

Muldoon also had an abiding hatred of the Labour Party and what he thought was its economic incompetence in government. He was therefore unashamedly prepared to use ANZUS and the US connection for party-political purposes, despite the fact that he himself was neither particularly pro-ANZUS or pro-America. In the words of his head of department, Gerald Hensley:

> He certainly pushed the nuclear ship [visits]. It was in your face ... I have never thought he was especially pro-American ... I mean he wasn't anti-American but ... he didn't particularly like the United States I always

> thought when we went there, but he did push the nuclear ship one; whether it was from sheer aggressiveness or not I don't know.[30]

Muldoon justified the early election on the basis of National MP Marilyn Waring 'crossing the floor' to support the introduction of Prebble's 1984 Bill, which sought to ban nuclear-powered as well as nuclear-armed warships from New Zealand waters. Waring followed this up with a letter to the chief government whip, Don McKinnon, saying: 'I have to advise you that I will no longer be available to attend any select committee or government caucus meetings for the remainder of the parliamentary term.'[31]

In my view, this was merely a handy excuse for Muldoon. Waring's actions hadn't led to the government's defeat on Prebble's Nuclear Free New Zealand Bill. Its introduction had been denied by the government, and in any event, there was little chance of it being defeated over any anti-nuclear issue before the scheduled end of the parliamentary term. Also, the government had a fallback position. The Leader of the House, David Thomson, had already told the House that Prebble's Bill would not get the consent of the governor-general while the National was in office.

It was typical of Muldoon to try to make Waring pay a price for her principled stand, carrying the burden of responsibility for a decision that belonged to him and him alone.[32]

The truth is that he was tired and he simply ran out of steam. He had lost control of the economy and his caucus, and had had enough. And, as the election result clearly showed, the New Zealand electorate had also had enough of him.

Hensley summed up Muldoon's mindset this way:

> when [Labour] brought in the Nuclear Bill and [some of the government caucus] looked like breaking ranks I think he concluded rather fatalistically that he'd rather die sort of standing up than spend the next three or four months on his knees. I don't think he expected to win that election ... His intellect and his political virtue really faded after the 1981 election. They were never as much in evidence again. He was increasingly tired ... but anyway, things got increasingly out of control. He was I think in those last two years fighting the last battle for the RSA generation. He thought New Zealand in the fifties was about as good as it gets.[33]

What is clear is that Muldoon's confrontational style contributed to the 'macho' anti-nuclear policy devised by the Lange government. In addition, as Bassett has confirmed, it hardened anti-American sentiments within the Labour Party:

> Few people knew of the American reluctance to play along with Muldoon. Unfairly, in retrospect, Labour supporters were inclined to suspect there was an American desire to dabble in New Zealand politics. More than a touch of anti-Americanism [could be discerned] within Labour's growing anti-nuclear stance.[34]

Whether the policy divide between National and Labour on defence was a major election issue for voters in 1984 is a moot point. They were faced with the continuing wage/price freeze, concerns about the state of the economy, and Muldoon's style. In the end, the mood was for change. In that environment, it became increasingly difficult for the government to 'sell' its defence policy, with the media increasingly simplifying the key choice to either support for the bomb or a firm commitment to anti-nuclearism.

What voters did confirm somewhat naïvely in the 1984 election was that they thought there could be a halfway house. About 80 percent of the votes went to parties favouring a continuation of ANZUS; and around two-thirds went to parties — including the Labour Party — that opposed the entry of nuclear-propelled and nuclear-armed ships. History has proved McLay right and voters wrong on this particular matter.

Although Lange personally — unlike the hard-core anti-nuclear element within his party — may initially have been interested in a 'halfway' solution, the Americans were not. They gave the government short shrift when it refused entry in February 1985 to the USS *Buchanan*, and New Zealand was effectively expelled from ANZUS.

CHAPTER 17

The Strategos Defence Review

Those within the Labour government who had commissioned the Strategos review of defence did so because the flaws in the structure and performance of the defence organisation were glaringly obvious even to the non-military eye, and the government did not trust most of those within that organisation to sort the problems out. Although this distrust stemmed partly from perceived opposition within defence to the government's anti-nuclear policy, and the resultant reduction in contact with the US military, the void between the two sides was deeper than this. Lange put it this way:

> In 1984, most of Labour's Cabinet and caucus were of a temperament which found military posturing ridiculous rather than intimidating. Our pride in our country was not bound up with military prowess. In New Zealand the armed forces did not have the standing which allowed them to dictate to the government. More than a generation gap was at work.[1]

In beginning our review in late 1987, the first thing Alf Kirk and I did was to have a good look at Cabinet's terms of reference.[2] Although at that stage they excluded defence policy, operational and command responsibilities and force structure, even without those areas the task was still likely to be massive, involving most of our time over the next 12 months. We also realised that we would need to employ numerous sub-consultants and extra staff, and rented more office space.

First, we had to fix our fee. Initially, I suggested that I be paid a fixed daily sum for three days' work a week, regardless of time spent; that my fellow Strategos directors should be paid for the actual time they spent on the review; and that other expenses, including sub-consultants' fees, should be passed on to Defence to pay at cost. This offer was declined on advice from the Treasury, which did not want an open-ended contract.

An amended proposal with a capped limit was subsequently approved. Defence ended up paying at least twice as much as it would have paid under my initial proposal, but even so, the final cost was still well under the agreed cap.

Another early issue was who was to be involved in the review. The defence establishment applied strong pressure to have a 'military expert' seconded to our team, but we rejected this on the grounds that it would compromise our independence. Their next suggestion was that any sub-consultants we employed should be subject to their prior approval. As a compromise, I agreed to 'advise' the Secretary of Defence who we were employing and the extent of that person's specific tasks.

Within days this process was tested and abandoned when I employed Michael Cox to carry out a review of defence real estate in conjunction with a Ministry of Works official. Cox was one of my former parliamentary colleagues and was ideally suited to the task. He had chaired my housing caucus committee; was a hard-nosed, practical person with a cost-accounting background; and crucially, could start work immediately. Within hours of my advising the secretary of his appointment, the minister rang me. The upshot of our conversation was an agreement that I could employ whomsoever I chose without having to advise anyone. This removed the possibility of any potential political or departmental 'interference'.

From the outset, we were aware that our prime audience was political and that the support of four particular Cabinet members would be critical: PM David Lange, deputy PM Geoffrey Palmer (a 'details' person, a lawyer and an expert on constitutional matters), Minister of Finance Roger Douglas (a 'big picture' person who had little interest in defence but needed no convincing that the organisation was riddled with inefficiencies) and Defence Minister Bob Tizard.

I was confident that the background and experience of the three main Strategos directors involved — with lesser input from other directors, Rob Campbell and later Brent Wheeler, who were busy on other reviews — meant we were up to the task. I had a background in law, politics and consulting. Alf Kirk had wide economic and accounting experience and had advised the prime minister on industrial relations matters. Strategos board chair Susan McAffer (whom I later married) had been involved in a number of political party campaigns, had wide experience in advertising and marketing and had been employed for a number of years as a ministerial adviser.

Because each of the four ministers had different interests, backgrounds and agendas, presentations to them had to be individually tailored. Lange was known to have a short attention span, so the objective was to get the key points across to him from one piece of paper in under 10 minutes. Gerald Hensley has recorded that he would go into Lange's office with a list of things requiring attention, determined to run through it the way he had been able to do with Muldoon, but he could never do so with Lange:

> After about two or three points he would be reminded of an extremely funny story about a colleague or something and away you'd go and three quarters of an hour later he was still sitting there and it didn't matter ... it was immensely entertaining ... he was almost ambivalent about everything including himself, and so his office management ... often verged on chaos.[3]

In complete contrast, Palmer was interested in the detail of issues such as the civilian/military relationship, the review team's options for Defence headquarters, and overall accountability. Douglas's approach was to listen but he rarely commented. Later, he made it clear that he would have supported substantial cuts to the defence budget.

Tizard was the only one of the four with a military background, having served as an air force navigator towards the end of World War II. He was a fierce supporter of the government's anti-nuclear policy, but also understood the implications of being outside ANZUS, and the cost of the government's more independent stance. He was a sceptic by nature but had a genuine understanding of the wider defence issues involved in the review. Also, because of his experience as a former finance minister he knew that any savings we identified were likely to take longer to capture than others anticipated, and that in any event they might not finish up with defence as Lange had promised.

Our contract required us to report to Tizard and Douglas (Douglas was later replaced by David Caygill).

Most of Alf's and my early time was spent with people in Defence headquarters, the organisation's power base. There was a Defence Council; a Secretary of Defence; a Chief of Defence Staff (CDS); a Chiefs of Staff Committee; three services (navy, army and air force) chiefs but with no coherent combined direction); and a Ministry of Defence covering the total organisation. Defence HQ employed 1450 people (900 more than the former CDS and Secretary had said they thought necessary) and a joint CDS/Secretary of Defence management structure which meant that the answer to the question 'Who manages?' was unclear.

The Defence Act 1971 was based on the underlying theory that the defence system was an integrated whole in which each of the three services functioned as a component part. The single service boards set up under the 1964 Defence Act had been abolished in 1971.[4]

The Secretary of Defence was the permanent head of the ministry. His tasks included financial planning and expenditure, the coordination of the business of the ministry and 'inspection' of the administration of the three services. He was also the principal civilian adviser to the minister of defence but had no responsibility for the command or administration of the services.

The Defence Council was paramount in both policy and command terms. As a result, the CDS's statutory power to command the three services through the relevant service chiefs was constrained, particularly as each service chief also had a right of access to the minister if opinions differed.

The CDS's role was also blurred with that of the Secretary of Defence because of their joint functions in relation to execution of Defence Council decisions; and coordination and supervision of the ministry's activities, policies and functions. The privileged position of the chiefs meant that they had a central role in the policy advice process, but were expected to implement that policy under the command of the CDS. The result was a strong focus on single-service concerns, rather than the overall interests of the total defence force.

While the command structure within each service was relatively clear, policy advice and delegation of command on a defence-wide basis were not, because of confusion and blurring between the respective roles and responsibilities at the top.

As I was the 'face' of the review team, the defence hierarchy expected me to front all initial meetings, with the impression clearly conveyed that the opinion of anyone else (my 'hirelings') was not to be taken seriously. While I was greeted with salutes and responses of 'Yes sir, no sir', Alf, who never wore a tie and invariably turned up to even the most important meetings wearing a garish fairisle jumper, was greeted with 'Hello, Alf.'

What the defence people didn't know (or had forgotten) was that Alf was an accountant and auditor who had specialised in military history, and among other things had spent time in the Inland Revenue Department as a compliance officer. He was also our analytical brain, so he and I were happy for defence to 'take him lightly'. While they were fawning over me, they should have been worrying about the information he was quietly extracting from them.

The areas that were excluded from our terms of reference caused problems almost immediately. When I asked the head of the navy, CNS Admiral Domett, for information on in-shore patrol craft, his response was: 'I'm not going to answer that. It's not within your terms of reference.' He was equally unmoved when I told him that military operational equipment was. He was clearly of the view, along with a number of other senior defence personnel, that professional military judgement took precedence over the opinions of uninformed civilians.

To give Domett his due, at least he was being consistent. He had earlier told Prime Minister Lange — following a verbal request at the time of the 1987 Fiji coup to ready the RNZN *Monowai* in case the evacuation of New Zealand nationals became necessary — that he was not going to comply. His answer had remained the same when Lange's instruction came in writing, insisting, as he was entitled to, that any 'instruction' would need to come from the Defence Council.

I wasn't prepared to put up with that sort of nonsense from the CNS or anyone else, and approached the CDS, General Mace, about the matter. Mace had an upright stance, the looks and demeanour of high office, and was extremely adept politically. His reaction to CNS's refusal was in keeping with his Strategos-designated nickname 'the silver fox'. 'Do you want me to sack him?' he asked. 'No,' I said. 'I only want answers to my questions.' As a result our terms of reference were completely revamped, with all areas now open to us.

Mace knew which way the wind was blowing and had quickly realised that he and the defence establishment would make little progress with us or the government unless they cooperated fully. He readily accepted our extended terms of reference and the reasons for them, as I had put them to the Defence Executive Committee:

> The last point I wish to make ... [relates to] the extent of our inquiry. This is important because it has been suggested that matters of operational or

> command responsibilities or force structure are outside our review. Although this may eventually prove to be the case in some areas of activity, the first thing that we have to decide is whether what is being done is consistent with the policy objectives of the 1987 White Paper, produced in the aftermath of the anti-nuclear policy and the resultant reassessment of New Zealand's strategic and security policies, and secondly, whether it is being done by the most economical means to maintain operational effectiveness. Any activities that are not consistent with the 1987 policy are *prima facie* a wasteful use of resources.

After this, the navy became 'the silent service', answering any questions put to them in a prompt and straightforward way, but without providing any additional information. If a question needed to be rephrased or asked in a different way to elicit the information that was obviously being sought, that wasn't the navy's problem. They hoped their tactic would see us move on to other things or, better still, go away, but we didn't.

This was not our last issue with the navy. Alf Kirk visited the Australian navy's Garden Island dockyard in Sydney, where discussions were held, among other things, on the possibility of extended Australia/New Zealand dockyard cooperation. He reported to me that the issue of the RNZN frigate *Southland*, which was scheduled for an imminent major refit in the UK, had cropped up. Everyone had agreed that the vessel was so elderly, and so lacking in equipment terms alongside the RNZN's other three frigates, that it didn't warrant the cost of a major refit. Alf went on to say that if a much less costly *minor* refit were to take place instead, at the Devonport naval base in Auckland, the Australians would be prepared to provide input. Alf's final comment was that unfortunately it now appeared to be too late as sailing arrangements were well advanced.

I didn't agree, and immediately contacted the head of the Devonport dockyard for confirmation that a minor refit could be handled there. After a bit of procrastination he said yes. I then rang Admiral Berlyn, head of the Sydney dockyard, to find out exactly what Australia was prepared to contribute. After speaking to his minister, Kim Beazley, he quickly confirmed that Australia could cover about 15 percent of the overall project in specialist areas.

Because I saw a joint venture with Australia as a good practical opportunity to test trans-Tasman cooperation, I wrote to the minister of defence advising him that in our view a major refit of the *Southland* was not warranted, and why. I told him about the option of a minor refit at Devonport with Australian help. I then flew off to visit defence establishments in the UK and Norway, leaving Alf to handle the flak from the navy, which was considerable because the government cancelled the UK refit and decided not to proceed with a minor refit either. In due course the *Southland* was decommissioned.

However, the navy's 'silent service' approach was positively effusive compared with the air force. Several within the RNZAF's senior hierarchy were deliberately obstructive, invariably late in responding to questions seeking information, and at times their conduct bordered on the unprofessional.

Their initial exasperated response to our team's persistent questions was 'If you spent more time visiting our bases you would understand why we do things this way.' And in due course we did. But when senior staff began to realise the extent of the inefficiencies we were uncovering on the bases, and the frustration of air force personnel in having to cope with them — which they were not shy in talking to us about — they shifted tack. Now, we were told, we needed to spend more time at HQ so that the advice being tendered on the bases could be put into proper context.

At my first meeting with senior RNZAF officers I was given a copy of *The Hunt for Red October* and told that if I read it, I would understand how the air force worked. The book is a good read and I enjoyed it, but it didn't help me much in resource management terms, which is what our review was all about! Later, the same officer was not quite so demonstrative after I had visited the Hobsonville air force base — adjacent to the Whenuapai base in Auckland, with him and the base commander.

Hobsonville was slated by us for closure but I found out that substantial work was still taking place on site to provide extra bomb storage capacity and to construct a highly specialised weapons testing facility. It seemed an obvious attempt to bolster the case against closure, so I recommended to the minister that work should stop. He agreed, and the base was eventually sold, despite the air force pleading that it be retained as the take-off point for the RNZAF's Orion surveillance aircraft. I asked Jack Healy — the former head of the Department of Transport who had gone to PNG with me several years earlier on Pacific Forum Line business — for his view. His succinct report confirmed that the Orions could be stationed almost anywhere.

Unlike the top echelons of the navy and the air force, the army was a treat to deal with. Its people were open, it was possible to debate issues with the Chief of General Staff (CGS) and his senior officers in a rational way, and the final Strategos report clearly benefited from their input. However, I heard several years later that the review itself and the transition that followed had not been easy for the army either. In 1998 Brigadier Roger Mortlock addressed the Foreign Affairs, Trade and Defence Parliamentary Select Committee, which I was chairing. When he had completed his submission he stood up, saluted me and said, 'Sir, you put us through absolute hell. We needed it, and we are the better for it.'

At the time of the Strategos review the army had three serious enemies. One was the army itself — with continual internal debates, conflicts and disagreements over equipment priorities and capabilities. Its other enemies were the other two services, in an environment where there was no joint force consensus and therefore a continuous contest between the three of them for a bigger share of the limited defence budget.

An example was the army's desperate need for a logistics supply ship. But as this required sponsorship and funding from the navy — whose priority was to upgrade its own fleet — nothing was happening. The army summarised the situation in a response to a question from us:

> There is little point in having Army reaction forces optimised for deployment in the Southwest Pacific if the strategic and tactical air and sea operational and transport capabilities are insufficient for their deployment and support.

We recommended a joint forces approach to priorities and funding, but it took two further defence reviews — Defence Beyond 2000 and the F-16 report in 2000 — for this to begin.

As we had anticipated, Alf and I were involved almost full time on the Strategos review during 1988, with substantial input from a new staff member and from our board chair, who coordinated work-in-progress and kept the whole exercise on track. Alf and I visited camps and bases and talked to military and civilian personnel. Meanwhile, sub-consultants carried out more than 30 detailed studies of different aspects of defence resource management.

Trans-Tasman defence relations

The stand-off between New Zealand and the US over the government's anti-nuclear policy created two problems and one substantial opportunity for the Australian government. One problem was how to stop the 'Kiwi anti-nuclear disease' spreading to its shores. The other was how to deal with New Zealand now that it had been effectively ex-communicated by the Americans. The opportunity, which Australia embraced, was to consolidate its own military ties with the US.

Under Bob Hawke's leadership Australia had reaffirmed its commitment to ANZUS in 1983, and in a speech to Parliament in September of that year Foreign Minister Bill Hayden said a recent government review of ANZUS had led to a firm and unequivocal reaffirmation of the alliance as fundamental to Australia's national security and foreign and defence policies. He added that Australia could not be expected to be influential in matters such as arms control, arms reduction and disarmament initiatives if it did not involve itself in nuclear deterrence.[5] The speech was a clear message to the Australian and the New Zealand public that the Australian government would not be adopting the New Zealand government's anti-nuclear policy.

The initial reaction of the Hawke Cabinet to the US imposition of sanctions against New Zealand had been to follow suit.[6] Instead, it took steps to strengthen the trans-Tasman defence relationship in the belief that this approach would encourage New Zealand to remain an active and capable supporter of regional security, and would reduce the risk of New Zealand's anti-nuclear policy spreading within the region.[7]

Australia largely achieved this objective, with Kim Beazley, who had become minister of defence following the Hawke government's re-election in December 1984, commenting later: 'New Zealand had a chance to isolate itself but then chose not to.'[8] Beazley then visited New Zealand in April 1985 for defence talks and was aware of the need to counter any public perception that his government was 'ganging up' on the Kiwis. His view was that, given the strength of anti-nuclear sentiment in New Zealand, and the evident determination of the Lange government to stick to its policy, the Australian parliamentary Opposition's suggested approach of issuing ultimatums to New Zealand and even threatening economic sanctions would prove counter-productive.[9]

On his various visits to New Zealand, Beazley discussed cooperation on a submarine project, suggested extra bilateral military exercises and training assistance, and offered to upgrade intelligence links — despite the American restrictions — by commissioning special reports for New Zealand on regional issues. The *quid pro quo* was that New Zealand had to agree to maintain, among other capabilities, an infantry battalion, a blue-water navy, a quality maritime surveillance capacity and an air combat force.

The overall result was a substantial improvement in defence cooperation between the two countries. However, New Zealand's rift with the US did affect the conventional wisdom in Canberra and Wellington that the strategic interests of the two countries were identical.[10] This was no longer the case.

In our review we went further than the 1987 White Paper in acknowledging the importance of New Zealand's defence relationship with Australia. There were several reasons for this. One was that Australia's defence capabilities were a crucial part of New Zealand's security and were closely interwoven with New Zealand's commitment to the South Pacific. Another reason was that New Zealand was unlikely, given its small size, to be able to accomplish much militarily in the region without Australian support. A prime objective of foreign and defence policy therefore needed to be to ensure that Australia remained interested in New Zealand's security, and this had far-reaching implications for New Zealand's force structure, equipment and training. The review team therefore contended that a prime objective of New Zealand's foreign and defence policy should be to ensure that Australia remained interested in New Zealand and the trans-Tasman security relationship.

That said, the relationship has never been easy, particularly for New Zealand. As we recorded in our report:

> The complexity of the New Zealand/Australian relationship should not be understated. New Zealand has always been wary about becoming too closely identified with Australia. Australia has always been puzzled by New Zealand's continued determination to make its own way in the world. However, the two countries have tended to cooperate when this was perceived to be mutually beneficial.[11]

The ANZAC frigate project

During 1988 Alf Kirk and I had a number of meetings with senior Australian Cabinet ministers and officials. The officials in particular made it clear that they were not universally supportive of the extra cost and effort Australia was having to bear as a result of Beazley's determination

With Alf Kirk in Canberra, 1988.

to keep New Zealand close.[12] They consequently adopted a hard line on the ANZAC frigate project, which contemplated the construction in Australia of eight vessels for the Australian navy and four for New Zealand.

When I met with them in Wellington the Australian officials said they saw New Zealand's participation in the project 'as a litmus test of its commitment to the trans-Tasman defence relationship'. Failure by New Zealand to purchase its four frigates, they said, would be interpreted as an unwillingness to play a credible role as a defence partner in the region and as a signal that it was in the process of withdrawal from the 'community of friends.' Further, non-involvement would be taken as a clear sign that New Zealand was not prepared to recognise that Australia was paying a substantial price in monetary and non-monetary terms to ensure that New Zealand remained a credible defence partner. That price, which Australia was prepared to pay, had extended to a commitment that New Zealand would not find comparable ships at a lower cost from other sources.

There were consequently wider issues for us to consider on top of the military suitability of the frigates. Another was the series of agreements signed by the prime ministers of the two countries in August 1988 which accelerated, widened and deepened the original closer economic relations

(CER) agreement consummated five years earlier. At the 1988 signing, the two PMs asserted that they had removed 'virtually all impediments to achieving a single trans-Tasman market' and saw the package as an 'historic achievement', building an 'economic relationship unequalled by any two sovereign countries' and heralding 'a trading environment which, as far as possible, is unencumbered by Government regulation and direction'.[13]

Although the original CER agreement had provided for the removal of virtually all tariffs and quantitative restrictions on goods moving between Australia and New Zealand by 1 July 1990, the document contained restraint of trade provisions. In regard to defence, Article 18(a) was particularly relevant at the time of the Strategos review. It stated:

> Provided that such measures are not used as a means of arbitrary unjustified discrimination or as a disguised restriction on trade in the area, nothing in this agreement shall preclude the adoption in either Member State of measures necessary … to protect its essential security interests.

In 1988, Article 18(a) was being used to exclude New Zealand businesses from access to most Australian defence contracts. If the article were waived, New Zealand businesses could compete for Australian contracts as if they were Australian. This degree of participation, the Australian officials pointed out, would not be confined to a share of the work flowing from the construction of the ANZAC ships, but would also extend to other defence contracts, 'provided participation in the ANZAC ship project was on an acceptable scale'. However, if it were not, Australian Defence Secretary Tony Ayers said at my meeting with him, 'New Zealand would not even get the contract for the tea urns.'

When it came to deciding on the replacement of the RNZN's four ageing frigates and whether New Zealand should buy from Australia, there were consequently strategic, commercial and political implications to be considered.

Ultimately, our recommendation was that New Zealand should enter into a contract — with suitable safeguards and undertakings — for the purchase of two ANZAC frigates, with an option to acquire a further two at a later date. This recommendation was accepted by the Lange government and the two frigates were ultimately purchased. The option to acquire two more remained in place until the National government decided in 1997 to reduce the frigate fleet from four to three vessels.[14]

The Clark government subsequently settled on only two frigates, supplemented by a range of multi-role vessels.

It was interesting to note the wariness of some New Zealand politicians to be seen to be getting too close to Australia, particularly in the aftermath of the US/New Zealand stand-off. On one of our visits to Canberra we had identified Paul Dibb as someone we wanted to talk to for our review. Dibb was director of the Joint Intelligence Organisation and had recently completed a *Review of Australia's Defence Capabilities*. He was therefore a very useful person for us to consult.

I invited him to Wellington and his visit was cleared by Beazley. I had not sought any approval at our end. Although the visit was supposed to be kept low key, within hours of his arrival I received a call to say the prime minister wished to see me. Without needing to be told, I could tell that some Cabinet ministers had heard about Dibb's visit, probably from defence staff, and had concerns. Were we getting too close to the Australians, some clearly wondered?

My fallback position with the prime minister — if this became necessary — was that I had the authority to consult whomsoever I chose, and a budget to match; and regardless of what politicians thought, we needed Dibb's input.

But none of this was necessary. Lange's opening remark was: 'I hear Paul Dibb is coming over.' I replied: 'Yes, he's going to talk to us about his views on the civilian/military relationship, and is spending a few days in New Zealand after that having a holiday with his family.' And that was the end of the matter.

Lange had obviously been pressured by some of his colleagues to find out what was going on and, if necessary, to issue an instruction to cancel Dibb's visit. As it was, and because he hated confrontation, all Lange wanted was to be able to report back that he had spoken to me about the visit, and it was all okay.

Analysis and solutions

One of my meetings in the UK resulted in contact with the facilities management company Serco. This was after UK officials had told me that Serco's approach, which involved the coordination of a range of 'non-fighting-force tasks', was saving on average around 15 percent of camp and base management costs.

At the time Serco was a small, well-managed company and had no business interests in either New Zealand or Australia. Following my meeting with the company's CEO and visits with him to some of the camps and bases where Serco's systems were in place, I offered him a return business-class ticket to New Zealand. A condition of the offer was that he should visit nominated camps and bases and write a report on facilities management for inclusion in the final Strategos report. He accepted my offer, and Serco subsequently established a presence in New Zealand and Australia.

Back home, with policy reconsideration now open to us, we came to an early conclusion that the defence of New Zealand's sovereignty was dependent on two fundamental objectives — the security of the South Pacific and defence cooperation with Australia — and that other objectives flowed from these. We were also aware that the 1987 White Paper had set out a more independent stance internationally for New Zealand and that the government's anti-nuclear policy was an important part of this.

In resource management terms, we also concluded that defence officials were acting within a set of inadequate structures that did not properly define their tasks or give them enough autonomy. They had this in common with much of New Zealand's state sector.

A central requirement for us was therefore to isolate those issues unique to defence, and to remember that traditional business management practices do not necessarily co-exist with the skills needed to — for instance — command a ship or a battalion in conflict.

The review team accepted that defence's special features had to be accommodated, and that its structures and spending might need to be adjusted rapidly in the event of an emerging threat. However, we were not convinced that these factors negated our applying the general thrust of the reform principles being carried out through the rest of the state sector. These conclusions were fortified by the knowledge that savings could be achieved from a more businesslike approach to its management, and that any resources released could be used to improve military capabilities.

We eventually decided the best way to proceed was with a marriage of state-sector reform principles and defence needs. This became our starting point for restructuring the New Zealand defence system, and its broad application underpinned the review's analysis.

The first principle was that policy and advisory roles ought to be separate from the administration and operational aspects of each department. This is to ensure that there is no monopoly on policy advice and, more importantly, to ensure that policy is not the exclusive preserve of the operational agency. It did not preclude ongoing feedback to the policy agency, but is an attempt to prevent advice being tailored to meet the needs of the operational agency rather than the needs of the consumer of the service. In the context of defence, this meant the military view had to be continually tested in the light of wider government objectives, and the policy debate needed to be conducted within a framework that avoids the risk of capture by either military or civilian points of views.

The second principle was that objectives ought to be stated in such a way that all parties involved in providing public goods and services are clear about their roles. This required clear definition of roles and division of responsibilities between each functional part of the agency, between commercial and non-commercial activities, between civilian and military advice, and between policy and management.

The third principle was that accountability should be maximised. This derived from the process of clarifying objectives. The essence of accountability was to be able to measure and assess performance against objectives and to attribute accountability clearly. From the viewpoint of effective resource management, this meant having mechanisms in place that were capable of assessing whether the taxpayer is getting value for money. In the context of defence it meant:

- leaving military operations to the military, subject to the control of the minister to meet the constitutional requirement for the subordination of the nation's military forces to the authority of Parliament, and making those military decision-makers fully accountable for those activities;
- defining military outputs (i.e. the provision of operationally capable forces);
- making policy advisers responsible for policy so there is no confusion between it and military or commercial functions'; and
- applying business criteria to the assessment of the performance of those responsible for commercial functions.

The fourth principle was that there should be competitive neutrality so as to minimise costs and provide the appropriate set of incentives and sanctions to enhance efficiency. This was achieved by removing any special advantages and disadvantages that prevailed within the state sector. From the viewpoint of the defence system, it entailed placing as much as possible of supply on a commercial basis. The clarification of objectives and the improvement of accountability were crucial preconditions for this to work.

The fifth principle was that managers ought to be allowed to manage. Experience had shown that major improvements resulted from:

- clarifying lines of authority;
- translating overall organisational objectives into clear objectives for individual personnel';
- reducing layers of management and paperwork;
- delegating decision-making;
- pursuing decentralised systems in areas such as personnel, finance, purchasing and inventory management; and
- improving management information systems.

For defence, this meant that once clear objectives and accountability mechanisms were in place, military personnel could be given management responsibility.

The application of the thinking behind the State Sector Act 1988 and the Public Finance Act 1989 were crucial and resulted in the setting up of a line of agency relationships designed to make it easier to assess whether agreed goals had been achieved.[15]

The introduction of these changes, and the way they were applied to New Zealand defence, provided a sharp divergence from, for example, Paul Dibb's *Review of Australia's Defence Capabilities*, which we had studied in detail.[16]

The conclusion we came to, considering the long list of problems uncovered and the special characteristics of defence, was that the resource faults within the system could not be overcome without a process of substantial integrated reform, including:

- reorganising Defence HQ;
- decision-making being based on defence-wide rather than single-service thinking;
- rationalisation of defence locations;
- introducing proper financial management information systems;
- fostering an environment that imbued the whole defence system with an understanding that cost was not just a function of the purchase price of goods, but that labour, existing goods, land, buildings and money also carried a cost.

The changes implemented by the government on our recommendations included the abolition of the Defence Council, an organisational split of the total existing defence structure into the Ministry of Defence and the New Zealand Defence Force as two separate legal entities, and the handing over of the whole NZDF budget to the Chief of Defence Forces (CDF). The latter move has been a resounding success — despite the CDF initially telling us he was petrified about having to assume this responsibility. The Secretary of Defence has no responsibility, authority or accountability for the management of the NZDF, which is in the hands of the CDF.

The organisational split was much more controversial, and was unusual in two respects. First, it resulted in New Zealand becoming 'the only country on the world with two defence departments — one to reflect and one to fight'.[17] Second, while other public-sector departments were also split along policy and operational lines, the two functions were generally kept within one agency, or else the policy function remained within the government sector and the operational activities were set up in some kind of Crown entity.[18] However, the issues we faced were not as straightforward as they were with other government departments.

This was because of the need to marry defence's special characteristics with the output-based management and delivery systems which by the time of the review had become a fundamental aspect of the moves to reform the public sector. These systems were ultimately enshrined in the 1989 Public Finance Act, designed to align resource management authority with the people responsible and accountable for delivering goods and services. Although many other countries have now moved to adopt such processes, during the mid-to-late 1980s New Zealand was unique in this regard.

Submissions on the Defence Bill 1989

By March 1990, in an indication of the government's determination to have defence reforms well in place before the election later that year, the Defence Bill 1989 had progressed through most of its stages on the way to coming into force on 1 April 1990. There were only three oral and six written submissions, basically because the government had said it was going to implement the general thrust of our report and had already introduced a number of the administrative recommendations. Most of the submissions were from former military personnel uniformly unsupportive of the reorganisation.

The two most contentious features were the CDF/Secretary relationship and the abolition of the Defence Council, with the most comprehensive submission coming from Denis McLean, who had extensive foreign affairs and defence experience and had only recently retired as Defence Secretary (or more accurately had not been reappointed at the end of his term because of his alleged opposition to the government's anti-nuclear policy). Before that, Lange described him as 'patrician in appearance, stamped with all the niceties of scholarship and manners'[19] and tried, unsuccessfully, to shift him from defence because of his views.

McLean was our civilian point of contact in the defence establishment, and on the eve of our reporting date I had succeeded — with more than a little gentle persuasion — to get him to support the military/civilian split we recommended. He told me on that occasion that he was sorry he would not be there to implement the report's recommendations. But within days he had changed his mind — after, I suspect, a combined frontal attack from the senior defence hierarchy. My response — perhaps slightly intemperate but representing my deep disappointment at his change of heart — was to write to him immediately and reverse the quotation by English novelist Edward Bulwer-Lytton, who wrote in 1839: 'Beneath the rule of men entirely great, the pen is mightier than the sword.' My own comment was short and to the point: 'Your change of heart only goes to prove that the sword is in fact mightier than the pen.'

The reaction of the Opposition National Party to our report was an undertaking to revert to the Defence Council structure once it was back in government, and to introduce civilian/military contestability at a much lower level within the overall defence organisation. National won the 1990 election, but did neither.

Post-reporting matters

After I had presented copies of the report to the government, Alf Kirk — whose contribution to the review had involved marathon day-and-night bursts of writing things up on a whiteboard, invariably followed by a week or so off with pleurisy — was physically wiped out. His last effort was to write 'The Defence Review Anthem' which is reproduced below. The tune is vaguely reminiscent of the national anthem and the text typifies its author's incisive wit and the growing irrelevance — at that time — of the

New Zealand military hierarchy and their civilian counterparts in a world that had all but passed them by.

The sixth verse has been omitted on the grounds of decency.

God of Nations we entreat,
Don't let Quigley sink the fleet.
Close the messes in which we eat,
Or toss us out onto the street.

We were having so much fun,
Taking turns to fire the gun.
Going for the occasional run,
Enjoying our places in the sun.

We guard Pacific's triple star,
From the shafts of strife and war.
Quigley thinks that threat's afar,
And took away the cookie jar.

It will be a frightful day,
When we have to earn our pay.
Some will leave straight away,
Others will just fade away.

We all thought it would be a farce,
The data we sent was pretty sparse.
But the review team wasn't on grass,
And put a boot up our arse.

Our report had been sent to an officials' committee for comment and was now before the Cabinet Economic Committee. I was asked to appear before that Committee with Lange in the chair. However, when I said I needed to see the officials' report before I could usefully comment on it, the agenda item was immediately adjourned to allow this to happen.

When the second committee meeting took place, Lange's leadership was under intense pressure and the new finance minister, David Caygill, was in the chair. Lange saw me in the corridor on my way to the meeting and called out: 'I've helped you, Quig. You'll help me too, won't you?' It was a sad occasion and we talked briefly. I then thanked him for what he had done for New Zealand and headed off to the meeting.

There, the only issue in contention was the auditing of aspects of military performance by civilians. This was vigorously opposed by the military, wrongly conceded by the committee, and resulted in long-term difficulties in the relationship between the Ministry of Defence and the NZDF. Prior to Gerald Hensley becoming Secretary of Defence after the election of the National government in 1990 — with his earlier appointment stymied by Helen Clark — there were three successive Secretaries of Defence between December 1988 and September 1991, with all of them attempting unsuccessfully to deal with the dysfunctional relationship between the two bodies.

The working relationship between the Secretary representing the ministry and the CDF representing the military was particularly bad, with a subsequent CDF writing: 'We perhaps perceived [the first Secretary] as wanting to reform regardless of what the outputs were. He perceived us as a bunch of extremely conservative people who would resist change in any form. We all talked past each other in one way or another.'[20]

In fact that particular Secretary was disliked intensely because of his desire to put into effect the government's intentions from the review. 'Those intentions weren't resting very easily on the Defence Force.'[21] Another more practical reason — in my opinion — was that all the initial secretaries prior to Hensley's appointment were there for relatively short time-frames, with the military determined to see them off.

A major part of the early problem with the implementation of our recommendations was that although the legislation required the Secretary and the CDF to 'consult', there was no statutory provision that required the military to hand over relevant information to the ministry, despite the Cabinet Policy Committee's decision in 1989 that there should be. The performance audit issue I had fought and lost before the Cabinet Economic Committee also caused major problems, with the military's vigorously expressed view that the evaluation of any function, task or responsibility of the NZDF by the ministry implied that the military couldn't be trusted to carry out their own audits and assessments. As a result, as I had warned the Cabinet Committee might happen, there was a misunderstanding of what the audit function was designed to achieve.

Gerard Hensley believed the 'output evaluations represented the core of what the Quigley Review originally intended of the audit and assessment function, but the way the two organisations were set up made this impossible to achieve for nearly a decade'.[22]

A scary movie.

When the Ministry of Defence and the NZDF had been in place for over 20 years, a recommendation I made in 1999 that it should be the subject of a re-evaluation was taken up by the Clark government. This is discussed later.

What the Strategos report did not contain were my comments — outlined in an eight-page letter to the prime minister — on 'a number of issues too sensitive for inclusion . . . to avoid too much public criticism of those in the system'. However, in view of the military's subsequent opposition to the report's main recommendations and government naïvety in leaving some key implementation issues to the defence hierarchy, these comments should have been made public when the report was released. Had they been, the New Zealand public would have been outraged at the waste of taxpayers' money by the military and the obvious indifference of some of the defence hierarchy to that waste.

CHAPTER 18

National's Defence Backflip and the Road to MMP

As the 1987 election approached, many within the National Party thought that Labour was headed for defeat as another one-term government. However, it was re-elected with an increased majority of one, providing it with 57 MPs compared to National's 40. Although National won back Pakuranga and East Coast Bays from Social Credit, achieving a net gain of three seats and increasing its overall vote to 40 percent (from 35.9 percent in 1984), Labour did much better, with 48 percent of the overall vote compared with just under 43 percent in 1984.

The figures in part hid the fact that National was suffering from continuing disillusionment among its traditional supporters. This was particularly evident in blue-ribbon seats, where voters clearly thought they could teach the party a lesson by either not voting — the overall turnout was down to 89.1 percent compared with 93.7 in 1984 — or in some cases voting for Labour because they supported what it was doing; or protest-voting for another party without the risk of National losing the seat.

Other reasons were Muldoon's continual harking back to his 'achievements' as prime minister; Bill Birch's ongoing lauding of 'Think Big'; caucus divisions over policy direction; and dissatisfaction over promotions and demotions.

As a result, National's majority in supposedly ultra-safe seats such as Fendalton, Remuera and North Shore plummeted respectively to 311, 406 and 920. Other close calls were in Wairarapa, where the final majority was 34, and Invercargill, 552. In contrast, in my former Rangiora electorate, where National supporters knew their votes were crucial, Jim Gerard increased his 1984 majority of 346 to 2132.

Following National's election loss there was a widespread move, mainly among the younger and less conservative wing of the party, to change the party's leader. Their view was that Muldoon represented the past and should be replaced. However, Muldoon would not go voluntarily and eventually a direct leadership challenge took place in November 1984. The two main candidates to replace him were Jim McLay and Jim Bolger. McLay was a free-market proponent with a relatively liberal social outlook. Bolger was more traditional and pragmatic, but less conservative than Muldoon. McLay won the contest with slightly over half the votes and Bolger became his deputy.

McLay's first major challenge was Muldoon himself, who refused to accept any of the 'elder statesman' portfolio positions offered to him, insisting on a more active role. Their relationship deteriorated further when McLay began to outline a major departure from Muldoon's economic policies. Eventually Muldoon was demoted to the bottom of the backbench membership list, no. 38 — where, among other things, he wrote the book *Number 38*.

When Muldoon eventually realised there was little chance of his retaining the leadership, he threw his support behind Bolger. This was despite his statement to a senior caucus member shortly after National's defeat in 1984, when George Gair had announced he was going to challenge for the leadership and Bolger was also expected to run, that he despised Bolger. This was taken to be a judgement on someone who, as Muldoon saw it, had been a coup leader but could be quickly and easily pressured back into line. Don McKinnon described Muldoon's view of some of his colleagues in an email to me:

> In many discussions I had with Muldoon he never believed anyone was as good as him, not put that crassly, but he had a disparaging word or phrase to say of *all* leadership contenders going back to 1985. Yes, he openly despised all the earlier 'colonels' coup' [members]. Playing one against the other was part of his DNA. The only support he ever gave openly, and to some aggressively, was for MacIntyre after Talboys vacated the deputy role.[1]

Nevertheless, Muldoon was happy to use Bolger later as a stalking horse to oust McLay. There was considerable media speculation that McLay would be replaced before the end of 1985, but the rumoured challenge failed to eventuate and McLay remained leader until early 1986 when, in an attempt to rejuvenate the party's upper ranks, McLay demoted Gair and Birch, who had both put their own names forward in 1984 for the position of leader before eventually withdrawing. Both were highly respected within the party and caucus for their ability and long service, and now aligned themselves with Bolger.

On 26 March 1986, Gair, Birch and party whip Don McKinnon presented McLay with a letter signed by a majority of the National Party caucus asking him to step aside. Bolger received a majority in the caucus vote that followed, and Gair became his deputy. After his defeat, McLay was appointed shadow minister of justice and shadow attorney-general, but was given a ranking of 10, below Muldoon, who came back into the front bench at number 8. McLay retired from Parliament at the 1987 election and in 2009 became New Zealand's permanent representative to the United Nations.

In its 1987 election manifesto National had promised to 'repeal those sections of the [Labour government's anti-nuclear legislation] which prevent New Zealand participating in collective efforts to make the world and our region safer and more secure'. This policy was a clear commitment based on principle rather than opportunism, and won respect and support for that reason. However, when Labour was re-elected, many in the National caucus put its loss down — wrongly, in my view — to its opposition to the anti-nuclear policy.

Faced with this clear major policy difference between National and Labour in the run-up to the 1990 election, and also an apparent softening of US stance towards New Zealand, National had a change of heart and adopted Labour's anti-nuclear policy.

Although some may argue otherwise, the facts are that National's advertising guru, Mike Wall, formerly of Colenso Communications, had convinced the caucus by early 1990 of the need for a policy change. His line was: 'Do you want to go into a political campaign with a mushroom cloud on television and the caption "Vote National" underneath it?' That mushroom cloud became the one thing Bolger thought would prevent him from becoming prime minister. Wall argued that Labour would zero in on this every day during the election campaign, this was enough for the soft underbelly of the National caucus to become anti-nuclear adherents.[2]

The party's credibility was further damaged when Bolger, immediately prior to the National's policy somersault, unequivocally undertook to the former New Zealand Chief of Defence Force, Sir Ewan Jamieson, before Jamieson left on a study visit to the US, that a policy reversal was not on the cards. Jamieson had sought a meeting with Bolger because he knew National's 1987 commitment to reverse Labour's legislation would be a major point of discussion while he was in the US. His record of his meeting with Bolger is that:

> I called on Bolger because I wanted to know for sure what the policy was. He spelt it out. As soon as possible after we come to power, [he said,] we will change the Nuclear Exclusion Act to such an extent that all ship visits will again be possible and we will, having done that, return as soon as possible to a fully participating role within ANZUS. I then said, now, are you firm on that? If the people in Washington ask me, am I going to get egg on my face if I say that is what you're saying and you have a change of heart? He said no, no.[3]

However, after the election, in the face of increasing disarray within Labour, National rose again in the polls and stayed there until it won 67 seats in 1990: a majority of 37 seats, the largest number in New Zealand's parliamentary history. But despite this, National's percentage of the overall vote was less than Labour's in 1987, which had produced a 19-seat majority.

Faced with ballooning public spending, National took some bold initial steps, particularly when Ruth Richardson was finance minister, to rein in expenditure and to put the country's books in order. As a result, and also because of the impact of Labour's earlier massive reforms and an export-led recovery, New Zealand began to prosper again. Unemployment fell through the 1990s, after peaking at 10.9 per cent in 1991; and the budget was brought into surplus in 1994.

The expectation therefore — among most pundits and particularly in the National caucus — was that the 1993 election would see them re-elected comfortably. But the electorate delivered a substantial shock. Disillusionment with the government was reflected in a low voter turnout of under 83 percent; an increase in support for New Zealand First of over 8 percent; and a loss of 17 National seats. Labour had increased the number of its MPs by 16 but there was not much enthusiasm there either, as its share of the overall vote went down marginally compared with 1990, largely due to an increase of over 18 percent in the support for the Alliance Party.

Initially it appeared as though there would be a hung Parliament, with National unlikely to be able to establish a clear majority. But when special votes were counted and the Labour MP for Eastern Māori became the Speaker, National had a majority of two, although with its overall vote down from almost 48 percent in 1990 to fractionally over 35 percent.

An unreliable ally?

After the 1990 election National's earlier backflip on Labour's anti-nuclear legislation was made worse in credibility terms, particularly in the eyes of senior US defence personnel, by a ham-fisted attempt to repeal the anti-nuclear propulsion provisions in the Act. In 1991 the government appointed a high-powered Committee on Nuclear Propulsion to examine the safety aspects of nuclear-powered ships and the risks they might present to the public on visits to New Zealand ports. The committee's key conclusion, in its December 1992 report, was that

> the presence in New Zealand ports of nuclear-powered vessels of the navies of the United States and the United Kingdom would be safe. The likelihood of any damaging emission or discharge of radioactive material from nuclear-powered vessels if in New Zealand ports is so remote that it cannot give rise to any rational apprehension.[4]

The committee also noted that there was a serious lack of understanding and knowledge, and much misinformation, in the minds of the public on the issue. However, once again poll politics prevailed and the government resiled from amending the Act.

Together with National's earlier reversal of its 1987 policy stance, this decision confirmed, in the eyes of the Americans, that New Zealand — even under a self-styled conservative government — was still an unreliable ally. Admiral Crowe, US Commander in Chief Pacific 1983–85, said he was not surprised. 'I never thought it would [reverse its policy in 1987],' he said.[5] The sanctions the US had imposed against New Zealand continued.

A further government decision was to conduct a Cabinet Review of Defence funding that resulted in cuts to operational and personnel spending of 19 percent in real terms in 1990–98. This was contrary to the Lange government's undertaking to the defence hierarchy to allow savings generated by the Strategos review to be reallocated to higher priorities within defence, and was a major factor in a progressive decline of the NZDF's capabilities.

Don McKinnon, minister of foreign affairs in the Bolger and Jenny Shipley governments, has described to me in graphic terms the difficulties he and the minister of defence faced in dealing with successive ministers of finance during the 1990–99 period, when — unlike the situation in Australia — there was no strong constituency within the Cabinet in support of defence:

> Ruth Richardson had taken over the Treasury portfolio and was antagonistic towards defence chiefs. She felt they were just mouthing the same issues and policies they had been for twenty years. She saw no sophistication in the way defence had changed and took some persuading that on issues like peacekeeping you first needed highly trained soldiers and then you trained them even better to be a peacekeeper. You were not looking for low-cost pot-smoking bearded peaceniks waving a banner labelled 'peace'. There was a continual downward pressure on the defence budget and no real recognition of just how expensive military equipment was and how it played a part in causing us to pull away from many things we probably could have managed a whole lot better ... When Bill Birch became Treasurer, it was even worse ... and became even more embarrassing as we moved into the Bougainville issue.[6]

In an attempt to regain some defence credibility, the government published a Defence White Paper in 1991, and a Defence Assessment (DA) was also produced. The White Paper was 'an early statement on the direction in which New Zealand's policy will move' ... to 'bring New Zealand back to its correct place in the international community'.[7]

The Defence Act 1990, following the Strategos recommendations, required the Secretary of Defence, in consultation with the CDF, to submit a DA to the defence minister from time to time, reviewing the different options for achieving the government's defence policy goals. DA91 noted that:

> In the view of our ANZUS partners, full membership [of the alliance] is not consistent with our anti-nuclear legislation. This effectively decouples New Zealand from the Western alliance. Without full membership the

> defence force's ability to work with Australia, the United States and others will remain constrained.[8]

The assessment acknowledged that, while the impact would be lessened if New Zealand were to define its defence interests purely in terms of the South Pacific, the NZDF's diminishing professionalism might encourage Pacific Forum countries to look more to Australia for their security assistance. The problem would be even greater if a national strategy were adopted which aimed to support distant as well as regional interests.[9]

The government opted instead for a strategy of 'self-reliance in partnership' and attempted to 'build a minimum credible defence force'. But there were problems even with this approach, because any defence strategy had to take account of two fundamental issues: the wide geographic spread of the country's interests, and its small population and fiscal base.

Given that the direct defence of New Zealand's territory was (and still is) viewed as a low priority — by planners and the public — thinking had to focus on an indirect strategy based on the defence of the country's interests abroad. But, as the assessment correctly noted, there was little enthusiasm to fund this, given competing demands from other elements of New Zealand's external policy, such as its diplomatic establishments and the foreign aid programme.

Defence planners responded by trying to make 'clearer sense' of New Zealand's huge geographic ambit by avoiding talking in terms of two separate and uneasily matched categories: 'the South Pacific' and 'Beyond'. They replaced the two categories with a perspective that looked progressively outwards from New Zealand in order to devise appropriate responses to a variety of interests.

The starting point was to look at the capability to deal with low-level threats to New Zealand, its territorial waters and its exclusive economic zone (EEZ); and then to move out to the country's maritime environment and its common interests with Australia and its Pacific neighbours. Next, the focus was on more distant but no less important interests in Southeast Asia, Northeast Asia and the Northern Hemisphere.[10]

In terms of its approach to the Southeast and Northeast Asia regions, the 1991 document was much more outward-looking than the 1987 White Paper, which had been written in the aftermath of the ANZUS split. The later paper strongly reaffirmed New Zealand's dependence on a stable and secure Asia-Pacific region and the importance of being able to make a credible contribution to deterring and, if required, assisting in defeating challenges to regional stability. These policy imperatives were presented as a significant determinant of defence force structure, and a reconfirmation — in contrast to the Strategos recommendations — of the need for a range of military capabilities across all three services. The conclusion was that New Zealand's defence force was reasonably well matched to its strategic position and to the range of external interests it was intended to support.

This was consistent with the underlying view — which Strategos disagreed with — that defence needed to be structured on the basis of an 'insurance/balanced force' approach.[11]

By the time DA91 was written, funding was starting to become a problem, with that document recording that 'the consistency in planning and funding which is the prerequisite to efficiency, still eludes us'.[12] The assessment went on to note that consideration would have to be given to adjusting or eliminating capabilities that contributed least to priority defence tasks. A series of reviews followed to explore possibilities, ranging from air combat to self-defence for naval and land forces.

While these reviews were under way, consideration was given to the development of an even closer defence relationship with Australia. DA91 had emphasised the importance of the trans-Tasman relationship by acknowledging a commonality of interest between the two countries that was reflected in their approach to collective security. However, the document recorded that this did not mean the two counties were 'a complete strategic entity', as neither wanted the relationship to be the dominant determinant of force structure.

This reluctance, which has been an ongoing feature of the trans-Tasman connection, was questioned at one point by the Australian minister for defence, Senator Ray, and CDF General Gration[13] when both defence forces were financially pressed. Ray suggested that Australia could take over certain responsibilities from New Zealand and that New Zealand could cover one or two of Australia's major capability areas.[14] Gration went further, arguing that the logic of further cooperation was inescapable:

> Given the costs of modern military forces and the constrained defence funds likely to be available to both countries, it seems clear that both countries will have to be selective in the capabilities they can maintain in their forces. As priorities must be set, it seems sensible that both countries not only

> cooperate more closely in matters such as training and logistic support, but also develop their force structures to be complementary to a greater degree than in the past.[15]

In the end Australia and New Zealand did enter into a formal Closer Defence Relationship Agreement (CDR) in 1991, but despite this, and the stated intention of the Bolger government to rehabilitate New Zealand defence in the eyes of the international community, the government was still unable to establish a clear support base within the New Zealand electorate for more money for the NZDF, or support for a particular set of military capabilities.

In the face of continuing cuts in NZDF spending, the CDF and the Secretary of Defence reported to the government in March 1996 that current NZDF activities could not be sustained, and that either a review of funding or significant cuts to military capabilities were required. Doing nothing was not an option, they wrote. This advice formed the basis for a subsequent DA and the 1997 Defence White Paper.

However, by the time they were published, the Mixed Member Proportional (MMP) electoral system was in place; National had formed a coalition government with New Zealand First; I was back in Parliament as the chair of the Foreign Affairs, Defence and Trade Select Committee; and I had my sights firmly set on a further review of New Zealand's security and defence environment.

MMP: Major electoral reform

The pressure for changes to the electoral system had been building since the 1978 election, propelled by the outcome for Social Credit, which was widely perceived as unfair. That party received around 16 percent of votes, but won only one seat. Elements within the Labour Party were dissatisfied too. At the elections in 1978 and 1981 Labour had gained more overall votes than National, but still had not won enough seats to form a government. During the 1984 election campaign Labour promised, if elected, to appoint a Royal Commission on the Electoral System to look at proportional voting systems, and it did so in 1985. The commission's 1986 report, *Towards a Better Democracy*, noted that a Parliament in which only the two main parties ever got to govern might not be the most democratic system, and proposed a referendum on the issue.[16] The commission proposed 10 criteria for a fair voting system, noting: 'The best voting system for any country will not be one which meets any of the criteria completely but will be one which provides the most satisfactory overall balance between them, taking account of that country's history and current circumstances.'

The 10 criteria, in no particular order, were:

- fairness between political parties, with seats in the House roughly reflecting the number of votes received;
- effective representation of minority and special-interest groups;
- effective Māori representation;
- political integration for all groups within society;
- effective representation of constituents with accountability;
- an effective and understandable system, with voters having the power to make and unmake governments;
- an effective government able to act decisively and fulfil its responsibilities;
- an effective Parliament independent from government control;
- a system with effective political parties that can formulate policy and provide representation; and
- a system that has legitimacy because it is fair and reasonable.

The commission recommended that New Zealand adopt the MMP system established in Germany in 1949, which it considered likely to work well here.

A political party would be entitled to a share of MPs proportional to its share of the party vote if it reached one of two thresholds. It would need to win either a minimum of 5 percent of the nationwide vote, or at least one electorate seat. Every eligible voter would be entitled to two votes — an electorate vote and a party vote — and a party's total number of seats in Parliament would be filled with a mix of electorate MPs and list MPs. Electorate MPs would be elected using the traditional first-past-the-post voting system, with the candidate getting the most votes winning. The rest of a party's MP entitlement would be made up from its party's list.

A broad-based influential lobby group, the Electoral Reform Coalition, was set up in mid-1986 to lobby for a referendum on the voting system to accompany the general election in 1987. But major government procrastination followed, and it wasn't until the 1987 election leaders' debate that an undertaking was extracted from Lange for a referendum on MMP at or before the next election. Despite this, the matter didn't proceed, amid ongoing divisions within the Labour government over the possibility of change. In an attempt to calm the internal discord, Geoffrey Palmer, Labour's deputy leader, stating at the party's April 1989 regional conference, that the issue was 'effectively dead for the immediate future' but that it might be revisited 'in another 20 years'.[17]

Palmer soon replaced Lange as prime minister and was himself replaced by Mike Moore just before the 1990 election. At the pre-election leaders' debate Moore and Bolger both came under pressure on electoral reform, and Moore promised a referendum before the next (1993) election. Bolger, who had previously been criticising the government's inactivity, also promised a referendum before the 1993 election.

When National won comfortably in 1990, it was consequently stuck with another policy commitment — one with the potential to undermine its years of success under the FPP system.

However, in 1992 a non-binding referendum took place, with the government promising that if a majority supported change, a binding referendum offering a choice between FPP and the most popular reform option would be held during the course of the 1993 general election. Although only around 55 percent of eligible voters took part in the 1992 referendum, 84.72 percent voted for change. In the second part of the referendum, voters chose between MMP, the Single Transferable Vote system (STV), the Supplementary Member system (SM) and, the Preferential Vote system (PV). After an extensive education campaign explaining the various options, MMP received nearly 70 percent support.

Prior to the 1993 run-off vote between FPP and MMP there was fierce lobbying on both sides. I was actively involved on the side for change. Both National and Labour had displayed arrogance over the years when they were in government and I wanted them taught a lesson. And also because the FPP system was patently unfair in denying a voice in Parliament to smaller parties with opinions and policies that differed from those of National and Labour.

With a much higher general election turnout of 85 percent in 1993, MMP won with a margin of 54 percent. This meant New Zealand would have a new voting system in place at the 1996 election that would dramatically improve the prospects of third-party representation in Parliament.

CHAPTER 19

Contemplating a Return to Politics

Moving to Sydney

Strategos had completed contracts with Defence, Justice, Treasury, Police and the Fire Service for the Labour government but by now senior MPs were increasingly preoccupied with internal conflict. Douglas was on one side, pushing for further economic and social reform, and Lange was on the other, increasingly concerned about the social cost of what the government had already done. As a result, it lost its appetite for further reform and the sun set on further government contracts for Strategos. With National likely to win the 1990 election, and few prospects of work for me from it, we restructured our consultancy. Michael Cox joined it, and three other shareholders departed.

I began to look for other income opportunities

During the 1989/1990 Christmas holiday period I received an approach from Sydney. I was asked if we were interested in investing in a company in return for a 25 percent shareholding and an ongoing monthly consultancy retainer. I was interested, but before making a decision I sought advice from businessman Peter Allport on the company's financial position, viability and potential. On our behalf Peter visited Sydney, spent time with company personnel, went through the company's books, and reported back that the business was solid, with considerable potential.

I replied, 'If it's such a good investment I want you to put some of your money into it too.' He did, and another New Zealand entity also came to the party, putting in the same amount as us for another 25 percent of the total shareholding.

When the money was paid, we moved to Sydney with an *Evening Post* billboard providing unexpected and unwanted publicity:

But by early November 1990 — despite the capital injections and substantial expenditure cuts — the company's forecast for the year to the end of June 1991 was for a substantial loss. By February 1991 things looked even worse. Further substantial cash injections were clearly needed, but as none of us were interested in throwing good money after bad, receivership followed. When things settled down, the other New Zealand company that had entered the picture at the same time as us picked up what was left of the business. Fortuitously, our monthly consulting fees had almost covered our original investment.

While in Sydney I had contacted Col Gellatly, head of the NSW Premier's Office, and his New Zealander deputy, Ken Baxter.[1] Both knew my background. They were progressively reforming the New South Wales government bureaucracy and asked if I was interested in applying for the position of director-general of the Department of the Attorney-General and Justice. I answered yes and lodged an application, and a date was set for my interview. However, in the meantime I was at a social function and got chatting to the recently retired attorney-general, John Dowd. He knew about my application and said I was the frontrunner, but added: 'I don't think they are going to fill the position.'

But the selection process continued. Before my interview I obtained references from Roderick Deane and Ross Sayers, chairman and chief executive of the State Railway Authority of New South Wales. I had first met Ross in New Zealand when I was managing director the Hugo Group and he was involved with New Zealand Rail. His reference was supportive, saying I had a clear, perceptive mind and was an excellent strategic thinker.

Deane wrote that I had the ability to see problems and solutions with clarity, that I had considerable personal drive and a natural enthusiasm for tackling big projects successfully, and that 'while [I was] a demanding manager to work for', I was always equally prepared to listen to good argument and analysis.

Then before the interview Gellatly told me that the Courts Division was going to be split off as a separate department and that I could have either this or the residual Attorney-General's Department. I opted for the latter.

I had been asked to submit a paper before I met the interviewing panel on the management of the courts, and in it dealt with the notion that 'a judge is master in his or her own court'. While I accepted this contention from the perspective of judicial independence, I argued that courts still had to be run efficiently and effectively, and that for this reason judges had to adhere to administrative guidelines. The judge on the panel challenged this view but I vigorously defended it, to the undisguised pleasure of the lay selection panel members.

Within days, Gellatly phoned and asked if I was available to meet with Attorney-General Peter Collins 'to see if you and the minister are compatible'. Collins arrived late for the meeting in the company of the acting head of the department who — to my surprise and annoyance — sat in on the interview.

From Collins' first question — 'How do you get on with your former National Party parliamentary colleagues?'— it was obvious I wasn't going to get the job. Jokingly, I put this down to being too tall for Collins, who allegedly is so self-conscious of his lack of height that he had a built-up desk and chair in his office, so that he didn't have to look up to anyone he was meeting with.

Gellatly was furious when I was turned down. He asked if I was interested in heading a new State Owned Enterprises Office being set up to mirror the SOE initiatives of the 1984–90 New Zealand government. I might have been, but before anything further was progressed, I asked him to find out whether my appointment to any senior government position was going to be acceptable to the NSW Cabinet. It clearly wasn't, as no other job offers eventuated.

In retrospect this wasn't surprising — I had been warned that some of my former National Party colleagues believed that my working for the Labour government (through Strategos) in New Zealand was akin to treason. The depth of this antagonism had shown up during a visit to Parliament to update ministers on the progress of the Strategos defence review. By chance Alf Kirk and I met Winston Peters in the foyer and he — dressed immaculately as usual in a dark pinstriped, double-breasted suit — challenged me with 'What are you doing here?' I don't remember my reply, but clearly recall his retort: 'When we're back in government, we'll remember who you worked for.'

After I had visited Oslo during the course of the defence review I was asked if I was interested in becoming their country's honorary consul in Wellington. I said yes, but again nothing eventuated. The coded message I read in this was that some of my former colleagues had had their say on this too.

Back in Wellington

A little before moving to Sydney we had sold our first Wellington house to Sylvia Cartwright (who later became chief District Court judge, then a High Court judge and eventually governor-general) and her husband Peter. We bought a house in Wellington's Upland Road within a short distance of the cable car. It was the classic 'worst house in the best street' scenario, with great views of the university and across the city to the harbour.

We decided to lease it given our impending move overseas, and a tenancy was arranged with the number two diplomat in the German Embassy. Before the lease was signed, a senior French diplomat also looked through the property. He saw our print of Stanley Palmer's 1985 painting *J'Accuse*, which depicts the artist's view of the aftermath of the *Rainbow Warrior* bombing. The diplomat, who obviously appreciated the subtlety of the painting, said with a slightly embarrassed laugh, 'If I lease your house, you must leave that painting here.'

While we were in Sydney I began to receive coded messages from the new chairman of Colonial Mutual Life in New Zealand that if I wanted to continue as a director, I needed to come back home instead of flying in from Australia for board meetings. This prompted us to move back to New Zealand.

I had resigned from Hugo in 1989 to avoid any conflicts of interest arising between it and the consulting work Strategos was doing, but I still

Reaction to the Rainbow Warrior bombing

held some other board positions. However, as National was now back in office, and there were few consulting opportunities available, we decided to auction the Hawkestone Street office.[2]

Interest was strong initially with three parties obtaining valuations, but as auction day approached, these buyers had disappeared. It turned out council staff were advising potential buyers that there were doubts about the building's status as an office, with its commercial zoning being called into question by various locals.

I went to the council and politely asked how the problem could be solved. I was told they would like to investigate the matter properly, but didn't have the staff available. So I offered to do the research myself, and about six months later was able to confirm to the council's satisfaction that the building had unrestricted 'existing commercial user' rights as an office. When we did eventually sell, the price — although not too bad — was about $80,000 less than it would have been.

America calling

Out of the blue one Saturday morning I received a call from Richmond, Virginia. I was asked if I would act on behalf of Ethyl Corporation, one of America's top 500 listed companies, to support its efforts to introduce a manganese-based product codenamed MMT as an additive for unleaded petrol in New Zealand. As the job involved extensive contact with politicians and relevant department officials, and was well paid, I agreed. The association proved a good one. Ethyl's people in the US and Sydney were easy to work with; I visited the company's head office in Maryland; and made many new friends. After several years of difficult negotiations the product was eventually included in the New Zealand Fuel Regulations.

I had been recommended to Ethyl by the head of a fuel marketing company in Wellington who had followed my political career. The same person recommended me shortly after to Tractebel, a long-established large international company based in Belgium that specialised in energy and infrastructure projects. My job was to look for takeover possibilities for Tractebel Asia in New Zealand and to act as that company's agent there. Again, this proved to be an interesting assignment, which only came to an end much later when contract negotiations that would have resulted in my client acquiring a major energy infrastructure business in New Zealand were abandoned at the eleventh hour as a result of an inter-Tractebel company takeover.

Time in the UK

Towards the end of 1995 we visited Cambridge in the UK for three months. Before leaving New Zealand I arranged with the university to give lectures there on the impending change to New Zealand electoral system, the Labour government's economic reforms; and New Zealand's social welfare system.

I also contacted John Groom, head of the International Relations Department at the University of Kent, and the editor of *The Round Table: The Commonwealth Journal of International Affairs* in London, and gave presentations on welfare reform in Kent, and in London on economic reform in New Zealand.

The London address was later published in *The Round Table*.[3] In discussing the key steps taken by the Lange government (and carried on by National for a period after the 1990 election), I said that they were based on the four cornerstones of price stability underpinned by the Reserve Bank Act, fiscal responsibility underpinned by the Fiscal Responsibility Act, a competitive and open economy, and a flexible decentralised

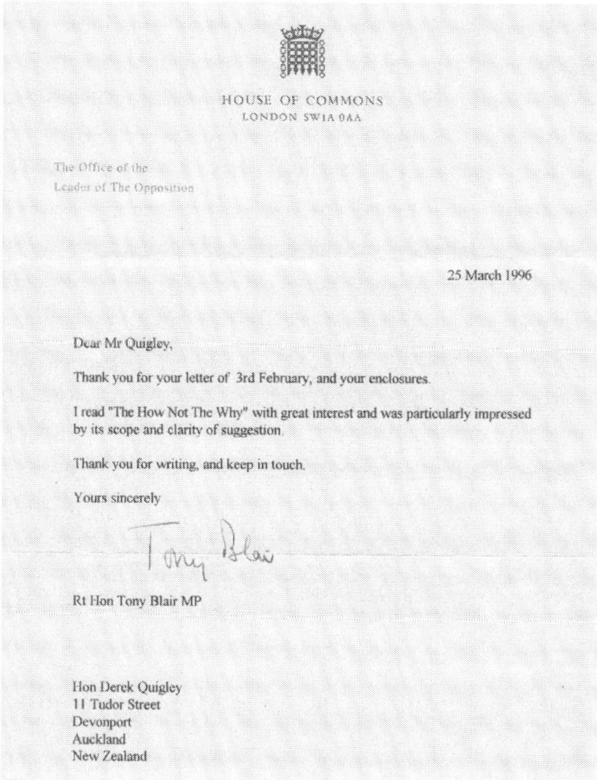

HOUSE OF COMMONS
LONDON SW1A 0AA

The Office of the
Leader of The Opposition

25 March 1996

Dear Mr Quigley,

Thank you for your letter of 3rd February, and your enclosures.

I read "The How Not The Why" with great interest and was particularly impressed by its scope and clarity of suggestion.

Thank you for writing, and keep in touch.

Yours sincerely

Tony Blair

Rt Hon Tony Blair MP

Hon Derek Quigley
11 Tudor Street
Devonport
Auckland
New Zealand

Correspondence from Tony Blair.

labour market. The overall result, I said, was that in just over 10 years New Zealand had gone from virtual bankruptcy to a situation where it could claim, with some justification, to be one of the most internationally competitive countries in the world.

The benchmark for that claim was the five criteria for European Monetary Union membership: a government deficit of no more than 3 percent, public debt of 60 percent of GPD or below, a 10-year bond yield of no more than 2 percent of the average of the three lowest countries, a stable currency, and inflation of 3 percent or less. New Zealand qualified in terms of all five criteria.

While we were in Cambridge I also took the opportunity to write to Tony Blair, then Opposition leader, sending him several one-page papers on aspects of the New Zealand reform process. I received a personal acknowledgement from Blair. I also arranged to meet with a number of MPs and their party people in London. What was most notable was the enthusiasm Labour was showing, and the 'Conservatives' lack of interest in the whole political process. Although their next election didn't take place until 1997, it was clear to me that John Major's Conservative government was tired and on the way out, and they knew it.

An approach to form a new party

Meanwhile, back home, National was in trouble electorally over broken promises in a number of important areas, with Muldoon telling Bolger in caucus in 1991 that he (Bolger) presided over a government that had broken more promises than any other he could remember, and denouncing the majority of his fellow MPs as 'spineless' for not being prepared to honour election promises and for not forcing ministers to do so.[4]

I was approached by Brian Nicolle, a political activist and supporter of Roger Douglas and the reforms he had orchestrated during the 1984–90 period, to see if I was interested in forming a new political party with Douglas.

The approach raised several questions for me to consider over the next few months. Was I interested in becoming actively involved in politics again? As an early decision was yes, I had to decide with whom. There were effectively only two options: either National or a new party with Douglas.

Going with National would potentially be easier — it had a well-established political presence and I had been associated with it since 1950 at branch, electorate, division and national level. I was a strong public supporter of its expressed private-enterprise philosophy. And yet by the 1990s I was *persona non grata* in the eyes of a number of my former parliamentary colleagues, who regarded me as one of the main architects of Muldoon's electoral demise. I had also compounded my unpopularity in my early days as a consultant by turning down two approaches from Bill Birch to do some policy research for the party.

In addition, I had been indiscreet enough to make occasional public comments in support of some of the Labour government's reforms — which really wasn't surprising since I had long been pushing National to implement similar policies. In fact, I had voted for Labour's re-election in 1987, not because I supported that party's basic philosophy but because — like many other New Zealanders — I knew the reforms they were undertaking were desperately needed. The Labour government had had the guts to grasp the nettle and implement change, and its reforms, which were not ideologically motivated, were designed to improve New Zealand society.

My final indiscretion, as far as some of my former colleagues were concerned, was my audacity in carrying out a number of high-profile department reviews for the Labour government — working for 'the enemy'.

The problem from my point of view was that I didn't think National was completely rehabilitated. Initially, during McLay's leadership, there had been nascent signs that the caucus was getting back on track, followed by a burst of much-needed further reform after the 1990 election, but after the party's near loss in 1993 it had reverted to a status quo mindset.

I then began to look into the history and performance of some of the 'third parties' that had been around during the period since my first involvement in politics. The three I chose to examine were Social Credit, the Alliance Party and New Zealand First.

I wanted to look at how each had fared under the old electoral system; and, more importantly, to consider whether a new political party based on the policies Douglas and I would be advocating was likely to attract enough support to make a difference. I was conscious at the time that Douglas — like me — was also *persona non grata* within his former party. However, as he had been doing further work in developing an overall comprehensive policy package along the lines I supported, I was definitely interested in talking to him.

Social Credit

Social Credit had been about for years before it officially became a political party in 1953, with its origins among influential people in the Auckland Farmers Union and its political offshoot, the Country Party. Its policies were based on the writing of British engineer C. H. Douglas, whose theories had gained international adherents in the 1920s and 1930s.

Douglas believed that the monetary system was inherently defective. He drew attention to the fact that public and private debt, taxation levels and the cost of living had all been increasing, and contended that there was no real security for individuals or the nation. The basic reason was a 'chronic gap' between the amount of purchasing power in the hands of the people who want to buy goods and services, and the prices that sellers had to charge to earn a fair return on the goods and services they produced.

To remedy this situation, Social Credit supporters proposed that a credit authority be set up to ascertain, through a national survey, the extent of the gap, and then to direct the amount of extra purchasing power required, which should be issued 'debt free', to balance production and consumption. The extra purchasing power, they said, could be issued in many ways, but their proposal was that it should be used by the government to reduce taxation, increase social security benefits, subsidise retailers who would accordingly reduce their selling prices to agreed figures, and for public works of a non-commercial nature.

They further argued that monetary reform was required to avoid world wars, inflation, poverty, unemployment and social problems.

In New Zealand, the first attempt to spread Social Credit policies was through some Country Party MPs, and, after Labour became government in 1935, through MPs within that party, such as John A. Lee. Lee was one of Labour's early advocates of 'state credit', based on the concept of zero interest rates to finance large-scale public works and housing, to reduce unemployment, taxes, rates and the cost of debt servicing.

In 1954 when Social Credit fielded 79 candidates it attracted over 11 percent of the total vote, but under FPP this didn't translate into any seats in Parliament. What it did do was create concern within the National government, which set up a royal commission to look into monetary, banking and credit systems in the hope of derailing Social Credit. The commission reported in 1956 that it found little substance in Social Credit's theories, but came up with two recommendations: that the Reserve Bank needed clear goals and objectives, and that the government should have more explicit responsibility for monetary policy.

If anything, the government's attempts to discredit its economic theories strengthened Social Credit's support, particularly in the Far North. In the Hobson electorate in 1966 Vern Cracknell, who had been steadily increasing his support over successive elections, won the seat from National with 48 percent of the vote, thanks to a 3.7 percent decline in support for Labour. On a nationwide basis Social Credit attracted almost 15 percent of the overall vote, but only won this one electorate.

It was the first time since 1943 that a candidate for a party other than National or Labour had been elected. But the success was short lived — National regained the seat in 1969 when Social Credit's nationwide vote fell to 9 percent. It declined to below 7 percent in 1972 when the Kirk Labour government was elected.

With no one in Parliament to advocate its monetary theories, and declining public support for them anyway, the indications were that Social Credit was on its way out. But in 1975 it actually increased its overall vote, despite National's support being up by over 6 percent and the Values Party attracting over 5 percent.

Social Credit's additional support — and National's too — was largely at the expense of Labour, which shed over 10 percent of its 1972 vote, helping candidates like me in Rangiora to win seats.

The party's big success came in early 1978 in Rangitikei, where Bruce Beetham, a university lecturer and former Hamilton City mayor — who had come second to National's Sir Roy Jack in 1975 — won the by-election precipitated by Jack's death. Beetham's win was despite National and Labour both fielding strong candidates.

Beetham was joined in Parliament in 1980 by another Social Credit MP following a second disastrous by-election for National and Muldoon. This time it was in East Coast Bays, which should have been safe for the government. However, the retiring MP had become increasingly unpopular locally and as a result had had to defend his seat in 1978 against not just Labour and Social Credit, but also against an independent National candidate who polled over 3500 votes. The by-election figures show that the Labour vote collapsed in favour of Social Credit, with most of the 1978 independent National candidate's votes going to that party too.

A crucial feature of Social Credit's support by this time was less to do with its monetary policies — which in any event were hard for the public to understand and were often labelled 'funny money' — than with the party as a vehicle for protest. It was the only viable alternative to National and Labour in an FPP environment. And although the party's high-water marks were in 1978 and 1981, with over 16 percent and nearly 21 percent respectively, because it had no brand other than its fading one-dimensional policy of monetary reform, it was always at risk.

In 1984, with an invigorated Labour Party under David Lange and the arrival of the New Zealand Party on the electoral scene, Social Credit's vote slipped to under 8 percent, despite the party holding the East Coast Bays seat and narrowly winning the supposedly safe National electorate of Pakuranga. Perhaps sensing that its monetary ideology had had its day, the party hierarchy undertook an unsuccessful rebranding attempt at its 1985 conference with a change of name to the New Zealand Democrat Party. Both of its MPs were defeated in 1987.

Social Credit's eventual demise emphasises that for a political party to remain viable it needs two things: an enduring and acceptable brand, and an overall coherent approach to politics that encourages confidence in what it stands for and the people who represent it.

The Alliance Party

The Alliance (under various names and groupings) also established a sizable parliamentary presence, as a result of the defection of Jim Anderton from the Labour Party. Anderton was an old-style socialist, well to the left of mainstream Labour ideology. Although he had aspirations to lead the party, he couldn't mount enough caucus support to get into Cabinet after the 1984 election. He then became an outspoken opponent of the government's reforms and a critic of its leadership, and when he was suspended from the caucus for voting against selling the Bank of New Zealand, he resigned from the party in April 1989, claiming: 'I didn't leave Labour, it left me.'

Anderton and others formed NewLabour on 1 May 1989 — May Day. In a first for an MP defecting from his party, he was re-elected in 1990 as MP for Sydenham.

Anderton's defection from Labour came as no surprise to me. I first met him at Christchurch Airport when he was president of the Labour Party and we were both on our way to Wellington. He asked me about the changes I had introduced to housing policy and my reasons for them. I explained why borrowers from the Housing Corporation had been given the choice to buy a new or an existing house, and why I had accelerated the option for existing state house tenants to buy the properties they were renting. It was all completely anathema to him.

Although Anderton explained the reasons for his rift with Labour being because the government had become too centralist/market driven — which he genuinely believed — I saw his defection as more about repositioning himself in the expectation of a change in the electoral system. And time lends my theory credence as NewLabour, formed under the banner of 'democratic socialism' as an alternative to Labour's policies, became part of the Alliance Party grouping in 1991 when it merged with the Democrats, Mana Motuhake and the Greens, plus two defecting National Party MPs who were opposed to the Bolger government's initial post-election reforms.

The enlarged Alliance had three basic policy pillars: left-wing economics, environmental issues, and a range of Māori agendas. Its two electoral strengths were its green policies — which were beginning to take on a life of their own — and Anderton as a popular individual and politician who was seen to represent a particular type of ideology.

My view was that the Anderton-type ideology wasn't likely to last, given the nature of New Zealand society, and indeed it became increasingly irrelevant in a post-Muldoon era in the face of the benefits that were starting to flow by the mid-1990s. This was despite the Alliance's good showing in the 1992 Tamaki by-election following Muldoon's retirement from Parliament, when as a vehicle for protest it nearly won the seat. (Coincidentally, I had initially taken out nomination papers to stand there myself under a banner of True Blue National after being approached by some Tamaki party members, but eventually decided against it — fortuitously, as I would undoubtedly have split the National vote and delivered an Alliance win.

Although the Alliance grouping attracted strong support in 1993, capturing 18 percent of the vote, in an FPP environment it only won two seats — Anderton's Sydenham seat and Auckland Central. Anderton became deputy prime minister after the 1999 election. Prior to that, the Greens had given notice in 1997 that they would leave the Alliance prior to the 1999 election, which they did. They had remained with that grouping until then on the principled basis that their three MPs had been elected as Alliance members. The Alliance was the smaller coalition partner in the first Clark term, but split during 2002 into what Anderton and his allies called the Progressive Party. In 2002 no Alliance MPs were elected but Anderton and one colleague were returned to parliament under the Progressive banner.

New Zealand First

Unlike Social Credit and the Alliance, both of which had a strong ideological basis, New Zealand First was and still is a populist party trading on the personal charisma of Winston Peters and the old-style national conservatism conveyed by its name. The party came into existence in 1993 after Winston Peters resigned as a National Party MP in protest at National's economic policies and his frustrated leadership ambitions — and the inability of the National Party caucus to handle them.

Peters was a caucus colleague of mine from 1978 to 1981. My recollection of him then is less about his contribution to policy and caucus discussions than his long-drawn-out Electoral Commission and High Court battle to confirm his election as MP for the Hunua seat following the 1978 election, his support for Muldoon during the Colonels' Coup, and his impeccable suits and coiffure.

But what Peters does have is longevity and presence, and a belief in his own ability. After losing Hunua in 1981 he was elected in 1984 as the MP for Tauranga, a safe National electorate, succeeding Keith Allen, and in December 1986 gained nationwide notoriety by raising in Parliament what became known as the 'Maori Loans Affair', where the Department of Maori Affairs sought to borrow money offshore to fund Māori development.

This was the first of a number of headline issues Peters raised, and resulted in his appointment to the Opposition front bench after the 1987 election. By early 1988 he began to feature in the preferred prime minister polls with 2 percent initially, 9 percent two months later and 17 percent by July, significantly ahead of Bolger. A poll of National Party voters had him at 38 percent as preferred party leader, ahead of Bolger on 32 percent.

Despite expressing pro-market tendencies in his 1979 maiden speech, Peters began not only to oppose the Labour government's reforms but also those being advocated by, in particular, Ruth Richardson. 'Maybe this is the opening round in the formation of the Win Peters Party,' she remarked.[5] How right she was.

Peters attracted further media attention in 1987 when he commented publicly that there was a chronic lack of political leadership in New Zealand and that it wasn't the exclusive domain of the Labour Party. This resulted in his demotion from the front bench, but when he was re-elected as the MP for Tauranga in 1990 with a majority of 9314 — the largest of any MP — he was appointed to the National Cabinet as minister of Maori affairs, with the lowly ranking of number 17. This positioning eloquently conveyed Bolger's unstated message to him.

But Peters, undeterred by demotion, was soon publicly disagreeing with the direction of some government policies, and in October 1991 he was dismissed from Cabinet after a speech in which he claimed that New Zealand had an 'Erebus economy'.[6] He immediately shot back up in the preferred prime minister ranking to 17 percent. In 1992, after he had launched another attack and the party moved to expel him, his support rose to 28 percent.

When the National Party took steps to prevent Peters standing for the party in Tauranga, he lodged a successful High Court challenge and resigned as an MP. He contested and won the resulting Tauranga by-election as an independent, and in July 1993 launched the New Zealand First Party.

New Zealand First fielded 88 candidates in the 1993 general election, attracted 8.4 percent of the overall vote and returned two MPs — Peters in Tauranga and Tau Henare in Northern Māori.

A persistent and adept self-publicist, in 1994 Peters tabled 1860 pages of documents in Parliament related to the 'Winebox Affair'. His 16 previous attempts to do so had been blocked by the government. The documents, sourced from the Cook Islands, were carried in a cardboard winebox, giving rise to the popular name. They involved allegations by Peters of impropriety and incompetence by New Zealand's Serious Fraud Office (SFO) and Inland Revenue Department (IRD) in relation to what Peters alleged was criminal conduct associated with tax planning undertaken by some of New Zealand's largest companies. A commission of inquiry was set up in September 1994 and headed by former Chief Justice Sir Ronald Davison.

The commissioner eventually reported in 1997 and found no grounds supporting the allegations of fraud and corruption, but the inquiry itself was extensively litigated after it had reported, and four findings by the commission in relation to one of the 60 transactions examined were overturned. Changes to tax laws relating to the claiming of foreign tax credits followed, along with new rules for disclosure to the IRD, and penalties for non-compliance.

Who was responsible for Peters' 'defection' from the National Party caucus and his subsequent establishment of New Zealand First? There are two obvious candidates: Peters himself, when his leadership aspirations within National were not progressing; and Jim Bolger, who gave the impression that he didn't know how to handle him.

CHAPTER 20

The Formation of ACT

With MMP locked in as the new electoral system for the 1996 election, it was a good time to look at forming a new political party. Voters were struggling to distinguish between the policies of National and Labour, and the advent of new parties would provide more policy options. Both major parties had been guilty of breaking promises in government, with the result that politicians polled alongside used-car salesmen as the least-respected occupational group in the country. There was a strong perception that MMP would deliver a fairer and more representative electoral outcome, as the large parties were forced to go into coalition with high-polling third parties, and that would help restore confidence in Parliament as an institution.

Roger Douglas and I shared significant political synergies, and both still enjoyed a degree of respect among potential voters for what we stood for in policy terms. The time seemed right to look at joining forces to create a new right-wing, free-market political party. As the two leaders of ACT, we had different backgrounds. Roger had come from a long line of trade union activists, with his father and grandfather both Labour MPs. As an MP from 1969 to 1990 he had been the youngest person in 50 years to become a Cabinet minister, in 1972 aged 34. In his maiden speech in Parliament he had spoken against foreign investment and in favour of government intervention in the economy. Both were mainstream Labour dogma at the time.

But by the time I was first in Parliament Roger's policy approach was based on a belief that successive National governments had consistently failed to tackle New Zealand's growing social and economic problems, and that because of this, the country's welfare system was failing low-income people. He was intent on changing this, but was frustrated in doing so because most of his time as an MP up until then had been in opposition.

In contrast, my initial nine years as an MP were in government, so when I was given a job to do, I was able to get on and do it. The outcome, in the words of Marilyn Waring in caucus one day, was that 'If every Minister ran their portfolio like Quigley runs Housing, we will be in government for ever.'[1]

The problem ACT faced in its early days was that Douglas, who was the party's best-known public face, was reluctant to take on the job as leader. After 21 years as an MP he had had enough, and wanted to spend more time at home with his family. He was also enjoying being away from the often vitriolic personal criticism showered on him by some of his former Labour colleagues who regarded his reformist policies as anathema to their basic ideology. Additionally, his ideas were in high demand among the New Zealand business community and overseas, where they were respected.

Talking to him much later I realised he didn't have leadership ambitions with all that that entailed. When I asked why he hadn't sought to be prime minister he replied he had briefly thought about it, but was aware that leaders invariably had to compromise their views to keep everyone happy, and he wasn't prepared to do that. And, like me, he had no time for personality politics.

As ACT's other founder, I had no desire to be the leader either, so we looked for someone else to take on the role. Craig Heatley was the obvious contender. He was young and personable, had presence, was a successful businessman, and was a strong supporter of Douglas's policies. More importantly, he would have been seen as a new, non-political face at a time when most existing politicians were not well regarded. But despite initially being mildly interested in leading the party, after two days in Dunedin campaigning with Douglas, Heatley realised that politics was infinitely more difficult than the business world. He decided it wasn't for him.

Roger had retired from Parliament at the 1990 election and had become interested in the Canadian Consumers and Taxpayers Group and thought New Zealand could benefit from having something similar. Brian Nicolle and Priscilla Tate — who had been Labour Party activists in the Auckland Central electorate when Richard Prebble was the local MP and were strong supporters of Douglas and his policies — also became crucial to the eventual formation of the political party ACT New Zealand.

Nicolle and Tate established an informal organisation to cater for people who were interested in politics but not necessarily in either of the two main parties. They arranged regular public meetings addressed by keynote speakers, which attracted numerous people who later became ACT members. Interviews and advertising were also arranged through a private radio station, BBC Radio, which was owned by Alan Gibbs, an Auckland-based merchant banker and later a key figure in the formation and funding of ACT.

In 1992 people paid to hear Douglas and me discuss key social and economic issues at a public meeting in Auckland, using David McLoughlin's book *The Undeveloping Nation* as a basis for our conversation.[2] At that meeting Douglas floated zero tax as an option. Later this concept was included in his book *Unfinished Business*, with input on the financial side from Rodney Hide, who at the time was working as an economist for Gibbs.[3]

This meeting led to the formation of the Association of Consumers and Taxpayers, a ginger group to promote open-market policies using *Unfinished Business* as its marketing tool, and to comment on economic matters and other political issues of the day. It was set up to test the water and to become the basis for new political party if a proportional representation voting system was adopted. Craig Heatley, Sky TV founder and in 1986 the youngest person (age 31) to feature on the *National Business Review*'s Rich List, was an association foundation member along with Douglas and me, and other enthusiasts. Heatley and Gibbs were key in assisting with the funding of the fledgling group, with Heatley the public face of the entity's eventual bankrollers.

Heatley's motivation — like that of Gibbs and the other financial backers — was to progress the reform policies Douglas had pursued in government in the interests of all New Zealanders. To suggest that they were only interested in their own personal financial advancement, as some like Nicky Hager did in his book *The Hollow Men*, is complete nonsense.[4] If there had been any truth in that, I for one would never have been involved with ACT. What the funders' support did allow was for the association's office to be set up and staffed, and for several of us to campaign nearly full time for the eventual political party.

Following the November 1993 vote in favour of MMP, Priscilla Tate became the association's first staff member, initially working part time from home, but by January 1994 she was employed full time in the association's Queen Street office. By March 1994 Heatley, by now also virtually full time, had employed a marketing expert who had worked for his Sky TV interests and for Coopers and Lybrand. She reported directly to Heatley.

ACT policies

During 1994, association members were asked if they wanted to form a political party and the response was positive. The name ACT New Zealand was overwhelmingly supported by association members. By 1995 all the functions of a political party, including media, policy formulation, party administration, publicity and membership building, were in train, with a mix of former National and Labour MPs involved.

Roger Douglas and I honed a well-coordinated set of policies based on our shared belief that for a more open-market economy to function properly, consumers should have a more significant role. We wanted them to be able to exercise the maximum practical degree of choice and freedom in terms of access to, for example, quality welfare, education, health care and retirement income, regardless of their circumstances. We saw the state having a less dominant role in the provision of those services, but instead providing the necessary regulation and supervision to see that no one fell through the cracks.

As we also believed that New Zealand would gain considerably from lower government spending and taxation, we advocated a single, flat tax rate of no more than 19.5 percent for individuals and companies. We believed this was fairer and simpler than the existing system; would encourage hard work, energy and thrift; would make New Zealand more internationally competitive; and would bring Kiwi capital, companies and people back home. Finally, in conjunction with the superannuation policy we were advocating, we saw a low flat tax rate — with appropriate alternative support for non-earners — as the key to providing security and wealth for New Zealanders in their retirement.

In terms of implementation, we envisaged that in return for people paying substantially less tax, they would be required to take out various forms of welfare insurance, and for that to work properly, there would need to be a degree of compulsion.

Compulsory superannuation had been in place in Australia for some time and was in place in New Zealand briefly during the 1972–75 parliamentary term. But the New Zealand scheme was replaced by National Superannuation, later renamed New Zealand Super, a universal scheme funded from taxation. Our proposal was designed to solve the growing retirement funding crisis by providing for all those in employment — other than the already retired who would have their pensions and health care paid for out of general revenue — to save a percentage of their earnings until they had put away a sufficient sum to buy a basic pension in retirement.

Those who had not been able to save enough by retirement age would have their pension entitlement topped up when they did retire. Unlike some employer top-up superannuation schemes which were calculated to phase out completely on a contributor's death, we proposed that individual contributions would remain an estate asset on death.

Compulsory health insurance, which we also advocated, was already in place in some overseas countries, with Singapore's system working well. New Zealand already had compulsory workplace and accident cover through ACC.

John Stuart Mill, in his treatise *On Liberty* in 1859, advocated a different approach to state-provided education, claiming: 'A general State education is a mere contrivance for moulding people to be exactly like one another.' To this end ACT proposed an education voucher system, whereby taxpayer funds would be paid directly to parents or to the school of their choice to provide access to better education for their children.

Education vouchers were regarded by some as a radical innovation. This was despite their contemplated purpose of providing better education for, in particular, children from low-income families, and the fact that they were in operation in various forms overseas.

Milton Friedman took up the case for vouchers in an interview, stating that their purpose was 'to enable parents to have free choice … to provide competition and allow the education industry to get out of the 17th century and into the 21st century, and have more innovation and more involvement'.[5] Presidents Reagan, George W. Bush and Trump have all followed his advice with various policy initiatives.

The compulsory elements in ACT's policy mix differentiated it from the policies of extreme neoliberal advocates of the far right who championed unrestricted free markets, wholesale deregulation and the abolition of government controls and regulations, believing that without intervention, the provision of appropriate goods and services would flow automatically.

In contrast, as one commentator put it, 'In Douglas's welfare state, you get more welfare but much less state.'

ACT's policies were attacked from two quite different directions. One group, the traditional supporters of state-provided services, claimed that vouchers were designed to destroy the state education system; that compulsory health insurance would resemble the flawed American health system; and that tax cuts were regressive and would only benefit the rich, who had already made far too much money from Douglas's earlier reforms.

Critics from the other side were led by market reformer Roger Kerr, executive director of the New Zealand Business Round Table. He labelled the party's superannuation proposal 'centralist' and wanted ACT to advocate voluntary savings. Kerr was like a dog with a bone in terms of policy purity, and had earlier criticised part of my AGPOL '83 speech in which I had suggested that there should be taxpayer retraining and relocation support for unemployed people. Kerr argued that this should be a market, not a state responsibility. He maintained that compulsion generally was completely inconsistent with what a party like ACT should be advocating.

In an attempt to overcome these criticisms, ACT launched a series of expensive advertising and marketing campaigns to improve the party's position in the polls. However, the individuals involved, although clever conventional marketing people, had little or no understanding of politics and were surprised when their efforts failed to improve ACT's rating. The focus shifted to attempts to find a 'silver bullet', when the reality was that what the party needed was good, old-fashioned message consistency based on intelligence, rather than slogans.[6]

However, from here on, until the election campaign started, media presentations continued to be run and paid for by the party's funders, with limited input from Douglas or me. As a result, the original advertising and marketing mistakes were compounded, with the result that the overall consistency of the original Douglas/Quigley message was substantially watered down.

Learning from Italy

Later in 1994 I went to Québec City to present two papers on energy reform. I took the opportunity after that to go on to Rome to study the formation of Silvio Berlusconi's Forza Italia party. Berlusconi became

Italy's prime minister in May 1994 as head of a coalition government. In Rome I met with existing and former politicians, political and media commentators, party strategists, ministerial staff, diplomats and ordinary Italians. The report I produced in June 1994 contained major lessons for anyone contemplating forming a political party.

Italy had been unstable electorally but stable politically since the end of World War II, with a series of coalitions that were, in reality, one-party governments because of the dominance of the Christian Democrats in each of them. Corruption and incompetence were rife, particularly during the 1980s. In addition, between 1990 and 1993 Italy experienced its first real economic recession since the war. Debt was about 114 percent of GDP and still rising at the time of my visit.

A series of referenda had been held to break with the old FPP electoral system and a new process was in place by early 1994. The left had won key local government elections in 1993, and were placing considerable emphasis on consultation and consensus. Initially they were expected to win the 1994 national election. However, as time went on, although the left presented themselves as supporting social democrat policies, centre-right parties were partially successful in emphasising their communist roots.

Enter Berlusconi, at the time one of Italy's few new successful business-people of the past 20 years. He was stridently anti-communist and had a vast commercial empire of TV stations and print media, supermarkets, investment houses and sporting interests. In September 1993 Berlusconi expressed concerns for Italy's future and was talking about the need for politicians to change. He also hinted that he might get involved himself in some way, though gave the impression he was not seeking political leadership. However, my research showed that the decision to form a 'non-political' party had been made in July 1993, by which time Berlusconi had decided to run as its leader.

The name Forza Italia — with 'Forza' meaning 'strength'— had been chosen by September 1993 but was not announced until three months before the election. The party was effectively up and running long before that, but was deliberately not launched until December 1993, when the party's strategists were fairly certain about the 1994 election date.

Berlusconi was very experienced in product campaigns and brought a similar approach to politics. His media outlets were an important part of the political sales campaign, which in large measure focused on him personally as a business winner and therefore a prime minister in waiting. Sophisticated polling and media techniques were used to gain an understanding of the thinking of 'Little Italy' (the lower middle class who watched his TV stations and followed his sports team), and to garner their support.

Forza Italia did its own polling, using in-house expertise from Berlusconi's companies. Outside pollsters were disregarded because of their preconceived views and traditional (flawed) approach to politics. The internal pollsters carried out motivational studies to gauge people's reactions to certain TV presentations, establishing that the 'average' Italian was pragmatic, had no ideology, and was looking for a problem-solver. They confirmed that a big policy vacuum existed, and therefore that a big potential policy market was waiting to be filled.

Armed with these findings, Berlusconi had sufficient confidence to run with 'rightist' policies, despite the fact that 'the right' had, up until the collapse of the Berlin Wall, been regarded in Italy as akin to the devil. His approach was helped by the perception that the existing political parties were seen as closed shops, pushing their own views, with no opportunity for outside participation. Berlusconi was consequently intent on doing several things differently.

One was to change the way political messages were framed. Another was to get close to the people, which was not the normal Italian political approach. Berlusconi's campaign style was always positive and pitched at the individual. His problem-solving approach was based on his business experience and he worked to build a constituency for a business-friendly government.

The party's policy presentation took the form of a statement listing about 45 problems and their solutions, with each problem and its solution capable of being seen in isolation. Opposing parties were largely ignored. The approach was deliberately modelled on US presidential elections, with the focus on one man — Silvio Berlusconi.

Image and brand, not ideology, were important. This approach was designed to develop an unstoppable bandwagon more than a political party. It capitalised on the existing dislike for politicians and political parties. Part of the strategy was 'to create a rightist supermarket of products' by bringing previously diametrically opposed parties into a coalition with Forza Italia. This finally delivered enough seats to form a government, but required a careful campaign strategy to maximise the potential to win seats in specific electorates. It also projected Berlusconi as a unifier.

Key to getting Berlusconi's ideas across to 'Little Italy' was the formation of special 'clubs'. These were the bridge between Berlusconi and the people and around 14,000 were eventually formed, with one person I interviewed describing them 'as a bit like Tupperware parties'. Initial contact was via toll-free phone lines. People were encouraged to participate in a 'free association' and to sign up with a 'winning' team. The clubs functioned as 'opinion groups', designed to give individuals an opportunity to help solve Italy's problems. A mystique was deliberately built up; the clubs were themselves closed shops through which Berlusconi communicated with members, either directly or by phone.

In relation to candidate selection, Forza Italia's research showed that about 70 percent of people had a clear preference for brand new political faces, with 86 percent expressing no confidence in existing political parties. The polls also showed that people were prepared to accept a lack of political experience, and by election day new faces were seen as an 'adventure' worth engaging in, albeit a slightly risky one.

Head-hunters and straw polls were used to pre-select new, clean candidates who were then fully briefed and carefully trained. Only those who could present well on TV were allowed on that medium. Yet the thrust of the campaign was not through the candidates. According to one of the three key strategists (I spoke to two of them), '70–90 percent of the impact of the campaign was image, name and leader, not candidates.'

The image was of the new Italian miracle, with Berlusconi portrayed as the person who could liberate Italy from its past. He was a problem-solver who could identify with ordinary people. In addition to his promise of an economic miracle, Berlusconi also promised 1 million new jobs over two years and a more efficient school system. He talked of business, house, family, jobs — and freedom from the oppression of government. 'We are the people who work; we have no time to develop economic models,' he told his supporters.

The party launch was held in a relatively small room, with attendance by special invitation. Not all those invited could get into the hall, which created the impression of a massive overflow of support and was broadcast throughout Italy by a satellite link with all the Forza Italia clubs. Berlusconi spoke from the aisles for 15–20 minutes without notes, against a backdrop of a clear, blue sky and rousing campaign music. One non-supporter remarked, 'Berlusconi wasn't a political success; he hijacked people's emotions.' This comment summed up the campaign approach, which was completely foreign to traditional Italian politicians. Nothing of the like had ever been seen before by the Italian electorate.

The party had been launched only three months before the election. When I asked whether this timing was right in retrospect, the response was 'Basically, yes.' Three months was not long to get the party machine up and running, but equally it didn't give the Opposition much time to mount a counter-attack.

'Will he last?' I asked. My question was addressed to a former Italian finance minister who had stood against Berlusconi in 1994. He replied: 'If he lasts one year, he will probably last for 10. The Christian Democrats [who had been in government for years] are so keen to get back into power that they will probably do anything to be part of a winning team.'

History has since shown that, for all his business success and the brilliance of his party's formation and launch, Berlusconi went the way of many other Italian politicians when he got into a position of power.

Rules and leadership

Back in New Zealand, one of my tasks before ACT was registered as a party was to draw up a set of party rules. These were drafted with detailed unpaid input from a leading Auckland lawyer. They provided for the election of a board of trustees which would have ultimate authority on issues such as party leadership, the selection of parliamentary candidates, and the order of candidates on the party list.

Initially, a small number of party members bitterly contested these provisions, arguing that the party membership, not the board, should have the final say on the order of the party list. However, the rules were approved unchanged in November 1994 at the inaugural conference of the association and the party, with ACT New Zealand officially registered with the Electoral Commission in February 1995.

While I was away, Roger Douglas, in his capacity as the party's de facto leader, had begun looking around for an existing politician to lead ACT, with names like Maurice Williamson from National and Phil Goff from Labour discussed. However, Richard Prebble, who was highly regarded by influential people in the business community for his work as a Cabinet minister during the 1984–90 reforms, was asked to lead the party.

I had been in Parliament with Richard for nine years earlier but I did not know him at all well on a personal basis. Like many National MPs

I had regarded him as Labour's 'rottweiler', continually looking to seize upon a sign of government weakness and/or an apparent division, or to savage the ideas of a government MP. I had figured in the latter category during the debate on my Community Service Bill. Naïvely, I had thought I would have cross-party support but, to my surprise, Prebble rubbished it in classic debating form.

Muldoon regarded him as the most irritating of his opponents, who was 'Always at it. Always a bother to us. Even if some thought he was mad the way he carried on, we never knew what he was going to come up with next.'[7]

But Richard Prebble was never mad. He is highly intelligent, was raised in a caring and supportive family full of equally intelligent people, and was a key minister in the economic reforming troika led by Douglas during the first term of the Lange government. In that capacity, and in the face of the economic crisis the government had inherited, he is reputed to have successfully convinced his Cabinet colleagues, to the surprise of some officials, to implement more fundamental reforms than even they were recommending. His brilliance, which attracted strong private-sector praise and support, was his capacity to get things done.

Richard eventually agreed to become leader on two conditions. First, that his candidature was put to the test in a poll of members. Second, that as leader he had authority to rewrite party policy as he thought fit. In a postal vote, party members were asked who they wanted to lead the party. Prebble won, in a vote split between him and me (despite the fact that I had not sought to lead the party). The vote also showed that the party's support base came fairly equally from both National and Labour.

Richard Prebble's upfront and aggressive reputation came with him when he became ACT's leader in 1996. This, together with the fact that the party was already perceived as extreme right wing, led to a watering down of the original policies Douglas and I had devised. They were replaced with what was considered to be a more 'saleable' package set out in a new manifesto written by Richard.[8]

Campaigning on the North Shore

As I had been actively campaigning for ACT, and because of Douglas's refusal to stand for election, I came under considerable pressure to put my name forward. Initially I refused, as we had just moved to Auckland and were still settling in. But eventually I agreed and put my name forward for the North Shore seat.

The campaign was a fun affair, with my approach initially designed to push the name Quigley rather than ACT, as I was better known than the party. One of our 'up National's nose' events was to float a large dirigible with 'Vote Quigley' prominently displayed on it above the National Party's annual conference on the North Shore.

Our campaign activities and advertising caused consternation among the North Shore National Party hierarchy and in particular Wayne Mapp, who was standing for the party for the first time in what had been George Gair's blue-ribbon seat before he retired from Parliament in 1990. The Nats needn't have worried, as their hastily organised poll showed that I had no chance of winning the seat.

The nearer we got to election day, the better the party polled — particularly as a result of the campaign Richard Prebble devised around his bestselling book *I've Been Thinking*[9] — and eventually eight ACT MPs were elected, with 6.10 percent of the list vote and Richard Prebble winning Wellington Central. In North Shore, Mapp won easily with 15,763 votes and I came in second with 5415 votes (14.8 percent of the valid votes cast). The party vote for ACT in North Shore was 13.75 percent — a major contributor to the party's overall success. I was again an MP, this time because of the party list.

However, my reasonably high individual vote, and indeed Prebble's of 14,269 (or 34.78 percent of the total votes in the Wellington Central electorate) raised an interesting question about the best way for a party to elect the maximum number MPs under MMP. The party vote is the key to achieving this, because an electorate win (other than in a situation where a party gains less than 5 percent of the party vote) doesn't actually add to the party's total number of MPs.

We were still learning how to work with MMP in 1996.

CHAPTER 21

Operating in a New Electoral System

The 1996 election had produced a close and inconclusive result. National had 44 MPs and Labour and the Alliance a combined total of 50 MPs. The other three parties in Parliament were New Zealand First with 17 MPs, ACT with eight MPs and United with one MP. This meant Winston Peters and New Zealand First became the 'kingmakers'. Whichever party they agreed to go into coalition with would lead the government.

After two long months of negotiations a coalition government was formed — to the surprise of many — between the previously antagonistic National and New Zealand First. Bolger remained prime minister and Peters became deputy PM. As this was New Zealand's first coalition government since the 1930s, the arrangement took some getting used to.

It didn't take long for the cracks to begin to show. Around the middle of 1997 the country was clearly becoming disillusioned with Bolger's leadership and the continuing antics of some of New Zealand First's Cabinet ministers. The Māori electorates had been longstanding Labour strongholds but in 1996 all five had been won by New Zealand First, with two of its MPs — Tau Henare and Tuariki John Delamere — joining Peters in the coalition Cabinet. Henare, who with Peters had been part of the original New Zealand First parliamentary team, was the party's deputy leader and, along with the other four Māori seat MPs, formed what became known as the 'tight five'. The image they portrayed was of the front row and locks of an All Black rugby scrum, and the controlling force in the government.

The media showed them wearing dark glasses and swaggering like gang members. This didn't go down well with National Party caucus members, who became increasingly frustrated over the undue influence New Zealand First was exercising within the Cabinet; and with the public at large as more and more New Zealand First MPs became embroiled in controversy.

A move developed within the National caucus to replace Bolger with Jenny Shipley, a supporter of Ruth Richardson's reformist policies. Shipley was thought to be better able to handle Peters and New Zealand First.

ACT MPs were actively supporting moves within the National Party caucus to replace its leader. At a function later in 1997 at the Wellington residence of National MP Gavin Herlihy — probably organised to discuss the matter — Prebble made a strong case to do so. One of the National MPs present was Wayne Mapp, who recalls being surprised that ACT seemed to think they could virtually demand that the Nats change its leader to suit their own agenda.

Support for change continued to build, and at ACT's 1997 Christmas party in early December, which was attended by a number of National MPs, the issue was openly discussed late at night. I remember telling some of the younger National MPs I felt the performance of the coalition government was a disgrace, that it was debasing Parliament in the eyes of the public, and that the National Party and its MPs were being tainted by association with New Zealand First. 'But how can we govern without them?' they asked. I replied: 'Some of them will probably still stay with you.'[1]

On 8 December Bolger resigned as prime minister in the face of majority caucus support for Shipley, and she became New Zealand's first female prime minister. Bolger stayed on in Parliament until 1998, when he resigned to become New Zealand's ambassador to the US. I thought this appointment was somewhat incongruous, given his and his party's flip-flop on Labour's anti-nuclear legislation.

Bolger's resignation as an MP triggered a by-election in his Taranaki-King Country seat in May 1998, with ACT mounting a vigorous campaign in the electorate. ACT's candidate was Owen Jennings, one of its existing list MPs and a former Federated Farmers chair. He came close to winning, with National's 1996 majority slashed from 10,223 to just 988.

Select committee changes

ACT had not become part of the coalition government because of policy differences between it and New Zealand First, but undertook to support it on matters of confidence and supply. This left ACT free to promote its own policy agendas, to disagree from time to time with government decisions, and to exercise leverage in certain areas. I was one of the beneficiaries of this leverage: in return for ACT supporting National's nominee for the position of Speaker, I became chair of the Foreign Affairs, Defence and Trade (FDT) Select Committee.

That committee had become moribund over recent years and I was determined to change this. I drew up a comprehensive list of subjects I wished it to cover over the next extended period and sought outside comment. Terence O'Brien, a former diplomat and at the time director of the Centre for Strategic Studies, was one of the people I contacted. He responded that, with such a detailed agenda, the committee would need extra help beyond that provided by Parliament's clerk's office. I agreed, and within days O'Brien came back to me saying that he had found an ideal candidate. Robert Ayson was a New Zealander who had just finished his doctorate in war studies at King's College in London and was currently looking for work, but he was likely to be snapped up soon.

Armed with a copy of the agenda I had drawn up for the committee, and outside support for it from people like Sir Frank Holmes, I went to see the clerk of the House, David McGee, to seek funds to employ someone. McGee said no select committee other than Finance and Expenditure had received extra funding in the past, but in view of the work ahead of FDT he was prepared to approve my request. Thus Robert Ayson became a special adviser to the FDT Select Committee on a full-time basis for almost two years.

The composition and operation of select committees in the new MMP environment created some interesting issues. Select committees are creatures of Parliament, not governments, in recognition of the separation of powers between the legislature and the executive, and as such are expected to operate on a non-partisan basis. Even so, when I was an MP under the FPP system National usually had a majority on most committees and appointed the committee chair.

Select committee reports then were a standard caucus agenda item. Committee chairs were expected to raise any potentially divisive or controversial issues there and in that forum obtain caucus approval before proceeding. This allowed the government effectively to dictate committee agendas and the content of committee reports back to Parliament. It was no different under Labour, according to Geoffrey Palmer, a constitutional law expert who spent 11 years as an MP including five as deputy PM and one as PM — all before MMP. Palmer wrote, on the basis of his observations, that parliament — as opposed to the government — played a limited role:

> Each week MPs of the governing Party met in caucus and in secret settled their policy. Once adopted, all members were obliged to vote for it in Parliament. Parliament became a rubber stamp — it determined nothing. It was just a talking shop. The positions were pre-determined elsewhere and the control just about total, to an extent still not possible in the United Kingdom.[2]

The introduction of MMP changed this in a number of ways. For one thing, the number of MPs in Parliament rose from 99 to around 120. Another factor was the wider spectrum of political parties and diversity of views represented in both the executive and Parliament as a whole. As well, an earlier overhaul of Parliamentary Standing Orders had led to automatic referral of most legislation to select committees, which also now had the authority to initiate their own inquiries. This aspect, in addition to considering legislation and departmental estimates, was to become a major part of the FDT's operations under my chairmanship.

Defence Beyond 2000

The FDT's Defence Beyond 2000 inquiry attracted considerable parliamentary and public attention and was the subject of an interim report to the House in 1998 and a final report in 1999.[3] It had been preceded by two other inquiries, *New Zealand's Place in the World* and *New Zealand's Role in Asia/Pacific Security*. Both had involved substantial input from Robert Ayson, and considered a comprehensive range of perspectives from a combined total of 47 oral and/or written submissions. Their conclusions provided a broad base for DB2000.

The FDT Select Committee noted that Australia's Foreign Affairs and Trade Policy White Paper *In the National Interest* (1997)[4] contained an overarching policy statement that enabled defence analysts' perceptions of threats to Australia's national security to be put into a wider perspective. 'In contrast,' DB2000 noted in its interim report, 'in New Zealand, military planning is not integrated into broader security policy planning with the result that competing demands for resources are not fully contestable.'

The committee consulted widely within and outside the traditional defence establishment. This was a major break with convention and the interim report drew a comment on this from the government: 'We are not accustomed to debate these issues.' The fact that the committee challenged several of the government's defence and foreign policy positions ultimately led to friction.

Colin James, in an article in 1999, wrote that a New Zealand foreign affairs committee can be safely discounted as amusing, perhaps even interesting, but irrelevant. Few voters care about foreign affair issues. However, he went on to write:

> But in the past few years 'peace' has pushed foreign affairs into the living room with disquieting television images of mayhem and oppression ... By the time the cabinet woke up to the tack [Quigley] was taking, his committee was far outside the bounds of polite political debate. All sorts of people not normally listened to in the development of defence policy made submissions. Suddenly amateurs are in where the professionals don't want them — the ranking of defence expenditure and priorities. Not literally, of course. By proxy through the likes of the Quigley committee.[5]

As a result of this friction, both the consultative process and the debate that followed were stymied, with the committee's access to anyone other than the most senior defence personnel finally severely constrained by political directive. Towards the end of the committee's hearings even single service chiefs were only allowed to appear before the committee in the presence of the CDF. All this was a pity because, as I know from long consulting experience, those working within an organisation — if given the opportunity to speak frankly — have a better idea than outsiders, and even their bosses, about what works, what doesn't work and why.

A substantial part of the interim and final DB2000 reports questioned aspects of the government's 1997 Defence White Paper and the Defence Assessment (DA97) on which it was based.

Prior to the completion of the 1997 White Paper with its overall theme of continuity and reconfirmation, CDF and the Secretary of Defence had advised the minister of defence that either a review of funding or significant cuts to military capability were required, with this advice forming the basis for both DA97 and the 1997 White Paper. However, despite this, the White Paper concluded that New Zealand had a defence force reasonably matched to its strategic position and to the range of external interests it was intended to support, that the NZDF's existing structural framework was appropriate, and that the present policy framework still met the country's requirement. As a consequence, there was no need for a new defence policy. As the prime minister wrote in the foreword to the White Paper:

> Cabinet had directed officials to develop investment proposals that matched fiscal realities; [saying] it wanted to find the right level of funding for defence 'that would ensure that not only is its investment in people and equipment sufficient to maintain professional military standards but that it would be supportable by successive Governments over the longer term.[6]

But funding had also been highlighted as an ongoing problem in a briefing paper completed by the Secretary of Defence for the minister of defence on DA97, which provided a comparative analysis of six different force structure options, noting that all would require a funding increase in the near term that would be difficult for the government to accommodate.[7]

In an attempt to maintain a balanced force approach, Cabinet had chosen a mix of capabilities: three frigates, retaining the air combat force, and four rifle companies in each of two battalions. This decision was significant in that it reduced the naval combat force from four to three frigates, and confirmed the continuing existence of an air combat capability, which had been the subject of debate for years.

Specifically, on the air combat force, the White Paper recorded: 'The current fleet of A4 Skyhawk fighters, while old, has been upgraded to provide an effective platform for their key roles of support for land forces and anti-ship missions well into the next decade.'[8] This meant the Skyhawks were not scheduled to be replaced until between 2007 and 2011.

But by 1998 it was obvious that the defence funding regime was still inadequate, and that further capital injections were required. Defence's difficulties were compounded by a decline in the value of the New Zealand dollar, which had by then been largely responsible for a 27 percent increase in the cost of the 1997 20-year capital estimate. The problem was exacerbated by government instructions that the NZDF was to remain within 1997 funding guidelines.

Further reprioritisation of all projects took place in November 1998 to arrive at a list of high-priority projects that could be financed within the guidelines. Projects categorised as Priority 1 (those considered fundamental to restoring the capabilities of front-line force elements) included armoured vehicles, combat aircraft, the C130s and a third frigate. Twenty-seven projects dropped below the indicative funding level and were placed in categories Priority 2 to 5. Many were said to be more critical, but that no money was currently available to fund them.

The inclusion of the combat aircraft and a third frigate in the Priority 1 list — when they had been outside the five-year window identified for high-priority projects 12 months earlier — had significant political implications. It demonstrated to me and to a number of other non-government MPs that, contrary to the prime minister's statements in the foreword to the White Paper, his government was still not committed to developing investment proposals that matched fiscal realities or to a structural framework for defence that successive governments would be able to support over the longer term.

The reasons for elevating the air combat capability and the third frigate to Priority 1 became evident shortly afterwards. On 30 November 1998 a revised 10-year capital plan had been presented to Cabinet, with other papers. One item focused on acquiring 28 F-16A/B aircraft from the United States, and this was approved. Another item sought approval to acquire a third frigate from Australia, but was declined.

In a further demonstration of fiscal unreality, Cabinet also agreed to maintain the funding envelope as set out in the 1997 Defence White Paper. This turned out to be explosive stuff for the FDT Select Committee in the context of DB2000.

The FDT committee adopts a different approach

In terms of national security strategy, the FDT Select Committee saw security as involving more than defence. It regarded the combat capabilities of the NZDF as just one way to secure the external environment. Others included diplomatic initiatives such as preventative diplomacy, the pursuit of arms control and disarmament, addressing global environmental concerns, and providing development assistance. The committee also recognised the need to balance the allocation of resources in terms of the conduct of foreign relations and whole-of-government priorities.

The committee therefore saw a need for defence to be incorporated into broader strategic planning to promote the country's overall security and enhance New Zealand's reputation as a successful, open and secure trading nation intent on actively playing a constructive role within the international community. The aim of this broader strategic planning approach was to achieve five national security outcomes: a secure New Zealand; a stable South Pacific region; a strong relationship with Australia; a role in both Southeast Asia and Northeast Asia; and a global approach to collective security and the international community.[9]

While these five security outcomes were similar to those spelt out in the 1991 and 1997 White Papers, some committee members believed that New Zealand needed a new policy approach for the Asian region.

Government policy at the time was based on the 1997 White Paper, which stated that continued stability of Southeast Asia was one of New Zealand's most important security goals and second only to the common security of Australia and New Zealand. However, the select committee noted that the criteria for military engagement by New Zealand were now quite different from what they were during the Cold War, and that a broad-based international consensus was now important before a country committed to the use of armed force.

The majority of the committee were of the view that New Zealand was not well placed to contemplate taking sides in any of the larger conflicts that could break out in Asia.[10]

Although major differences of opinion had been anticipated between members of the committee, this was not the case. Initially I was assumed to be right-wing/pro-defence. In contrast, the Alliance Party committee member was perceived to be at the other end of the spectrum and only interested in the NZDF engaging in peacekeeping in a limited number of specific countries, and certainly not alongside US forces. But there were many points of agreement between us.

The committee was unanimous about the urgent need to upgrade the army, with the top re-equipment priority being deployable land-force elements. The rationale for this was simple. In an army report made available to the committee[11] it was noted that at the time of the first Gulf War the New Zealand Army had been incapable of being allocated any task more arduous or complex than, say, a static garrison or prisoner-of-war handling function. The committee was told by CGS in April 1999 that the army was not able to field or sustain a battalion-sized force that was mobile and capable of protecting itself while carrying out tasks. We consequently recommended that the government's proposed timetable to upgrade the army — with its focus on 'the Army after next' (that is, by 2015) — was completely unacceptable.

The committee's DB2000 reports challenged traditional thinking on aspects of the government's defence policy, and formed the basis of a different approach to defence by the Labour-led coalition government after the 1999 election. They also represented a substantial degree of cross-party support, despite the fact that the final report contained two minority reports — one by the three government members, and the other a short statement by the Alliance Party to the effect that it

> supports the recommendations of this report with the exception of that part of Recommendation 1 which relates to the development of closer relations with French forces in the Pacific; and all of Recommendation 2, on developing closer defence relations with Malaysia and Singapore.[12]

The reasons for the minority report by government members were basically political. The final report was presented to Parliament in August 1999, shortly before the general election in October. It contained a number of recommendations that challenged aspects of the government's defence policy, and its general thrust had been publicly endorsed by Helen Clark, Leader of the Opposition. Government committee members were brought back into line by ministers and consequently sought to distance themselves from some of the recommendations.

In contrast, the committee's interim report, published a year earlier and long before most MPs had begun to think about the forthcoming election, was unanimous, other than on two minor matters relating to the role of the Territorial Force and the form of basic training for recruits.

A comparison of the committee's unanimous views in the interim report with those of government members in their final minority report illustrates this. The interim report records:

> We consider that there should be a shift in national security policy towards the provision of a more sharply focused range of military capabilities, structured to maximise their operational and political impact, and with the

> capability to operate safely and effectively in medium level conflict. Major elements of all three services can play effective roles in a reshaped NZDF, but some make a broader contribution to the national interest, and are therefore more cost-effective.[13]

The committee went on to say that NZDF resources were spread too thinly and needed to be concentrated on a different range of affordable and sustainable capabilities, which it listed in order of priority: land forces; fixed wing, rotary wing and maritime transport forces; maritime patrol forces (naval and air force); and air strike.[14] It acknowledged national interest arguments in favour of retaining an air combat force but unanimously recommended one of two options be adopted:

> either to disband the jet training and strike capability on purely financial grounds, or to replace the current A4s with more modern combat aircraft on the basis of their capacity to contribute to the advancement of the country's national interest considered alongside competing [defence] expenditure priorities . . .[15]

The government responded (as required under Parliament's Standing Orders) to the committee's interim report recommendations to the effect that the 1997 White Paper had identified a continuing need for an air combat capability; that it had decided to replace the existing air combat fleet with 28 F-16s 'on very favourable terms'; and that '[t]his had enabled the acquisition to be accommodated within the current Defence Long Term Plan without displacing other important acquisitions'.

Government members of the select committee promptly delivered a minority report accordingly:

> [We] view retention of the Air Combat capability as essential to provide future Governments with policy options for meeting a wide spectrum of New Zealand's security requirements. These include protection of our maritime approaches, making an appropriate contribution to our defence relationship with Australia, and promoting and enhancing regional and global security and co-operation . . . [We] view the lease of F-16 aircraft to replace the Skyhawk fleet as a sound decision, both in military and economic terms.[16]

Despite their unanimous support in the interim report for 'a more sharply focused range of military capabilities', they also wrote:

> Government members believe that the present selective balance in our defence force capabilities is both affordable and wise. New Zealand is able to afford a two-battalion infantry-based army as proposed in *Army 2005*. It can afford a combat-capable navy of three or four surface ships [i.e. potentially one more than policy provided for] and a military sealift capability. And it can afford an air force able to undertake strategic transport, maritime surveillance and air combat. All are set out in the 1997 Defence Assessment.[17]

Regardless of these differences, as Arthur Grimes and James Rolfe recorded in their 1999 paper prepared for the Treasury:

> A careful reading of the Select Committee's reports and the Government's response could safely lead the reasonable reader to conclude that there is [less] difference between the positions held by the two parties than much of the commentary makes out. Both the Government and the Select Committee accept the need for effective armed forces able to play a role in the international arena ... This means that the differences are probably as much of rhetoric rather than of substance and that the short-term size and shape of the armed forces will depend as much on funding as on political decisions.[18]

Grimes and Rolfe also commented that the select committee's reports were 'the most coherent recent non-government analysis of defence policy'.

Several years after I left Parliament I was told by a reliable source that the government members' minority report was not in fact written by them but had been farmed out to a former senior air force staff officer to write.

Actual committee differences

There were two issues where there were differences of opinion between me personally and some other committee members. One concerned the prohibition on nuclear-powered ships docking at New Zealand ports. The other was over a Labour MP's bill that had been referred to the committee for consideration. It sought pardons for five New Zealand servicemen executed for desertion and mutiny during World War I.

During the course of DB2000 a number of witnesses sought changes to New Zealand's anti-nuclear legislation, and in particular to the prohibition concerning nuclear propulsion. The committee sought advice from Alan Poletti, a nuclear physicist and member of the original 1992 committee on nuclear propulsion chaired by Sir Edward Somers.

When Poletti appeared before the committee on 11 December 1997 he provided members with an update of the original Somers Report. He said all the committee's findings were as valid in 1997 as they had been in 1992: nuclear and safety experts had been universally positive; and opponents of visits by nuclear-propelled ships had been unable to refute the logic or the statements in the report. He concluded:

> Concerns for their safety is not a valid reason for keeping nuclear propelled vessels out of New Zealand. New Zealand's foreign policy needs to distinguish between nuclear and other weapons of mass destruction and nuclear propulsion and energy and peaceful nuclear technology. Treating them together destroys New Zealand's credibility as a developed and sophisticated nation.[19]

I agreed with Poletti's comments and urged the select committee to recommend changing the provision on nuclear propulsion, but mine was a lone voice. The committee's decision was: 'We recommend that there should be no change to the New Zealand Nuclear Free Zone, Disarmament and Arms Control Act 1987.'[20]

The second and only other substantial disagreement within the committee was over the appropriate way, in 1999, to deal with a series of injustices that had taken place some 80 years earlier.

The member's bill seeking pardons for five members of the New Zealand Division who had been shot — four for desertion and one for mutiny — raised the issue of how to reconcile the mores of that time with modern-day thinking. The solution I proposed, which the committee agreed to, was to refer the matter to an outside expert. I recommended Sir Edward Somers and the committee and the government agreed.

Some background will be helpful. After its campaign in Gallipoli, the New Zealand Division arrived in France in April 1916 and remained there until the end of the war, under the overall command of the British Army. This meant that offences by New Zealand soldiers on active service — treachery, mutiny, cowardice, desertion and sleeping on duty — carried the penalty of death. Up until the armistice in 1918, a total of 31 New Zealand soldiers were sentenced to death, though 26 sentences were commuted. The member's bill related to the remaining five.

After investigating the matter thoroughly, Sir Edward wrote that in the light of the knowledge at the time, he was unable to conclude that there was sufficient evidence of a miscarriage of justice in any of the five cases. There was not enough evidence at the time to justify a pardon, and he believed there was not sufficient evidence to warrant such a course. While a pardon by statute was within the power of Parliament, he concluded, in the absence of clear evidence justifying it, such a solution would break new ground.

However, he wrote:

> A statement to the House, similar to that made by the Minister for the Armed Forces to the House of Commons on 24 July 1998 in respect of British servicemen executed during the First World War, might be an acceptable course in the case of the five New Zealand soldiers.

In conveying Sir Edward's findings to me as committee chair, the minister of defence advised that Cabinet, at its meeting on 11 October, had approved the following:

> [T]he Government proposes (given that the Parliament has risen for the 1999 general election) to table Sir Edward's report in the House by the 18th of this month as required by Standing Orders. Should the new Government consider it appropriate, a statement could be made in the House next year (similar to that made in the UK House of Commons) recognising that the passage of time has raised doubts about the stigma of condemnation, that those executed were unquestionably men of bravery and courage, and that they themselves were victims of war. At that stage, a decision on the future of the member's bill will need to be taken by him, should he be re-elected.

The member was re-elected, and in due course the Clark-led coalition government that won the 1999 election granted a posthumous pardon to all five soldiers.

CHAPTER 22

Other Involvements as an MP

In addition to my chairmanship of the FDT select committee and my involvement in activities that flowed from that position, there were a number of other matters I was able to focus on. One was what I regarded as the undemocratic and racial anomaly of Māori seats in Parliament and what appeared to be the endless Treaty of Waitangi claims process.

As mentioned earlier, separate representation for Māori in Parliament dates from 1867 when four seats were established as a temporary measure. These were allocated on the basis — at that time — of a potential Māori voting population of 50,000 while there were 250,000 Europeans, represented by 72 seats. Equal representation would have given Māori 14 seats. The number stayed at four as the total number of electorates increased over time, and after 1935 they became safe Labour Party seats for a long period of time. Until 1975, the qualification for enrolling in a Māori electorate required a person to be 'more than half caste'.

Changes to the Electoral Act in 1975 removed the reference to fractions of descent and placed the emphasis on 'self-identification'. This flowed from the acceptance of two standards by Statistics New Zealand in the five-yearly census for the definition of Māori: an ideal and an operational one. The ideal definition was: 'A person is said to have Māori ancestry if they have any Māori ancestors, no matter how distant.' The operational definition was: 'A person is said to have Māori ancestry if they claim to have Māori ancestors, no matter how distant.'

This was the situation that applied when I was re-elected as an MP in 1996, but it changed in 1998 when Statistics New Zealand decided that the ideal and operational definitions should be combined and brought into line with the 1993 Electoral Act and the 1974 Māori Affairs Act. Both Acts have the definition that Māori means a person of the

Māori race of New Zealand, and includes any descendant of such a person. Consequently, since 1975, following each census, Māori are also able to switch from the Māori electoral roll to the general roll and vice versa.

A further major change to Māori representation took place with the passing of the 1993 Electoral Act, which provides for the number of Māori seats to be linked to the number of Māori electors on the Māori roll, using the same population quota that is applied to general seats.[1] As a result, at the time of the 2017 general election there were seven Māori electorates.

Separate representation for Māori became, over time, linked to claims for settlement of Māori grievances under the provisions of the Treaty of Waitangi, which had the potential to continue ad infinitum as pressure built for some earlier, supposedly binding settlements to be revisited. In my maiden speech on my return to Parliament I raised the need for claims to have a finite completion date, and — in the interests of racial equality as proposed by the royal commission on the electoral system if MMP were introduced — for separate parliamentary representation for Māori to be abolished.

One Māori MP, Tau Henare, accused me during the course of my speech of being a racist. I took strong exception to this and a vigorous exchange took place in the House, which resulted in the intervention of the Speaker.

Over the next several months I continued to push for resolution of these two issues and prepared a member's bill titled the Treaty of Waitangi (Final Settlement of Claims) Bill, which drew a successful ballot and was eventually debated in Parliament. I put a lot of time into drafting the Bill and consulted widely on its content, including having discussions with the race relations commissioner. The purpose of the Bill was to provide a timeframe and a context within which all Treaty claims must be settled, so that the focus could shift away from past grievances and start looking to, and planning for, the next stage of race relations discussions in New Zealand.

I saw an end-point for the claims process as the first step in getting New Zealanders to start thinking about the changes required to take race relations to a higher plane, and I wanted the timeframe to be enshrined in law. I nominated the turn of the century (2000) as the cut-off time for lodging claims with the Waitangi Tribunal, and 2005 as the date by which claims must be settled.

The Bill also recognised that the end of the claims process had to be seen in the broader context of race relations generally, with particular emphasis on where New Zealand stood as a nation, what needed to be done to achieve this goal, and by what process people of all races might be brought together.

The issue of separate Māori seats was only obliquely addressed in the Bill, but was listed as one of the matters to be considered in establishing 'equality between all races in New Zealand'. For the purposes of this consideration, the intent of that phrase was defined in the Bill

> as a situation in which New Zealand is one country with many people united in a single legal system that recognises differences between the races where such differences are essential to secure the adequate development and protection of particular groups and individuals; and to provide for members of a minority to be free, in community with other members of that minority, to enjoy the culture, to profess and practise the religion, and to use the language of that minority.

The reaction to the Bill was interesting. ACT MP and former Māori activist Donna Huata supported it strongly. Henare had by now changed his tune and congratulated me, saying these things needed to be talked about. In contrast, National Cabinet minister Nick Smith accused me of political opportunism. Smith was a 10-year-old in Rangiora when I was first elected to Parliament, and during the 1996–99 Parliament was the MP for Nelson. Although he is extremely bright, his parliamentary career has been dogged by occasional questionable actions, and his comments on my motives in introducing the Bill were in this category. I was furious that he had questioned my integrity and, to his apparent surprise, told him so in no uncertain manner.

The Bill caused considerable soul-searching among New Zealand First MPs, several of whom were Māori. At one stage they contemplated voting for it to be referred to a select committee, but their antipathy towards ACT finally won the day and they opposed it. Most National MPs supported the Bill in private, but still inexplicably voted against it.

Since then, National has continued its approach of electoral convenience on this topic. It had a specific election policy in 2008 to settle all Treaty claims by 2014 and to abolish the Māori seats after that. Instead, after the election it agreed with the Māori Party, as part of the coalition government agreement, to establish a constitutional advisory panel to consider, among other things, the Māori electoral option, and Māori representation in Parliament and in local government. The panel was required to make its recommendations by September 2013.

However, on 11 December 2011 National signed a relationship accord and confidence and supply agreement with the Māori Party — when it again needed Māori support to form a government — undertaking not to remove the Māori seats 'without the consent of the Māori people'. This made a mockery of the process of the advisory panel, which was still considering its brief.[2] All of this was completely consistent with the longstanding history of the National Party to put pragmatism before principles, especially if the former might aid their continuing control of the Treasury benches.

Battling the bureaucracy

Another matter — and one I concluded successfully — was of a more quasi-personal nature. When I first became a Cabinet minister one of my office staff was a bright young woman named Vicky who had just left school. She had stacks of personality, and I kept in touch with her over the years. After I left Parliament in 1984, Vicky met a Peruvian diplomat in Wellington. They married, spent time in Lima when the husband was posted back there, and later returned to Wellington following another posting. In Lima, Vicky had her first child, and help at home was provided by a live-in Peruvian housekeeper/babysitter who, for purposes of anonymity, I will call Maria.

When the family returned to Wellington, Maria accompanied them. After Vicky had a second child, followed by a separation and eventually divorce, Maria stayed on with the family, playing a crucial role in raising the two children while their mother studied and worked to support the four of them.

However, as Maria had no legal family of her own in New Zealand and only a Peruvian passport, she did not satisfy the Immigration Department's criteria for permanent residence. This meant she risked being sent back to Peru. Vicky approached me to see if I could help. I immediately suggested that Maria apply for New Zealand residence so that she was in the system, and consequently able to stay at least while her application was being processed.

Maria was of Peruvian Indian ethnicity and did not know her parents. The only 'family' she had was the woman who had raised her, whom she called Aunty. Although the people she was in contact with in Lima knew who her parents were, they refused to tell her, so she was unable to access any official records. Surprisingly, none of this seemed of interest to the New Zealand officials who were processing her application, and in due course it was declined.

Tuariki John Delamere, the immigration minister at the time, had discretion to approve the application and I asked him to review it. After hearing nothing for some time I approached his office to ask about progress. The official replied offhandedly that the matter had not been placed before the minister yet, 'but he won't be approving it anyway'. And he didn't.

More determined than ever, I organised an appeal and approached Peter Bennett, a personal friend and a former New Zealand ambassador to Peru, for support. Peter knew the family, and Maria and her background. He also knew Peru and was familiar with the country's social structures.

I also gained support from the Catholic Church and other community leaders. These documents emphasised the close links between Maria, Vicky and her two children; the time they had been together as a virtual family unit; the support Maria had provided during the marriage breakup; and the fact that she had nothing and no one to go back to in Peru.

Finally, we received verbal advice that our appeal had been successful. But the news coincided with Maria receiving word that 'Aunty' was terminally ill. Maria had saved enough money to fly to Lima, but needed official documentation to enable her to get back into New Zealand. I mistakenly thought this could be arranged quickly through the minister's office, but underestimated the resistance that our successful appeal had generated.

Initially, I was polite in my approach to the minister, but when that didn't work, I resorted to raising my voice, questioning his competence and his lack of compassion. Still I had no success. In desperation I rang the Immigration Department CEO and explained the situation. Within hours, all the requisite documents were issued.[3]

Maria flew to Lima to find that 'Aunty' had died 10 days earlier. A small consolation was that she had left Maria her Lima house. However, before Maria returned to New Zealand, the rest of the Peruvian 'family' insisted she sign it over to them.

When Vicky's children were self-supporting, Maria was able to complete the childcare studies she had been doing part time and get a good job. In due course she met and married a quiet young man from a large New Zealand Catholic family, moved with him to Australia, and now has children of her own. The transformation in her personality over the years is amazing to see. When I first met her, she lacked confidence, was quiet and shy and couldn't understand why a former Cabinet minister painted his own house and did alterations to it. That was something former ministers certainly didn't do in Peru! Today she is outgoing and active in the community and, along with her husband, provides huge support to their family.

It was a pleasure to have been able to help her.

Accident compensation (again)

Another area I was able to concentrate on when I was back in Parliament was accident compensation. My initial involvement followed an approach from Paul O'Connor, the 'whistling bailiff' whom I had got to know while practising law in Christchurch.

Paul wanted me to try to obtain compensation he had been denied by ACC. He had been involved in a car accident in which his vehicle was hit by another from behind. He had sustained neck injuries and eventually lost the sight in one eye. ACC covered the cost of treating his neck injury but declined his claim for loss of sight, claiming that it was the result of a pre-existing condition. Paul disagreed, and wanted ACC to reimburse him for the costs of specialist medical care and provide ongoing disability payments.

I contacted the corporation's CEO and the very large O'Connor file was delivered to my parliamentary office. I came across an early memo between two staff members who thought Paul was lying. Although there was no evidence in the file to justify this conclusion, it had clearly coloured their views on the claim, which they recommended be declined. Their stance had been upheld on review. I recommended Paul lodge an appeal.

At the appeal I mounted two arguments. The first was that the statements in the medical reports and documents on file justified a decision in Paul's favour. The second argument rested on a point of law and was to the effect that even if the facts of the case did not justify a decision in his favour, the corporation was 'estopped'[4] or legally prevented from denying

Paul's claim because of the blatant bias displayed by the two corporation employees.

The estoppel allegation raised difficulties for the appeal authority because of its flow-on implications. The easy and practical way out, which it adopted, was to uphold the appeal on the first ground, and not to have to rule on the estoppel argument.

Another issue that attracted my interest and was peripherally related to accident compensation was a decision of the Court of Appeal in 1998. *Daniels v Thompson*[5] dealt with appeals by four plaintiffs in separate actions claiming exemplary damages. Claims for exemplary damages, sometimes called punitive damages, are brought by way of civil as opposed to criminal proceedings against a defendant and are punitive in nature. Their origin is said to lie in two cases decided in England in 1763, *Huckle v Money* and *Wilkes v Wood*, where individuals were awarded substantial damages for improper interference in their affairs by public officials. The awards were set to punish and deter the defendants and to express the jury's outrage at their conduct.

I have often thought that the relationship between exemplary damages and accident compensation might be a good thesis subject for my unfinished LLM degree.

Such claims were at one stage increasingly being seen as a way to circumvent the statutory prohibition on claims for damages for personal injury after the introduction of New Zealand's accident compensation legislation.

All four actions brought under the umbrella of *Daniels v Thompson* involved allegations of sexual offending, with the defendant in one case having been sentenced to nine years in prison for rape. In the second case a child's guardian had been sentenced to two years in prison, suspended for 12 months, after pleading guilty to a charge of sexual violation. In the third case the defendant had been sentenced to six and a half years for sexually, physically and emotionally abusing his daughter. In the fourth case the defendant — a registered psychologist — had been acquitted on nine counts of sexual abuse. In all four cases before the Court of Appeal the plaintiffs were claiming the civil remedy of exemplary damages.

The majority of the Court of Appeal acknowledged that as the accident compensation regime had removed civil liability for causing personal injury, 'It [was] not appropriate for the Court to circumvent that policy by altering the role of exemplary damages.'

It further ruled that the plaintiffs' damages claims were 'an abuse of process' because they effectively meant the defendants were being tried twice on the same charges. The four conclusions of the majority were:

- There should be an absolute bar on civil proceedings claiming exemplary damages where the acts relied on as the basis for an award had been the subject of a conviction in the criminal Courts.
- A claim for exemplary damages should be struck out as an abuse of process if the defendant had been acquitted and essentially the same acts which constituted the criminal offending were relied upon.
- To similarly prevent an abuse of process it would be appropriate to stay the civil proceedings if it appeared a criminal prosecution was likely in respect of the subject-matter of the claim for exemplary damages.
- Section 26 of the New Zealand Bill of Rights Act 1990 did not bar an award for exemplary damages. What was prohibited was a second trial for the same offence.[6]

A detailed reading of the majority conclusions revealed a radically restrictive approach to exemplary damages claims, with the veiled implication that they should not be used to circumvent the prohibition that the accident compensation legislation had imposed on suing for personal injury.

Justice Thomas — in his minority judgment in *Daniels v Thompson* — thought this was too radical an interpretation of the law. He stated that while accepting an award for exemplary damages would be exceptional, he preferred the 'non-restrictive' approach recommended in the *1991 Ontario Law Reform Commission Report* and the 1993 Law Commission for England and Wales consultation paper titled *Aggravated, Exemplary and Restitution Damages*.

I agreed with Justice Thomas's view and sought to either ameliorate the impact of the majority decision or overturn it, using 'the highest court in the land' (Parliament) as the forum.

With the help of Crown counsel I drafted a member's bill based upon the statutory amendment included in the Law Commission for England and Wales consultation paper. My Bill was lodged, but as for all member's bills, any discussion in Parliament depended on its being drawn out in a ballot. And since my Treaty of Waitangi Bill had already been drawn, the chances of a second one was fairly remote. I began to think about other options.

The opportunity came through my membership of a specially constituted Select Committee on the Accident Insurance Act. I was lying awake in bed one night when the thought suddenly occurred to me that an amendment to that Act might be possible. I approached the Clerk of the House but he said what I contemplated was too remote from the legislation currently before Parliament.

Undeterred, I went back to the Crown counsel, who was confident he could draft something that would be within the scope of the legislation, and he did. I then had to convince the other key MPs — particularly the two hard-working and intelligent Labour members on the select committee, Ruth Dyson and Lianne Dalziel, with whom I had established good working relationships — to support my amendment.

Next, I had to make sure the government did not rule the amendment out using its financial veto. I had known the minister sponsoring the legislation, Murray McCully, for many years and we got on well. As luck would have it, he was interested in a deal involving ACT support for another part of the legislation, in return for which he was happy to agree not to rule my amendment out on financial grounds. I now had a majority to pass my amendment through the committee stages of the House.

The minister of justice, Douglas Graham — clearly egged on by his officials — was less supportive than McCully, and I had occasion when moving my amendment to thank him for his 'grudging support'. I told the House that the amendment would provide justice to victims of rape and sexual abuse in particular, and went on to outline my reasons for disagreeing with the majority judgment of the Court of Appeal in *Daniels v Thompson*.

I argued that the procedures in the criminal and civil courts were quite different, with different standards of proof. In one jurisdiction the whole case is run by the Crown and in the other by the plaintiff, and the two jurisdictions were accorded a quite different status.

My amendment — which passed into law — clarified that:

- nothing in the Accident Insurance Act prevents a claim being brought for exemplary damages for conduct that has resulted in personal injury covered by the Accident Insurance Act or former Acts;
- an award may be made even though the defendant has been charged, acquitted, convicted, discharged without conviction, charged but the charge has not been dealt with, or the limitation period for bringing a charge for such an offence has expired.

But that was not the end of the matter, as certain plaintiffs in *Daniels v Thompson* had appealed to the Privy Council (under the name of *W v W*) and this case had been heard but no decision had yet been delivered when my amendment went through Parliament. The fact that Parliament had 'intervened' when the matter was still before the courts — in this case having been heard but awaiting the judgment of the Privy Council — was viewed by some as unacceptable — in fact Solicitor-General John McGrath accused me at a social function immediately after the amendment had been passed of being 'a constitutional disgrace'.[7]

By passing my amendment, Parliament — as the highest court in the land on policy — reasserted its authority over the Court of Appeal in terms of policy-making. What the amendment did not do, and was not designed to do, was restrict a court's right to 'interpret' and 'clarify' policy as and when needed.

Bad blood and medical procedures

Another important ACC amendment was passed through in my name under the heading of 'Personal injury caused by medical misadventure' during consideration of the Accident Insurance Amendment Bill. Credit for the amendment, which I acknowledged when I introduced it, rightly rests with Ruth Dyson and Lianne Dalziel.

The issue led to a redefinition of 'personal injury' in the Accident Insurance Act to include an infection suffered by an insured as a result of a medical misadventure and passed on to his or her spouse or dependant. The select committee had been alerted to an ACC claim lodged by a pregnant woman who had contracted HIV from her partner. The corporation had accepted her claim but had declined to cover her child, who had also been infected while *in utero*. A court had upheld this claim but ACC was considering an appeal.

The amendment, moved in Parliament by the Labour committee MPs, overrode this possibility by clarifying the law. But when the government opposed it and I voted on ACT's behalf with the government, the amendment was lost. Later, Lianne Dalziel came up to me and asked: 'Why didn't you vote for our amendment?' When I replied that I realised I should have, she said: 'Well, fix it.' And that is what I did next day, following a substantial degree of further negotiation with McCully and his officials, and further muted objections from the minister of justice. Graham claimed that the change was too major to be brought about by way of a 'mere amendment', but I pointed out that the select committee had already considered the matter in detail and the majority of its members were in favour of the change on social policy grounds.

Registration of foreign doctors

An issue I took up with my fellow parliamentarians across all political parties — this time without success — was foreign doctor registration. I was motivated by the unfair situation I came across whereby numerous highly trained overseas doctors were unable to practise in New Zealand without having to qualify again from scratch, or in some cases having to work under the supervision of doctors substantially less experienced and less qualified than them.

Registration problems were not confined to the medical profession. I lost count of the foreign taxi drivers whose cabs I rode in who answered my question 'What professional qualifications do you have?' with answers such as engineer, pilot, chemist, lawyer, physicist, economist, doctor and so on. The registration of foreign doctors seemed to me to be the easiest issue to solve. How wrong I was, despite the fact that every MP I approached agreed that a problem existed.

My focus was to try to establish a set of universally acceptable registration criteria, initially using as a basis existing criteria from Commonwealth and OECD countries. This was turned down so I tried a few other approaches. All were knocked back for one reason or another by different MPs, until I finally ran out of time as the 1999 election approached.

Since then, considerable progress has been made on the matter, particularly because of New Zealand's shortage of doctors. A comprehensive system is now in place to assess a candidate's suitability to practise in New Zealand.

Entertaining foreign diplomats

One event that had lapsed before I became chair of the FDT Select Committee was its periodic hosting of a social function for members of the diplomatic corps. I reinstated this and it was a huge success. It also had unintended consequences when a number of the diplomats reciprocated the committee's hospitality by inviting me to visit their country as a guest of government.

In Hawaii, the US Navy invited me aboard one of their nuclear-powered submarines, and there I witnessed in its main control centre — following the 1997 escalation of tensions in the Gulf as a result of the expulsion of US weapons inspectors from Iraq — the military buildup and surveillance of flights in and out of Baghdad airport. With all types of aircraft flying everywhere, it was easy to see how an inattentive operator might push the wrong button and down a passenger plane by accident.

During a visit to Germany I led a small delegation — that included the head of the Treasury and the governor of the Reserve Bank — to study the impending introduction of the Euro. All our meetings there were brilliantly organised, with access to senior politicians and officials, and attendance at a performance of the Berliner Philharmoniker, which was a real treat.

In China I travelled with Paul East, who was excellent company, and General Mao, our host representing the Chinese military. The general had considerable style and used his rank to advantage. They flew us first class and the accommodation was excellent. If a particular restaurant happened to be closed, as happened on one daytime excursion when we arrived very late, it was immediately ordered to reopen and, in recognition of the general's authority, did so extremely promptly with the full menu available to us.

In Taiwan, in addition to my meetings with senior politicians and officials, we enjoyed a guided tour of the Taipei National Palace Museum. The museum derives from the same institution as the museum in the Forbidden City in Beijing, the contents of which were moved on numerous occasions during times of conflict and war. It covers about 80 hectares on the outskirts of the city and afforded an opportunity to see some of the more than 650,000 pieces of the largest collection of Chinese artefacts and artwork in the world, including ancient bronze castings, calligraphy, scroll paintings, porcelain, jade and rare books that span 8000 years of Chinese history.

Of all the countries visited, Japan and China stand out as the most interesting because of what I was able to see and learn about their different cultures. My wife joined me on the Japanese trip and the host country covered all my costs on these trips but not hers, which was appropriate. Initially, however, this caused problems in Japan. Assuming (wrongly)

With Susan and Paul East in China, 1999.

that it would operate as a cashless society, I had taken very few yen with me and planned to use my credit card for most purchases. I quickly found that 'cash was king', and there was a limited number of ATMs.

Eventually our interpreter got the hang of dealing with me. She would say:

> Tomorrow you have an appointment with the Secretary for Defence at 2pm. I suggest we meet in your hotel lobby at 12 noon; have lunch at a [nominated] restaurant that specialises in eel [or tuna or whatever]. Your wife's meal will cost 2000 yen which I will need in cash. Is this acceptable?

My answer was always yes, and the food was brilliant.

One unusual event I witnessed in Tokyo was the after-office-hours delivery of several cartons of new computers to a shop opposite our hotel. Because the shop was closed when delivery took place, the cartons were neatly stacked and left in the street overnight. To my amazement, they were still there next morning and were taken into the shop when it opened. I doubt whether the computers would have sat on the footpath overnight in many other countries.

With Susan in Kyoto, 1999.

We visited Kyoto over a long weekend, choosing it because of its history, beautiful buildings and gardens. Kyoto is located in a valley in the eastern part of the mountainous region known as the Tamba Highlands, with hot summers and cold winters.

The original city was arranged in accordance with traditional fusui, with the main business district located to the south of the old imperial palace. Although ravaged by wars, fires, and earthquakes during its 11 centuries as the imperial capital, Kyoto was spared much of the destruction suffered by other Japanese cities during World War II. US Secretary of War Henry L. Stimson famously intervened to remove Kyoto from the atomic bomb target list in order to save this cultural centre, which he knew well from his honeymoon there and from later diplomatic visits. Kyoto is consequently one of the best-preserved cities in Japan.

At least in theory, Japan still had — at the time of our visit — no conventional defence force, despite the fact that my official hosts were the Japanese military. What the country did have was an extremely large and sophisticated 'self-defence force' — which in 2020 ranked fifth out of 138 countries in terms of global firepower — made up of unified ground, maritime and air self-defence forces that had a combined budget larger than France and about the same size as that of the UK.

Following Japan's defeat in World War II, the public demanded not only total disarmament and the removal of all military leaders from positions of public influence, but also a constitutional ban on rearmament. The 1947 constitution therefore renounces war as an instrument for settling international disputes and declares that Japan will never again maintain 'land, sea, or air forces or other war potential'.

Despite this, subsequent Cabinets have interpreted these provisions as not denying the nation's inherent right of self-defence. As a result, with the encouragement of the US, Japan has developed its unique self-defence force.

CHAPTER 23

Defence in the Spotlight Again

I had decided to retire from Parliament at the 1999 election. However, before and during that campaign, Helen Clark, Leader of the Opposition, foreshadowed substantial changes to defence if she became prime minister. In particular, she said, she would ask me to review the F-16 contract the National-led coalition government had signed with the United States.

Labour and its coalition partners won the election, and even before being sworn in Clark asked me to meet with her. At that meeting in her Auckland home I was asked to carry out two reviews: one for the F-16 contract, and the other, a much larger job, a review of the whole New Zealand Defence Force. Initially Clark said that she expected me to recommend cancelling the F-16 contract 'if the cost is not too high'. This was consistent with her publicly expressed view in December 1998 that '[t]he whole thinking and strategy behind [acquiring the F-16s] is warped'.[1] She clarified — at my request — that 'cost' included non-financial considerations, and the terms of reference were drawn up accordingly.

My contract employer for the F-16 review was Mark Prebble, head of the Prime Minister's Department and brother of ACT leader Richard Prebble.

The F-16s in question were originally destined for Pakistan but the US had cancelled their delivery in 1998 when that country exploded its first nuclear bomb. New Zealand then contracted to acquire the aircraft to replace the RNZAF's existing fleet of 19 A-4 Skyhawk attack aircraft.

The first Skyhawks had entered service in New Zealand in June 1970, and by 2000 five of them had been in service for 30 years. Although they had been substantially upgraded, their design dated back to the 1950s. In the words of Sir Wilson Whineray, who chaired the Air Combat Capability Policy Study in 1998:

> I find this to be a long time, and while upgrades have meant that the aircraft have roughly kept pace with technology trends, this study has clearly shown that the Skyhawk is inadequate as an air combat capability in the modern world. These [inadequacies] are largely due to the limits of its ageing airframe, with its lack of speed and manoeuvrability. In the business [world], no corporate could be remotely competitive using equipment nearly 40 years old.[2]

The F-16 had, by the year 2000, become the standard multi-role combat aircraft around the world. Those offered to New Zealand had been built in the early 1990s and were unused apart from test flight time. They had a full airframe life of up to 30 years, and without doubt offered a significant improvement in capability over the Skyhawks, particularly in the close air support and air interdiction roles. They could also be readily fitted with electronic counter-measures and target pods, both regarded as essential in the medium to long term, although the plane's existing configuration met the role and operational capability requirements for most foreseeable lower-order peace enforcement contingencies over the next 10 years.[3]

Under the terms of reference for the review, in assessing the consequences of cancellation, deferment, amendment or confirmation of the project, I had to consider the wider implications any decision might have for air-strike capability. This matter had been the subject of ongoing questioning for a number of years. When it became clear to me very early in the review that cancellation would be tantamount to disbanding the air-strike capability, I raised this with key ministers — Clark, Goff as minister of foreign affairs, and Mark Burton as minister of defence. Clark and Goff refused to accept this as a possibility.

At the meeting with Clark where this was raised, on 9 February 2000, Mark Prebble, Heather Simpson, Graham Fortune (Secretary of Defence), Neil Walter (head of foreign affairs) and an MFAT scribe were present. There were no NZDF people there. I arrived at the meeting at the agreed time, but subsequently found out that several key issues relating to the F-16 acquisition contract, my review, and the political ramifications of the overall matter had either been discussed before I arrived, or were discussed after I had left.

Fortune noted after the meeting:

> Clark says there are four options: confirming the acquisition/lease; lease/buy fewer aircraft; keep the A4s/no F-16s; do away with the air combat capability. She accepted a more detailed review would be desirable before the fourth option was considered. She did not like options one or two. She suggested that Quigley should focus on option three for the time being, with a deeper review of the need for an air combat capability being investigated. She was attracted by the savings that would be generated by selling the A4s and Aeromacchis and buying pilot training from the Australians.
>
> Clark explains: 'I am leading a fragile coalition, where the majority is to [my] left' and 'taking the F-16s will be extremely damaging to Labour and the Coalition'. Clark thinks withdrawal can be handled diplomatically and expects the United States to understand the limits of a country of less than four million to maintain a credible defence force. She is not interested in any 'US sweeteners' as they would 'not solve her political difficulties nor her belief that the capability is not needed'. Clark also asked questions about detail, exit costs, numbers of F-16 and how they are calculated, and about what US officials might or might not have said or offered, other defence acquisitions — especially from the army.[4]

Meanwhile, in blissful ignorance of this, I told the meeting my two early conclusions were that the acquisition deal was a good one financially, and that its cancellation would result in the air force's air-strike capability being disbanded. Clark was emphatic — that would not happen while she was prime minister. Instead, she suggested, perhaps it would be better to get rid of the navy's frigates. I said, 'If you do that you will lose all credibility.'

The meeting was not helpful as far as my review was concerned. It was obvious it was not going to be easy to get through to Clark on the wider implications I was obliged to consider. I decided to get on with the review and talk to her again when I had all the information in front of me.

Unlike the situation with the FDT Select Committee DB2000 inquiry, during the F-16 review I at least had access to most of the information and people I needed. I also had a 'top secret' security clearance so I could receive briefings on the strategic environment from MFAT and the External Assessments Bureau of the Prime Minister's Department.

What I didn't have — on specific instructions — was direct contact with Canberra or Washington, or with US official representatives in New Zealand. I was required to avoid any risk, particularly in the case

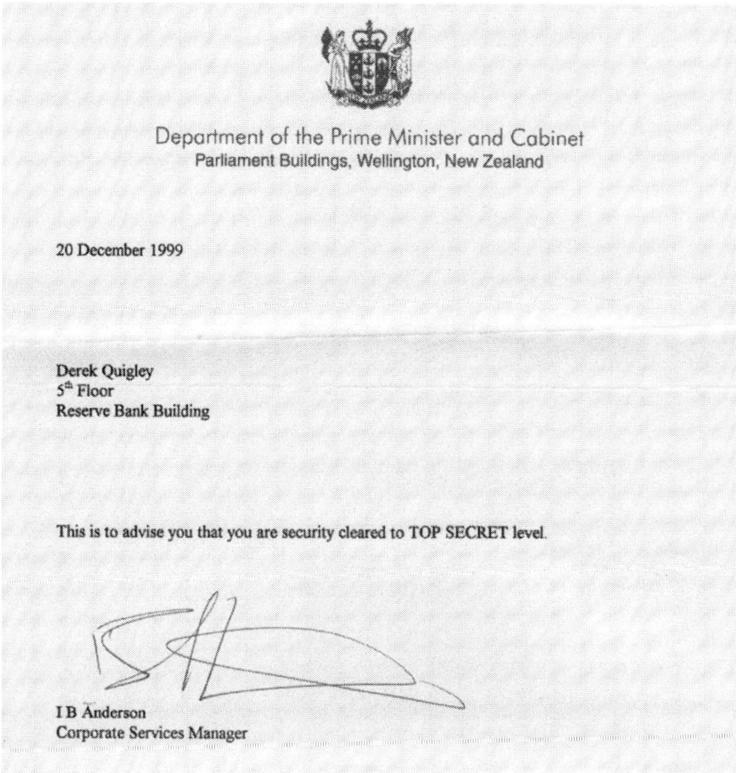

Department of the Prime Minister and Cabinet
Parliament Buildings, Wellington, New Zealand

20 December 1999

Derek Quigley
5th Floor
Reserve Bank Building

This is to advise you that you are security cleared to TOP SECRET level.

I B Anderson
Corporate Services Manager

Clearance to pry.

of the Americans, of 'building up their expectations that the contract might be confirmed'.[5] However, I did have input from an independent economist and unlimited assistance from two excellent Treasury officials.

One of the tasks of the Treasury people was to check and collate information obtained from Defence. This proved to be difficult, as noted in the Treasury memorandum that accompanied my final report: 'There are substantial risks around some of the figures provided to the Treasury by NZDF. [They] have changed a number of times during the review and on past project cost experience, are likely to be underestimates.'[6]

As I began to move towards final recommendations, a number of key matters emerged that suggested the possibility of a new contract being negotiated with the US administration for fewer aircraft. It was clear that 28 strike aircraft was an excessive number for a relatively small country like New Zealand, when a critical mass was said to be a squadron of 18.[7]

It had become clear that the Americans were open to discussing a package containing fewer aircraft.[8] The contract contained two five-year break points and no compulsory purchase clause, meaning New Zealand could quite legally tell the Americans to 'take them away' if that was what was wanted either five or 10 years later.

I also looked at the possibility of leasing the aircraft rather than buying them. According to our calculations the existing deal was a good one financially, but leasing would be even more favourable. A cost of at least $1 billion was projected for outright purchase (of all 28 aircraft) plus upgrades, compared with a basic lease and regeneration package (until at least June 2009) of $363 million.[9]

I was aware that New Zealand had made considerable progress through the latter part of the 1990s in overcoming the standoff with the US resulting from the anti-nuclear legislation. For me, part of the attraction of the F-16 deal was that it would be, at least in part, recognition of the ongoing rebuilding of the relationship. It was not about the possibility of New Zealand being readmitted to the American fold as an unswerving supporter of that country's defence and foreign policy. I believed that if New Zealand were to have a capable and relevant defence force, the NZDF and the people who served in it needed access to the type of security intelligence, general information, training, exercise opportunities, equipment, funding lines and technology that could only be provided by a close association with Australia and the US. It was also about maintaining the RNZAF's operational and technical expertise, upgrading operational capability and having the potential to expand that capability in the future if circumstances warranted. My view was that once the air-strike capability was disbanded, it would be lost forever.

I consequently began to work towards a package that would involve leasing fewer aircraft. When Mark Prebble realised where I was heading he tried to heavy me, because I was not now likely to recommend cancelling the F-16 contract. He suggested that my contract with him was at risk of cancellation, and also that I would not be given the wider defence review after all. But Helen Clark, to her credit, told Prebble — and he passed this on to me — that she was quite happy for me to provide her with independent advice.

Despite the recommendations of the Strategos review 12 years earlier, no prioritisation process had been put in place in relation to defence project spending. The process still involved consideration of bids on an ad hoc basis, or when something was needed for an urgent deployment or regarded as 'an attractive acquisition opportunity.' The F-16 contract was a case in point.

Although I knew the F-16 contract would create immediate cashflow difficulties and affect the funds available for other defence projects, this was symptomatic of a much deeper problem within the NZDF. For some time it had been trying to maintain the so-called 'balanced force' approach, but it didn't have the money or appropriate policy direction to do so.

In my view, a thorough overall assessment was needed of what the government required of the NZDF. The general thrust of my F-16 report of 6 March 2000 — like the Strategos review and the two DB2000 reports — was aimed at addressing these problems. My two key recommendations were:

- That the government consider approaching the United States government with a view to renegotiating the F-16 package to include a lesser number of leased aircraft; and that
- All defence projects be reviewed as a matter of urgency, on a project-by-project basis, with a view to reprioritising and funding them on the basis of their capacity — judged from an NZDF-wide perspective — to advance New Zealand's national interests.[10]

Before presenting my recommendations I provided the prime minister with a detailed one-to-one briefing. I gave the same briefing to Goff and Burton, with the former's staff member David Shearer also present. Shearer later commented to me: 'Ministers had never had such a comprehensive briefing before.'

The meeting with Clark occurred immediately before officials were due to travel to Washington to try to obtain an accurate figure on the cost of cancelling the contract. I had been unable to do this because of constraints imposed on me over who I could talk to.

Clark listened to my presentation without comment, then asked whether I thought I should be going to Washington with the officials. I said I hadn't considered going, but could do so if that was thought to be helpful. She said she would phone me back that evening. When she did, it was to say it had been decided I shouldn't go in case my presence built up American expectations. She then asked me to repeat my briefing to the officials who were going.

Next morning Mark Prebble greeted me by saying I could now write up the detail of my wider defence review contract. Brian Lockstone, who had helped me draft the F-16 report, commented that feedback from senior journalists was that the prime minister now thought the F-16 review entailed much more than she had originally realised.

When I briefed the officials before they left for Washington, they told me they had been instructed not to initiate discussions during their visit about fewer aircraft, but to listen to what the Americans had to say. When they returned several days later they had obtained accurate cancellation costs (about $11 million) and options for fewer planes. But by then the government had decided to cancel the contract, and did so.

There were several reasons. One was the politics of the issue. The Labour caucus showed little support (and the Alliance none) for the F-16 package, or for that matter for the air-strike force, which had never actually been used in combat since the RNZAF had acquired it.

Another was money. Even though the lease costs were now substantially lower than the purchase price originally contemplated, the financial meter was running, with large payments due sooner rather than later. These were payable quarterly and would have amounted — as I outlined in my report — to more than $254 million by the end of the first five-year lease period.

The third reason was timing, in relation to other urgent defence priorities. The F-16 package had brought the air combat force's replacement forward from the date contemplated in 1997 when the defence capital plan had already increased from $4.4 billion to $5.6 billion between then and Cabinet's approval of the project in November 1998.

The overall financial result, because of a decline in the value of the New Zealand dollar between the time the contract was signed and its cancellation, was that the government actually made an overall profit from the cancelled F-16 deal.

Despite Clark's unequivocal statement to me that her government would not disband the air-strike capability while she was prime minister, by June 2000 it had decided that the core requirement for the NZDF was to have well-equipped, combat-trained land forces able to act as effective peacekeepers, supported by the RNZN and RNZAF.

Following further reviews, the government disbanded the existing air combat force and at last set up a process to prioritise all defence projects, and to fund them on the basis of their capacity, judged from an NZDF-wide perspective, to advance New Zealand's national interests.

An interesting postscript dates back to a matter I raised with Kim Beazley in 1988 during the course of the Strategos review. It concerned the consideration of joint trans-Tasman pilot training, which was accepted by Beazley as a matter worth investigating. Ultimately the idea was rejected on spurious 'operational and sovereignty grounds', but it raises an interesting question: would the RNZAF still have an air combat capability today if its top brass had been adopted a more cooperative approach to recommendations of the Strategos review, instead of continually fighting them?

The price of my providing an independent F-16 report, rather than one framed to accord with the wishes of the Labour and Alliance caucuses, was that I was not invited to carry out any further defence reviews. However, I at least retained my status and credibility as an independent adviser!

Defence policy and structure

In June 2000 the government announced its new direction for defence in a Defence Policy Framework Statement, against the background of the F-16 cancellation decision and the various reviews discussed earlier. The statement was said to have been guided by and built upon the 1999 FDT Select Committee DB2000 final report,[11] aimed at outlining the government's goals and priorities for defence and providing a framework for future decisions about military capabilities, resources and funding.

In the wider policy context, it recorded that defence was but one aspect of New Zealand's foreign and security policy, and that the government would work to promote a comprehensive approach to security.

The statement noted that resources were spread thinly across a range of capabilities not all of which could be well sustained. The greatest needs were to:

- upgrade the army's mobility, communications, surveillance and fire-support capabilities;
- provide effective air and naval transport capabilities; and
- maintain effective maritime surveillance capabilities of the air force and navy within the New Zealand EEZ and those of Pacific Island states.[12]

The statement represented a major policy shift and effectively ended the 'balanced force' approach (at least for the time being) which had been adhered to by successive New Zealand governments.

On 8 May 2001 the Prime Minister announced what she described as a plan for 'a modern, sustainable defence force matched to New Zealand's needs', with the following key components:

- a joint force approach to structure and operations with the objective of improving co-ordination between the three services;
- a modernised army based on two light infantry battalions;
- a naval fleet with (eventually) two ANZAC frigates, a multi-role vessel with long-distance and Southern Ocean capabilities, and new inshore patrol craft;
- a refocused air force with no air combat force arm; and
- a sustainable funding plan.

The plan was said to be based on comprehensive reviews of New Zealand's strategic position and capability requirements, and on the expectation that it would meet New Zealand's strategic needs and allow the country to contribute usefully to international operations 'where the Government decides to engage'.[13]

It had taken successive New Zealand governments 13 years and three defence reviews to finally put in place a mechanism that Strategos started in 1988, to link defence policy, priorities and funding.

The Hunn review

Following the recommendation included in DB2000 that accountabilities and structural arrangements within New Zealand Defence should be reassessed (i.e. the creation of two separate legal entities in 1990), the Clark government commissioned the *Hunn Review*[14] after the 1999 election. Its recommendations were received in 2002.

The review found a broad consensus among those interviewed that some parts of the organisational model on which the 1990 Defence Act was based had worked, but the separation between policy formulation 'by civilians' (Ministry of Defence) and the management of operational delivery by the military (NZDF) had not delivered the promised benefits. Paragraph 17 of the report's executive summary reads:

> It is the contention of this review that the fundamental premise is wrong. The objective in contemplating a defence structure should be to meld the

> military and civilian contributions into a single stream of advice and operations, not to keep them in separate boxes. Whatever justification there may have been at the time, the situation has changed in the 12 years since the current system was introduced — responses to international security issues have developed, there is a growing emphasis on 'jointness' and governance models have been reconsidered.

The report's principal conclusion was that the key components of the 1990 Act should be radically redesigned and replaced, and that 'Any changes ... should be based on a reconsideration of all the factors impinging on defence policy and implementation and should incorporate much more than a single set of managerial concepts — as tended to be the case in 1989/90.'[15]

Reactions to Hunn's report were varied. Graham Fortune, Secretary of Defence 1999–2006, believed that any problems with the existing defence structure were because the original Strategos recommendations had not been implemented in full.[16] This had inevitably led to an uneven balance of responsibility and division of labour between the CDF and the Secretary. In his opinion the problems were neither structural, requiring large-scale reorganisation, nor personality based. 'The responsibilities given to CDF and the Secretary are largely appropriate and the two Chief Executives, both in the recent past and now, work collegially,' he wrote.[17] In other words the initial problems — in his view — had now been overcome.

The Treasury also expressed reservations, making two important points First, that NZDF's resource management had been the most effective of any armed force the Treasury had looked at internationally. And second, unless accountabilities were very clear, an organisation with effectively two heads was inconsistent with the key strengths of New Zealand's public management system and put at risk the very real gains in resource management made by the NZDF over the past decade. The proposal would need to be very carefully designed to avoid the problems of confused accountabilities that led to the separation of the two organisations in the early 1990s, Treasury officials argued.

In my view, the New Zealand structure has significant advantages. The fact that the ministry and the NZDF are legally independent entities means the Secretary has no responsibility, authority or accountability for the management of the NZDF, while the CDF does.

No changes to the relevant parts of the Defence Act have followed.

The Auckland City Complaints Commissioner

After the F-16 review I was asked by Christine Fletcher, who had been in Parliament with me during the 1996–99 Parliament but was now mayor of Auckland City, to become the city's mayoral complaints commissioner. I accepted.

At my first meeting, Fletcher expressed concern over a liquor licence that had been issued to what in law was a massage parlour but in fact had a long history as a brothel. Night-time activity and noise had increased substantially since the liquor licence had been issued, and the property was in a part-residential/part-commercial zone. The file I was given contained a considerable number of complaints.

The first thing I noticed was that the surname of the police officer who had signed off the approval on the liquor licence application was the same as one of the New Zealand directors of the Melbourne-based company that owned the premises. I contacted the district police commissioner and asked for the matter to be investigated. In due course I was told that everything was above board and that the common surname was a coincidence.

Next, I found that the council employee who had investigated the application and recommended its approval was no longer employed by the council — she was now employed by the company that owned the massage parlour.

I was at home one evening writing up my report when I received a phone call. The male caller declined to provide his name, merely saying that he was 'a friend'. He asked if I was reviewing a particular massage parlour liquor licence, and when I confirmed I was, he said: 'You and your family need to be careful. The people who own the business have more money than the government has just put in to bailing out Air New Zealand and they are very ruthless.'

I ignored the threat and duly lodged my report with the mayor. As I had no legal protection if defamation proceedings were issued against me, and no hard evidence that corruption had been involved, I stuck to outlining the facts I had uncovered and left it to the council to decide what to do. It did nothing.

Shortly after that, Christine Fletcher lost the mayoralty to John Banks, and following a review of the city's finances by my former Cabinet colleague Bill Birch, my annual contract lapsed. However, I stayed on as commissioner 'to be approached on a case-by-case basis as appropriate'.[18]

Banks in turn lost the mayoralty to Dick Hubbard in 2004, at which point I wrote to the new mayor asking if he wished me to resign. He asked me to stay on, but no more files have been referred to me. I wonder if I'm still Auckland's mayoral complaints commissioner?

Visiting fellow at ANU

Looking for a further challenge, we moved Canberra in 2004 where I became an unpaid visiting fellow at the Strategic & Defence Studies Centre at ANU. This provided me with an office, ongoing access to lectures on interesting topics, research and secretarial assistance, and unrestricted contact with staff, students and about a dozen other visiting fellows who were eminently skilled in various aspects of Australian, trans-Tasman and international defence and security.

One was Robert Ayson, who had worked with me in Parliament and was head of the centre's undergraduate programme. Another was Paul Dibb, whom I had previously consulted during the Strategos review. Although I found Canberra a brilliant city for intellectual stimulus, with its prestigious university, foreign embassies, defence establishments, Houses of Parliament and interesting people, I soon found out that I was more of a practitioner than an academic. However, I enjoyed presenting seminars on the New Zealand reform process, writing papers, authoring *The War Against Defence Restructuring*[19] and making submissions to an Australian defence management review chaired by Catherine Livingstone, at one time chair of the CSIRO, Telstra and the Commonwealth Bank.

In my oral submission to her committee I began by outlining what I saw as the four assumptions that any consideration of defence should take into account. First, that a country's defence policy and defence force should be appropriate to its place in the world. Second, that in an environment of limited resources, a direct link between defence policy, priorities and funding is necessary in order for efficiency and effectiveness to be optimised.

Third, that although the operational performance of a defence system doesn't lend itself easily to measurement by standard accounting or general commercial yardsticks, it is important to be able to relate expenditure decisions to results in some way. And fourth, in most defence establishments, savings can be achieved by adopting a more businesslike approach.

Livingstone was particularly interested in why the structure of New Zealand defence had been changed. I told her the split into two separate entities was basically about clarifying accountability. When Livingstone reported, she recommended that further consideration be given to the New Zealand defence organisational split, but the Australian defence hierarchy disagreed, and the matter went no further.

CHAPTER 24

ACT in Parliament

With Prebble's manifesto as the party's policy umbrella, ACT's main approach during the 1996 campaign was 'presidential', based around Prebble himself, supported by other candidates throughout New Zealand. This, plus the party's substantial private-sector funding and a decline in National's vote from 35.05 percent in 1993 to 33.87 three years later, was sufficient to enable ACT to elect eight MPs, despite the fact that it was a new party with no parliamentary funding and limited media support.

But once in Parliament it never built on its presence there to became a large viable force able to challenge National and remove New Zealand First completely from the political scene. This was in large measure because of the way it conducted itself. With no coherent strategy or a brand based on *Unfinished Business* to bind all of its MPs together, most of them soon began to focus on their own areas of interest. The result was that ACT was quickly seen as just another political party at a time when large numbers of voters were looking for something completely different.

When I became an MP again I had been away from Parliament for 12 years and was the oldest member, at 64. As a list MP with no electorate responsibilities I decided to spend my time — when not attending to normal parliamentary duties — promoting ACT's basic policies and helping the party become a major political force. But this proved extremely difficult.

ACT's team of MPs were a brilliant lot, with a mix of genders and experience. Seven had university degrees, with the only non-graduate, Owen Jennings, a former national president of Federated Farmers and well known and respected in the rural community. However, with no clearly identifiable policy package like the one Douglas and I had devised, the party was rarely on message.

The first to break ranks was Rodney Hide, who has a string of university degrees and on his best days is a brilliant speaker. He had decided that the road to success in politics was to become a household name by championing causes the public could identify with. His initial focus was on the benefits enjoyed by his fellow MPs and their former colleagues. He soon became known nationwide as 'Parliament's perk buster'.

Initially, Prebble tolerated this, but with long experience as a headline seeker himself, he was soon looking for ways to get into the media too. When I asked why he wasn't focusing on basic party policies, the answer was along the lines that 'Talking about them won't give us the coverage we need'.

Richard is intelligent and hardworking, was an ardent ACT supporter, and extremely supportive of his parliamentary team — as I personally found out when I had to take time off for prostate surgery. But he was also too impatient and not committed to the ACT policies I had helped to put in place. I saw this as a waste of a golden opportunity to build ACT's support base, and was annoyed by Hide's off-message headline-seeking. I began to wonder why I had bothered coming back into politics. So I got on with the big-picture issues where I thought change was needed.

Fortunately, I had been able to convince Brian Lockstone to join me as my PA. Like me, Brian was very unhappy with Prebble's and more particularly Hide's approach, and when the coalition government started to fall apart he suggested I should consider joining the government on 'a lend-lease basis'.

I was lukewarm and the idea went nowhere, although Bolger and I met briefly to discuss the possibility, with him, I suspect, hoping I might bring some additional ACT MPs with me to bolster his fragile coalition. At our meeting I told Bolger I thought National's coalition with New Zealand First was damaging his and his party's reputation, and then asked him if he thought his leadership was secure. 'Of course it is,' he replied, which showed — as events soon illustrated — that I knew more than he did about that particular matter.

ACT still had a narrow window of opportunity to establish a permanent, sizable place in Parliament, as the Taranaki–King Country by-election result showed. Along with the other ACT MPs, I was actively involved there to remind voters of the policy differences between ACT and the National/New Zealand First coalition government.

With the by-election giving the party's MPs a nationwide publicity boost, they were soon back to headline seeking. That this wasn't working was illustrated by the results of an in-house independent survey of the comparative media effectiveness of ACT's eight MPs in terms of positive coverage for the party during the 1996–99 Parliament. It saw me come out on top as a result of my work as chair of the FDT Select Committee and my other parliamentary initiatives. Although this established that my contribution had helped to maintain ACT's profile, it was of little long-term help to the party when I didn't stand for re-election in 1999.

In 1999 ACT increased its number of MPs to nine due to an increase in its list vote of 19,051 from three years earlier, but Prebble narrowly lost Wellington Central. An interesting feature of the result there, in purely tactical voting terms, was that the 15,988 electorate votes he received might have done substantially more for ACT if they had been list votes.

In 2002 ACT again returned nine MPs with slightly fewer list votes due to a substantial decline in voter turnout, down from 84.8 percent three years earlier to 77 percent. But the 2002 result showed a disaster waiting to happen for ACT.

National had gone from 44 MPs in 1996 to 39 in 1999, and New Zealand First from 17 to five. In 2002, while ACT still had nine MPs, National experienced a massive decline in support, with its MP numbers dropping to only 27. The beneficiary was not Labour, which only increased its MPs by three, but instead New Zealand First, which came back from five MPs to 13. United Future, a new centrist party led by former breakaway Labour MP Peter Dunne, won eight seats in 2002, following a credible TV performance by its leader on the eve of the election.

While ACT almost held its list votes in 2002, National shed 204,623, New Zealand First gained an additional 122,986, and United Future won 124,853.

Why didn't ACT pick up the votes that went from National to New Zealand First and United Future? In my view, it was because ACT had no clearly identifiable brand, and as a result its credibility was suspect. Also, even those voters who were thought to be ACT's hard-core supporters in fact weren't. As subsequent events illustrated, most of them were only voting for the party in the hope that it might return to its earlier ideals and policies. If it didn't, and a more attractive alternative came along, they would jump ship.

And that's what happened when Don Brash become National's new leader and started to expound a new policy direction for that party. In the

2005 election ACT dropped from nine MPs to two, avoiding annihilation only because Rodney Hide was gifted Epsom.

What ACT had needed long before 2005 was for the party's founding philosophy and core policies to be coherently and consistently communicated, and for the benefits that would flow from their implementation to be properly explained. But this never happened, and at ACT's annual conference in 2000 Roger Douglas condemned MPs who 'run any fickle line capable of grabbing short-term votes and attention', with Hide clearly in his sights. Hide, for his part, pointed out that focusing on economic theory — which in fact was not the basis of Douglas's criticism — attracted no media interest, whereas 'the so-called stunts are particularly well-reported'.[1]

The impact of Don Brash

Don Brash had stood previously for National as an electorate candidate and finally entered Parliament as a list MP in 2002. A former governor of the Reserve Bank and an advocate of open-market policies, he replaced Bill English as party leader in late 2003. He was seen as honest, economically literate and a new face in politics. Importantly, he was also seen as a 'non-political politician'. His focus was on core party policies, ideology and unifying New Zealand. In his Orewa speech in January 2004, which attracted wide-ranging headlines and attention, he said:

> [T]he topic I will focus on today is the dangerous drift towards racial separatism in New Zealand, and the development of the now entrenched Treaty grievance industry. We are one country with many peoples, not simply a society of Pakeha and Maori where the minority has a birthright to the upper hand, as the Labour Government seems to believe.[2]

Although these sentiments differed little from those expressed previously by Bill English, they resulted in an unprecedented 17 percent boost for National in a public opinion poll shortly after. The Treaty of Waitangi was mentioned far less frequently in the speeches and press releases of the Clark-led coalition government after that.

Brash was supportive of ACT's original policies, and later, for a brief time, became ACT's leader. He advocated lower taxes, an end to Waitangi Treaty settlement claims, the abolition of the Māori seats in Parliament and a range of market-orientated initiatives. The message he conveyed was that this time — if National became the government — what he was outlining would be implemented, not just talked about.

ACT supporters liked Brash. 'He is a new kind of politician . . . not part of the club . . . he is honest, sincere and energetic. He has a vision of a New Zealand that is rooted in the future, not the past.' These comments, which certainly accorded with my views of the man, were made by Brian Nicolle, a key figure in the formation of ACT.

Brash drew support from a wide range of sources. Nicky Hager's book *The Hollow Men*[3] lists Brash support from Douglas, Prebble, Hide, Judd, Bassett and Richardson; from committed Labour people such as David Caygill and Margaret Austin; from Barry Coleman, owner of *National Business Review*; from pro-business advocates such as Roger Kerr and reformers like Roderick Deane; from moneyed people like Gibbs, Myers, Heatley, Shirtcliffe and Friedlander; and from religious groups like the Exclusive Brethren.

However, the inference Hager drew was that these supporters were not committed to a better New Zealand for everyone; they were only motivated by their own personal interest. Consequently, he argued, any ideas they might have about the need for a different policy approach to a range of fundamental issues like better economic management, more efficiently delivered social services, better race relations, freedom and choice, and the role of governments weren't even worth considering.

But what Hager's book does illustrate is how political leaders can be run ragged to a point of exhaustion and diverted from their core beliefs. Once Brash became leader he was continually pressured to meet more and more people with 'brilliant ideas'; to respond daily in the media to myriad issues; and crucially to adopt a different strategy — in the interests of winning — where some of his policies were thought to have the potential to scare potential voters off. The result was an exhausted leader who began to make mistakes and, as a consequence, to agree to some of his core policy beliefs being 'sanitised'.

The underlying assumption associated with sanitisation is that voters are gullible and can be manipulated; that they are only interested in hip-pocket politics; and that they can somehow be made to believe that political promises will be paid for by someone other than them. But my experience is that voters are not stupid. They want to be told the truth and mostly can't be 'bought'. If they could be, Michael Bloomberg's $1 billion spend on his Democrat Party nomination campaign would have seen him, not Joe Biden, contesting the US presidency in November 2020 against Donald Trump.

Brash didn't quite make it in 2005 for two main reasons. First, because he didn't stick to his policy beliefs when the electorate was looking for firm leadership and clear policy differences; and second, because he was caught out on the eve of the election being evasive about the source of some of the party's advertising funding, and his intention to repeal parts of Labour's anti-nuclear legislation.

But what his leadership and the 2005 election result did achieve was the election of an additional 21 National MPs as voters flocked back to the party. The extent of this swing saw National's list vote increase by 464,503 and its number of MPs go from 27 to 48. In contrast, ACT's list vote dropped from 145,078 to 34,469 and its MPs to two; New Zealand First shed 107,797 list votes and its MPs went from 13 to seven; and United Future dropped from eight MPs to three.

A notable feature of National's 2005 campaign was its tactical voting decision. From the introduction of MMP it had urged supporters to give both of their votes to the party. It had obviously been studying the opinion polls since Brash became leader and concluded — on the basis of the 37 polls between 7 July 2004 and election day — that ACT had no chance of achieving the 5 percent threshold and therefore would not have any MPs unless it won an electorate. National saw the chance to get rid of a political irritant and decided not to support Rodney Hide's bid for the Epsom electorate.

In what turned out to be a hostile campaign, the National Party president wrote to Epsom voters asking for two ticks for National and echoing its nationwide election pitch: 'If centre-right voters give ACT their party vote, National may be prevented from being the largest party in Parliament, and Labour may end up staying in power.'[4]

But many National voters ignored the president's letter and Hide won the seat with a majority of 3102. However, National increased its list vote substantially while ACT's dropped.

The 2005 election result also led to the demise of Don Brash as National's leader and his replacement by John Key.

National moves to the left

Key was another near-new face in politics, with a personality that was portrayed as the full leadership package: intellect, charm, compassion, vision, international experience and a successful private-sector track record. To boot, he was a state-house kid turned millionaire merchant banker.[5] In Richard Prebble's view, John Key was 'the candidate from Central Casting — he never forgets his lines.'[6]

Key could have been New Zealand's most successful modern-day prime minister, but, despite his undoubted success in winning elections, with Bill English's help in managing the economy, he failed to live up to his potential.

In the 2008 election, when he first became prime minister, National's list vote rose from 39.19 percent in 2005 to 44.93 percent, and its MPs went from 48 to 58. Hide again won Epsom, and because ACT had secured 3.65 percent of the list vote it returned five MPs. In contrast, New Zealand First achieved a 4.07 percent list vote but because it hadn't won an electorate, it finished up with no MPs.

The increase in ACT's vote from 1.51 percent three years earlier was due to Douglas standing for the party for the first time, and was an indication of his continuing voter appeal. The tragedy was that he hadn't stood in 1996.

The reaction of the National Party hierarchy to Douglas's election was an interesting reflection of how their strategy had returned — in the post-Brash era — to status quo politics designed to win elections rather than solve New Zealand's growing social and other problems.

John Key showed National's new approach when he refused to have Douglas in his Cabinet because of his 'radical right-wing agenda' of cutting taxes, offering education vouchers, privatising the health system and slashing government spending. Key and his colleagues were obviously not interested in the ideas of someone whose reforms two decades earlier had saved New Zealand from near bankruptcy, and were unswayed by the international accolades that had been showered on Douglas.

National's strategy was to become a more centre-left party by attempting to cannibalise the New Zealand First vote now that that party had no parliamentary representation; to attract support from Labour's right-wing base now that it had moved further left under Helen Clark; and to limit the rise of ACT.

National had mistakenly assumed that ACT's near demise in 2005 was due to lack of voter appetite for its reformist policies, and had obviously forgotten why its own support had surged under Brash's leadership. It had consequently decided to avoid being associated with Douglas and the policies he stood for. However, it was still prepared to offer minor parties support in individual electorates, provided they stayed minor.

This approach appeared to work in 2011 despite New Zealand First coming back in that year's election with eight MPs. National was able to form a government with support from three Māori Party MPs and one each from ACT and United Future, with no need to call on New Zealand First.

In 2014 National was even more successful, with an outright majority on election night of 61 in a Parliament of 121 MPs. However, when all the votes were counted it finished with 60 MPs — the most any party had secured since the introduction of MMP. Labour's list vote dropped to 25.13 percent, the lowest since the introduction of MMP and its worst percentage of the overall vote since 1922.

Although Labour now appeared to be a declining force, New Zealand First now had 11 MPs. Nevertheless, National was again able to form a government without them.

But there were three potential concerns for National from this result. First, there was still a sizable centre-right vote that it hadn't captured, demonstrated by support for the Conservative Party, which secured 3.97 percent of the vote but no seats in Parliament. Second, voter turnout was down to 77.9 percent and there was no guarantee any returning voters would favour National. But as the 2017 election approached — with Key still prime minister — National looked likely to win again.

Richard Prebble summed up Key's performance in 2016 in one of his regular *New Zealand Herald* opinion pieces — on the day the Labour Party celebrated its 100th birthday — with the comment:

> John Key is the best ever Labour prime minister the country has ever seen. We thought Helen Clark straddled the centre ... but he has taken it to a whole new level. Fundamentally he has squeezed Labour out to the left and they don't know how to respond ... It's pretty easy to be in favour of the status quo ... but to be a radical politician of reform, that requires real talent.[7]

Despite his unquestionable PR skills, John Key never demonstrated that particular talent when he could and should have. I consequently rate his prime ministership as a failure because of this.

Even after Key handed over the leadership to English, the expectation was that National might still win in 2017. English appeared confident with a message to National voters to support the re-election of David Seymour, ACT MP and party leader since October 2014, in Epsom, and the United Future candidate in Ohariu, and give their list vote to National.

But National's support — at around 50 percent just before Key stood down — dropped to the mid-40s as election day approached. The same polls showed that neither ACT nor United Future was registering anything other than marginal support and on that basis were unlikely to have more than one MP each after the election. The big beneficiary in the polls was Labour, following Jacinda Ardern becoming party leader on 1 August 2017. From then on, it was clear that National's only chance of retaining government was in coalition with New Zealand First. But on past performance, this looked an unlikely prospect.

Voter turnout in 2017 was 79.8 percent. National's vote dropped to 44.3 percent and its MPs from 60 to 56; Labour's vote increased to 36.9 percent and its MPs to from 32 to 46; and New Zealand First and the Green Party finished up with, respectively, nine and eight MPs. ACT was the only potential coalition partner for National but again it had only one MP — David Seymour — so National found itself back in Opposition.

ACT's vote had dropped to 0.5 percent and the party looked like a lost cause, but in the 2020 election it returned 10 ACT MPs after Seymour again won Epsom and ACT secured 7.9 percent of the party vote.

Seymour had gained support for the party in its own right and also at the expense of National, with that party's list vote down to 25.6 percent and its MPs down from 56 to 33. New Zealand First secured only 2.6 percent of the list vote and was again out of Parliament. The electorate still appeared to be in love with Prime Minister Ardern, with Labour securing 50 percent of the list vote and electing 65 MPs.

A major feature of National's poor election performance was its succession of leadership changes, with the party finally regaining traction when it selected Christopher Luxon as its leader in November 2021. Labour changed its own leader prior to the 2023 election, with Ardern replaced by Chris Hipkins.

In the run-up to the 2023 election National began to regain support, with a poll in early February 2023 giving it 39.6 percent and ACT 13.7 percent. If these figures were replicated on election day, the two parties together would have sufficient MPs to form a coalition government. But a week out from election day, National's hopes of getting a clear National–ACT win were diminishing with a *New Zealand Herald* poll on 6 October

2023 showing New Zealand First rising in the polls and ACT's support declining. The poll percentages then were: National at 35.8, ACT at 10.6, Labour at 26.8, the Greens at 12.3 percent and New Zealand First at 5.7.

This meant National and ACT would need New Zealand First to form a government if that party stayed over the 5 per cent threshold. And this is what happened, with National electing 48 MPs, ACT 11 and New Zealand First eight. A three-party coalition government was eventually formed.

The result was a particularly good one for National as it had successfully managed, late in the campaign, by officially endorsing New Zealand First as a potential coalition partner in addition to ACT, to divert some of ACT's support towards New Zealand First. By doing so, it finished up in government with two minor coalition partners rather than one, ACT New Zealand, with its market-orientated right-wing libertarian policies that National had eschewed ever since its first election win in 1949.

CHAPTER 25

New Zealand Today

Around the world tensions are rising; climate change is wreaking havoc; civil war, unemployment, hunger and water shortages are driving mass migration; Europe is struggling to deal with a belligerent Russia and its reliance on its oil and gas; the Middle East is again in turmoil; the US is losing its status as world leader; and numerous nation states — even before the Covid pandemic — have become more self-focused and internally divided.

By comparison, New Zealand is stable and its long-term prospects look good. Demand for its exports seems likely to remain strong as the world's population grows and pressure for high-protein food products increases. As at 31 January 2022 New Zealand was outperforming the average of OECD countries in income, jobs, education, health, environmental quality, social connections, civic engagement and life satisfaction, with its ranking also ahead of the likes of the US, Japan and Singapore, according to the OECD's Better Life Index.[1]

It is also rated one of only 24 so-called true democracies in the world, second only to Norway in 2024.[2] It regularly comes first or near first in terms of an absence of government and business corruption, and is ranked as a business-friendly country because of its openness to international trade, free-market economic reforms and reputation in encouraging foreign investment. It came second behind Iceland in the 2022 Global Peace Index for low crime rates and high religious tolerance, and is regarded as having a good human rights record. New Zealand is among the top 10 countries in the world to raise children, and purports to have in independent foreign policy.

But all that aside, how have successive New Zealand governments performed in terms of their fundamental responsibilities to their people as defined by Thomas Hobbes in *Leviathan*?[3] There Hobbes listed the first responsibility as providing the safety of law and order and protecting citizens from each other and from foreign foes, and the second as providing goods and services that individuals cannot provide for themselves.

The answer is not well, as three examples show.

First, New Zealand is ranked as having the worst levels of family, interpersonal and sexual violence of any OECD country,[4] with remedial action not becoming a policy priority until 2017. In July of the following year a new Family Violence Act came into force, followed in September by the announcement of Te Aorerekura: The National Strategy to Eliminate Family Violence and Sexual Violence, with a 25-year timeframe launched in December 2021.[5]

The strategy brings together nine government departments and agencies to improve the way they work together to prevent and respond to family violence. They must coordinate strategic policy, investment, evidence and best-practice approaches, and monitor and resolve tensions that arise.

To oversee the process, an interdepartmental executive board was set up, consisting of the heads of the nine departments and agencies. It is charged with providing ministers with advice to support system-wide decision-making designed to reduce family and interpersonal violence.

But progress has been slow. In mid-2023 the auditor-general stated:

> I am concerned that after nearly five years working together under new structures … agencies have not made more progress in the way they operate. This work needs more urgent focus … transforming the way agencies work individually, together, and with tangata whenua and others remains a challenge for all those involved. Agencies need to agree with tangata whenua, community advocates, and non-government organisations on how they will work in partnership with each other.[6]

He went on to identify some issues that risked undermining trust between agencies, community partners and tangata whenua, including a lack of agreement on protocols for sharing sensitive information, and agencies not always learning from the experiences of community partners to improve programmes and responses for people affected by violence.

Why is progress so slow?

There are several reasons. One is the assumption that because violence is a product of other problems — such as, for example, inequity, experiencing violence at an early age, and the adverse impact of colonialism — satisfactory solutions will not be achieved until a range of long-term problems have been resolved.

Another reason is contained in the relevant Cabinet paper. Individual agencies are to remain responsible to their respective portfolio ministers for implementing and progressing actions. With this approach and the strategy's long timeframe, there is likely to be loss of focus as ministers change, elections take place, and officials concentrate on their core portfolio responsibilities. The danger is that the process will devolve into endless meetings and more and more reports. Caswell Consultancy has already reported to the auditor-general that there were at least 136 reports on family violence and sexual violence between 2010 and early 2020.[7]

But despite this, there seems to be no progress in reducing the problem. According to research, over that same period family violence incidents increased by 60 percent, with a prediction that they could rise by another 35 percent by 2025.[8]

A further reason is that the focus of the strategy is on long-term solutions rather than on violence today. The reality is that violence is unacceptable in any form, in any community and in any culture. It is a fundamental violation of a victim's human rights, and as such is everyone's responsibility, including that of governments, to reject and prevent it.

One way that should help is to place greater emphasis on prevention by early identification of violence where it is occurring, followed up by immediate intervention.

Is a different approach like this possible? I suggest that it is. The approach I am suggesting is designed to overcome the two issues of lack of political direction and lack of urgency, and also to build on a more active wellbeing and prevention approach by the police, who are already designated as the key domestic agency charged with keeping New Zealanders safe.

My proposal would require a minor amendment to the Police Act to mandate prevention as a specific stand-alone legal role requirement as opposed to, as is currently the case, a function. It would require the police to take a more active role in violence prevention in the conduct of their own activities, and also provide them with the authority to take over the lead role in coordinating and progressing the prevention activities of the other eight agencies involved in the current 25-year plan. Finally — and this is crucial — it would oblige the police to become more actively involved with neighbourhood support groups to take advantage of their local knowledge of where violence is occurring.

Currently, despite a range of community-orientated prevention initiatives over the years, New Zealand Police, under the Police Act, is primarily an enforcement and prosecution agency, not a preventive agency.

My suggestion involves a 'before the event' approach, which community policing is supposed to achieve. Neighbour support groups would retain their independent status, to differentiate them from traditional reactive policing. Their prime responsibility would be to know their individual areas intimately, work with the police to convey the message that criminal activity, and in particular family violence, is completely unacceptable, will not be tolerated, and will be severely punished if it does occur. Any necessary enforcement action will continue to be a police responsibility.

The second example of where New Zealand could do better in terms of government Hobbesian responsibilities is with state-provided education and health. New Zealand's state education system is in a state of deep malaise, with some of the largest educational disparities between demographic groups in the OECD.[9] And in the case of health, although most New Zealanders enjoy high overall health status, and despite at least seven major reforms of the health and disability sectors since the 1980s,[10] there are still significant inequalities for Māori, Pacific peoples, the disabled and those on low incomes.

This raises the question: are different approaches worth considering in these areas too? Again, I suggest the answer may well be yes. The current policy approach to reducing inequity is strongly focused on two ethnic groups, Māori and Pacific Island people. But this ignores the fact that there were at least 213 ethnic groups from 196 countries in New Zealand a decade ago.[11] Although these figures will have changed since then, what has not changed is that inequity is not just confined to Māori and Pasifika.

In the *Weekend Australian* in July 2020 Noel Pearson, an Indigenous Australian land rights activist and a history and law graduate, wrote of the danger of prioritising one particular ethnic group ahead of other people:

> By separating Indigenous disadvantage from white and migrant Australians allows a pall of 'exceptionalism' to be cast over the constantly depressing and outrageous out-of-step numbers that characterise Indigenous disadvantage. It's as if [Australia] — inured to the bad numbers — has come to accept that little can be done.[12]

Pearson went on to record that inequity and poverty need to be addressed as country-specific problems, not just Indigenous problems.

But this is not how successive New Zealand governments have attempted to solve these problems. My question is: why are other disadvantaged New Zealanders accorded second-class status and consequently second-class attention? In the case of Māori, the answer seems to be that over time the Treaty of Waitangi has become a vehicle to consider issues well beyond its original intent. The right to adequate health care and appropriate education are basic human rights to which all New Zealanders are equally entitled. To break the disadvantage cycle, logic suggests that individuals who need help should have access to it, regardless of their race.

The third Hobbesian example concerns the responsibility of governments to protect their citizens against actual or potential foreign foes. But according to the minister of defence in mid-2023, the New Zealand Defence Force is 'not in a fit state to respond to future challenges'.[13] Given this, as well as New Zealand's responsibilities in the Pacific and to Australia in relation to its defence alliance with that country, the question is: what can New Zealand contribute to both that can make a positive difference in the region?

In an article titled *A New Role for New Zealand in the Pacific,* published by Massey University's Defence and Strategic Studies Centre,[14] I suggested that there could be substantial benefits if New Zealand were to take over the coordination of remedial climate action in the Pacific on behalf of Australia and other interested parties; and further, that consideration should be given to the formation of an ANZAC Defence Force so that the NZDF has the capacity to engage — if this becomes necessary — in modern intense high-technology warfare.

But what of other policies?

Beyond the Hobbes fundamentals, how do successive governments rate in prioritising them? This was the issue I attempted to deal with when I was a finance minister, but the answer is still 'not well at all', particularly as some of the key questions that determine the nature of the economy and the wellbeing of its people are seldom — if ever — discussed. For example:

- Should New Zealand reconsider its commodity-dependent export mindset given its small population?
- Is it sensible to be so trade dependent on China?

- Is New Zealand still safe from attack by foreign foes given that distance and isolation no longer necessarily provide protection?
- Is New Zealand's prohibition on anti-nuclear propulsion still justified when it will likely be repealed immediately if war breaks out in the region?
- Do New Zealand's government and governing systems need to be rethought?

A robust political system needs to have appropriate separation between the legislature, the executive and the judiciary to provide checks and balances on how the government exercises its power, and to maintain accountability and impartiality. But successive New Zealand governments have failed in terms of separation of these powers, as one of the country's leading constitutional and administrative lawyers, Philip Joseph, has pointed out:

> When formulating cabinet policy and attending to portfolio responsibilities, ministers exercise executive functions, but when introducing, debating and voting on Bills, and defending the government's record on the floor of the House, they exercise legislative functions as members of Parliament.[15]

This conflation of executive and legislative powers represents a major departure from the ideal. This ideal is realised only in relation to the judicial branch of government, which is legally independent of the political executive.[16]

Is it time to encourage more executive accountability by re-establishing a workable Upper House-type body? Since 1951, New Zealand has had a one-chamber Parliament, with accountability of the actions of the executive limited by the absence of an authoritative independent body to scrutinise and, where appropriate, revise legislation emanating from it.[17]

Should we look at changing New Zealand's three-year general election cycle to four or five years? From my observations this short cycle encourages political parties to campaign on short-term, feel-good issues and avoid 'hard' decisions that might harm their re-election prospects. A longer election cycle would also, hopefully, reduce the dominant role of political party elites in policy formulation, and encourage the development of more meaningful policies.

Another option is to look at strengthening Parliament's select committees. The current system has a number of limitations. One is the small pool left for committee membership after all the executive positions have been filled. Another is that the workload of backbench MPs is already heavy. And importantly, select committees are not where most MPs want to be. They want to be in the executive after the next reshuffle if they are in the governing caucus, or after the next election if they are in the Opposition caucus. The New Zealand system consequently creates serious motivational conflicts for backbench MPs.

A further option is to strengthen the potential for public servants to offer free and frank policy advice to incumbent governments. This would be contrary to the current division of responsibilities between ministers and the public service, as described here in a Treasury report:

> On public policy, it is elected representatives such as Ministers who make 'value judgements' on behalf of the population when they make policy decisions. It is not the job of public servants to make value judgements, and the Treasury does not take a position on these matters. However, the Treasury can support elected representatives in making value judgements by identifying the normative issues at stake and the tradeoffs and tensions between different values.[18]

This artificial division is, in my view, a constraint on the potential of governments to produce good outcomes, and is different from the way I operated as a minister. What became clear to me was that policy was a crucial part of most considerations. No one has a mortgage on good ideas, and officials working within a system are often the people who know what works and what doesn't, and what changes would help. They need to know they are being listened to and that their views are being taken seriously.

Three examples illustrate what happens when policy is left in political hands and not regularly updated. The first concerns New Zealand's historically much vaunted social welfare system, with a government-appointed review team reporting in 2019 that it was in need of fundamental reform:

> The current social security system was set up in a different time and no longer meets the needs of those it was designed to support . . . Urgent and fundamental change is needed. This will be challenging because the problems are large and the system complex . . . The experience of using the system is unsatisfactory and damaging for too many of the highest-need and poorest people.[19]

The second example shows what happens when monopoly service providers are left unchecked and without competition. The three biggest expenditure items in the government's budget are education, health and social welfare. In 1972 they cost $4500 per person in 1990 dollars, but by 2020 the figure was over $12,000 per person.[20]

The third example is the housing accommodation supplement, which was introduced in 1991. It illustrates how one policy impacts on others and the difficulty of initiating meaningful change, particularly when around 350,000 recipients are involved. In 2019 the *Child Poverty Action Group Report* stated:

> . . . while the name of the Accommodation Supplement suggests it is supposed to assist with housing support, successive governments have actually relied upon it to assist with overall income adequacy, regardless of the supply of appropriate affordable housing . . . for . . . years, governments have called upon the AS to fill the large gaps left by an inadequate welfare system and low minimum wage . . . [U]nsurprisingly, the AS fails miserably in this mission for which it is not fit-for-purpose.[21]

Officials are obviously aware of the need for reform, because as at 2 June 2021 they were seeking guidance from ministers on the objectives of the review they had been instructed to undertake. They commented in late 2022: '[T]here are a number of areas of concern.'[22] In 2024 there still appears to be no workable solution.

Another option for consideration is creating a new Ministry for (say) Policies and Priorities. This would be a super-ministry, and was the end game of what I was contemplating when the 'Quigley concept' on expenditure priorities was produced. It would have wide-ranging powers to investigate and comment on, as appropriate, policy performance across agencies, and would provide an additional way of improving the accountability of ministers and the executive by obliging them to take increased ownership of not just individual portfolio policies but also the relevance of those policies to overall government objectives. It would also strengthen the obligations of officials in relation to the Public Service Act 2020 to offer free and frank advice,[23] and to support the development, implementation and delivery of policy.[24]

My suggestion for a more active overall policy role by officials isn't new. For example, under the Defence Act 1990, which followed the

Strategos review, the Secretary of Defence has functional responsibilities to formulate advice, in consultation with the CDF, on defence policy; and to prepare, also in consultation with the CDF, and submit defence assessments to the minister, including a review of different options capable of achieving the government's policy goals.

These defence assessments — particularly since the two DB2000 select committee reports which opened up defence policy to public inspection, and emphasised the importance of security being considered in a wider context than previously — although admirable in their content, have still not gone far enough in illustrating how policies in other portfolio areas seemingly unrelated to either defence or foreign policy need to be considered together, and coordinated and progressed on a whole-of-government basis.

Today, the essence of security involves the ability to prevent, withstand and manage crises and situations under heightened contingencies. As a result, national security includes issues like protection against pandemics and infectious diseases; combating terrorism and organised crime; ensuring safe transport, energy and reliable food supplies; countering the devastations of climate change; engaging in initiatives for peace and global development; and so on. The objectives are to safeguard the life and health of the population and the functions of society; and to maintain fundamental values such as democracy, the rule of law, human rights and basic freedoms.

In order to achieve then, a country's political independence and autonomy must be secure and territorial integrity must be maintained. Day-to-day responsibility for different types of essential services is now spread among a variety of actors who all need to maintain the capacity for a proactive rather than a reactive response. Crises and threats can arise quickly, but can also involve a slow sequence of events. Whatever the timeframe, effective cooperation is crucially important in strengthening that ability.

Conclusion

This has been a long journey. I was 17 when I first became interested in politics, and now I am 92. New Zealand society has evolved and changed over those years, and continues to do so. As a small country it wants to be, and be seen to be, a relevant and respected part of the international community.

Like politicians anywhere, New Zealand's political leaders continue to face new and interesting challenges. They must respond to people's changing wants and needs and safeguard their lives and health, as well as society's valued institutions, while maintaining fundamental values like democracy, the rule of law, human rights and basic freedoms.

Politicians today face additional international security issues such pandemics and infectious diseases, the devastations of climate change, terrorism, food and energy security and ongoing international conflicts.

In this book I have sought to explain some of the background and thinking that informed my work as a politician and consultant on national and international issues over many decades. I hope what I have written may help people understand some of the challenges politicians face, and encourage them to contribute to the nation's future so they can justifiably feel proud of who they are as individuals and as New Zealanders.

APPENDIX

My Alternative Economic Plan

1978–81

1. To build on the base of the past three years and step beyond existing policies.
2. To escape the trap of inflation and New Zealand's slow growth structure by reducing costs and creating greater efficiency in the domestic sector.
3. To improve productivity and the international competitiveness of the New Zealand economy.
4. To promote a minimum level of sustained growth at an annual rate of at least 3 percent of GNP in real terms.
5. To progressively reduce inflation down to the OECD average by 1981–82.
6. To reduce the overseas exchange transactions deficit with a view to its elimination by 1981–82.
7. To reduce the internal deficit before borrowing to a sustainable level by 1981–82.
8. To improve economic policy formation and implementation at ministerial and officials' level.
9. To reduce public-sector expenditure in real terms and increase the efficiency of that expenditure.
10. To develop an economic climate which will encourage private-sector expansion.
11. To achieve the maximum levels of employment consistent with the attainment of the foregoing objectives.

IMPLEMENTATION OF OBJECTIVES

Statement of Intent

The government intends to achieve its primary objectives of improving productivity and international competitiveness by taking the necessary policy decisions required to establish a more competitive economic pricing system within New Zealand.

Moves to date include (inter alia):

a. The introduction of a more competitive banking system.
b. The removal of price control.
c. The encouragement of overseas investments in New Zealand.
d. An exchange rate adjustment which will ensure export profitability. To avoid the loss of the competitive export advantage and stimulus to local manufacturing flowing from this adjustment, it will almost certainly be necessary to:
    i. Contain wage demands.
    ii. Impose a (temporary) ban on general wage orders (GWOs).
    iii. Amend the GWO legislation to exclude consideration of price rises stemming from exchange control alterations and/or movements from direct to indirect taxation.
    iv. Announce that import controls will be progressively dismantled and replaced by tariffs (with adequate protection against dumping).
    v. Introduce demand management policies to restrict consumption spending and encourage investment in exports.
e. The removal of restrictions on competition by:
    i. Progressively delicensing over a wide front but particularly in transport and the processing industries.
    ii. Removing as many producer subsidies (direct and indirect) as possible and progressively eliminating the balance.
f. The progressive but staged removal of import control over a period of (say) five years and a movement towards protection by tariffs.
g. The encouragement of the export sector by:
    i. Facilitating the transfer of resources by providing reallocation assistance, redundancy payments, retraining, etc.
    ii. Increasing tax on consumer goods.
    iii. Granting priority for loan finance for those industries having a growth potential beyond the New Zealand domestic market.

h. The boosting of confidence and the encouraging of investment in the public sector by:
    i. Abolishing death duties for estates up to (say) $250 000 where dispositions are spouse to spouse or parent to child.
    ii. Announcing a commitment to minimum levels of sustained growth at the rate of at least 3 percent of gross national product (GNP), in real terms.

i. Announcing a commitment to:
    i. Cut red tape.
    ii. Reduce public-sector involvement.
    iii. Strengthen the private sector.
    iv. Follow up this commitment by a well-advertised public auction of surplus government plant and machinery.

j. Carrying out a well-publicised review of existing government departmental programmes and functions.

k. Reaffirming the government's commitment to the maintenance of firm monetary control as a key element in future policies aimed at restoring overall economic stability by:

l. Introducing and/or maintaining measures to reduce the internal deficit.

m. Placing greater emphasis on indirect rather than direct taxation, thus encouraging investment and saving and discouraging consumption.

n. Reemphasising government's intention to remove consumer subsidies.

o. Asking for cooperation from all sections of the community in achieving the foregoing objectives. To obtain this cooperation it will be necessary to spell out the advantages of success and the disadvantages of failure. The size of the projected internal and external deficits will have to be publicised as will the risk of massive increases in inflation, plus the possibility of losing international trading competitiveness and international creditworthiness.

p. Emphasise (internationally) that New Zealand is taking steps to restructure its economy; is stable politically and therefore a good investment prospect; is a producer of quality export products which are internationally in demand in a world which is short of food.

Notes

Preface

1 Brian Easton, *The Commercialisation of New Zealand* (Auckland, Auckland University Press, 1997).
2 OECD (2019).

Chapter 1: The National Party

1 'National Party', from A.H. McLintock, *An Encyclopaedia of New Zealand* (1966): https://teara.govt.nz/en/1966/political-parties/page-11
2 This was confirmed in discussions with Sid's son, Eric Holland, who was an MP with me.
3 Michael Bassett, 'The National years 1949–99', *Dominion*, December 1999.
4 Malcolm Templeton (ed.), *An Eye, an Ear and a Voice: 50 Years in New Zealand's External Relations 1943–1993* (Wellington: Ministry of Foreign Affairs & Trade, 1993), p. 52.
5 *The Reserve Bank and New Zealand's Economic History* (Wellington: Reserve Bank, 2007), p. 16.
6 Ibid.
7 Derek Quigley, *Economic Reform: New Zealand in an International Perspective* (The (UK) Round Table, 1996), p. 310.
8 *Hansard*, September 1950, pp. 2784–85.
9 John R. Martin, 'An age of the Mandarins? Government in New Zealand, 1940–51', in Samuel Furphy (ed.), *The Seven Dwarfs and the Age of the Mandarins: Australian Government Administration in the Post-War Reconstruction Era* (Canberra: ANU Press, 2015), pp. 81–106.
10 By 1978 the Construction Department had become the Construction Division of the Housing Corporation. Its main task was to draw up plans for state houses, which were then built by the private sector. One of my early policy moves as Minister of Housing was to disestablish this division.
11 This was after being pressured by several senior MPs and party officials.
12 Barry Gustafson, *His Way: A Biography of Robert Muldoon* (Auckland: Auckland University Press, 2000), pp. 89–90.

Chapter 2: Farmer, Student, Lawyer

1 From my official army records.
2 Ibid.
3 The stone was reappropriated to London four months later, but returned finally to Scotland in 1996.

Chapter 3: Entering Parliament

1 John Blumsky attracted a lot of New Zealand and international attention in 1979 when he was the only journalist in Antarctica to report on the devastating crash of Air New Zealand flight TE901 into Mt Erebus.
2 Hugh Templeton, *All Honourable Men: Inside the Muldoon Cabinet 1975–1984* (Auckland: Auckland University Press, 1995), p. 48.
3 Barry Gustafson, *His Way: A Biography of Robert Muldoon* (Auckland: Auckland University Press, 2000), p. 175.
4 *NZ Parliamentary Debates*, vol. 407, 1976, pp. 3674–96.

Chapter 4: Making Progress as an MP

1 The Cultural Revolution was a decade-long social-political movement in the People's Republic of China that began in 1966. The aims of the ruling Communist Party were to reinforce Maoist thought as the dominant ideology within the party, and to ensure

communism was dominant. Mass purges of capitalists and 'bourgeois elements' were carried out to eliminate 'old ideas, old culture, old customs and old habits'. Estimates of the eventual death toll range from 1 to 2 million.

2 Peng Xizhe, 'Demographic consequences of the Great Leap Forward in China's provinces', *Population and Development Review* 13(4) (1987): 639–70. Estimates of the number of deaths vary widely. The 'Three Bitter Years' of the Great Chinese Famine were 1959–61.

3 Maotai was served on official occasions during feasts when foreign heads of states and distinguished guests visit China. It was at the time the only alcoholic beverage that Chinese embassies presented as an official gift.

4 The Berlin Wall was built in 1961 by the German Democratic Republic (GDR or East Germany) when Germany was partitioned into East and West. Its demolition by ordinary citizens began on 13 June 1990.

5 Michael Bassett & Judith Bassett, *Roderick Deane: His Life & Times* (Auckland: Penguin, 2006), pp. 68–69.

6 Barry Gustafson, *His Way: A Biography of Robert Muldoon* (Auckland: Auckland University Press, 2000), p. 189.

Chapter 5: 1978

1 Malcolm Fearn was an extremely competent and experienced private secretary who served a number of housing ministers. He became senior private secretary to Sir Robert Muldoon 1982–84. When National went into Opposition in 1984 he became executive assistant to a succession of National leaders, including Muldoon, McLay and Bolger. Malcolm was also, for a time, state director of the National Party in Victoria, Australia, and before that director of administration for the Liberal Party in Victoria.

Chapter 6: Attempts to Control Government Spending

1 The Lange government introduced the minister/CEO accountability provision and the Bolger government a much more open disclosure regime.

2 Tony Garnier, *Election '81: An End to Muldoonism?* (Methuen, 1981).

Chapter 7: Other Ministerial Responsibilities

1 Section 13 of the relevant Act states: 'Any moneys that remain in the War Damage Fund after all claims or outstanding claims against the Fund have been settled or provided for and all advances made ... have been repaid shall be applied in accordance with the appropriation of Parliament for the purpose of granting financial assistance to persons suffering loss or damage by reason of any earthquake or other disaster.' War Damage Act 1941 (5 Geo VI 1941 no. 17), p. 184.

2 *Report of the Committee on Taxation in New Zealand*, 1967.

3 Appropriation Bill – Financial Statement, *Hansard*, 15 July 1980, pp. 1676–80.

Chapter 8: The Law and the Arthur Allan Thomas Case

1 Jim McLay emailed me on 18 June 2017: 'You are correct that many of the "Think Big" projects were 'rubber-stamped'; but, that said, I do recall the lengthy battle (over several Cabinet and committee meetings ... regarding the Methanol plant when, eventually (after Muldoon had delayed the final decision to continue his pressure on individual ministers), the matter was decided by just one vote (if I recall, David Thomson switched sides).'
My own recollection is that it was Warren Cooper's vote that tipped the decision in favour of the Muldoon camp.

2 Paragraph 10, memo to Prime Minister Kirk from Attorney-General Martin Finlay, 1 November 1973.

3 Barry Gustafson, *His Way: A Biography of Robert Muldoon* (Auckland: Auckland University Press, 2000), p. 291.

4 Adams-Smith to Muldoon, 10 January 1979, Recommendations section, paragraph 5, p. 18.

5 Ibid., pp. 18–19.

6 Ibid.

7 McLay confirmed to me in his email of 18 June 2017 that his initial view was that the matter should be referred back to the Court of Appeal.
8 Gustafson, *His Way*, p. 291.
9 Adams-Smith to Muldoon, December 1979, Recommendations section, paragraphs 2 and 3, p. 18.
10 Memo, Solicitor-General to Prime Minister Muldoon, 10 December 1979.
11 Ibid.
12 Jim McLay, email to author, 18 June 2017.
13 *Report of the Royal Commission to Inquire into the Circumstances of the Convictions of Arthur Allan Thomas for the Murders of David Harvey Crewe and Jeanette Lenore Crewe, 1980* Wellington: Government Printer, p. 18: https://web.archive.org/web/20110609174212/http://homepages.paradise.net.nz/r.christie/thomas_royal_commission_1980.pdf
14 Ibid., p. 87.
15 Ibid., p. 116, paragraph 491 reads: 'That a man is wrongly imprisoned for 9 years, is a wrong that can never be put right. The fact that he is imprisoned on the basis of evidence which is false to the knowledge of Police Officers, whose duty it is to uphold the law, is an unspeakable outrage.'
16 Andrew Laxon, 'Police still hold firm to their case', *New Zealand Herald*, 29 May 2010: www.nzherald.co.nz/nz/news/article.cfm?c_id=1&objectid=10648147
17 Ibid.
18 Ibid.
19 Peter Williams, *A Passion for Justice* (Christchurch: Shoal Bay Press, 1997).

Chapter 9: The Colonels' Coup

1 Barry Gustafson, *His Way: A Biography of Robert Muldoon* (Auckland: Auckland University Press, 2000), p. 267.
2 Ibid., p. 270.
3 Michael Bassett & Judith Bassett, *Roderick Deane: His Life & Times* (Auckland: Penguin, 2006), p. 75.
4 Gustafson, *His Way*, pp. 217–18. Gerald Hensley confirms the 'peanut farmer' comment in *Final Approaches* (Auckland: Auckland University Press, 2006), p. 203.
5 Gustafson, *His Way*, p. 298.
6 Rob Talbot, email to author, 7 June 2008.
7 Hugh Templeton, *All Honourable Men: Inside the Muldoon Cabinet 1975–1984* (Auckland: Auckland University Press, 1995), pp. 151–52.
8 What may have led some of my colleagues and elements within the media to think otherwise may have been the result of Susan McAffer sprucing up my appearance to soften the hard-line public image I was starting to develop. Out went my heavy clod-hopper shoes, my steel-rimmed glasses were changed for softer-looking ones with much bigger frames, and my hair was cut differently.
9 Richard Long, 'Muldoon advises Quigley he should quit Cabinet', *Dominion*, 12 December 1980, p. 1.
10 R Long, 'Muldoon advises Quigley he should quit Cabinet', *Dominion*, 12 December 1980, p. 1.
11 Gustafson, *His Way*, p. 307.
12 Christchurch *Press*, February 1981.
13 Don McKinnon, email to author, 16 March 2020.

Chapter 10: Tourism, 'Think Big' and the Springbok Tour

1 Statistics NZ: www.stats.govt.nz/information-releases/tourism-satellite-account-2019
2 Hugh Templeton, *All Honourable Men: Inside the Muldoon Cabinet 1975–1984* (Auckland: Auckland University Press, 1995), p. 123.
3 Ibid., p. 124.
4 Gerald Hensley, *Final Approaches: A Memoir* (Auckland: Auckland University Press, 2006), p. 227. Hensley was the head of the Prime Minister's Department during both Muldoon's and Lange's time.

5 Templeton, *All Honourable Men*, p. 127.
6 *The New Zealand Official Year-book, 1981*: https://www3.stats.govt.nz/New_Zealand_Official_Yearbooks/1981/NZOYB_1981.html
7 Michael Bassett & Judith Bassett, *Roderick Deane: His Life & Times* (Auckland: Penguin, 2006), p. 91.

Chapter 11: Resignation from Cabinet

1 Tony Reid, 'The nays have it', *NZ Listener*, 23 January 1982.
2 Barry Gustafson, *His way: A Biography of Robert Muldoon* (Auckland: Auckland University Press, 2000), p. 320.
3 Michael Bassett & Judith Bassett, *Roderick Deane: His Life & Times* (Auckland: Penguin, 2006), pp. 91–92.
4 Hugh Templeton, *All Honourable Men: Inside the Muldoon Cabinet 1975–1984* (Auckland: Auckland University Press, 1995), p. 169.
5 The Cabinet decision awarding the contract to the joint venture consortium had provided for the tenderer to extend the validity of its bid if negotiations were completed satisfactorily before the water right situation had been resolved.
6 *Contractor* 32(9), October 2008.
7 The landowners considered the Crown had insufficiently compensated them when it compulsorily acquired their land to build the dam.
8 According to an email I received from Jim McLay on 20 October 2017, Muldoon took 'particular exception' to the word 'platitudes', which he wrongly attributed to me, not Bayley.
9 'Quigley writes to The Dominion', *Dominion*, 11 June 1982, p. 1.
10 Jim McLay, email to author, 20 October 2017.
11 *Dominion*, 11 June 1982.
12 Christchurch *Press*, 3 January 1983.

Chapter 12: A Backbencher Again

1 Michael Bassett & Judith Bassett, *Roderick Deane: His Life & Times* (Auckland: Penguin, 2006), p. 93.
2 Ibid., pp. 92–94.
3 Hugh Templeton, *All Honourable Men: Inside the Muldoon Cabinet 1975–1984* (Auckland: Auckland University Press, 1995), p. 176.
4 Shortly after my resignation, television ran a widely publicised news item setting out what I had lost in terms of salary, staff, free accommodation in Wellington, access to the ministerial car pool and so on. As a result, one of my supporters loaned me an electorate car until after the 1984 election.
5 *NZ Listener*, 23 January 1982.
6 *Australian*, 14 May 1982.
7 Templeton, *All Honourable Men*, p. 211.
8 Barry Gustafson, *His way: A Biography of Robert Muldoon* (Auckland: Auckland University Press, 2000), p. 338.
9 Ibid.
10 *Hansard*, Finance Bill, second reading debate, 6 December 1983, pp. 4637–38.
11 Bassett, *Roderick Deane*, pp. 82–84.
12 Ibid.
13 Robert Muldoon, *Number 38* (Auckland: Reed Methuen, 1986), p. 54.

Chapter 13: Research and the Bob Jones Party

1 The Meat Producers' Board (established 1922) became Meat New Zealand in 1998, then the New Zealand Meat Board in July 2004.
2 There were only three of us at the dinner and most of the time Mrs Thatcher and I argued quite aggressively about access for New Zealand produce to the UK and the EU now that Britain had joined that entity.
3 *Straight Furrow*, 2 February 1983.

4 The full speech was published in *Straight Furrow*, 8 June 1983, p. 5.
5 Dan Watkins had been a leading figure in the early development of the New Zealand agrichemical industry. *AGPOL* was the journal of the Department of Agriculture.
6 Barry Gustafson, *His way: A Biography of Robert Muldoon* (Auckland: Auckland University Press, 2000), p. 340.
7 Ibid., p. 341.
8 Hugh Templeton, *All Honourable Men: Inside the Muldoon Cabinet 1975–1984* (Auckland: Auckland University Press, 1995), pp. 171–72.

Chapter 14: The 1984 Election and Labour in Office

1 Jim McLay, email to author, 5 February 2018.
2 Richard Long, *Dominion*, 12 July 1984.
3 Report by Muldoon on 1984 general election to National Party dominion councillors, undated, p. 3.
4 Edmund Bohan, *Burdon: A man of our time* (Christchurch: Hazard Press, 2004) .
5 The European Economic Community (EEC), formed in 1957, was renamed the European Community (EC) in 1995 under the Maastricht Treaty of 1992. Under that same treaty the EC was absorbed into the European Union (EU) in 1993.
6 Capital Economics (Wellington), email to author, 24 May 2024.
7 Derek Quigley, *Economic Reform: New Zealand in an international perspective* (The (UK) Round Table, 1996).
8 David Lange, *My Life* (Auckland: Penguin, 2005), p. 173.
9 Michael Bassett & Judith Bassett, *Roderick Deane: His Life & Times* (Auckland: Penguin, 2006), pp. 107–15.
10 Hugh Templeton, *All Honourable Men: Inside the Muldoon Cabinet 1975–1984* (Auckland: Auckland University Press, 1995), p. 221.
11 Officials initially recommended a 15 percent devaluation but the politicians wanted 20 percent and officials agreed. Roger Douglas, phone conversation with the author, 13 April, 2020.
12 Templeton, *All Honourable Men*, p. 221.
13 Bassett, *Roderick Deane*, p. 113.
14 Michael King, *The Penguin History of New Zealand* (Auckland: Penguin, 2003), p. 593
15 For a more detailed analysis of the overall reform process, and what did and did not work and why, see Quigley, *Economic Reform.*
16 Jim McLay, email to author, 5 February 2018.
17 Bassett, *Roderick Deane*, p. 145.
18 State Services Commission, *New Zealand's Reformed State Sector* (Wellington, 1994), p. 2.
19 Ibid., p. 6.

Chapter 15: Life after Parliament

1 Hepatitis C was first identified in 1989 and by the year 2000 at least 25,000 New Zealanders were recorded as having being infected. Donor screening was not introduced until mid-1992.

Chapter 16: The Background to Labour's Anti-nuclear Policy

1 Strategos Consulting, *The New Zealand Defence Resource Management Review*, 1988.
2 https://nzhistory.govt.nz/politics/nuclear-free-new-zealand/testing-in-the-pacific
3 Michael C. Pugh, *The ANZUS Crisis, Nuclear Visiting and Deterrence* (Cambridge: Cambridge University Press, 1989), pp. 69–70.
4 www.congress.gov/bill/93rd-congress/senate-joint-resolution/248/text?overview=closed
5 Pugh, *The ANZUS Crisis*, p. 72.
6 Ibid., p. 74.
7 Greg Fry, 'Australia, New Zealand, and arms control in the Pacific region', in Desmond Ball (ed.), *The Anzac Connection* (Sydney: Allen & Unwin, 1985), pp. 101–03; *New Outlook*, January–February 1985, p. 13.
8 Australia and New Zealand signed the SPNFZ Treaty in 1985 and ratified it in late 1986. The US, the UK and France did not sign the three protocols until 25 March 1996.

9 Pugh, *The ANZUS Crisis*, p. 54, referring to a New Zealand National Archives note.
10 Ibid., p. 32.
11 Ibid., p. 75.
12 Ibid.
13 Ibid., referring to US Congress, 94(2) House Armed Services Committee, *Report of the Ad Hoc Subcommittee*, 4 June 1976, p. 3042.
14 Pugh, *The ANZUS Crisis*, pp. 78–80
15 Ibid., p. 78, referring to a New Zealand National Archives note.
16 Foreign Affairs and Defence Committee, *Report on the Inquiry into Disarmament and Arms Control* (Wellington, 1985).
17 Pugh, *The ANZUS Crisis*, p. 80.
18 Ibid.
19 TV2 and TV1 news polls, 19 and 29 September 1980.
20 Pugh, *The ANZUS Crisis*, p. 79.
21 *Evening Post*, 12 May 1982, cited in McKinnon, *Independence and Foreign Policy: New Zealand in the World since 1935*, p. 279.
22 New Zealand Labour Party, *Report of the Sixty-Seventh Annual Conference*, Auckland, 2, 3, 4 & 5 September 1983, p. 23.
23 Richard Kennaway, 'ANZUS alliance: Perspectives & priorities', in Jacob Bercovitch (ed.), *ANZUS in Crisis* (Christchurch: Canterbury University Press, 1988), p. 221.
24 Hon J.K. McLay, *Nuclear Arms: My View*, Wellington Cathedral Lenten Lecture, 27 March 1984.
25 Ibid.
26 Michael Bassett interview with Gerald Hensley, 10 April 2002.
27 Michael Bassett, *The Collapse of New Zealand's Military Ties with the United States*, Fulbright Lecture, Georgetown University, Washington, DC, 2 December 2002.
28 Marilyn Waring, *Women Politics & Power: Essays* (Wellington: Allen & Unwin, 1985), p. 109.
29 *NZ Parliamentary Debates*, 12 June 1984, vol. 456, p. 257. Also referred to in Marilyn Waring, *The Political Years* (Wellington: Bridget Williams Books, 2019), p. 338.
30 *Hansard*, vol. 456, pp. 317–18.
31 McKinnon's 'Notes' and McKinnon to Muldoon, 14 June 1984, referred to in Barry Gustafson, *His Way: A Biography of Robert Muldoon* (Auckland: Auckland University Press, 2000), p. 370.
32 David Lange, *Nuclear Free: The New Zealand Way* (Auckland: Penguin, 1990), p. 52.
33 Michael Bassett interview with Gerald Hensley, 10 April 2002.
34 Bassett, *The Collapse*.

Chapter 17: The Strategos Defence Review

1 David Lange, *Nuclear Free – The New Zealand Way* (Auckland, Penguin, 1990), p. 75.
2 Strategos Consulting, *The New Zealand Defence Resource Management Review*, 1988.
3 Michael Bassett interview with Gerald Hensley, 10 April 2002.
4 A detailed legal analysis of New Zealand's defence legislation is provided by Professor Matthew Palmer, Centre for Public Law, Victoria University of Wellington, in a paper attached as Annex F to D.K. Hunn, *Review of Accountabilities and Structural Arrangements between the Ministry of Defence and the New Zealand Defence Force*, 30 September 2002.
5 Alan Burnett, *The A-NZ-US Triangle* (Canberra: Strategic and Defence Studies Centre, Australian National University, 1988), pp. 101–02.
6 Bill Hayden, Australian Minister for Foreign Affairs, news release, 10 December 1985.
7 Hugh White, *Living Without Illusions: Where Our Defence Relationship Goes from Here*, paper presented at the Otago Policy School, 2001, p. 1.
8 Kim Beazley, *ANZUS Alliance*, official *Hansard* report by the Joint Standing Committee on Foreign Affairs, Defence and Trade, Canberra, 11 August 1997, p. 54.
9 Burnett, *The A-NZ-US Triangle*, p. 104.
10 Coral Bell, 'Australia's foreign & security policies', in Jacob Bercovitch (ed.), *ANZUS in Crisis* (Christchurch: Canterbury University Press, 1988), p. 156.
11 Strategos, *New Zealand Defence Resource Management Review*, p. 232.

12 See Jim Rolfe, *Australia–New Zealand Relations: Allies, Friends, Rivals* (Honolulu: Asia–Pacific Center for Security Studies, June 2004): https://apps.dtic.mil/sti/tr/pdf/ADA627510.pdf
13 Strategos, *New Zealand Defence Resource Management Review*, p. 233.
14 *The Shape of New Zealand Defence*, government White Paper (Wellington, 1997), p. 8.
15 Jonathan Boston et al., *Reshaping the State: New Zealand's Bureaucratic Revolution* (Auckland: Oxford University Press, 1991), cited in Anna Smith, in *Guns and Gold* (ed. Anne French), Wellington: Victoria University of Wellington through Victoria Link, 1999), p. 5.
16 Paul Dibb, *Review of Australia's Defence Capabilities: Report to the Minister for Defence* (Canberra: Australia Department of Defence, 1986).
17 Gerald Hensley, 'Reflecting on the Fourth Labour Government', *NZ Herald*, 30 April 2004: www.nzherald.co.nz/nz/news/article.cfm?c_id=1&objectid=3563688
18 Smith, *Guns and Gold*, p. 9.
19 David Lange, *Nuclear Free: The New Zealand way* (Auckland: Penguin, 1990).
20 Ibid., p. 10.
21 Ibid.
22 Hensley interview, 11 December 1998, referred to in ibid., p. 10

Chapter 18: National's Defence Backflip and the Road to MMP

1 Don McKinnon, email to author, 17 May 2024.
2 Don McKinnon, emails to author, 20 May and 28 July 2004. McKinnon resigned as Opposition defence spokesman when National adopted Labour's anti-nuclear policy.
3 Extract, Michael Bassett interview with Sir Ewan Jamieson, 1 June 2002.
4 *Report of Special Committee on Nuclear Propulsion* (Wellington, December 1992), Finding 1, p. 173.
5 Michael Bassett interview with Admiral Crowe, Washington DC, 5 December 2002.
6 Don McKinnon, email to author, 27 July 2004.
7 Jim Bolger, Prime Minister, Preface, *Defence White Paper 1991*, p. 5.
8 MOD/NZDF, *The Defence of New Zealand 1991: A Policy Paper*, p. 27.
9 Ibid., pp. 27–28.
10 Ibid., p. 53.
11 Derek Quigley, *The War Against Defence Restructuring* (Canberra: Strategic and Defence Studies Centre, ANU, 2006), p. 89.
12 *The Defence of New Zealand 1991: A Policy Paper*, p. 103.
13 I had met both Ray and Gration during the course of the Strategos review.
14 *Canberra Times*, 13 September 1991, p. 8.
15 P.C. Gration, 'The ADF in the region of the future', *Journal of the Royal United Services Institute of Australia*, vol. 12, no. 2, October 1991, p. 45.
16 *Towards a Better Democracy*, Report of the Royal Commission on the Electoral System (1986): https://elections.nz/democracy-in-nz/what-is-new-zealands-system-of-government/report-of-the-royal-commission-on-the-electoral-system
17 'Rod Donald takes MMP message across Tasman', SCOOP Parliament Independent News, 21 August 2003.

Chapter 19: Contemplating a Return to Politics

1 Baxter later moved to Victoria and headed the Victorian Premier's Office, where major reforms were carried out under Jeff Kennett's leadership.
2 Strategos had bought the building to provide more accommodation after we got the Defence review contract.
3 Derek Quigley, 'Economic reform: New Zealand in an international perspective', *The Round Table*, no. 339, vol. 85, 1996, p. 310.
4 Barry Gustafson, *His Way: A Biography of Robert Muldoon* (Auckland: Auckland University Press, 2000), p. 458.
5 Henry Cooke, 'A brief history of Winston Raymond Peters', *Stuff*, 21 June 2018: https://www.stuff.co.nz/national/politics/97547465/a-brief-history-of-winston-raymond-peters
6 Ibid.

Chapter 20: The Formation of ACT

1 Marilyn reconfirmed this in an email on 17 April 2020.
2 David McLoughlin, *The Undeveloping Nation: New Zealand's Twenty-year Fall towards the Third World* (Auckland: Penguin, 1992).
3 Roger Douglas, *Unfinished Business* (Auckland: Random House, 1993).
4 Nicky Hager, *The Hollow Men* (Nelson: Craig Potton Publishing, 2006).
5 Milton Friedman on education vouchers: www.edchoice.org/who-we-are/our-legacy/articles/milton-friedman-on-vouchers/
6 Priscilla Tate, email to author, 5 February 2013.
7 Ross Meurant, *The Beat to the Beehive* (Auckland: Harlen Books, 1989), p. 174.
8 *Values not Politics: ACT New Zealand Campaign Manifesto* (Auckland, 1996).
9 Richard Prebble, *I've Been Thinking* (Auckland: Seaview Publishing, 1996).

Chapter 21: Operating in a New Electoral System

1 Wayne Mapp was present at both functions and can verify these comments.
2 Geoffrey Palmer, *New Zealand's Constitution in Crisis: Reforming Our Political System* (Dunedin: John McIndoe), pp. 10–06.
3 *Defence Beyond 2000*, interim and final reports of the Foreign Affairs, Defence and Trade Select Committee (Wellington: New Zealand House of Representatives, 1998, 1999).
4 *In the National Interest: Australia's Foreign and Trade Policy White Paper* (Canberra: Commonwealth of Australia, 1997): http://repository.jeffmalone.org/files/foreign/In_the_National_Interest.pdf
5 Colin James, *NZ Defence Quarterly*, October 1999.
6 Jim Bolger, foreword, *The Shape of New Zealand Defence: A White Paper* (Wellington: Ministry of Defence, 1997), pp. 5–6.
7 Gerald Hensley, Secretary of Defence, in a briefing note to Minister of Defence on Defence Assessment, *Defence Background Paper: Evaluation of the Options*, Wellington, 6 June 1997, para 1.
8 *The Shape of New Zealand Defence*, p. 10.
9 *DB2000*, final report, pp. 17–18.
10 Ibid., p. 27.
11 Ibid., p. 89.
12 Ibid., p. 132.
13 *DB2000*, interim report, p. 21.]
14 Ibid., p. 5.
15 Ibid., p. 57.
16 *DB2000*, final report, p. 125.
17 Ibid, p. 114.
18 Arthur Grimes & Jim Rolfe, *Defence Objectives and Funding*, paper prepared for the Treasury (Wellington: Institute of Policy Studies, Victoria University of Wellington, 2000), p. 28.
19 Parliamentary Library, *Defence Beyond 2000*, I/DEF/POLETTV53.
20 *DB2000*, final report, p. 53.

Chapter 22: Other Involvements as an MP

1 M. Comrie, A-M. Gillies and M. Day, 'The Māori electoral option campaign: Problems of measuring "success"', *Political Science* 54(2), December 2002, pp. 45–58.
2 Unsurprisingly, the panel's recommendation on the Māori seats was that 'the current arrangement for the representation of Māori in Parliament should remain while the current conversation continues'.
3 After his time as an MP, Delamere became an immigration consultant. I hope he was better at that than he was as a minister.
4 Estoppel is a little-used legal principle that bars a party from denying or alleging a certain fact owing to that party's previous conduct, allegation or denial.
5 [1998] 3 *NZLR* 22.
6 Ibid.

7 When I wrote to McGrath to congratulate him on his knighthood and signed it with the addition of 'your constitutional disgrace', he replied that he didn't resile from his comment, but acknowledged that it was 'a bit hyperbolic'. John McGrath to Derek Quigley, 22 January 2007.

Chapter 23: Defence in the Spotlight Again

1 'Fighter deal on but doubt over frigate', *NZ Herald*, 1 December 1998. p. A1.
2 Derek Quigley, *Review of the Lease of the F-16 Aircraft for the Royal New Zealand Air Force*, 6 March 2000, p. 2.
3 Ibid., pp. 2 & 54.
4 Extract from Fortune's notes of the meeting made available to the author on 24 May 2005.
5 Derek Quigley, notes of conversations with Helen Clark and CEO of the Prime Minister's Department, *c.* late February 2000.
6 Quigley, *F-16 Review*, p. 38.
7 *The Shape of New Zealand's Defence: A White Paper*, Wellington, 1997, p. 30.
8 Document dated 5 March 2000 (in author's possession).
9 Quigley, *F-16 Review*, p. 52.
10 Ibid., p. 55.
11 *Priorities for Rebuilding the NZDF*, Cabinet Paper CAB (00)314, 9 June 2000.
12 Ibid., paras 30–32.
13 Pre-budget announcement, 8 May 2001, p. 1.
14 D.K. Hunn, *Review of Accountabilities and Structural Arrangements between the Ministry of Defence and the New Zealand Defence Force*, 30 September 2002.
15 Ibid., Executive Summary, para. 12.
16 Graham Fortune, telephone discussion with the author, February 2005.
17 Fortune to Hunn, 10 December 2001, p. 3.
18 David Walker, manager executive services, Auckland City, to author, 14 August 2002.
19 Derek Quigley, *The War Against Defence Restructuring* (Canberra: Strategic and Defence Studies Centre, 2006).

Chapter 24: ACT in Parliament

1 'Douglas reads Prebble the riot act', *Sunday Star-Times*, 12 November 2000.
2 https://www.scoop.co.nz/stories/PA0401/S00220.htm
3 Nicky Hager, *The Hollow Men: A Study in the Politics of Deception* (Nelson: Craig Potton Publishing, 2006).
4 Extract from National Party 2005 election brochure.
5 Hager, *The Hollow Men*, p. 277.
6 *The Letter*, ACT press release, 19 September 2005.
7 Richard Prebble, *NZ Herald*, 8 July 2016.

Chapter 25: New Zealand Today

1 https://www.oecdbetterlifeindex.org/countries/new-zealand/
2 https://worldpopulationreview.com/country-rankings/democracy-countries
3 Thomas Hobbes, *Leviathan* (Baltimore: Penguin, 1968).
4 Sophia Lawrence, *Rethinking the Narrative: Intimate Partner Violence in New Zealand Amicus Curiae*, Equal Justice Project, 3 May 2023: www.equaljusticeproject.co.nz/articles/rethinking-the-narrative-intimate-partner-violence-in-new-zealand2023
5 https://tepunaaonui.govt.nz
6 Report by the Office of Controller and Auditor-General, *Meeting the Needs of People Affected by Family Violence and Sexual Violence*, 27 June 2023: https://oag.parliament.nz/2023/family-violence
7 Carswell Consultancy, *Experience of the Family Violence System in Aotearoa: An Overview of Research 2010–2020*.
8 Cornish and Strange commenting on the 2021/2022 Police Annual Report, *Stuff*, 20 November 2022.

9 Michael Johnston, 'Children in New Zealand left rudderless by failing educations system', EducationHQ, the New Zealand Initiative, 30 January 2023: www.nzinitiative.org.nz/reports-and-media/opinion/children-in-new-zealand-left-rudderless-by-failing-education-system/
10 J. Cumming, *New Zealand Health System Review*, (New Delhi: World Health Organization Regional Office for South-East Asia, 2022).
11 New Zealand Statistics, 2014 census.
12 Noel Pearson, *Weekend Australian*, 25–26 July 2020.
13 Craig McCulloch, 'Changing global tensions prompt New Zealand to ramp up security and defence resources', quoting the Minister of Defence following the release of a defence policy and security document, RNZ, 4 August 2023.
14 Derek Quigley, *A New Role for New Zealand in the Pacific* (Massey University Defence and Strategic Studies Centre National Security Journal, 3 September 2023).
15 Philip A. Joseph, 'Separation of powers in New Zealand', *Journal of International and Comparative Law, vol. 5, no. 2* (December 2018).
16 Ibid.
17 When the Holland government abolished the Upper House it promised to reintroduce a more workable replacement but never did.
18 The Treasury, *Te Tai Waiora: Wellbeing in Aotearoa*, 24 November 2022, p. 45: www.treasury.govt.nz/publications/wellbeing-report/te-tai-waiora-2022
19 Government-appointed Welfare Expert Advisory Group. February 2019.
20 Roger Douglas, Robert MacCulloch & Hugh McCaffrey, *The March Towards Poverty: Why the Labour Government has much more to deal with than the economic consequences of Covid-19 in its upcoming budget*, Studies in Applied Economics, Johns Hopkins University, December 2020.
21 Child Poverty Action Group Report, *The Accommodation Supplement: The Wrong Tool to Fix the House*, Conclusion, 1 May 2019: www.cpag.org.nz/publications/accommodation-supplement-wrong-tool
22 The Treasury, Official Information Act response, 2 November 2022.
23 Section 12, Public Service Act 2020.
24 Section 11, Public Service Act 2020.

Image Credits

7 NZ National Party: 1949 election pamphlet. Alexander Turnbull Library, Wellington, New Zealand.
8 NZ National Party: 1949 election pamphlet. Alexander Turnbull Library, Wellington, New Zealand.
14 NZ National Party: 1951 election pamphlet. Alexander Turnbull Library, Wellington, New Zealand.
14 NZ Watersiders' Union: 1951 Loyalty Card. Alexander Turnbull Library, Wellington, New Zealand.
16 NZ National Party: 1951 election pamphlet. Alexander Turnbull Library, Wellington, New Zealand.
20 At Medbury school, aged 13. Personal collection.
26 With Mabel Howard, election night 1963. Star Media Limited, from Stuff Limited, June 2024.
31 Derek, Mac Maciaszek, Philip Davies and Neil Maclean, Christchurch, 2012. Personal collection.
41 1975 election campaign bus. Personal collection.
42 Another way to campaign. Personal collection.
63 New Cabinet Ministers, after 1978 election. Left to right: Wellington, Birch, Quigley, Muldoon, Cooper, Couch and McLay. Source: Unknown
78 No, you can't have more money. Personal collection.
111 I've asked them to remove the cap. Cartoonist, Tom Scott. Personal collection.
116 Delayed deputy PM vote to avoid wrong result. Cartoonist, Bill Wrathall.
117 Duncan finally makes it. Cartoonist, Sid Scales.
118 Cabinet reshuffle to bolster support for PM. Cartoonist, Bill Wrathall.
146 In full flight. Personal collection.
151 Note from Ben Couch following my resignation, 24 June 1982. Personal collection.
154 Hang on in there Derek. Copyright Bob Brockie. All rights reserved.
154 I need consistency. Copyright James R Lynch. All rights reserved.
155 Damn the National Party. Cartoonist, Tom Scott. Personal collection.
155 That's got Quigley safely tucked away. Credit, J Barr. 1984.
157 The wage/price freeze was supposed to shut them up. Copyright Eric Heath. All rights reserved.
167 Muldoon's reply to mine wishing him good health. Personal collection.
171 On the terrace of House of Commons. Left to right: Michael Ryle, Clerk of the Overseas Office, Rt Hon Bryant Godman Irvine MP, Quigley, and James Lamond MP. Source: S.47340. British Official Photograph. Crown copyright reserved.
199 Tree trimming in 1986 shortly after first heart operation. Personal collection.
225 With Alf Kirk in Canberra, 1988. Personal collection.
235 A scary movie. Cartoonist Tom Scott. Personal collection.
251 Reaction to the Rainbow Warrior bombing. Courtesy of the artist Stanley Palmer and Melanie Roger Gallery, Auckland.
253 Correspondence from Tony Blair. Personal collection.
299 With Susan and Paul East in China, 1999. Personal collection.
300 With Susan in Kyoto, 1999. Personal collection.
305 Clearance to pry. Personal collection.

All reasonable efforts have been made to clear copyright for images reproduced in this book. We will be happy to hear from any parties we have been unable to contact.

Index

Bold denotes photographs
Italics denotes other illustrations